D0990445

Ribbon Creek

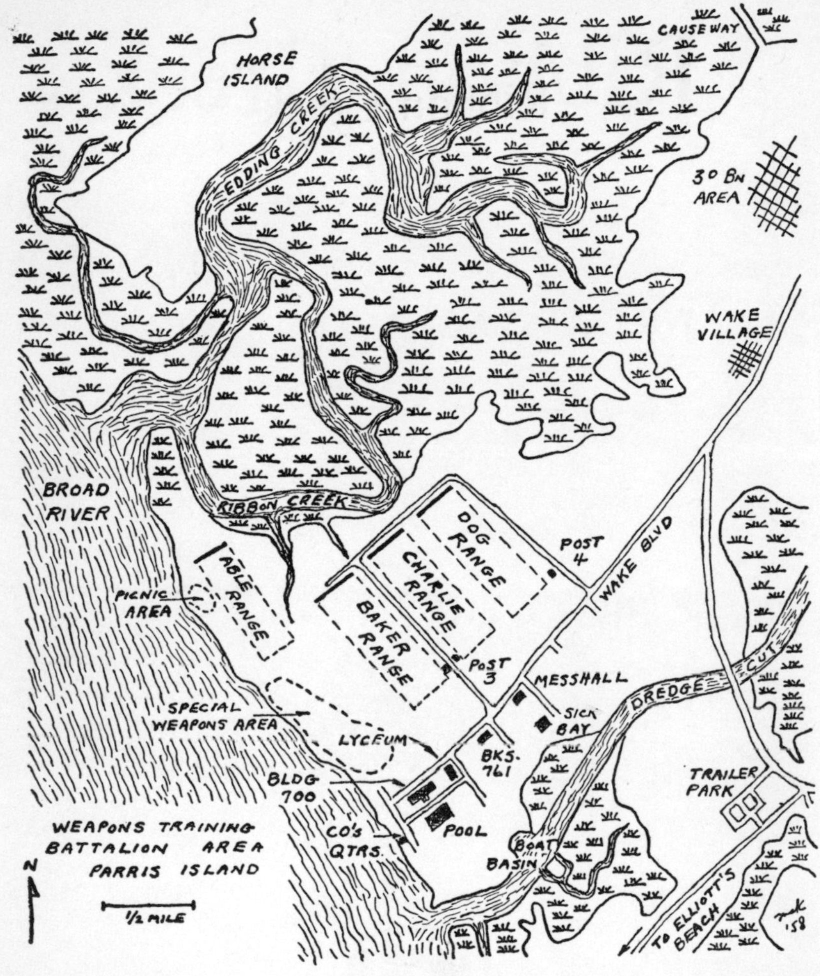
HORSE ISLAND
EDDING CREEK
CAUSEWAY
3D BN AREA
WAKE VILLAGE
BROAD RIVER
RIBBON CREEK
DOG RANGE
CHARLIE RANGE
BAKER RANGE
ABLE RANGE
POST 4
WAKE BLVD
PICNIC AREA
POST 3
MESSHALL
SPECIAL WEAPONS AREA
DREDGE CUT
SICK BAY
LYCEUM
BKS. 761
BLDG 700
TRAILER PARK
CO'S QTRS.
POOL
BOAT BASIN
WEAPONS TRAINING BATTALION AREA PARRIS ISLAND
N
1/2 MILE
TO ELLIOTT'S BEACH
'58

Ribbon Creek

WILLIAM BAGGARLEY McKEAN
Brigadier General
U. S. Marine Corps, Retired

THE DIAL PRESS 1958 NEW YORK

Library of Congress Catalog Card Number: 58-12776

The opinions or assertions contained herein are the private ones of the writer and are not to be construed as official or reflecting the views of the Navy Department or the naval service at large.

DESIGNED BY WILLIAM R. MEINHARDT
PRINTED IN THE UNITED STATES OF AMERICA
BY THE HADDON CRAFTSMEN, SCRANTON, PENNA.

TO THE MEMORY OF—

THOMAS CURTIS HARDEMAN
Born October 8, 1935
at Kippee, Georgia
Died April 8, 1956
in Ribbon Creek

DONALD FRANCIS O'SHEA
Born March 23, 1938
at Brooklyn, New York
Died April 8, 1956
in Ribbon Creek

CHARLES FRANCIS REILLY
Born December 15, 1937
at Ira, New York
Died April 8, 1956
in Ribbon Creek

JERRY LAMONTE THOMAS
Born February 5, 1939
at Columbia, South Carolina
Died April 8, 1956
in Ribbon Creek

LEROY THOMPSON
Born November 21, 1937
at Summerton, South Carolina
Died April 8, 1956
in Ribbon Creek

NORMAN ALFRED WOOD
Born September 3, 1938
at Bay Shore, Long Island, New York
Died April 8, 1956
in Ribbon Creek

Contents

Ribbon Creek

1

Viewpoints

SIX MARINE RECRUITS were drowned in Ribbon Creek, Parris Island, South Carolina, about 8:45 P.M., April 8, 1956. Their Platoon 71 was billeted in Weapons Battalion area for marksmanship training. Both platoon and area were under my jurisdiction as Commanding Officer.

Human frailty caused this tragedy. We had legal machinery available at Parris Island to take corrective action and make appropriate amends. But 1956 was an election year. General Randolph McC. Pate, Commandant of the Marine Corps, leaned on the panic button in his Washington headquarters. The press, Congress, and our general public became emotionally involved with the incident. On May 7 I was relieved of this, my last command, in the final weeks of my Marine Corps career in an administrative action from which there is no appeal.

Nearly to the hour, forty days after the Ribbon Creek incident five civilians died in head-on automobile collision eight miles north of Ann Arbor, Michigan. One of these was my eldest son. This second tragedy was also caused by human frailty, but it was scarcely noticed in Washington. There was no public outcry. Emotionally involved were close relatives, intimate friends, some University officials.

I give you this story of Parris Island, modern cradle of the Marine Corps, from my personal viewpoint, as a work of love.

I write for publication, to be sure, but I'm convinced this manuscript could be just filed away without losing its significance. Being in the throes of composition two years has given me deep insight into human nature and the dynamics of Marine Corps leadership. I hope this study—for it is a study—will have the same value for you.

As much as is humanly possible, I have tried to use the actual words of witnesses and participants, but I have taken the liberty of deleting or rearranging these words when it would make for clarity without sacrifice of meaning. Where the same person speaks at both Inquiry and Court-Martial but makes conflicting statements, I give weight to the former because his memory was fresher. My manuscript does not contain the usual scholarly footnotes because I feared it would make rough going for the reader. Consequently, the reader must trust my editing for not removing too much of the context which I've struggled to retain. Every line in this volume can be documented in the manner of a legal treatise or scientific research paper.

When I quote unrecorded conversations—or on rare occasions reconstruct them on the basis of my acquaintance with the speakers—it is with faith that these marines would verify the tenor of their remarks if it should be challenged.

My own observations and opinions are, of course, governed by the uncertainties of human fallibility. While I've done my best to restrain personal bias, true objectivity is a goal never achieved—were it in fact desirable. The physicist is a variable in his own experiments; the surveyor is a part of his most precise measurements. But in our view of Parris Island this is not pure liability. Sympathy and understanding come only through years of living with the people in their culture. Outsiders may drop in, absorb a bit of local color, go home to write about it; they're appreciated by all their readers except the natives. One bias to which I rigidly adhere: United States Marines are the finest among military elite. Still, I wouldn't dispute the proposition that the Marine Corps is continually in need of improvement and that it could do with a good keelhauling right now.

My primary source of material is personal experience and

observation: I lived on Parris Island thirty-three months before the Ribbon Creek tragedy; I participated actively in that Boot Camp's way of life; I kept close to my troops. Immediately following the recovery of the last body from Ribbon Creek, I sat down and wrote my own version of the story, which ran to 20,000 words. Following that, with unavoidable interruptions, I wrote a series describing Parris Island customs and people; this was completed within five months and added another 20,000 words. That manuscript I call "Ribbon Creek I."

Months later, providentially, I gained access to the complete record in the case of the United States vs. Staff Sergeant Matthew Charles McKeon. This starts with an appointing order for the Court of Inquiry dated April 9. The record of that Inquiry contains 345 pages to which are appended thirty-five exhibits. Then there is the endorsement of Commanding General, Parris Island, in which he uses sixteen pages to explain his viewpoint. There follow endorsements by the Commandant of the Marine Corps, Judge Advocate General of the Navy, and Secretary of the Navy. Next is the Secretary's appointing order for the General Court-Martial. The record of McKeon's trial uses 1,143 pages to which are added fifty-three exhibits. One of these exhibits is thirty-two pages; others are maps and photographs; there is a photostat of Matthew McKeon's twenty-page statement written when he was in shock. Finally, we have the Secretary's Court-Martial Order, composed for public consumption, which takes fifteen pages. All of this forms a seven-inch stack of legal-size paper.

This windfall of paper with which to document the full story aroused in me an extreme reaction. My psychologist friends will agree that I have in their terms an obsessive-compulsive personality: When I set out to tell a story I don't like to quit until I've included the last remote detail. This is analogous to the somewhat ribald doggerel we recited out in the Pacific: "No sparrow falls unheralded in Doug's Communiqué." It was interesting to me that French Huguenots built Charlesfort on Parris Island in 1562, three years before the founding of St. Augustine, and the following year murdered their commanding officer; that in 1564 Spanish troops captured a French expedition there and hanged the survivors only to suffer the same treatment from the French a few months later; that pirates and smugglers unquestionably used Parris Island waters for refuge; that the first English settlement of the Carolinas was made near there; that British troops occupied Beaufort during the Revolution; and that on November 7, 1861, from Parris Point one could have watched Flag Officer Samuel DuPont's ships and General Isaac Stevens' landing force establish a permanent stronghold in the Confederacy.

But history is just one small strand in an enormous hawser. There are institutions with their complexity and intrigue: an Exchange capitalized at $800,000; the golf course; the postwar Special Services empire with its education and information program; "varsity teams" with members whose amateur status and primary service as marines is open to challenge; the Depot Children's School and a bureaucratic maze that must be run to keep it going; charities, with two worthy organizations competing to lend money, often when the need is doubtful; accounting, a 113-member, loosely distributed clan that spends dollars to save pennies; taverns and clubs, at three social levels, not counting a refuge for women marines; Food Service and Maintenance with tentacles everywhere; the Chaplains' Center, bogged down in paper work but "organized" to dispense religion like aspirin or shoes; and ATs, graduate recruits being "processed" who form a convenient labor pool. The relationship of Parris Island institutions with those of Beaufort in business and politics is an entrancing case study in sociology. There is the wonderland of Staff, maximum centralization of decision (G-3 determines if it is raining on the parade ground), and delegation of responsibility without adequate authority, reminiscent of Lewis Carroll. There is the geography of Parris Island, sandbar in the swampland. And not least are interesting people: civilians who stay, like Heddie Chambers; marines who remain a full career, then join Civil Service; and those who come and go in the mill of "rotation."

All of these I attempted to field strip and lay out for inspection. After that I drifted into medicine, in wanton detail, and then tried to analyze the legal aspects of the narrative until—I thought—the results were worthy of a Law Review. This version went to some 280,000 words, which I call "Ribbon Creek II," and though it was opinionated and controversial, it was complete. But my editors convinced me no reader would sit still for that.

Since then, by deleting and condensing, I've come up with "Ribbon Creek III," which I hope is an acceptable version. Still you need to be warned on several points.

You're going to find inconsistencies. No two spectators view any scene alike. Records of every tribunal are actually fragmentary, as social scientists can assure you. My own observations are given as I perceived them on the spot—later I discovered many facts I wish I'd known earlier. During the Court-Martial, Chief Trial Counsel Sevier often "delegated" the examination of witnesses to an assistant; this is seldom apparent in the record. Hence, there are times when Major Sevier gets credit for the words of Captain Haden or Captain Otten, yet this is unimportant because Sevier continued responsible.

You're going to wonder about public reaction, or attempt to recall it. Rather than spread this all-important story through the book, I felt it would be less confusing to telescope it in the next to last chapter where it may serve you as a quick review.

You're also going to be confronted with an alleged "moral issue" soon after tragedy erupts: drinking vodka; non-swimmers drowning while swimmers are eaten by sharks; "treatment incompatible with accepted American standards of human dignity," such as "callousness, brutality, coarseness, verbal filth, personal humiliation, hazing, public ridicule, and lackadaisical attitudes" in supervision. Would you analyze this factor and form your own value judgments?

You're going to notice that the Commandant of the Marine Corps, the Commanding General of Parris Island, Drill Instructor Matthew McKeon, and seventy-eight marine Boots were all new to their jobs early in 1956. Do you think this coincidence had any bearing on the affair?

You will find the names of the six dead marines in italics, which I hoped would make for greater clarity. When I speak in the present tense it represents conversation or my own thoughts at the moment. In my description of life at Parris Island, I have attempted to stop the clock on April 8. General Pate insists that since then he has wrought many "improvements" through Brigadier Greene's Recruit Training Command and an additional Inspector General. While I'm skeptical of this, I'm making no effort to dispute that claim. Nor do I contend that any vestige of that social milieu of the Parris Island of my day still remains.

Parris Island, like the whole Marine Corps, resembles a flowing stream; it is never the same two consecutive moments. When we number our troops in thousands, we lose some and acquire others from one instant to the next. General Alexander Archer Vandegrift was much perturbed while Commandant because no one could tell him—truthfully—how many marines were in the Corps on any one day. And he didn't care *what* day. So my effort to stop the clock is no more than an abstract ideal. All of my thirty years' naval service are bound to tint the picture.

Major John Zimmerman, Marine Corps Reserve, wrote in *Naval Institute Proceedings* maintaining all marines are "characters." Most of the characters in this narrative are living. Practically none are fictional—and those few will be obvious. I have done my utmost to be sympathetic with all, but truth has its demands. My wife would prefer I destroy this account rather than offend anyone—but that in itself would be untruthful. Marines are combat soldiers; in combat people get hurt. If the shoe fits, you're Cinderella.

2

Trouble

"COLONEL, this is Patrick. We're in trouble."

"What's the scoop, Pat?"

"Some knuckleheaded DI took his platoon to the swamp. They're streaming back to Building 761, wet, cold, muddy. Some still lost."

"What platoon and battalion?"

"Don't know yet. Taylor discovered them and reported it to me. I'm on my way to investigate."

"Call me when you find out. Lock up the DI. Send those that need it to Sick Bay."

"Aye, aye, sir."

It's easy to tell time by TV. Sunday evening, the two big ones at the movies, the three small ones in bed—and for once they're asleep. Mom didn't stay awake through Ed Sullivan; the next program isn't for me. I go back to my den for another stint with the Bible, frankly, an exercise in four languages, not theology.

The telephone again. "Patrick, Colonel. It's Platoon 71, Third Battalion. I have some of the boys in Sick Bay, but they're all right. We took a muster and eight are still missing. Have notified the Provost Marshal, Depot Officer of the Day, Staff Duty Officer. Major McLeod is sending out search parties from Guard Company."

"Okay, Pat. I'll advise the Chief of Staff. You tell the Third Battalion Duty Officer. Call me if you need me or when there's anything new."

Back to the den. Mom is awake. We talk a few minutes, then: "I'd better put on a jacket and go see how they're making out." I walk out to the garage.

In retrospect I think of false cues: lost, missing, swamp. None had any serious connotation. We've had searches before. During my thirty-three months at Weapons Battalion we invariably got them all back. Usually it only means that my boys lose sleep. Like the ship's captain racked out in his sea cabin, of course, I was bound to have my slumber interrupted.

Usually my battalion is aroused to recover lost fishermen, though we're not mentioned in the Depot Search and Rescue Plan. Someone fails to take along an extra shear-pin for the propeller on his outboard motor and he doesn't know how to improvise, for instance, with a nail. Other times the fog may close in unexpectedly. We never hear about the missing until dark, nor do we often find them before daylight. But we search.

Yet with Boots the problem is different. With a medium-sized training load it is normal to have anywhere from three to a dozen recruits continually missing. While they seldom annoy Weapons Battalion, they irritate the Provost Marshal. These lads decide Parris Island is too rough and they take off. Ignorant of local geography, they may get out to the golf course; we can expect to see those after missing two meals. Other times they negotiate the swamp behind Third Battalion area. They used to be discovered on the road heading for Burton. But Colonel Austin Conner (Shifty) Shofner, when he was Depot Inspector, suggested we make alterations to the main gate: wire it in and erect floodlights. Shifty gained his experience escaping from the Japanese at Mindanao. And so in recent months the fugitive Boot winds up on Malecon Drive. It is Guard Company's responsibility to search for those missing.

But occasionally these runaways lose all sense of direction and come out of the swamp in the Rifle Range area. They're pooped out, muddy, and well chewed by insects (sand fleas are the trademark of Parris Island). Not long ago we found a boy in one of the School Range instruction sheds. He looked as though he had taken a terrific shellacking. We started an investigation expecting to charge someone, DI or fellow recruit, with maltreatment or assault. Then it turned out that bugs were responsible.

What to do when we find these truants? Treat them for exposure and shock—the medicos call it "symptomatic treatment." Upon recovery, we give them a fair trial and throw their fannies in the brig a few days for a reminder.

Naturally there are some who succeed in escaping from Parris Island, and after the routine waiting period these are posted as deserters. Upon their apprehension or surrender, they find themselves confronted by a general court-martial. But the FBI is only about ninety-nine per cent efficient and there are recurrent legends—entirely plausible—that the bones of some of those missing lie in the waters surrounding Parris Island. These would be drifters without intimate kin, or men enlisting under an assumed name.

Sited for line of fire to the northwest, our four rifle ranges, named by letters, have their impact areas in creeks and marshland. Manned by a marine, each six-foot-square target is fixed in a carrier which permits raising it for display and lowering it for masking. Hits are marked by spotters, small cardboard discs on wooden spindles, and also are signaled by raising larger colored metal discs attached to long poles. Just in front of the targets is a protective concrete wall reinforced with a heavy bank of earth thrown up between it and the firing line. Technically, only the wall and bank are "butts," yet marines persist in using that name for the whole target area.

I back the car out of the garage and drive toward C-Butts. I should remember to remind Mom again that the Old Man wants our garage doors closed—that way the junk and litter won't show. Besides, Butch left the light on when he took his bike out. I'll have to get after him. It isn't just the Depot Conservation Program; what about when I'm going to be paying the light bills myself? I can't get any of my tribe to turn them out, dammit! Well, this is probably another restless night. Our Guard of the Day will be tired out before we crank off at six in the morning. We could be lucky, though; the stragglers might be in already. It's obviously maltreatment. What was that knucklehead thinking about anyway? It was the Junior, of course—a new buck sergeant, maybe just a corporal. Another damn investigation with more paper work. I'll ask Third Battalion to take this investigation if it's just their boys involved. I turn off Wake Boulevard and reach the ammunition sheds on the road between B- and C-Ranges.

"Halt!"

I slam the brakes, then back up a few yards. The recruit is standing there at port arms. Okay, this is part of his training. "What do you do now, son?"

"Advance to be recognized!"

"No, no, boy. The next thing you say is, 'Who's there?' and I'm going to say, 'Commanding Officer.' Then what in hell are you going to do? I'm in civilian clothes."

"I'm not sure, sir."

"Go take a look at the tags on my car. I'll dim the lights."

He did and returned.

"Now, that was an officer's tag, No. 3. You might be satisfied I'm telling the truth. But you could ask to see my ID card. Here it is."

"Oh, no, sir! The DI told us never to touch anyone's ID card. He said to make 'em throw it on the ground."

"Look, son, goddammit! I'm not going to get out of this car and I don't have time to hold school. You take this card and look at it in the headlights."

He did and returned.

"Now. Has anything been going on around here?"

"Well, sir, cars and trucks and a fire engine drove by."

"Did you halt them?"

"Yes, sir. But they wouldn't stop."

"Very well, son. Now do you recall the General Order that says, 'To receive, obey, and pass on to the sentinel who relieves me all orders from the Commanding Officer, Field Officer of the Day, Officer of the Day, and officers and noncommissioned officers of the Guard only'?"

"Yes, sir!" He seemed to relax.

"All right. I'm now giving you this order and you pass it on to your relief: This will no longer be a challenging post tonight until after we secure the butts and you are properly instructed by an authorized member of the Guard. Do you understand that?"

"Yes, sir."

"Carry on!"

I drive into C-Butts and park.

Major Stanley N. McLeod, Depot Provost Marshal, is standing on a slight hummock 130 yards behind No. 12 target and directing the job. Scattered around him on the bank of Ribbon Creek are patrol trucks, the resuscitator with operator, an ambulance, and a fire engine with searchlights trained out over the tidal flats. Thirteen hundred yards to our front, broken by Ribbon and Edding creeks with their small tributaries, those flats extend to Horse Island. Three thousand yards to our right we can see the lights on Malecon Drive, where the causeway crosses this marshland. Two hundred yards to our left we know the flats border Broad River. At high tide the whole area is under a few inches of water. The marsh is covered with reeds which grow to a height of four feet. At all times the mud is soft and difficult to traverse.

Within calling distance of Major McLeod are Captain Charles Patrick, Weapons Battalion Officer of the Day; Technical Sergeant Johnny Taylor, Weapons Battalion Commander of the Guard; Lieutenant Robert D. Jones, Assistant Provost Marshal; and Mr. Thomas E. Peck, our new Fire Chief, decked out in shining white helmet and slicker. McLeod describes his search plan: One patrol is to the left working from A-Range pier through the brush toward us. Others are to the right patrolling the woods northeast of D-Range, in rear of Wake Village, and adjacent to Third Battalion area. With his voice-radio net McLeod has everything under control.

"Mac, are you going to work Malecon Drive and Horse Island?"

"Not yet, at least, Colonel. I'm already using all the men available in Guard Company. Don't want people sleeping on post later on. Besides, those boys haven't had time to get that far."

"Why the resuscitator?"

"Oh, the Chief wanted to bring it out. If we do need it, it'll be in a hurry."

Patrick walked over and saluted.

"You always have the guard when there's trouble, Pat. How lucky can you be?"

"This isn't so bad, Colonel. It turned out that one of the boys was in Sick Bay all along. The corpsman turned him in at Sick Call this evening. Taylor tells me another yelled over from across the creek. That means only six more to go."

"Better get Taylor back in the barracks area. Someone has to run the Guard. Trouble comes in bunches."

The Fire Chief strolled over.

"That's what you get, Peck, for having your picture with all that propaganda in the *Boot* Friday."

"Just part of the job, Colonel."

"Well, we turned you out on your first Sunday night to let you know there's seldom a dull moment around here."

Peck and McLeod reminisced about chores they did together at Bayonne. "Always something going wrong with that moth-ball fleet! Fires. Storms. Sometimes the shipkeepers forgot to slack off lines, then sure enough the tide would go out."

"Remember that hurricane? The woman I pulled off that tug must have weighed 300 pounds. And she wanted me to go back and rescue her pictures and dishes!"

I spoke to Chief Peck. "How about elevating one light on that engine? It will be easier for those boys to see it. Doesn't do any good in close on the water."

More small talk with McLeod. He obviously has the situation well in hand. As usual we turned out too many people for such a small job. But that might get it over a little faster and we may all get some sleep. Just more paper work for the investigators tomorrow.

Through the reeds and brush on this side of Ribbon Creek, jumping across a steep-sided drainage ditch, comes one of our missing boys. Ready hands heft him up on the near side. He is the one they yelled to before. He is soaking wet; there is mud on his clothing and one hand; he still has on his field boots and jacket, but his cap is missing; obviously cold, he appears to be in good shape. Not much perturbed, he seems proud of all the attention. A corpsman throws a blanket over him.

"Anyone over there with you, boy?"

"No, sir. I got lost from the platoon."

"Haven't heard any others yelling over there?"

"No, sir."

"How'd you get across?"

"They asked mc if I could swim and I said I could but I waded it okay."

"Send him to Sick Bay for a check. Have him scrubbed up. Get his name, Pat."

The corpsman bundles him into the ambulance and drives away. For years I've trained myself as a witness: to observe, to get the facts. I am wearing the watch Mom gave me last Christmas—and don't think to look at it.

Captain Patrick rejoins us. "Chaplain Bielski was sure mad at me. He really chewed me out because I didn't notify him. I apologized. I had to admit that I didn't even think of it."

"We don't need a chaplain. It isn't that kind of emergency. This is different from that electrocution. I'll have to talk with Tony; he's getting too eager. We only need him around to administer last rites. But that DI needs a chaplain; he can use a handful of pink sympathy chits."

One evening last summer I was out weeding the flowers. No. 3 Engine rolled and I went inside to the phone; it rang as I got there. Trouble over in Messhall 762. I was on the way. A recruit standing in water put his hand on the spud peeler. (It is highly probable that he was operating the machine contrary to orders, but that was vigorously denied both by the Duty Cook and recruit witnesses.) We found out later that the ground cable had been broken by piling bags of potatoes on it. The resuscitator crew was working on the victim when I got there. He didn't revive.

While displeased with the accident, which might have been avoided, and unhappy with the laxity of Food Service, over which I had no jurisdiction, I was proud of our emergency service. Everything clicked. The Duty Cook started artificial respiration within seconds. I wasn't long getting there, but when I arrived the Officer of the Day, Provost Marshal detail, ambulance with oxygen, Duty Medical Officer, and fire engine were on the job. The Mess Sergeant walked up a few minutes later. Captain Patrick was Officer of the Day.

That time we forgot the chaplain and Father Tony Bielski gave us the hell we deserved. (It's a good thing the youngster was a Protestant.) Later at the Old Man's weekly conference Ralph Wood complained that we didn't notify the Public Information Officer. The press got the story from the coroner and—as might be expected—it was jumbled.

By now the tide is ebbing rapidly. Mud banks become more exposed as Ribbon Creek narrows. I speak to Patrick. "Send the Guard truck out to Trailer Park and wake Sparks. Have him bring around a boat and patrol these different arms of the creek. You won't need to tell him to idle his motor frequently and listen for their calls. Some of those recruits may be over on the far edge of that loop." Then in jest an old seagoing expression, "Call me if the wind changes." This is no emergency. I head for my quarters.

Staff Sergeant George W. Sparks is often in the midst of trouble—either his own or ours. But whenever we need a waterman, Sparks gets the nod. We once had Wixson, master carpenter as well as shrewd boatman; Wixson died in an automobile accident nine months ago. Before that, we had John Clement, finest waterman in the Carolina Low Country, but he left Weapons Battalion fifteen months ago for Japan. Still we do have Sparks.

He's half Indian, half Irish. Back home in Washington State Sparks wears a hat to the state liquor store and a headdress for hunting and fishing: he gets a break with the law that way. Sparks started as a crewman in Marine Aviation. Then he went out to the old Fourth Regiment in Shanghai; they were shifted to the Philippines and later captured at Corregidor. Sparks spent thirty-three months as guest of the Emperor, mostly at Cabanatuan. Torture, disease, and undernourishment didn't improve him.

Sparks has two offenses in his service record for talking back to senior NCOs. In the movement north from In'chon after the Korean landing Lieutenant Colonel Allan Sutter stopped long enough to award him a deck court, which cost a stripe. Then he got into trouble at Camp LeJeune. When he came to us we found that Sparks just can't keep his hands off recruits. Nor would he stick to the lesson plan when we had him instructing on the School Range; he used scheduled time telling sea stories to the Boots. So we asked the talking doctors to look Sparks over. Now he's profiled S-3 (instability), which means he won't be assigned with troops any more. He'll soon have put in his twenty years; in the meantime there's always a job for him. We put him down at our dock where he can work alone repairing motors and keeping boats in trim. He's done a first-rate job there and he's available at times like this when we have trouble.

But Sparks' family situation worries me. His wife lives with five children in a trailer. Peggie, the eldest child and only daughter, is in the second grade with my Judy. Peggie had some kind of growth behind her eye. I first noticed it at the Battalion picnic out at Elliott's Beach over two years ago. We asked Chaplain Ed Hartz to investigate. Ed discovered that Peggie had had repeated medical treatment and surgery almost from birth. Dr. McMurray examined her at Beaufort Naval Hospital. He wanted to send Peggie on to Charleston and summoned Sparks to talk it over with him. Sparks held out for Bethesda, 600 miles away. That same afternoon he had his wife and the four little ones on the train at Yemassee. His only logistic arrangement was cashing a check. At least he has some financial stability—and on his pay, too. (When Mom wanted to go north in a hurry last fall, I had to call on Bill Scheper, president of Peoples Bank at Beaufort.) Peggie spent months in the hospital. The eye was removed surgically and then there was skin grafting. Just before Christmas she returned from her last session. There's still some drainage and the prosthesis isn't satisfactory. But she's a sweet and polite child—in contrast to my hoodlums. That was a nice thank-you note Mom got from Peggie after her recent siege at Beaufort.

Sparks only stays home to eat and sleep. When he's not working in the Battalion, he's out on Broad River fishing. Even during working hours, Sparks is frequently "testing a boat" or scouting around for some distinguished visitor whom he can take fishing. Last spring Hugh Keveling, Saline, Michigan, pharmacist, was my house guest. Sparks escorted Keveling and they returned with three cobia each weighing more than twenty pounds. But while they were on the river there was a minor adventure with sharks—Mr. Hugh didn't care to repeat the expedition though he stayed another week. Sparks always brings me a cobia at some odd hour when the last thing I want to do is skin the creature. But he forces me to go to work because the meat is so tasty.

Sparks is quite a decent craftsman. Since he got the boats in condition, we've been continually proud of them. He built bunk beds to wedge his sons in that trailer. The model shrimp trawler he made for Butch is a real prize. But I feel that Sparks is weak in personal responsibility. I've told him he reminds me of the Eskimo who abandons his aging mother on the ice. I'll never forget that command inspection made by General Pollock. Sparks didn't even own a green coat and the jacket he wore must have been issued at Tun Tavern. Anyway, he's a well-dressed marine now and he's sure handy when we need him.

Around midnight I am back at my quarters. Mom is awake and waiting up for me. I wore a thin sports jacket and am now cold. I pour us each a short nightcap.

"What is it this time?"

"Some goddam DI that sneaked by the talking doctors had his boys out in the mud back of the butts. Wish I knew what he was thinking about."

"Are they all back?"

"Not yet. Six of them are still lost. It's going to take hours for those goonies to wade in. No Boot has any sense of direction at night. There're probably two or three groups of them widely separated in that muck. They may come back toward the searchlights or we'll find them tomorrow between the asphalt plant and the incinerator."

"What will they do to the DI?"

"Oh, he'll get a court. Quite a bit will depend on Thompson—it's a Third Battalion platoon. Tommy's a levelheaded gent—back in Quantico I had him as a corporal instructing in the Platoon Leaders' Class. This isn't very serious. If the DI belonged to me I'd either reduce him under Article 15 or give him a summary, depending on his rank. They'll take him off the field, of course. Might send him out here to Weapons—we're getting our summer augmentation now, and it's always the left-overs."

"Why do DIs do things like that anyway? It invariably gets them in trouble."

"Woman, that's the question I'd like answered: 'Why?' My crystal ball always clouds up at a time like this. Come on! I've finished my drink—just what I needed. Let's go to bed; I may be getting calls all night."

We just reach the head of the stairs when the phone rings. It is Bill Buse, Chief of Staff. "The Old Man's worried about this. I'm bringing him out in a few minutes. He's dressing now."

"Okay, Willie. I'll be out there, but everything was going along fine when I left a few minutes ago."

"Is there anything we can do from here?"

"No. Major McLeod has all emergency equipment there with a full crew, even the Fire Chief. Guard Company has several patrols working. They've broken out too much already. Quite a few of my boys are out there, too. As far as I can see, it's just a matter of time."

"All right; we'll see you in a few minutes."

This time I put on my uniform and field jacket.

"So long, Mom. Get some sleep. May be depending on you later."

What the hell's the Old Man worried about? Of course, he's new on the job—hasn't been here three months yet. After he's been around longer he'll find out this is mere routine. Sure, from a public relations angle it's nice to see a couple of stars shining. It's good for the recruits to see him out on the line on record day. It's probably good for him to accept all those invitations to cocktail parties and dinners, ride in parades, sit in reviewing stands, make speeches, be anywhere someone wants a "dignitary." But he's either going to be selective and know when to refuse—or it'll kill him.

I drive over to the barracks and park in the usual spot. Inside, members of the Guard know even less than I do. As I walk out I see Bill Buse's car pull up; the Old Man is with him. They invite me in and we drive together down to C-Butts.

"Better park here, Willie; that ground's firm but there are ditches and ruts. Wouldn't want to hurt your new jalopy. The General's a field soldier—he can walk."

As we start toward the center of activity an MP comes over with a flashlight and guides the Old Man. McLeod briefs us. He sent for the DI and questioned him at length. It seems th DI took his platoon out of the barracks about Movie Call—at least that was the best way he could fix the time. They marched down toward A-Butts and then did a column right and came in behind B-Butts. Somewhere near that first target shed in C-Butts he did a column left. In fact he talks in terms of three successive columns left. He probably crossed Ribbon Creek, went some distance on the tidal flat, and then came back through the creek. Of course, he could have done a couple of those columns left in the creek. Anyway, some of his boys started yelling—maybe in the dark they got a little bit panicky—and he lost control. He talks about the Section Leader, a big Negro boy, struggling with him. Somewhere near here they came up out of the swamp in confusion. No trails have been found in the grass or reeds to indicate their path. Here on this side, of course, our vehicles and patrols may have obliterated them. Even in a planned night action it's always difficult to maintain direction, so we might not yet have the right scent. There's even the possibility he took his departure from D-Butts, but we haven't found any tracks up there either. That Private Cox we recovered two or three hours ago was on the flat a few yards down the creek from here. Negative reports from foot and boat patrols. There's a small group working the flat right now.

Captain Patrick calls me aside. Here is CWO Jesse L. Griffin, from Roads and Grounds, all bundled up and rigged for general quarters. "I've got a truckload of timber back on the road. Where do you want it? The best thing I could find was two-by-twelves."

"Timber? For what?"

"Someone at the Provost Marshal's Office called Maintenance and said to bring it out. I got the idea they wanted it to build a footpath across the swamp."

"If we get it for nothing, we'll take it. Won't we, Pat?"

"Sure. Go dump it in my back yard, but don't invoice it."

"Can't do business that way. They're going to be on my neck in the morning because I loaded it out and didn't sign a receipt. I had to cut a lock."

"Well, someone's getting eager. There's no need for any timber down here. Take it back and see if you can find out who's your friend that gives you useless work in the middle of the night."

The Old Man stands around a long time. He is awfully quiet. Finally he starts to shove off. "I'll be back at daylight, Bill. Can we give you a ride to the barracks?"

"No, thank you, General. I have the Guard truck here."

General Burger and Colonel Buse disappear in the darkness. I watch the car drive away.

Sparks is yelling from across the creek. He found some tracks. It seems that they were in two widely separated places near the edge of the stream. From what I can gather, at least some recruits went to the northward. The other marks were apparently made by that boy Cox. We can see the tide has passed low water slack and started to flood.

Sergeant Taylor, Commander of the Guard, comes out and I have a talk with him. After getting the report from the Corporal of the Guard he drove into the butts, turned off his lights, and listened. He heard noises down near the water and turned his lights back on. Someone yelled they were being blinded, so he turned the lights off again. The platoon was in foul shape, completely out of control, wet and muddy. Some recruits were carrying their buddies. The DI was excited. He talked about the Section Leader jumping on his back and their going down twice together—then he hadn't seen the Section Leader any more. Taylor instructed the DI to get a head count on the platoon and get them back to barracks. He took one man to Sick Bay. Taylor doesn't indicate he thinks anyone could have been drowned. Nor do I believe he has such an idea now. He's a pretty stable character and doesn't panic easily.

Looking backward I think, "How stupid can you be?" But since then the facts—as near as we'll ever know them—have pretty well jelled. It was something like a problem in combat intelligence. Captain B. H. Liddell Hart, British military writer, would call it "the fog of war." Fragmentary information flows in slowly; beware rumor; remain objective. Time and again in our military schools we tell of the panic-stricken, shell-shocked man who swears that he is the sole survivor of his platoon, company, battalion. Later it is learned that casualties were few and the operation successful. Besides, every good soldier is a born optimist—he has to be. Tell a patrol that the odds will enable but one member to return; each glances at the others and says to himself, "Those poor bastards!" Colonel David M. Shoup, who was in command that first night at Tarawa and got the Medal of Honor for it, had to be an optimist when he was there holding the bag. In addition to being optimistic he is a first-rate amateur gambler, which also helps. One of the Second Marine Division Staff told me about getting ashore after dark, crawling over bodies and through wire, finally locating him. Dave's first words were: "This is the goddamnedest crap game I've ever been in."

Unfortunately, I was ignorant as well as optimistic. Otherwise, we might have had the show on the road one tide earlier—though the final result couldn't have been changed. Nor until later did I know how wheels were turning. Over in Beaufort the grapevine was far more effective than our voice-radio. Marines went from house to house, quietly. "There's trouble over at Weapons. I can't tell you what it's all about. You'd better get back to the Battalion." Through the night my troops kept filtering in: watermen, fishermen, boatmen, just-general-handy-men. Knuckleheads, misfits, low GCTs, psychiatric cripples, problem children, admitted screwballs, but MARINES. Some were later reported to me for failure to be in their places of duty at the appointed time. All were volunteers. We shall see the individuals as they work. There was one who directly disobeyed my orders—but what are you going to do? It reminded me of that time we pulled into Noumea after the original movement to Guadalcanal, where we left the First Marine Division short of the rations, ammunition, fuel, and equipment which remained in our ships' holds.

I gathered some 400 marine strays in *Hunter Liggett*. Wounded or not, they felt they had been kidnaped. All wanted to get back to their outfits. A staff officer with the Navy, without command, I rounded them up by virtue of my seniority and duty to submit a muster-roll on them. Their spirits reached the nadir that day Admiral Richard Kelly Turner, Amphibious Force Commander South Pacific, directed marine effectives be transferred to *Fomalhaut,* a cargo ship, and be used as stevedores on resupply runs. One lieutenant was particularly emphatic:

"Major, I've got to get ashore up there. My gang can't get along without me. I have plenty of spare parts and a repair trailer in that ship. They need me. What can I do?"

"All I can tell you to do is carry out your orders. Stay with that ship and help work her!"

"What would happen if I jumped ship at Guadalcanal?"

"If you ever quote me, I'll say you're a damn liar. But I've never heard of a marine court-martialed for deserting *toward* the enemy."

Captain Flanagan of *Fomalhaut* was unhappy. Weeks later I heard through the grapevine that only a few marines failed to escape from his ship on her return to Iron-Bottom Lagoon.

Likewise, my boys deserted their stations and duty and came out to help their Old Man.

I walk over to the bank of Ribbon Creek, stand a short distance from Major McLeod, take an occasional glance, and listen. Mac had sent for the DI again. There he stands, bareheaded, scrubbed up, in starched utilities, the prisoner-chaser a few paces behind him. His crew cut is an example for any recruit. He appears calm and most serious. But Mac seems to get only repetition; our orientation is no better. I finally go over to Captain Patrick.

"Pat, have all the boats out and manned at daylight. They can see all over the flats at high tide. We won't open fire until we have those recruits in—and even then I want the Provost Marshal to give us an 'all clear.' You know where to get me; call me if anything at all develops. I'll see you about daylight."

Back to the barracks in the Guard truck. I drive my own car over to the quarters. Mom stirs. "Did you get them all in?"

"Nope. Six still missing. I'm beginning to feel that we're not necessarily looking for warm bodies."

It was a good thing I slept; the relaxation would keep me going later. There was no need to set the alarm clock: after one hour fifteen minutes on the pillow, I glance out the window. It is morning twilight. First a quick shave, then back to C-Butts.

Now it is full daylight. The tide is two hours before high water and our boats are working all over the swampy flat. Major McLeod briefs me on his patrols covering the perimeter of the area. One of our boats comes in and reports seeing some marines over on the left side of Horse Island. Our voice-radio confirms what we feared: it is another patrol.

The Old Man comes out with Bill Buse, Chief of Staff,

trailing in his wake. General Burger watches our operations for a long time but has little to say. Buse tells me Major John Denvir Stith, Executive Officer at the Marine Air Station, has agreed to break out his Beechcraft at daylight and give us an air search. No sooner has Bill finished telling me this than Dennie buzzes us with his SNB and starts flying a pattern over the swampland. Finally the Old Man leaves after letting me know I can write my own ticket for anything I need.

There was talk between Bill Buse and me about notifying the newspapers. If this is merely a breach of discipline with no ill consequences, it would be well to keep quiet. As it is, Parris Island gets its share of unfavorable publicity. On the other hand, should we need the coroner's services, the longer we wait the more untenable our position. Before the Chief of Staff shoved off he told me the Old Man was telephoning the Commandant of the Marine Corps at seven forty-five if we hadn't recovered the boys before then.

Deciding when to advise the press is a touchy subject. It is particularly delicate right now. In case someone has been hurt, there is going to be a horrible outcry when the story breaks. I just read in this month's Northwestern University *Alumni News* an article on "The Right to Know." Professor Scher, the author, is a true crusader. Right now he's counsel to a Congressional committee investigating charges that the Federal government is suppressing news of its operations. I agree with him on public matters—and this affair may become one of those—but when it comes to protecting individual privacy I'm old-fashioned.

Suppose Sergeant Bucko—first-rate DI, twenty months on the field, excellent combat record—one morning loses his temper with Private Stumblebum and clobbers him. Bucko is caught in the act, given a fair trial, convicted, and punished. Reporting this not only intrudes on the Sergeant's privacy, it gives a bad name to the Marine Corps. Little does the public care that Bucko has already trained 420 good marines this cruise and is still being forced to pay for one dereliction. (He should have been removed from the field before this—a DI can only tolerate so much—but we're usually short of people.) Nor will the public infer that Stumblebum's parents might have applied child psychology by whacking their textbook across the fatty part of his back. No! The hue and cry is: brutality! If one DI is brutal they conclude all DIs are brutal. And when each year we number platoons in hundreds and recruits in thousands, there's bound to be a great deal of "laying on of hands."

Yet truth will out. If we have a real news story it will break. It's a shame our Public Information Officers don't acquire a professional nose for news. If our Parris Island PIO, Captain Ralph Calvin Wood, had the traits of a reporter he'd be out here now getting the scoop. He complained when we failed to notify him about that boy being electrocuted; now he'll attempt to gather information at his desk.

Army Major Eugene Lewis when we were together in Washington during World War II delighted in chiding me about Marine Corps press relations. Lewis claimed that a marine rifle squad consisted of a squad leader, six privates, and one Public Information NCO. Actually, when we had General Robert Livingston Denig handling the press during that war, relations were superb—but in the ten years since, no one with his talent has held the job. Too many of our more senior officers are afraid of the press. They figure it an unwarranted intrusion when the reporter is exercising his "right to know." They seem to forget he'll write a story anyway and with a little understanding they can gain his co-operation. More serious though is the fact that each fears the next higher echelon. That begins with our own PIO. He fears the Chief of Staff, who in turn figures we have the right to slant and censor every story. So it goes. Thank goodness that's out of my province. Ralph Wood can talk with Bill Buse and Joe Burger. Doubtless they'll pass the buck to the Commandant—and if the story breaks in Washington we're losing friends among local newsmen.

Before I came in the service, I was raised on the Salt Lake *Tribune*. Old-timers like Billie Igleheart, City Editor, and John Derks, Sports Editor, taught me a good deal about their profession—and then warned me to stay out of it. That and later experience has made me sensitive to both sides and has taught me one inflexible law: You can't profitably crumb on the Fourth Estate. If there have been any casualties, we had better cut in the reporters soon.

Obviously riled about something, Tom Peck, our Fire Chief strolls over and disrupts my train of thought. "How's it going, Chief?"

"I've seen everything now. A while ago I figured we'd better get some fuel. That engine'd been running all night to give us power for those searchlights. So we phoned for fuel. What do you think we got?"

"You gave me a tip. Instead of diesel, it was probably heating fuel."

"You guessed it. That's the first time in my life I've seen a fire engine dance."

"What are you going to do now?"

"Well, we've got one engine off service for maybe a week—which I don't like—but those bastards did it and they're going to be the ones to make the repairs."

I toy with the idea of relieving Captain Patrick as Officer of the Day. By now he has been up more than twenty-four hours and constantly on the move. The last time I noticed him, he looked pretty well tuckered out. But a glance at the ambulance shows where he is now: Half reclining, laid out for inspection, he is partially covered with a hospital blanket and the ambulance driver has the heater on. He rests about half an hour and that keeps him going.

Negative reports continue from foot and boat patrols. I go over to Major McLeod. "Mac, do you have a grapnel on the fire wagon?"

"It's worse than that, Colonel, there isn't one on the Island. I asked Mr. Griffin to make a couple for us in the Maintenance Shops. They should be ready in another hour."

"Well, I guess if we had them at each Boat Basin no one would know where to find them. A grapnel isn't something we need every day."

"The Sheriff has a good one. Should I call his office and ask them to bring it over?"

"Go ahead, but let's not raise any alarm."

Someone comes up on the radio net. Major Stith just landed on Parris Island at Page Field. Do we want to send up with him someone better acquainted with the area? We do and shall. Six or eight of my boys are standing around waiting for something to do, such as taking their turn in a boat. Clark happens to be at the right end of their semicircle, lucky Pierre. "Do you want to take an airplane ride?"

"Yes, sir!"

"You know the ground here and what's going on. Hop in the Guard truck and get out to Page Field. Major Stith will be waiting for you. Give him the dope and see if you can locate anything."

"Aye, aye, sir." He's gone.

In that waiting group I see one of our problem children. He had nine years in the Army before he joined the Corps—so maybe he was raised in the wrong environment. Give him something unusual and he'll work himself to exhaustion. (I imagine he is an excellent combat soldier.) But burden him with endless routine, such as instructing on the School Range, and he's a constant source of irritation. While he's shrewd enough to keep himself from being clobbered, he's continually in hot water over trivia: just a little bit late, dismisses his outfit too early, careless about paying his bills—probably allots too much of his budget to beer. Then there are his wife and child; there seem to be difficulties at home; I know that they've both been to see the chaplain several times. This is another example of a good marine who shouldn't even try to be a family man. Before the war we discouraged married men in the Corps. We refused to enlist any in the lower grades. For years there was an article in the *Marine Corps Manual* that said in effect: Service to the Corps comes first, family life is secondary. Then the pay was such that juniors couldn't afford a wife; now our pay scales are arranged to encourage marriage. But as the saying goes: "If the Marine Corps wanted you to have a wife, you'd have been issued one." Marriage is certainly a detriment to our mobility.

Major McLeod suggests we make a short reconnaissance and refresh our knowledge of the terrain. We drive to the low-numbered end of B-Butts, get out, look around, speculate on what route the platoon took. Then we go to A-Butts, study Ribbon Creek, note the condition of our small homemade pier, and climb up on the end of the butts where we can survey the whole landscape. We return to his station wagon just in time to pick up an emergency message: Fire Call.

"Want to go to a fire?"

"Hell, no. Do you have to?"

"Peck's at the Fire Barn; I can skip this one. I'll send Lieutenant Jones out."

"Then let's get back and see what's going on."

En route he checks in with his office and has a conversation about the DI. He mentions his name, McKeon, and pronounces it exactly the way some careful linguists pronounce mine! (Later I found out that Matthew McKeon pronounces his surname McEwen. The family claims Irish origin. But genealogists could probably show that we're distant cousins, out of the MacDonalds of Glencoe—those that could run fast enough to escape the Campbells.)

"What did you say that guy's name was?"

"I've been trying to keep it from you, Colonel."

"Damn you! I'm going to find a culprit named McLeod even if he spells it with two *c*'s."

Two sheriff's cars are at our CP. Deputy O. C. Michael brought over the grapnel and our boys started to drag, though the water is still quite high. Sheriff J. E. McTeer followed in Michael's wake. I climb in a car with them, frankly to get warm. But it turned out I was to receive a most needed education.

Sheriff McTeer is a Southern gentleman of the old school. He doesn't make a practice of barging over to Parris Island and telling us Yankees how to do our jobs. But he has had years of valuable experience here in the Low Country recovering bodies. He breaks the news gently just by telling some of his stories. He particularly emphasizes the fact that a body is invariably found quite close to the spot where the man goes down. This is true even in a strong tideway. Then he tells us about floaters. He estimates it would take four days in this season and weather for enough gases to form to raise a body. Then we worry about fish and crabs. He has an answer to that, too. If a body were clothed, it could most probably rise even though exposed flesh might be well cleaned off. That raises yet another question which none can answer: Quite a few in that platoon last night were partially undressed.

Finally Sheriff McTeer tells about shrimpers. He figures the best way to retrieve a body is to drag with a shrimp net. He has used that method time and again. Would it be all right if he tried to get someone over? It would! He tells about Rutledge Elliott, always ready to lend a hand. If his trawler and crew are ready, McTeer could have them on their way in short order. He calls his office on the voice-radio:

"Jim, I want you to call Rut Elliott. Put the telephone receiver against your radio and I'll talk to him. Then you listen and tell me what he says." The call is completed.

"Rut, this is McTeer. There's been some trouble over here on Parris Island. Could you bring your boat over and drag this stream?"

"He says, 'Where are you?' "

"What's the name of this place?"

"Ribbon Creek."

"We're out at the Rifle Range, on Ribbon Creek. We're up the stream a piece. You'll see us on the bank."

"He says he knows where it is and he'll be over as soon as he can get underway."

"How long will it take?"

"He says he has to go all the way around the Island. It'll be an hour and a half after he casts off."

"Many thanks, Rut. I know the boys over here will appreciate it."

Sheriff McTeer is also Beaufort County's self-confessed champion mud-flat runner. He gained that skill hunting marsh hen. He wants to cross over Ribbon Creek and do a little scouting, if we can find him some rubber boots and utility clothing. Ragley takes the Guard truck to the barracks and borrows some utilities from Private Campbell, who wears the largest in the Battalion. McTeer changes, we call in Sparks, and the two go across to the tidal flats.

They find several trails, but there is no way to know whether they were left by recruits or searching parties. Then they spend some time following one that particularly interests them. This trail leads down to the creek from the marsh on the far side to a point some fifty yards below where we are standing. The tide is at just about the stage it must have been when the platoon marched in. Tracks in the spongy mud disappear in the water. It will be some time yet before we realize their fateful portent.

3

Thumping

MAJOR JAMES K. YOUNG commanded Weapons Training Battalion eight months until I took over July 3, 1953. The first thing Jim did when I arrived was hand me a three-page memorandum without heading, date, or signature. He told me this was passed by hand from each Battalion Commander to his relief. The paper was headed "MALTREATMENT." It stated the policy of Major General Merwin H. Silverthorn, then Commanding General at Parris Island. This is an abstract of that policy:

> Any Drill Instructor that strikes a recruit except in self-defense, will be tried by court-martial. It is the policy of the Commanding General to try maltreatment cases by Special or General Courts-Martial. This policy should not be construed as detracting from the discretion inferred upon convening authorities by law. When a Commanding Officer is informed of maltreatment, the Drill Instructor concerned, regardless of rank, shall be confined as soon as possible, and all recruit witnesses shall be segregated. It is well known that many Drill Instructors have escaped punishment because they or their friends frightened the recruits into false testimony or into refusing to testify to actual facts. In every case of this nature, speed in investigation and awarding punishment is essential. Commanding Officers must assure recruits that they may feel free to testify as to the truth and that little or no delay in their recruit training will result.

But I was never convinced Silverthorn meant what he said about "detracting from the discretion" of Battalion Commanders.

Frequently in his Tuesday morning conferences he spoke caustically about those who insisted upon exercising their legal prerogatives administering nonjudicial punishment or referring minor cases to trial by summary court-martial, even though these actions were swift and certain. We were given to understand—unequivocally—that while the law gave us discretion, Silverthorn didn't. Should any of us feel that deviation from his policy was essential, we would visit him privately in his office and obtain his permission in each instance. Silverthorn reminded us often that General Lemuel C. Shepherd, Jr., then Commandant of the Marine Corps, sent him to Parris Island for the specific purpose of eradicating maltreatment.

Unfortunately, General Silverthorn's policy failed to have the desired effect. Company officers overlooked minor acts of maltreatment; to take notice of them would upgrade those acts to criminal. Battalion Commanders meeting a recalcitrant DI at office hours would tend to write "excuse accepted" on the punishment sheet and then give the offender a tongue lashing. Even when more submissive COs ordered a special court-martial in rather serious cases, it was nearly impossible to sustain a conviction. The court was normally composed of two company officers and a DI from another battalion. They were too close to the accused DI—too aware of his problems—to be objective. It took months for me to realize these acquittals hinged on semantics.

One mid-day Bob Krugh, my Battalion Adjutant, was driving me to Mainside for an Exchange Council meeting. As we passed West End Infirmary a recruit platoon was standing at rigid attention near the door. Toward the rear of the platoon a DI was slapping a recruit in the face hard enough to snap back his head. Bob stopped the car and I grabbed the DI by one arm, the recruit by another. We loaded them in, took them straight to their Battalion Office, and handed them over to Captain Charles Patrick, who was then Executive Officer. Lieutenant Colonel Carl A. Nielsen, Battalion Commander and an old-timer who followed the book, ordered trial by special court-martial. Bob Krugh and I were witnesses; counsel harped on our distance from the scene, which in a car closing the range is difficult to estimate. Recruits standing beside and behind the victim were also witnesses. The verdict: not guilty. Hearing that, I was rather disturbed until eventually I could figure it out. A Parris Island court required spilled blood or broken bones to meet its criterion of *maltreatment*.

That word didn't impress me until I came to Parris Island. In fact, I had to look it up in the Code: "Any person subject to this Code who is guilty of cruelty toward, or oppression or maltreatment of, any person subject to his orders shall be punished as a court-martial may direct." In explanation *Manual for Courts-Martial* says:

> The cruelty, oppression, or maltreatment must be real, although not necessarily physical. To assault and to subject to improper punishment are examples of this offense. The imposition of necessary or proper duties and the exaction of their performance will not constitute this offense even though such duties are arduous or hazardous or both.

When this abuse was interpreted by general courts-martial, whose members were further removed from intimacy with DIs, one might predict that convictions for maltreatment would be more certain. But this was not the case. It took weeks for law specialists to hold a pre-trial investigation and schedule the trial. Then when the DI did come to trial, prosecution witnesses were his own recruits. Except for those few with an ax to grind or a sprinkling of mild neurotics, who were usually discredited during cross-examination, the normal recruit was staunchly loyal to his old Drill Instructor. When all the evidence was in, most courts had "reasonable doubt." Acquittals exceeded convictions. Threats of trying recruits for perjury were of no avail.

During Inquiry into the Ribbon Creek incident Thomas P. Costello, counsel for Matthew McKeon, said: "It seems to me that there is so much proof and evidence produced here to the effect that Staff Sergeant Matthew McKeon was informed about maltreatment that there must be an awful lot of it, else why the necessity of so much warning concerning maltreatment?"

Attorney Costello scored a point. When I arrived at Parris

Island we had a special detention squad room for DIs awaiting trial. After all, they were noncommissioned officers and it is Marine Corps tradition not to lock up an NCO unless he is a real criminal—we usually take his stripes away before we consider throwing him in the brig. Anyway, maltreatment was sufficiently prevalent to warrant a DI pokey. Out at Weapons Battalion we had Platoon 40 assigned as permanent target pullers and police detail. One DI after another in Platoon 40 had been accused of maltreatment, while investigations and trials went on for more than six months. It was a sorry outfit; we were happy when that platoon was transferred.

Courts-martial for maltreatment were continuous during the thirty-three months preceding Ribbon Creek. To protect the individual privacy of the accused DI, newspapermen were rarely informed of these. But court-martial didn't solve the problem. One trouble was that the offense was variously defined at different command levels. Besides threatening court-martial and elaborating on the penalties for those convicted, Post Regulations merely said: "Maltreatment of recruits reflects serious discredit on the command. It is therefore essential that all possible precautions be taken by all members of this command to preclude maltreatment in any form. Maltreatment is considered to be a serious offense." Standing Operating Procedure for Recruit Training Battalions (Male) was more explicit:

> Maltreatment of recruits is prohibited. Personnel guilty of maltreatment will receive severe disciplinary action in view of the subordinate status of the recruit and the absolute necessity of just and equitable treatment in the development of a recruit into a marine. Some examples of maltreatment are:
>
> Abusive treatment.
>
> *Striking* another person in the service is an offense against regulations. Correction of a recruit's clothing, equipment, manner of posture by a Drill Instructor is not maltreatment unless it is done in an abusive manner. Instructors at all times are responsible that corrective action is not abusive and that it cannot be misconstrued by the recruit as striking or a threat thereof.

Hazing does not develop in a recruit pride of being a marine, and in many forms it is dangerous to health. Among many practices considered to be hazing are: scrubbing decks with tooth brushes; lockerbox drill; calisthenics with pockets loaded with sand; platoon belt lines; conduct of physical drill to the point of exhaustion; the deliberate creation of nonconstructive work; use of the position of attention as a punishment; running up and down ladders; pulling the cap over the eyes; scrubbing the recruit with sand, canvas or other materials; inhaling smoke and drinking water.

Any interference with the privilege of routine medical treatment at Sick Call, or emergency treatment at any time, is maltreatment.

Light or no-duty chits will be respected both as to express and implied meaning.

Profane, obscene or abusive language is prohibited by the Uniform Code of Military Justice.

Irregularities.

Mail will be delivered promptly and recruits will be allowed to receive, read and retain newspapers, periodicals and books.

Guard duty has two functions, security and instruction. It will not be used for punishment.

Mass punishment. A platoon, or a portion thereof, will not be disciplined for offenses committed by individual recruits.

Interruption of sleep. The period between Taps and Reveille is designated for the uninterrupted sleep of individuals in their billets. No recruit not on duty is to be disturbed during these hours except in cases of emergency. This does not preclude the quiet awakening of bedwetters at periodic intervals.

Shouting. Orders and commands will be given only as loudly as is necessary for recipients to hear. Shouting at a recruit may constitute hazing.

Exploitation.

Financial dealings with recruits involve gifts, loans, bribes, donations, testimonials and holding of monies or other valuables.

Collections. Money will not be collected from recruits by permanent personnel except as authorized by the Commanding General.

Extortion is unlawfully influencing a recruit to the advantage or profit of the extortionist.

Promising certain station for profit.

Procuring civilian clothing or jewelry or services for recruits.

Requiring recruits to perform personal services: This includes washing, folding, ironing or stowing of laundry; shining shoes; cleaning individual weapons or equipment; making bunks; cleaning rooms and similar services.

We have one other source document concerning maltreatment, Lesson Plan No. 1, Drill Instructors' School. While not a regulatory publication, it could be used as a threat to the DI:

Many Drill Instructors have a fear that the "Brass" is out to get them. They develop this fear through hearing of investigations of innocent DIs; they do not distinguish between investigation and punishment. They should understand that under circumstances in which persons are injured that an investigation is mandatory—at Parris Island or anywhere else.

Stress fact the CG and Bn COs recognize errors in judgment are possible, also that every effort is made to help a DI in difficulties or trouble, but that it is impossible to whitewash maltreatment. The DI who understands his authority and responsibility will do his job without worry or fear. However, there are some Drill Instructors who say they don't know what "maltreatment" is, that they are afraid to do many things which they consider proper for fear of being accused of maltreatment. Any question of this nature can be resolved easily.

What is maltreatment? (Unnecessary rough physical or mental treatment.) Ask yourself the question, "Is the action which I am contemplating (regardless of who carries it out) designed to hurt the recruit in order to punish him for past misdeeds or to insure his future compliance or to assert my authority?" If the answer is "yes," don't do it. Now, some few will want a further definition of "hurt." The only answer here is, "Do it to yourself; if it hurts, it's hurt." Don't stick your neck out by maltreating; this does not mean that training should be soft, far from it. Maltreatment can be mental or physical or both.

The DI does not punish, but may use extra instructions of constructive nature.

That last admonition is the crux of our problem—only the Battalion Commander may administer punishment legally. But the Marine Corps leader instills discipline and thus builds morale in his outfit by precept and example through rewards and punishment. All of this indoctrination for the DI is negative: he is told what he can't do; he isn't told what he can do. If the recruit needs correction, the DI can legitimately "chew him out" —in a soft voice, without profanity, obscenity, or abuse. Beyond that, he must "run the recruit up" to the Battalion Commander, which requires filling out a punishment sheet, scheduling Office Hours, and bringing along witnesses. Needless to say, formally arraigning minor offenders has traditionally been judged the sign of poor leadership. If a DI should visit the Battalion Commander frequently with his problems, he wouldn't be long on the field.

Legitimately the DI has one loophole: extra instruction of a constructive nature. Emphasis is on "physical conditioning" since commanders in the field habitually deplore the physical condition of our recruit graduates. Recruits making errors in the manual of arms might be required to double-time around the parade ground, or hold the rifle out horizontally with one hand. There are push-ups, knee-bends, physical drill under arms, double-timing in place, and even duck-walking that can be done openly without criticism. Except in the most sultry weather, it is tradition that recruits run to and from formation; this is not criticized. Company officers tend to overlook the game of chasing seagulls or finding a group of recalcitrants staring at the Iwo Jima monument, ostensibly imbuing themselves with tradition.

But that is about the limit of the DI's disciplinary tools to be used openly; the remainder must be surreptitious. Since one DI is continuously with the troops, while most "supervision" comes during Working Hours, and since the DI can insure the privacy of his hut or squadroom by establishing outposts—if he is that cautious, the only limit on informal punishment is ingenuity—and the avoidance of telltale marks. Even then a steady flow of minor injuries treated at Sick Bay are attributed with a straight face to flying locker-boxes.

There have always been plenty of buckets on Parris Island. For years each new recruit had to draw one with his initial issue. These were useful—inside—to place over the recruit's head while he stood at attention. A variation was to make him smoke a cigarette with his head in the bucket. Cigarettes themselves were useful: they might be smoked under a blanket, or held in the mouth by the lighted end, or chewed up. Making the punishment fit the crime, DIs gave this treatment to those who tried to steal a smoke without the smoking lamp being "lit." There was bunk drill, elbows-and-toes treatment, countless minor effective tortures useful so long as the perpetrator wasn't caught and the victim didn't squeal.

By rule and tradition we lay hands on a marine only to correct his posture or the position of his rifle. There was even a time when those exceptions were not permitted. Then each DI carried a swagger stick, which he laid on the recruit instead of hands. Eventually swagger sticks were replaced by exceptions to the rule. In 1954 the swagger stick returned—as a badge of office. But the "no hands" rule with recruits is extremely difficult to enforce; the DI is sorely tempted. Moreover, he considers his charges children. We all spank our kids, don't we? Though I don't advocate corporal punishment in general, I'm convinced that its moderate application would make useful citizens of many misfits we send back to civilian life through the Aptitude Board.

Years ago in Port-au-Prince the 53d Machine Gun Company had a new first sergeant, William E. Safley. One morning at Reveille a hung-over private refused to get up when the corporal called him. This was reported to the sergeant who also called him and met with refusal. The sergeant took his problem to the first sergeant who went into the squadroom, upended the bunk and, when the private got to his feet, knocked him down. At Office Hours these three witnesses appeared with the accused, who was wearing a dressing on his cheek:

COLONEL: What do you have to say?

ACCUSED: Sir, the First Sergeant hit me.

COLONEL: He didn't hit you hard enough; five days bread and water.

SERGEANT MAJOR: Right face, forward march.

COLONEL: First Sergeant, you did the right thing. You're excused. *(He turned to the corporal and sergeant.)* As for you two, you're keeping your stripes on probation. My noncommissioned officers are going to be obeyed. If the private is too big for one corporal to handle, the corporal nearest him will lend a hand. Let me worry about complaints from any Congressmen. Dismissed.

Master Sergeant Thomas Brokaw was a DI at Montfort Point when we had segregated recruit training. An ex-sparring partner of Jersey Joe, one look at Brokaw is enough to inspire military courtesy. While inspecting the magazine area one day he confided in me, "Ah din have no trouble wid da boys. Co'se, once in a while I had ta take 'em out in da woods and talk to 'em."

Staff Sergeant Matthew McKeon was being cross-examined at the Court-Martial:

Q. Now, speaking of slapping, you say you had other platoons. Is that the way you handled your other platoons? Did you handle your platoon in combat that way?

A. No, sir. By slapping them?

Q. Yes. They were in a little different status, weren't they?

A. Well, in combat or outside of combat when I was a squad leader or fire team leader and a man in my fire team or squad goofed off, we fell into a little knuckle drill.

We see a newspaper picture of a state governor being made honorary member of a college professional fraternity. He is handed a suitably inscribed pledge's paddle. We all know the brothers use those paddles for purposes other than collecting autographs. We have initiations in social, fraternal, and service organizations. Even the Boy Scouts have an "ordeal" in the Order of the Arrow. Only when someone gets hurt do we raise the cry of "hazing." Then we say the American way of life is respect for the dignity and worth of the individual. In that light, any form of hazing is wrong. But is it? I believe that humiliation and indignities—within bounds—make for a better man. I believe they give him a stronger feeling of group membership—

belonging. In the Marine Corps we strive for group-belonging expressed in teamwork. The well-being of the individual is subordinate to that of corps and country.

At Weapons Battalion record day provides a good show. The recruit's score is chalked on his helmet liner, cap visor, or the back of his shooting jacket. Before the platoon marches off from the firing line it is divided in two groups: qualified and unqualified. The first section moves off, heads up, squared away. The second section follows in the wake at a respectful distance. These recruits wear their shooting jackets backward or as skirts, trouser legs are rolled up, caps are reversed, rifles are slung with muzzles toward the deck. One evening I saw a platoon headed for chow; it had fired record that day. The leading section was in perfect cadence and really looked proud. Bringing up the rear was a small group with thumbs in mouth, skipping, wearing towels as diapers. Probably I should have stopped and taken the name of the DI, but I figured his originality might have some effect.

There was an incident I experienced at Weapons Battalion when a recruit lost blood. Firing the Browning Automatic Rifle was in progress on Special Weapons Range. This recruit had a stoppage. Instead of just raising his hand, he started to turn around—which hazards everyone on the firing line. One of my coaches took an original form of immediate action: He clobbered the recruit with a cleaning rod. After Dr. Ernie Ferrell sewed up the scalp, we had Office Hours. The recruit was impressed with his error. I ruled that my coach acted in line of duty; that his action, though slightly rough, was effective.

An official indignity forced on the new recruit is the haircut. He marches in a naked line at Hygienic and takes his turn in a straight-backed chair. In twenty seconds it's all over; he's completely bald. One commanding general questioned about this explained that recruit haircuts were required for sanitary reasons, but he didn't mention that the hospital corpsman, who sees each recruit just before the barber, eliminates pediculosis from the pubic hair with a quick shot of DDT. Father August Weigand, CSSp, visiting Parris Island, took me to task because recruits' heads were shaved. He thought it unnecessary humiliation:

"How long do they keep them shaved?"

"They just do it once, Gus. In three weeks they'll have a nice crew cut."

"Well, if there were good psychological reasons, I'd go along with it."

"How long was your head shaved in the novitiate, Gus?"

"Two years." He changed the subject.

Recruits, of course, still fail to understand. Colonel Nelson Reeve had a good example before the Aptitude Board. The lad had just been advised that he was to be discharged and sent home:

"Do you have any questions?"

"Yes, sir. Do I get embarrassment pay for this?"

"Embarrassment pay?" Reeve thought of all the new pay laws: severance pay, mustering out pay, travel pay, dislocation allowance. "What do you mean?"

"The boys at POU told me I'd get embarrassment pay while my hair was growing back."

Then this classic requires a bit of explanation. The ex-recruit who wrote the following letter had a real problem. Recruiting had been difficult and the Marine Corps was required to lower dental standards. At the time this letter was written previous higher standards still applied to the Marine Corps Reserve. The man addressed his problem to the Commandant of the Marine Corps:

23 July, 1948

DEAR SIR,

I would like to get some information from you, and I would like you to answer me a question, why wasn't I excepted in the Volunteer Marine Corps Reserve. Heres the story—

I enlisted in the Marine Corps 30th June 1947 to serve 3 years. I wanted to be a Marine ever scince I was a kid. I wanted to be a twenty year man. So I joined up. Sent me to Parris Island. They kicked the shit out of me, like they do all "boots." for a week. Then the "D.I." calls me and two other fellows from my platoon, and says to pack our gear. We were to go to Casual Co. I knew right then & there. The bastards were going to send me home, I get to Casual Co. and hang around for another week, and then they sent me home with a medical survey, General Discharge. All my hair was off my head. And when I got home. I was so fucken humiliated, I got pissed at the Marine Corps. They said I did not have enough teeth. Now what I want to know is, do you fight a war with your teeth? They could of at least fix them for me. But no, they send me home, and humiliate me. I was discharged on the 17th July 1947. People made fun at me. And boy was I pissed off. So exactly one year later, I went to Newark New Jersey to enlist in the Volunteer Reserves. Before that I sent a card to the Commandante Vandergrift. And he sent it to Newark. I got a letter and an enlistment blank to fill out. I fill it out and send it to Newark. A while later I get a letter say to report to the recruiting office at Newark with my original discharge. I get there and I just about to sign all the papers. when the sergeant calls the Captain in charge, and says, "Sir, this man received a medical survey discharge." So the Captain, "well we can't take you in the Reserves," *but,* he says, "we can take you in the Regulars." Now what kind of shit were they handing me. First they throw me out of the Regulars, then they said I could go back in the Regulars. I told him, I wouldn't go to that fucken island if you gave me a $1,000. So he says, "well son, thats all we can do for you." So please answer me this question, why wasn't I excepted in the V. Reserves. I would like to get in the Rerserves very much.

I'll enclose the letter they sent me in regards to the enlistment in the V. Reserves.

Please answer.

Thank You Very Much,

We hold the DI responsible for making marines out of his boys; then we limit his authority to talking—so long as it's nice, pure talk. Depot General Order No. 161 enjoins us to suppress obscene and profane language. We are told that vulgarity weakens our powers for communication, but this doesn't convince either DIs or recruits. My prediction is that we'll never make profanity unpopular with marines. As a youngster I saw *What Price Glory?* on the stage; every punctuation mark seemed to be a "godammit." Then the captain asked the old Frenchman, "Is it rape or seduction?" Another report came from Floyd Gibbons, who quoted the gunnery sergeant in France as saying when his troops went over the top, "Come on, you sonsofbitches! Do you want to live forever?" The only writer I remember who used mild words in describing marines was John Thomason, but he had a gift for translating marine language into parlor talk. There was the time he spoke of his DI's asserted rank relative to God and said, "Come to think of it, I don't believe he ever mentioned God—at least in that manner."

We had out in San Diego a pink-cheeked private named Bettis. He couldn't finish a brief sentence without calling up a few violent oaths. Our Company Commander was George Maynard, who had years of practice in Santa Domingo, China, and Nicaragua. George was an accomplished master of cursing in four languages—including classical Latin—but he said it made him blush to hear Bettis talk. Aboard ship I've overheard young sailors and marines spout obscenities until even I was amazed at their proficiency. But they did it in conversational tone and without obvious self-consciousness. I can't believe they meant to be profane or vulgar. Most crimes require intent; they had none, hence no crimc.

It seems to be a tradition: tough soldier, rough talk. There's not much hope for effective legislation against tradition. Actually, it seems to give a lift to our *esprit* and I can't see any real harm in it, though most wives complain when we're first home from a long stretch in the field. If language helps to make a marine feel that he's tough, I'm for it.

Withholding a recruit's mail is unquestionably abusive, but even there the DI has a problem. It is fine to say that the boys may read their home-town newspapers and any magazines they receive, yet they don't have time to read much more than letters and the *Marine's Guidebook*. Then the DI has a prejudice against sweets, particularly soft drinks and candy (pogey-bait), especially when his platoon is firing the Range. His sharp eyes prevent Boots purchasing sweets when they file through the exchange, but Mom mails him a box of fudge and cup cakes. This practice is so widespread that General Silverthorn instituted a "cookie locker" for each platoon. Theoretically recruits had access to their packages at times approved by the DI. Actually this food was liable to get rather stale at the Rifle Range. And when the DI did grant a dispensation the owner shared generously with his platoon-mates.

Extortion is another form of maltreatment that has existed since Parris Island became our Boot Camp. Extortion is continually being suppressed but it can't be eradicated. Recruits are often told it is tradition to give their DIs a "going away present" in gratitude for what they have acquired during their training. The DI tells of family problems, his boys are sympathetic. The basis of extortion rackets is that each recruit has in his pocket a few dollars he is unable to spend. Outside the messhall, for example, he hands the newsboy a quarter or a dollar and tells him to keep the change, which may help the Boot feel that at least he's superior to somebody. Then we have another factor: Thousands of men each with a few spare dollars means thousands of loose dollars. Graft at Parris Island is like *cumshaw* in China, it seems engrained in the way of life. The big difference over here is that we can pass laws against it and at least try to enforce them. Still it's quite a chore to keep ahead of the DIs: They invent a new approach every minute.

Occasionally DIs get emergency leave for serious illness or death in the family; they need only tell the platoon that they haven't any money for the trip home. DIs' babies are delivered at the Beaufort Naval Hospital with regularity; what is more fitting than a present for the proud father? Some DIs levy a tax on the platoon for permission to go to the movies; the money is placed in a bucket in the middle of the squadroom and left there when the platoon falls out. A few of those scroungers are known to have had the nerve to plank a stack of dimes on the bar at the Staff NCO Club and then brag about it.

I was talking with Jim Young, my Executive Officer. "Jim, did your DI ever shake you down when you came through here?"

"Hell, yes! Our platoon paid for a fine silver service—though we didn't see it. He was going to get married when we graduated. Then I ran into him on Iwo thirteen years later; the sonofabitch was still a bachelor."

One DI let it be known that his car was about to be repossessed; he owed $700. Imagine his surprise a few days later—the evening of pay day, to be exact—when he found a paper bag in the front seat of his car. It contained exactly $700. This came to light, however, and the DI was court-martialed.

A racket grew up during the schedule for taking commercial photographs at the Rifle Range. As each recruit came out of the Nissen hut he was approached by a "collection agent": "One dollar, boy, guarantees your picture in the home-town paper." This character must have made quite a haul. The editor of a Long Island weekly heard the story and raised the issue, but the culprit was never identified.

This shakedown is connected with a legitimate racket: photography. Each recruit has an official government photograph taken for his ID card and Service Record Book. He is also privileged to go to the Exchange and sit for a so-called portrait. But that isn't enough. He marches on schedule through one Nissen hut where he has a picture taken for the "yearbook." That publication is printed for a group of platoons and in addition to the individual pictures is made from plates used over and over. These contain a picture of the Commanding General with a message from him, a history of Parris Island, local scenes. The books sell to the recruit at five dollars a copy; they're alleged to have untold "public relations" value. When my son finished basic training at Fort Knox we received a similar book from the same Atlanta firm.

But even that isn't enough. Into another Nissen hut, on schedule in prescribed uniform, our recruit goes for a second commercial photograph. One copy is donated by this firm for use by the Home Town News Center and many of these do appear in the local paper. Then Mamma gets a proof along with sales letter and price list: "We know you're proud to have your son in the Marines and do want a picture of him in uniform." A predicted number of parents fail to respond to this letter. Then at the strategic time—which can also be predicted by experience—

these get a second letter: "We know how much you want that picture, just for you this is our second price."

Of course there's no need to be completely cynical about photographs: The Depot Exchange gets its rake-off and that money winds up in the Recreation Fund. In one year its percentage from the second firm exceeded $10,000. Looking at it another way, it saves the taxpayer that much for athletics and entertainment.

Our Iwo Jima monument on the right bank of the Potomac was purchased mainly by recruits. We give them "an opportunity" to contribute to charity and it seems there is always some drive going on. At the Fall Festival, mainstay of the Parris Island Welfare Chest, recruits by hundreds line up to win a home-baked cake on the wheel-of-fortune at the Officers' Wives Club booth. There, at least, they get something tangible for their money while DIs co-operate by lowering the barrier on sweets.

Magazine subscriptions afford another lucrative enterprise. It is unfortunate that this deal involves both the Marine Corps *Gazette* and the *Leatherneck,* which contribute so much to the Corps. This story begins in Washington. There, from appropriated funds, the Quartermaster General purchases annually a large block of copies of both magazines for distribution to posts and stations. But the continued success of any publication depends upon guaranteed circulation. Local Recreation Funds are "encouraged" to purchase additional bulk subscriptions. Then, with implicit pressure from higher up and tacit approval of Headquarters Marine Corps, agents of both *Leatherneck* and *Gazette* organize an unofficial sales force at Recruit Depots. At Parris Island the Depot and Battalion Sergeants Major sell the *Leatherneck* while Depot and Battalion Field Stripers (Chief Drill Instructors) peddle the *Gazette*. Every platoon attends a regularly scheduled sales talk for each magazine. From the official viewpoint members of this captive audience are under no pressure: They exercise their own free will. The salesman follows an approved "lesson plan"—then gathers in his commissions. (Alone or in concert, Sergeant Major and Field Striper have the power to give any DI a rather hard time.) Recruits buy.

We say the magazine salesman follows the official lesson

plan. One of my corporals told me about his experience with Platoon 34. His DI assembled the platoon, turned it over to the salesman, shoved off. After the salesman finished his speech outlined in the lesson plan, he had just one buyer. He then double-timed the Boots through the boondocks near the Dredge Cut and southwest of Second Battalion area. After this exercise several boys saw the light; after a second exercise the whole platoon was sold.

During my first year on the Depot sales amounted to $390,000. Commissions for the sales force were $49,000. For acting as sales managers, the Depot Field Striper received $6600 and the Depot Sergeant Major got $8800. Actually the Depot Sergeant Major admitted getting $12,000 but claimed he split $3200 among DIs. It's the old motto: "*Semper Fidelis,* we got ours." I often wonder whether Internal Revenue can say the same.

Now when the recruit sends the magazines home, or to the girl-friend, it isn't so bad. But every Boot gets an address change upon completion of training. For several years these magazines used to accumulate in the Post Office and then be sold for old paper. Just recently CWO Clayton D. Sketoe became Postal Officer, discovered the problem, and did something about it. But the pity is that recruits can read these magazines in their recreation rooms—anywhere in the world—free.

When Captain Charles Patrick, Officer of the Day, called me Sunday night and reported the plight of an unidentified recruit platoon, there was no need to make a formal study of the problem, I could give a split-second decision: "Lock up the DI." On the face of it, this unknown NCO was guilty of maltreatment. I had heard many stories about DIs taking their platoons on night marches through swamps—and the area behind Third Recruit Training Battalion seemed favored. There were rumors that some DIs had narrow escapes when they concealed the muddy boots and soiled clothing of their troops. We even heard that some Company Commanders discovered such evidence but couldn't or wouldn't find any witnesses to support their hypothesis. It was generally known that on the Elliott's Beach hike DIs enjoyed playing "air raid" in areas where their boys were sure to get lathered with mud, but no one seemed to object to that practice.

To my knowledge, no similar marches had been conducted at Weapons Battalion, though in the summer of 1955 one reserve officer from Philadelphia did exercise his troops most of the night at Elliott's Beach and bring them to the Rifle Range next morning for record firing, whipped. We did have a minor riot—or gang fight between two platoons—the evening of Washington's Birthday 1954 in which I am morally certain at least one DI was involved. Lieutenant Richard McLaughlin, Liaison Duty Officer in our Recreation Area, was inspecting at the time and nipped the fracas in the bud. I headed the Board of Investigation which met for three days and endeavored to sift out facts. We were quite unsuccessful. Recruit witnesses paraded through the courtroom and told us bare-faced lies; they were particularly careful to protect all DIs. In the Ribbon Creek case I hoped recruit witnesses would be separated quickly and that investigators might have an opportunity to pry from them a few truths. After all, we had this character red-handed.

4

Platoon 71

Recruit platoons at Parris Island are numbered serially as they form during the calendar year. Platoon 71 was activated in a regular assembly-line process at Recruit Receiving, February 23. Since the previous day, Wednesday, was a legal holiday, some of the group had been billeted overnight at Casual Company; others came by bus from Yemassee that morning. CWO Alexander Welter is in charge of Recruit Receiving but he spends more time signing papers than looking over the forlorn rabble disgorged at the door of this waiting room from vehicles of the Palmetto Bus Line. Welter's NCOs herd the boys into the room, seat them on backless benches, collect their travel orders, ask routine questions, type a roster of the new platoon, check names with noses, herd the outfit outside, and turn it over to a waiting DI. From then until graduation eleven weeks later the burden is on him.

Platoon 71 seemed much the same as any other. Good American names on its roster might have been drawn from a jury panel or college football squad: Beneshefski, Daszo, Grabowski, Hartman, Kochis, Martinez, McGuire, Mihalcsik, Nehrenz, Vaughn, Whitmore, Zeigler. There were but one Brown and Jones, no Smith or Miller. No two Boots had the same surname. New England Yankees with hazy knowledge of the War Between the States met unreconstructed Rebels who would talk of nothing else. There was a strong leavening from Great Lakes states and Appalachian foothills. There were country boys, city boys, boys from industrial towns—who would term themselves neither.

Probably seventy-seven civilian boys formed Platoon 71. But there are continual changes during training. Minzello was the first casualty: he went to Regimental Infirmary within forty-eight hours. By the end of the first week, before the platoon "went on schedule," it acquired six men from Platoon 59: Acker, Blair, Brower, *Hardeman,* Hendrix, *Reilly.* These men had been slow learners. That same day Private *Thomas* joined from Platoon 67; he had lost some time in Sick Bay. Early in March the DI sent Schempp and Strawderman to POU; neither had been tested with the GCT because of reading deficiency. By mid-March Bush, Cummins, and Hagey were dropped to Sick Bay. A week later Myers joined from Beaufort Naval Hospital. And so on April 8 there were seventy-nine on the DI's roster. Divided according to religion they were: Protestant 56, Catholic 22, Jewish 1; normal experience would indicate the distribution five light in Catholics. Available records tell nothing of race, but two Negroes were drowned: *Thompson* and *Wood.* Privates Barber, Butler, and Leake, who later testified, were also Negro.

How many recruits of Platoon 71 made the march into Ribbon Creek? It is doubtful that we shall ever know. The platoon roster which Major Holben submitted at the Inquiry shows seventy-eight. The one that Sergeant Huff brought to the Court-Martial indicates seventy-nine. Sergeant McKeon in the confession he made to Sergeant Cummings about seven-thirty the morning of April 9 stated seventy-five marched into the creek and three were at the hymn-sing. But Private Pool testified at the Inquiry that he returned from the hymn-sing, joined in the field day, and made the march. When Captain Patrick received his original head count, eight were missing. Later Private Cox returned from across the creek and sometime that night one of the missing was located in the Rifle Range Sick Bay: He had turned in there shortly after supper and did not make the march. The first roster shows Private Dunn transferred from the platoon; the second lists him a member. The specification under Charge II, modified by the Judge Advocate General and approved by the Secretary of the Navy, alleges McKeon marched seventy-four men into Ribbon Creek. My audit of all records would show the true number as seventy-eight. Beyond doubt there were seventy-seven. No one seemed to worry about a few warm bodies more or less.

Platoon 71 spent the rest of February, one week, "forming." Many of these procedures we shall view more closely elsewhere, and so here we'll preview them rapidly. From Recruit Receiving, the DI led his new platoon in a ragged formation to Hygienic where they left their civilian clothes, became "skin heads," emerged dressed in apparently oversized utility clothing and lugging seabags. Still in ragged formation with the embarrassed DI unable to keep them closed up or in step, they went about half a mile along Panama Street into Third Battalion area. Here they were assigned double-deck bunks in Nissen huts, dropped their seabags, drew mattresses, pillows, bedding, and locker-boxes. Most of the week they spent waiting in line for the "bucket issue" (principally toilet articles) at the Exchange, screening at POU (Psychiatric Observation Unit), physical examination, dental examination, issue of seasonal clothing, the "No. 1 Lecture" by some chaplain—divided for the moment according to religious faith—inoculations, the General Classification Test. Medical Records, Dental Records, Service Records were opened for each Boot, who spent considerable time answering questions and signing papers. Meanwhile the platoon was organized into squads, there was a place in formation for each lad to stand, marching improved as the DIs shouted at them while going from place to place to wait in line. They quickly learned protocol of the chow line.

Three Drill Instructors "picked up" Platoon 71 the first day. All would be with them during training hours, one of the three would be with them constantly. Staff Sergeant Edward A. Huff was Senior DI. His assistants were Staff Sergeant Matthew C. McKeon and Sergeant Richard J. King, both of whom graduated from DI School February 3. That is a five-week course; attrition is heavy; training is intense. No DI takes over a platoon upon completing school; he must first understudy an experienced DI. But a large increase in the recruit training load was forecast—and already during the first eight weeks of 1956 more than 5,000 had been received at Parris Island. By virtue of Staff NCO rank Matthew McKeon could expect to have a platoon of his own in the next ten-week cycle. This was contingent, of course, on the ability he would demonstrate as Edward Huff's understudy.

Staff Sergeant Huff reported at Parris Island August 6, 1954. He went on the drill field in October of that year. While in Second Battalion he took through two platoons as Junior DI and one as Senior. Platoon 71 was the second he was with in Third Battalion but the first as Senior DI. At the Court-Martial he was questioned about service:

Q. Sergeant Huff, how long have you been continuously in the United States Marine Corps?

A. Approximately twelve years, six months, and about fifteen days, sir.

Huff was married and occupied Quarters 264, on the corner of Panama and Cuba streets at Mainside, about 250 yards east of the Administration Building and the same distance south of the Commanding General's quarters. Since he was senior in rank and also had sixteen months on the field, Huff "delegated" night and weekend duties to McKeon and King. Swimming instruction, for instance, is given at night; Huff never took his platoon to the pool.

Sergeant Richard J. King had a month less than four years' service when assigned with Platoon 71. He was unmarried and consequently had to live in a hut or room near the platoon when off duty and not on liberty. That meant when McKeon had the duty he and King frequently spent the evening together.

Staff Sergeant Matthew Charles McKeon was born at South Acton, Massachusetts, October 26, 1924. His parents now live in Worcester. He was the fifth of his mother's eight children, four boys and four girls. She lost her first husband after having two children. The family is stanchly Catholic. Matt didn't finish high school—he was expelled from school once—but left during World War II to go to work. With two brothers then serving in the Marine Corps and a sister an Army nurse, Matt stayed just eighteen months as a wire blocker: winding wire on spools, tying ends, maneuvering a fork lift to store and ship the spools. Before he was eighteen, Matt enlisted in the Navy, went through Boot Camp at Newport, Rhode Island, went aboard *Essex* and stayed throughout her gallant World War II career.

When the Navy finished bringing troops home from the Pacific in Operation Magic Carpet and laid up *Essex* at Bremerton in December 1945 Matt McKeon was "demobilized." He took a job in a machine shop operating a heading machine, putting tops on such things as bolts and piston rods. This lasted sixteen months; Matt's feet were itching all the time. In May 1948 he enlisted in the Marine Corps and went through Boot Camp at Parris Island. After that, as if he needed more seagoing experience, McKeon went to Sea School at Marine Barracks, Norfolk Naval Shipyard, Portsmouth, Virginia. From there he went in a draft to *Columbus,* flagship of Commander Naval Forces, Eastern Atlantic and Mediterranean. Based in England, she cruised from the Scandinavian countries through the Mediterranean. Late in 1949 McKeon was beached at Charleston, South Carolina, where he spent four months at the Marine Barracks.

While in Charleston, Matthew McKeon took a wife, Elizabeth, who had borne him a girl and a boy by the time he was assigned Platoon 71. They were now expecting their third child. Alice Bridget was born shortly after the Court-Martial.

From Charleston, McKeon went to Quantico and served two years with Schools Demonstration Troops. That outfit changes its name quite frequently though it has served the same purpose at least ten years. It conducts weapons demonstrations and assists in tactical problems of the Marine Corps Schools, where officers are trained at three levels of command; it assists in the testing and development of new weapons and equipment; and it presents spectacles for visiting dignitaries. Life in the outfit is rugged but professional training is superb. After a fourteen-month tour in Korea, McKeon returned to Quantico and spent more than a year instructing young officers in infantry weapons at Basic School.

Between tours at Quantico, Matt McKeon served in Korea, where he arrived in late 1952. While the situation was stabilized —a so-called active defense—First Marine Division was involved in much shooting. McKeon was Platoon Sergeant of a machine-gun platoon. He was questioned about this at the Court-Martial:

Q. What activity were you in?

A. Well, Hill 229—and then we were up around Boulder City at the end of 76 Alley, they call it. I don't know what the hill number was.

Q. While you were in combat, at any one time what was the largest number of machine guns under your command?

A. Well, just before we secured, we had to defend this little link—a finger.

Q. A what?

A. A finger running out over a patty there, and we had approximately as many as fifteen to twenty machine guns on it.

Between his first tour at Quantico and his experience in Korea McKeon remained a civilian four months, but he couldn't stay home while his buddies were fighting. When his enlistment expired during his second tour in Quantico, McKeon decided to make a career of the Marine Corps. He re-enlisted for six years and volunteered to be a Drill Instructor at Parris Island. He arrived there December 29, 1955, spent five weeks in Drill Instructors' School, and on February 4 was assigned to Third Recruit Training Battalion. Ninety NCOs started in Class No. 38 at DI School, fifty-five completed the course, Matthew McKeon stood fourteenth in his class. It could reasonably be forecast he would become an outstanding DI.

Some of us like to predict from test scores. October 8, 1952, shortly after McKeon signed his third enlistment contract, having been out of the service four months, he was given the General Classification Test for the second time. With 100 being average, McKeon's over-all score was 91; the profile: reading and vocabulary 93, arithmetic computation 90, arithmetic reasoning 99, pattern analysis 81. His last qualification with the carbine was 248 (sharpshooter), with the rifle 168 (unqualified), with the pistol 244 (marksman). Yet in DI School his final average was 84.9 with the average of 673 graduates about 80.

Without stopping to debate those recurring questions of equity and validity, we can accept as a fact that the way to promotion and pay in the Marine Corps is paved by the judgment of superiors. Matthew McKeon's superiors were pleased with his performance.

Lieutenant Colonel Robert Thompson, Battalion Commander, said: "I have a file of monitors' reports on Sergeant McKeon in which everything is marked from 'very good' to 'outstanding.' From my observation of Sergeant McKeon on the field I was most pleasantly surprised at his ability, his attitude toward being a Drill Instructor, and the readiness with which he came in and actually took over his duties with the platoon."

Captain Richard Grey, Company Commander, said: "I have made the comment to others that I thought he was one of the smartest Drill Instructors we had had in the Battalion since I had been there."

Master Sergeant Hershel Baker, Field Sergeant Major, said: "I'd say he was doing a very good job. I base this observation upon the conscientiousness with which he works with the platoon. He had—to me—a great amount of patience to correct individuals on errors and even when he gave them a break from drill—gave them time to have some water to drink or something—Sergeant McKeon was going over something to keep their minds open at all times. He was going over something he had already taught—a review on what he has done, which is an indication of a man being conscientious and that is what we look for in Drill Instructors."

Master Sergeant Hans Manthey, Chief Drill Instructor, said: "I had in mind giving—to make Sergeant McKeon a Senior Drill Instructor when he finished this platoon, sir. I based that observation on his manner, the way he handled troops, his bearing, and his being versed on the drill, sir."

Staff Sergeant Edward Huff, Senior Drill Instructor of Platoon 71, said: "Like I said before, sir, Sergeant McKeon, as far as I am concerned, is an outstanding Drill Instructor. He done his work—done it well—and to me he never seemed to complain."

Twenty-three members of Platoon 71 testified at the Inquiry, eleven made no voluntary statement when given that opportunity at the conclusion of their hearing (but it is highly probable that Counsel Holben discouraged testimony he didn't carefully guide). Another eleven, while generally slanting their views toward the Ribbon Creek incident, spoke highly of Sergeant McKeon. William Rambo was most direct: "Well, sir, I'd like to say that Staff Sergeant McKeon has been a great help to me and I'm pretty sure he has been for the rest of the boys. And he's always been good to us. He's been patient with us and he's trying to teach us certain things that we should know in Boot Camp. A lot of things that he has helped us on—I know he has me—and I'm grateful to him for that, sir. That's about all I can say, sir." The only harsh note among the voices of twenty-three recruits came from Hugh Mulligan—and he wasn't actually derogatory: "Well, sir, I believe that in the afternoon when I was laying on the grass with a few of the other recruits—I believe that Sergeant McKeon was displeased with that, sir. That's as much as I know." These men all spoke less than seventy-two hours after the tragedy. They spoke in defense of their DI.

Nineteen members of Platoon 71 testified at the Court-Martial fifteen weeks after the tragedy; eleven of these were repeaters from the Inquiry. None was actually hostile toward Matthew McKeon. In cross-examining them, Defense Counsel used many long, leading questions, but it is still possible to winnow out some of the witnesses' own words to indicate their feelings. Eugene Ervin said: "He was patient—very patient. He was, sir, in my opinion, one of the best teachers. He wanted us to be one of the best platoons, sir—I know that." Gerald Langone said: "Well, sir, I thought he was the best on the Island—in my opinion—and I think most of the men agreed with me, sir. He was always patient with us and whenever we got a break it was Sergeant McKeon that gave it to us—mostly. Whenever he was on duty he gave us frequent breaks. He always told us if we had any personal problems to come right up to him and talk to him about it. Sergeant McKeon told us quite a few times that he wanted the best that we could offer—at least we could try, try hard." Melvin Barber said: "To me he seemed like a very right person. I mean, he helped you if you needed any help—tried to help you. No, sir; he didn't flare up. He was a very patient person. But I have seen him smack a person on the head—in the back of the head." John Maloof said: "When the troops were at the Rifle Range and we tried to get into these sitting positions he said, 'Don't worry about it; you will get it.' He had ways of saying things that made your feeling a hundred per cent better all the time. He was always there helping us." Walter Nehrenz, Richard Drown, Joseph Moran, Carl Whitmore, and Ronald Geckle agreed, using similar words.

Dr. Charles Herlihy, Depot Psychiatrist, had Matthew McKeon in his office for a neuropsychiatric examination at 3:15 P.M., April 9. This is what Herlihy had to say at the Inquiry: "Sergeant McKeon was brought to my office dressed in fatigues and wearing the armband which indicated that he was in confinement in the brig. He was attended by a brig chaser. He took a seat in my office. He appeared quite dejected, remorseful—I think stunned is a more appropriate word—and he was depressed. By that I mean he showed slowing of his thinking and physical movements. He was alert, however, to a certain degree. He was a co-operative patient for me to interview. My examination proceeded very easily. He had no loss of his memory of recent or past events. He knew, certainly, why he was being examined and he was able to discuss with me quite clearly—but as I say, very slowly—the events which transpired on the day prior. He was able to relate to me the incidents which took place and the proceedings several days prior to these events and at no time showed any evidence of defective memory. He was clear and coherent and logical in his thinking and in his replies to my many questions. There was no evidence of any flight from reality—if I may use that term. That is, his thinking was not distorted, it was not confused, and he was not psychotic in a medical sense and not insane in a legal sense as far as I am concerned as the examiner. He was, I think, very appropriately moderately depressed over the events that had transpired. I would say on the basis of my examination—although I did not examine him specifically—he is at least average or better than average intelligence level. His judgment, as I could glean it in this psychiatric examination, has shown itself at times in the past to be based on impulsive thinking. He tends to act hastily and think about it later. There is no evidence of emotional disturbance or serious mental disorder of any type in the Sergeant's family background or in the Sergeant himself as far as the examination can determine. Medically, he certainly has some defect in his left limb."

After the "forming period," Platoon 71 "went on the schedule." From March 1 to 24 it stayed close to Third Battalion area or that Battalion's allotted share of the Parade Ground. The platoon had long hours of close-order drill with opportunity to sit down during lectures on military courtesy, discipline, sanitation, personal hygiene, first aid. The men learned how to make up their packs and how to lay them out for inspection. They had twelve hours' mechanical training with the Garand rifle. They went everywhere in formation, kept cadence, and were continually corrected in posture. Outside their huts when not in ranks they moved at double-time. They had shoe-shine drill and found out how to care for their clothing. Each had a *Marine's Guidebook* in his rear pocket and read it whenever opportunity afforded. Except for fitting of eyeglasses or dental appointments, the group was continually together, doing everything "by the numbers": going through the mess line, getting a drink of water, taking a shower, going to bed. Even in their bunks, at the DI's command the whole platoon would roll in unison from left side to right.

March 24 was the twenty-first training day. Platoon 71 had had "physical drill under arms" daily. It had been through the gas chamber. It hiked out to Elliott's Beach one dawn, bivouacked there overnight, hiked back. Results on the fifteen-day progress test had been rather good. Today was moving day; the platoon was headed for the Rifle Range. Packs were made up. Seabags were stowed, numbered on the bottom with chalk, and hauled out to the Range by van. Recruit sentries were constantly with those seabags and other platoon gear. At first these sentries thought they were lucky, they didn't have to march. After it was all over they thought differently; they spent hours on guard, standing in one spot. The two recruits who got a break—and they had blisters on their feet—rode with Sergeant Huff in his car, the trunk loaded with personal clothing, military gear, and a few pieces of luxury equipment—such as a coffeepot and steam iron—belonging to the DIs. Both McKeon and King marched with the remainder of the platoon in heavy marching order. McKeon was carrying a sawed-off squeegee handle which he used as a walking stick. En route they passed other platoons marching back to West End or to Mainside.

McKeon halted Platoon 71 at Nissen 299, the Liaison Hut, and received his billeting plan. The platoon was berthed in Barracks 761, a frame, H-shaped structure. It was assigned the lower-deck squadbay at the northeast end. His recruits found this far superior to their Nissen huts in Third Battalion area. It was less crowded, steam-heated, ventilation was better, and toilet facilities adjoined their squadron. The afternoon was spent moving in, policing up. By time for evening chow they were completely squared away. Before he went home for the weekend, Sergeant Huff let his boys know in emphatic terms that rifle marksmanship carries heavy weight in competition for "honor platoon." He would tolerate no goofing off at the Rifle Range. Each man had to give the best that was in him. Huff insisted that he was getting soft, but since they were faced with a tough schedule on the Range he would let them go to the movies that Saturday night.

Next day there were church parties, clothing to scrub, meal formations. The platoon drew shooting jackets, belts, and scorebooks in the afternoon. Generally speaking, it was a day of rest, but Reveille would sound at four-thirty next morning. That would provide adequate time to police up and get breakfast. The platoon had to be on the School Range at six forty-five.

CWO Ernest W. Kraay, distinguished marksman and veteran of twenty-seven years' Marine Corps service, operates the School Range. The first thing Monday morning he assembled in Weapons Lyceum his instructors and DIs from the ten platoons that had joined over the weekend. He emphasized co-operation between DIs and Range Instructors. He gave rules for ironing out disagreements and settling grievances. After that, he introduced to the DIs particular School Range instructors who would stay with their platoons for the next three weeks. Staff Sergeant Huff and his assistants teamed up with Technical Sergeant Elwyn B. Scarborough.

Scarborough is a native South Carolinian. His military service dates well back, but on account of "broken time"—occasions when he decided to take another fling at civilian life—he still has less than twenty years. His gray hair gives him a distinguished look, but his ruddy complexion is not wholly suggestive of outdoor work. Scarborough's personal life has for some months been filled with difficulties. There has been legal action over a family estate. His wife remains in Charleston, where she holds a job, while he lives in the barracks here. Though he has a car, he will usually spend a free weekend on Parris Island rather than drive up there. His military performance has been adequate.

Platoon 71 found the first two weeks on the Rifle Range were even tougher than they had imagined: Reveille before daylight, swimming after dark during the first week, often a day's work lasting eighteen hours. Recruits had to get into positions which stretched hitherto unused muscles. While coaches insisted this would give them the best balance during firing, it was hard to believe. If the physical strain weren't enough, there was *arithmetic!* They had to learn about what wind does to the bullet—and wind may come from any direction. Then they had to know how many clicks of what sight knob moves the bullet how many inches up or down, right or left—and that changes for every range. There was trouble with squeezing the trigger and knowing when to hold the breath. Slings cut into their biceps, chafed their forearms, burned their wrists. Limbering-up exercises didn't seem to help the soreness of their muscles.

When it appeared time to relax, they were always on the march. They went to Special Weapons Range and fired the .22 rifle. Back on the School Range they would resume "snapping-in." Then they would go to the Pistol Range. After that there might be a training film in the Lyceum—with alert instructors making them stand up when it looked as though they were falling asleep. The pistol Range seemed relatively close in, but it was more than a half mile from there to the messhall. Afternoons of their second week they fired the M-1 rifle. That was harder on strained muscles and gave their shoulders a pounding. Elbows were getting sore despite the fact there were heavy pads on their shooting jackets. Some even had sore ankles and knees.

Saturday, April 7, Platoon 71 fired in the morning. They seemed to be getting much better. Next week they would fire the full course four consecutive mornings, longer if the weather were bad. But that final morning would be for *record* and it is impossible to make honor platoon with poor marksmanship. Sergeant Huff figured this outfit was about average. He was particularly hopeful for improvement during the coming week. He knew that one can hardly gauge the outcome before then—and that no matter how good they are, the platoon needs to get the breaks in weather. Huff noticed that during the last two weeks discipline had been slacking off, but he figured it always happens at the Rifle Range—and gets even worse during the week of mess duty that follows.

Never has a DI been satisfied with the human material he is required to mold. Physically, recruits are either too amorphous or too rigid to suit him. Intellectually, they're either "wise guys" or stupid. Some time ago the DI School polled our Drill Instructors; two responses are significant:

	Agree	Disagree
Most recruits seem not to have been disciplined at home	245	59
We do not get as good a recruit now as when I went through Boot Camp	269	45

These complaints, of course, are perpetual. They started shortly after Robert Mullan at Tun Tavern in 1775 signed on the first draft. Mullan was proprietor of the Tavern, equipped with a substantial bar. But even though the recruiter no longer need qualify for a bartender's MOS, he retains that glib manner worthy of more sociable grog-sellers. The DI remembers his own recruiter—unfavorably—but the DI also has a complete mental block about his own ineptitude as a Boot. Then he suffers in training his own recruits—and cordially dislikes all recruiters. This selective amnesia revives that hoary gripe: "It wasn't like this in the *old* Marine Corps." But marines have no monopoly on this grievance. Naval history has been researched to antiquity. Our sailor's refrain goes approximately like this:

When Noah got the Ark all built
And she was sailing well,
The baboon said to the ape on watch,
"The Navy's gone to Hell!"

But it is consensus that discipline and morale—leaving those terms undefined for the moment—or at least precision in drill, posture, neat and smart appearance, decline while troops are at the Rifle Range. The environment is much different from the Parade Ground; marksmanship coaches and instructors spend more time with the recruit than does his DI; any real tense marine firing the rifle will probably miss the target. One of my predecessors claimed he had a system for limbering-up recruits, removing all pressure while they were at Weapons Battalion. That claim, within limits, sounds good in theory. There is just one trouble: None of my people know how to put it into practice. There must be discipline—strict discipline—on the firing line; yet the recruit's position should be relaxed. The pressure of competition—to make a good score—is always on, often as bad as buck fever in the new hunter. Recruits frequently leave the line in tears; a few have wounded themselves or committed suicide in their remorse. We agree, parade-ground snap isn't visible on the Rifle Range.

Discipline in Platoon 71 wasn't an issue during the Inquiry though Matthew McKeon said in his confession April 9: "I got the idea to take them out into the swamps that night thinking that I could teach them a little more discipline. About three fourths of the platoon was squared away but the remainder were foul balls." At the Court-Martial, Defense Counsel made discipline a major issue. Of nineteen recruit witnesses there, ten said it was poor, eight weren't asked about it, one said it was good. Let's hear what members of Platoon 71 thought of themselves:

Melvin Barber: "In my opinion, they didn't have too much

discipline in the platoon. They took certain matters very seriously and others they didn't." Louis Leake: "I didn't like the discipline in the platoon. They weren't taking it too seriously, sir." Eugene Ervin: "At the time, sir, my opinion was—even though I'm in the platoon—my opinion was that we were very poorly disciplined. I mean, we did have poor discipline, that's right, sir." Walter Nehrenz: "The first two weeks our platoon was here we had good discipline, but after that there wasn't good discipline." Richard Drown: "Well, sir, I wouldn't say they were exactly undisciplined. It seemed like they had the spirit when they wanted to have it; when they didn't want to have it they just didn't have it." Joseph Moran: "Well, it was not a disciplined platoon when we were on this Island, but it seemed when we were in Camp LeJeune and the men from 71 were spread out through a company of about two hundred men they seemed to show up very well." Gerald Langone: "Well, sir, it was very, very poor—exceptionally poor. They were not willing; they had no spirit." The dissenter was Carmac Brennan: "About discipline? I say the discipline was good, sir."

Edward Huff was questioned at the Court-Martial:

Q. What were your observations as Senior Drill Instructor with regard to their response to discipline and to the morale of the platoon as a unit?

A. Of the five platoons that I have had or worked with, Platoon 71 did not have the discipline that the other four platoons had that I worked with, sir.

Q. Would you regard their state of training with regard to response to discipline and command—as well as morale—as good or bad?

A. Just mediocre, sir.

Q. Were you satisfied with it?

A. No, sir.

Corporal Richard King was questioned about many things at the Court-Martial, but no one asked his opinion about discipline. Staff Sergeant Matthew McKeon, on the other hand, was permitted to elaborate:

"When we first picked up this platoon, we immediately put them in the shock and fear stage. That is, usually not any violence or anything, but we keep them moving all the time. Up until about a week before we went to the Range—maybe a few days before we went to the Range, you could see the platoon kind of slacking off. They had spirit, they had good morale in it, but I noticed the platoon was more or less working in groups. I suppose you could call it a buddy-buddy system. They weren't working as a unit—and they were told about it. Then we went to the Range. The big thing I could see was that the Drill Instructors weren't with them all the time. Tell them to fall out, and they would fall out, but their manner was slow. In shock and fear if a man was slow you could walk over him, but then they came out of the shock and fear stage, and maybe started coming outside too slow. For example, a man was falling out a little slow, the guy behind him instead of walking over him, he would slow up, and the one behind him, and the next thing you know they would all be walking. They would fall out and when they get out there maybe a quarter would be scratching their buttocks or looking up at airplanes, or whatever they might be doing when they all knew they had to fall in at attention. I would go up and correct them. I might ask if it was necessary to tell them the position of attention, and maybe give them a slight slap to put them in the position of attention. The kid would say, 'No, it isn't, sir,' and I would ask him what the position of attention is. Anyway little things like that was adding up and adding up, and out on the Range Sergeant Scarborough brought my attention. I didn't think it was that bad, but he said that he had had quite a few platoons out there on the Range, and he said this was without doubt the poorest disciplined platoon he ever had. And he talked to Sergeant Huff about it, and Sergeant Huff was pretty well perturbed about it, too. I could see the point. Well, the spirit and the eagerness to learn seemed to leave them. It seemed to have left them. I remember the first couple of weeks they were very eager to learn, and they could learn, and they picked up quite quickly, but now it seemed like instead of picking up something of value they were picking up these goof-offs: how to sneak a smoke, how to stay longer in the chow halls, and little things like that. They were picking up bad habits."

5

Weapons

CEASE FIRING sounded across the Rifle Range soon after eleven Saturday morning, April 7. That was the signal to begin one of the three or four Weapons Training Battalion parties we have each year. We selected this date because it was the last weekend the Parris Island Rifle Team would be home for nearly two months; we wanted to give our forty competitive shooters a good send-off. Next Thursday they would leave for Camp LeJeune to fire in the Eastern Division individual rifle and pistol matches, followed by the Elliott Trophy rifle and Edson Trophy pistol team matches.

Our shooters have been training since mid-January and their prospects look good. We had troubles in the beginning but Captain Norman D. Fournier has taken the helm and seems to be master of the situation. Our goal is to bring the Elliott Trophy back to Parris Island, where it first came in 1912. May 28 our boys will return and 300 shooters from all over the world will converge on Parris Island for the Marine Corps Matches—their bunks will be made up and waiting.

Left of the ranges and 300 yards south of A-Butts, just inboard of Broad River and our Weapons Demonstration Area, we have a small picnic grove shaded by live oak; the NCO Recreation Committee voted for a picnic there. They've whitewashed tree trunks, chopped down grass, improvised a burlap-screened latrine for the men—women and children will use regular plumbing in the butts—and we are now ready to go. More games are scheduled than can ever be played; there are favors for children. Master Sergeant Albert E. Fisher, senior NCO in the Battalion, went over to Beaufort and put the touch on Edwards' Five and Ten Cent Store. Edwards had some merchandise left over from Easter, which was last Sunday, and even had some toys from Christmas. Fisher came back with a good selection for the children.

Sergeant Major John L. Langston supervises the beer. Draft beer is much cheaper than cans and we don't have such a mess to clean up. Fourteen half-barrels were put on ice yesterday, under lock and key, in Mess Sergeant Aderhold's outside reefer. But no one is forced to drink beer. We have case after case of soft drinks. The recruit messmen who assist with the food will get their fill of cola for the only time they're in Boot Camp.

One marine serving beer now is my problem child; he seems to be enjoying himself yet keeping his pledge. Essentially a good soldier, he has been too friendly with the bottle. He came up to Office Hours so many times that he's back to private as the result of nonjudicial punishment. I didn't want to give him a court-martial because I was afraid that would lead to a bad conduct discharge, which would only send him out to Skid Row. So I gave him my standard lecture about the evil effects of alcohol on the growing boy, made him read the record of investigation into Ricochet's death from acute alcoholism—those pictures should have impressed him—then sent him to Father Tony to take the pledge. Many's the rummy I've tried to cure, few successfully; this may raise my batting average.

The Guard truck is out here loaded with food—and I know that Sergeant Robert Shelton, Chief Cook, has more like it back in the messhall. The troops and their guests dig in.

Just outside our picnic grove toward the Special Weapons Armory a volley-ball tournament is in progress. Between the grove and A-Range road there is a horseshoe pitching contest. Some of the women are watching those games, others are sitting at tables feeding their children, most interrupt their activities from time to time to round up the smaller youngsters.

Both mess table and beer dispensary are popular. For steins

we use old beer cans that have the top removed, lip smoothed. Saving beer cans begins in the Slop Chute ten days before any party; we have paper cups, of course, but they don't help the flavor. The force of the wind seems to be increasing enough to interfere with the games.

Sparks is in charge of serving beer right now, Whalen is his assistant. But we miss old Fuchs at that job; Fuchs went to Norfolk a few months ago. When I first noticed him he had an evening job in the Slop Chute at fifty cents an hour. Our system down there was for the bartender to put his change, receipts, and keys in the safe and then twist the dial when he closed at night; next morning the Steward—who was the only one with the combination—would collect the cash and make a quick inventory. One morning after pay day Fuchs was missing from Reveille Roll Call; there was no money in the Slop Chute safe. Al Hartkopf, Exchange Officer, was rather agitated until we got a phone call from Fuchs in Savannah. Fuchs assured the Sergeant Major that he had the money and would return on the next bus; he had gone on liberty late and slept in. Though he admitted being right well anesthetized, he kept his money in one pocket and Exchange money in the other. On his return he handed the latter over to the Officer of the Day. It took persuasion but I finally got Al Hartkopf to give Fuchs a second chance at the job. All went well for a month or two, then Fuchs was gone again—and stayed away longer. There was nothing for me to do but take away another stripe and keep him in front of the Slop Chute bar. Still Fuchs did a fine jack-of-all-trades job over in the Police Shed and enjoyed serving beer at all our parties.

Now the wind is really high. There are clouds of sand on the opposite shore of Broad River. All of our canvas is carrying away. Games have been secured and many of the women and children are leaving. About three o'clock we bug out to the Slop Chute, though not before the Rifle Range looks like a desert sand storm. The Slop Chute is a dingy, dirty basement under Squadbay No. 1. There isn't room for a large crowd, but it's all we have and we need shelter. We promised the troops beer, it must continue to flow.

This is a critical time for any Commanding Officer: his marines enjoy ganging up on him with deliberate intent to drink him under the table—but as a lieutenant one should learn to cope with the situation. Just last August the Chinese Marine Corps rifle team attempted the same tactic under the guise of the Oriental sport of *gambei*. While there is a parry for this, the heart-to-heart talk requires a riposte. Tongues are loosened; all too many want to confide in the Old Man. This talk is off the record, straight from the shoulder, often maudlin. Though the Commanding Officer must be wary, for 2,000 years troop leaders have had the same watchword: *in vino veritas*. The time is ideal to take the pulse of an outfit.

Corporal Delehanty is obviously enjoying playing request numbers on his trumpet; just a few days ago I had to clobber Sergeant Delehanty. That incident I'll never understand. He's a real squared-away marine who stands out at inspection; he has one of the best coaching records in the Battalion. Some months ago General Pollock noticed Delehanty holding skull practice for his recruits just before they went up on the line for rapid fire; now we require that procedure of all coaches. He earned meritorious promotions successively to corporal and then sergeant. He made the Depot Rifle Team. But what did he do last Sunday? He and a buddy took one of the boats out and fired a small-bore rifle into the picnic area at Elliott's Beach—endangering life after all the safety precautions we've taught them! Worse, they've been teaching recruits our Range Regulations for months. He's taking the reduction to corporal gracefully. Weapons troops were upset when he lost his baby about a year ago; his wife's back home now waiting for another. If he gets a medal at Camp LeJeune maybe I can stretch a point and return his third stripe.

By six o'clock all of the women and children have disappeared after eating a second meal. We're going to have quite a bit of roast beef left over; the fried chicken is gone. Hour by hour the crowd thins out; the flow of beer slows down. By nine o'clock only a few topers remain. Sergeants Langston and Fisher say they'll stand watch until we close the bar. We agree on eleven o'clock—if there's anyone left who can still take it. There will be plenty of beer left tomorrow for today's Guard, and some to turn back for credit. Having done my duty, I walk over to my quarters.

Weapons Training Battalion area is shaped roughly like a kite with its top to the north. It is bounded on the northeast by some imaginary property lines and Golf Course Road; on the southeast by the Dredge Cut; on the southwest by Broad River; and on the northwest by Ribbon Creek. The north-south axis is about 2,000 yards and the east-west about 2,500 yards. It is nearly flat, though one of the Parris Island peaks is at our flagpole, twenty-two feet above mean low water. The area contains more than 300 buildings which, except for eighteen sets of officer and NCO quarters, four maids' quarters, five messhalls, and Sick Bay, are under jurisdiction of the Commanding Officer. The only permanent structures are Building 700, Weapons Battalion barracks; Messhall 769; and Sick Bay, Building 771. The others are divided roughly half and half between temporary frame buildings and Nissen and Quonset huts. When the training load is high we put troops under canvas. Our capacity is about 8,000, limited only by the number of targets. Shooting from dawn to dusk in the long days of summer twenty-six relays have fired over the course, but we have to push them.

After I'd had the outfit a year, lacking the clear-cut directives I would have desired, I "deduced" the mission of the Battalion in the manner once taught at the Naval War College and wrote it in a Battalion General Order:

> To train each recruit so that he will use the M-1 Rifle with the confidence, accuracy, and aggressiveness which is traditional in the Marine Corps.
>
> To familiarize recruits with other individual and crew-served weapons required by current directives.
>
> To conduct requalification training with the rifle and pistol for marines permanently assigned to the Depot or serving with other units in the area.
>
> To conduct familiarization firing with guard weapons for those marines who require it.

To conduct training with rifle, pistol, and automatic rifle for the Marine Corps Reserve, Naval Reserve, and Coast Guard as required.

To select and train competitors to represent the Depot in the Division and Elliott Trophy Matches.

To organize and train teams to represent the Depot in rifle, pistol, and revolver matches in the Southeast.

To provide facilities and conduct intramural marksmanship competition.

To encourage and support civilian marksmanship in the area.

To conduct matches as directed by Headquarters Marine Corps.

To provide facilities and services for training of the Marine Corps Rifle and Pistol Team and for individuals designated for international competition.

To increase the individual military proficiency of members of this organization as may be consonant with the foregoing tasks.

To promote a vigorous athletic program which provides for maximum participation.

During my tenure as Commanding Officer, 66,057 recruits, 5,643 requalifiers, and 4,061 Reserves fired the rifle for record. I didn't keep figures on Coast Guard, Seabees, or firing with the carbine, pistol, and automatic rifle.

The first two months aboard I spent getting my spurs dug in while Staff threw at me all odd jobs designed for a colonel. There were a number of general courts-martial with me as President, though after the McDonald case I was habitually challenged peremptorily. Colonel Austin Conner (Shifty) Shofner had spent a year on the Exchange Council and wanted to get off; he played poker with the General, I didn't; I took the Council. Colonel Fenwick Nelson Reeve was senior member of the Aptitude Board, which met once a week; he needed an alternate; I volunteered. Colonel Francis Howland (Red) Cooper was being detached; he recommended a newcomer for chairman of the School Board; I was the newcomer. Ex-officio I was assigned as

Depot Munitions Officer and member of the Depot Development Board. Then I voluntarily relieved John Stevens on the Boy Scout Committee. It was worse than the time in Haiti as a second lieutenant when I had seven jobs. So it took quite a while to learn my primary job—in fact, I didn't finish learning.

Eventually I discovered some things I didn't like about record firing: the final examination in marksmanship. Coaches were setting the recruit's sights and keeping his scorebook. If a shot hit the butts, he'd be given another round. In sustained fire, targets were withdrawn at the end of the time limit, but five seconds later they reappeared with the command: "Fire out the alibis." If the recruit had any rounds left he had an alibi. Coaching was permitted illegally on the line. Recruits would fire ten shots sitting instead of five of them kneeling. If a recruit had a good group on the wrong part of the target the coach changed his sights and let him fire again. If that wasn't enough, there was "sample verification" in the butts—before the first relay was through firing offhand, everyone on the line knew where the verifiers were. The only trick they weren't using was firing the whole course at 200 yards prone.

Knowing all that, I was skeptical even yet. I studied the distribution of 2,400 scores recorded during April before I arrived. This is how they stacked up:

Number of Recruits	Score	Number of Recruits	Score	Number of Recruits	Score
91	192	78	212	19	222
87	191	61	211	21	221
95	Marksman	82	Sharpshooter	34	Expert
8	189	57	209	22	219
14	188	70	208	25	218

Large numbers don't distribute like this by chance with peaks at critical scores. Besides, my study of the records showed weather conditions made no difference in qualification percentage. I learned that firing continued as long as the targets would stay in the frames—recruits would get ninety per cent qualification in a hurricane.

I hadn't been raised that way. The Marine Corps tradition for fifty years of competitive and record marksmanship was strict honesty. During the thirties someone at Headquarters analyzed the distribution of record scores and found critical-score peaks not near as radical as mine; the Commandant raised hell. I remembered the time cheating was suspected in Panama; the Adjutant and Inspector hastened down there and all hands had to fire the course again. Policy was so firm that I didn't feel I needed or wanted to consult General Silverthorn about this, so I quietly lowered the boom.

That was the easiest job I've ever done. My officers were old-timers. I merely told them we would follow the rules—including the punctuation. There would be one verifier for each pair of targets. On record day the coach would be referee as long as the recruit was forward of the ready-boxes. Weapons Battalion officers left my office in smiles, happy that Parris Island would soon cease to be the victim of pointed remarks from other posts, like Camp LeJeune. Overnight, with no change in coaches or training methods, our percentage qualification dropped from ninety to seventy—and stayed there.

Now ever since Tom Andrews, Chairman of the Psychology Department at the University of Maryland and capable statistician, and Clyde Coombs, Professor of Psychology at the University of Michigan, intellectual heir of the late great psychometrist L. L. Thurstone, and originator in his own right of new methods for scaling human behavior, set me to thinking, I've had little reverence for percentages. But our public schools have cemented percentage stereotypes firmly in our culture: Seventy or seventy-five per cent seems to be passing. No one asks, "Percentage of *what?*" In baseball thirty per cent is a fine batting average, sixty per cent can win a league pennant. Any gambler can make his fortune, consistently winning fifty-one per cent of the time, assuming even odds and no take by the house. But the public thinks in terms of one hundred per cent for general purposes and one thousand per cent for baseball. Apparently General Silverthorn did the same. My guess is that in evaluating this attribute in comparison with his personal ideal ninety per cent was standard.

It's a good thing Silverthorn didn't convert his golf scores to that scale!

Silverthorn wasn't alone. Two years later, having been briefed by me on the Parris Island fiasco, without field study to back up his assumptions, Major John Mesko at his desk in Headquarters wrote this for the signature of Lemuel C. Shepherd, Jr., Commandant of the Marine Corps, and distribution to all Commanding Officers:

> I have noted with satisfaction the recent substantial increase in the over-all rifle marksmanship qualification percentage of the Marine Corps. This reverses the downward trend which had caused me so much concern during the past few years. The improvement can be attributed to the increased and personal emphasis being placed on marksmanship by Commanding Officers. Small arms skill can be improved still further if Commanding Officers insist upon highest standards and through their active and energetic supervision plus personal interest. I consider it well within our capabilities to qualify at least ninety per cent of all marines with the rifle.

That is autistic ideation. Shepherd (or Mesko) could raise the qualification percentage two ways—honestly: by lowering the standards or by lengthening considerably the training period. Even then I can't believe they'd do it with recruits.

Staffmen watched our percentages six weeks but were never willing to concede that reports for many months previous had a different basis. Then Silverthorn lowered the boom on me. He demanded positive action now. There was letter writing between offices without careful observation on the ground. Staff made the usual recommendations: closer supervision, more schools. Silverthorn relieved seven of my coaches by name on the basis of one day's performance while their cumulative records were superior to those of an equivalent group he permitted to remain. He relieved my Range Co-ordinator, Master Sergeant Irving Johnson, who was not a teacher but a scheduler. Then he threatened to march out a whole new outfit—from Commanding Officer to junior messman—each with *Field Manual 23-5, Rifle Marksmanship* in his pocket.

We tried hard. We drove our troops relentlessly. It was October and November, the weather wasn't good. So Silverthorn made me Officer-in-Charge of Weather, which hadn't bothered his golf. At last he ordered a slow learners' program. This gave an extra eight days' firing to those who on preliminary record had no hope of qualifying. The program lasted twenty-five weeks. During that time we fired 2,200 recruits over this special course and qualified fifty-four per cent. The only cost was in the recruit's missing his week of mess duty—but you'd think the only reason we have recruits at Parris Island is to do mess duty. Then Staffmen wrote a "brief staff study"; the program was abolished.

CWO Len Oderman took a long time convincing me that there are some marines who will never learn to shoot; no one can convince me that marksmanship is not the Corps' most vital asset.

In this training the knowledge and experience of the veteran is passed on to the newcomer. Unfortunately this is donc primarily by word of mouth. Only a small fraction of marksmanship technique has been reduced to writing and pictures. This is probably because it was developed in the main by our old Gunnery Sergeants. (By accepted definition the Gunnery Sergeant was a First Sergcant who couldn't read or write.) Those old-timers are leaving us now at a rate that should concern Staff. For example, our four top-bracket team leaders in competitive marksmanship will be forced out next year. There is considerable danger of the art being lost to the Marine Corps.

Here in Building 700 one gets his first indication that Weapons Battalion is not just another unit like a ship's detachment or a battalion in the Fleet Marine Force. Weapons is an institution. It has been rooting in this soil since World War I. The wise Commanding Officer doesn't take over and start swinging the ax; he spends plenty of time getting acquainted. Meanwhile, the troops test him for acceptability. Eventually he belongs. Then he can effect quiet changes and fight for improvements. Staff makes it necessary to fight: Staffmen seem to forget their country cousins. This reminds me of priorities in Fleet Admiral Ernest

J. King's Cominch Headquarters during the war; first came Eisenhower, then the Mediterranean, then Nimitz, then the South Pacific, then MacArthur. Lord Louis Mountbatten was just out at six o'clock. Weapons' comparative position is between Doug and Lord Louie: in or out at six.

Weapons Battalion in another sense recalls memories of living in Haiti: You had an electric stove but the cook wanted to use the charcoal brazier out in the yard. It was easier to learn the natives' way of life than to teach them yours, so when you adjusted to them the problem was whipped. Later you could induce minor changes like getting them to bathe regularly, serve from your left, or quit using an old sock to grease the frying pan. Theorists in military leadership would condemn the approach of adjusting the Commanding Officer to the unit instead of tailoring the unit to fit the personality of the CO. But it is a matter of fact that Weapons Battalion represents the cumulative growth of forty years' experience. This is true of both the physical plant and the methods used in training. Why learn by repeating old mistakes?

So I looked at the situation quietly, talked things over with Jim Young, my Executive, and usually had Jim put changes into effect. The first thing I noticed was that recruits, who should have been training, were doing all of the police work except that inside our own barracks; each half day at least one platoon reported to the Police Sergeant. My boys would throw a cigarette butt over the side of the arcade, some recruit would come along with a bucket and pick it up. We stopped that forthwith; then it took more than a year to get the place looking shipshape again. (This probably never would have been done, but General Pollock arrived and put the pressure on me.) There were thousands of signs, all prohibitory; every man in the outfit who owned a car had a parking place reserved, though many were in driving squads. For two years I pulled down signs and refused to let new ones be erected; any sign that stayed had to be completely justified: giving vital information or warning of danger. Grassy places were surrounded with miles of pipe railing, each section carrying a sign, "Don't Sit Here," and bent to the ground by sitting above the sign; the pipe went to salvage. When the Range was extended from twenty-five targets to 186, my predecessor, the late Captain

Joseph J. Tavern, permitted the construction workers to cut down all the old live oak, pine, and undergrowth. Each season we've been replanting between the ranges; last year we got in 328 trees, mostly oak, and 532 shrubs; we planted more than that this year but the Police Sergeant hasn't yet counted them for me.

The most profitable changes I made were in eliminating lost motion. Ten platoons would march over to the Pistol Range, where they could fire one at a time; now we keep them on a nearby School Range and call them over in turn. Monday morning of the first week was used to draw shooting jackets and scorebooks; now my duty supply man issues them Sunday afternoon on a schedule that leaves a minimum of waiting. Rifles must be inspected at the Armory upon arrival and just before firing, so recruits in droves waited at the door for hours; now we have an auxiliary School Range just outside the door; while the others are snapping in, recruits are called into the Armory four at a time. As my troops got the word, they continued this drive on their own initiative. I do believe that our effective training time has doubled.

Few people realize the cost of the Weapons Battalion operation. During my first year here shooting jackets alone cost $60,000; we expended $2,800,000 in munitions, though our allowance was $3,500,000—we couldn't use the remainder fruitfully.

CWO Alvin (Goober) Johnson is Battalion Munitions Officer. Besides requisitioning, stocking, and issuing ammunition, he is frequently called in as a trouble-shooter. For several years before World War II the Tenth Regiment used to come to Parris Island from Quantico for their artillery firing. Their gun positions were near Weapons Battalion or in Elliott's Beach area; their old impact zone is our golf course. Every now and then a 75mm dud is turned up out there; Weapons marines examine it and decide whether to blow it on the spot or bring it back to our area for destruction. We finally convinced Joe Frasca, golf pro, of the danger, and then found that he had some old "bombs" in his garage; out we went as an emergency task force to discover they were inert bodies of miniature aircraft bombs that once contained a shotgun shell to release a puff of smoke. But another time some ATs had a 75mm dud in their squadroom at Mainside and were taking it apart when a lieutenant discovered them; Weapons marines brought it out and destroyed it—it blew with a high-order burst. If that lieutenant had arrived a few minutes later, the Naval Hospital would have had to process an emergency requisition for more coffins.

Then there was a Beaufort civilian who carried in a Civil War cannonball and wanted my people to disarm it so he could keep it as a souvenir. My response was that if it were a Yankee projectile we'd reclaim it as Government property; if it were Rebel we'd take it as contraband. It blew quite nicely. But the best one was last summer when a civilian working on a grader turned up a jettisoned 500-pound aircraft depth-charge bomb while cutting a road for a new housing development near Beaufort. We got a written request from the property owner and permission from the Commanding General, then we illegally transited South Carolina's highways in Goober's car with fuse, detonators, and TNT blocks. The man on the grader had pushed the bomb once, backed off to give it a good shove, and then changed his mind. He watched us with some amusement, as did the contractor. When we had fire in the hole and drove down the road a good piece, the civilians looked like they thought we were chicken; when they measured the crater with their steel tape, they were impressed: it was twenty-two feet in diameter, eight feet deep. The contractor moaned, "I wouldn't have found enough of my grader to collect the insurance." The operator was silent.

Until November 1954 we continually had one officer and two enlisted marines designated as Explosive Ordnance Demolitionmen, which gave them respective extra pay of $100 and $50 a month. After that date I could only certify extra pay for a month in which they did their job; previously we blew dud grenades nearly every day. But neither Goober Johnson nor Sergeant Sparks got a nickel for the aircraft bomb—they had destroyed a mortar shell in our Demonstration Area the same month. Master Sergeant T. J. Collins, Ammunition Chief whom I could no longer justify for an EOD rating, came along with us anyway and admitted he would have destroyed the bomb without extra pay. Demolitionmen are crazy. As we drove back Collins said, "Yes, sir, Sir. I'll see that beautiful high-order bloom in my mind's eye for a long time." Goober Johnson had taken over the Munitions job when Willie Tate left—and, incidentally, Willie had taken over from Goober in the same job. When Goober's EOD rating came from Washington in July 1954 I wrote him this letter:

FROM: Commanding Officer
TO: CWO Alvin E. Johnson
SUBJ: Money
1. Goober Johnson's thirst may now abate,
Demolition pay begins this date.
W. B. McKEAN

During my tenure we've pushed competitive marksmanship as hard as we could within the limits set by Staff. Our philosophy has been that this is the finest way we know to develop outstanding coaches. We admit that achieving good marksmanship doesn't automatically insure good coaching ability—but it helps. This is a summary of how we participated in the all-Marine Corps program last season:

	Total Entries	Parris Island	Total Places	Parris Island	Total Medals	Parris Island
Individual						
Division Rifle	595	34	86	17	66	10
Division Pistol	298	7	43	5	32	1
Marine Corps Rifle	211	18	31	6	14	2
Marine Corps Pistol	120	7	44	4	15	1
Team						
Elliott Trophy	31	2				
Inter-Div Rifle	50	8				
Inter-Div Pistol	25	2				
Marine Corps Team	141	17				

Medals are awarded to nondistinguished shooters only; places go to all in the medal zone. In Division Rifle, Parris Island shooters, except one knucklehead, finished in the top half; in Division Pistol, Parris Island shooters were in the upper twenty per cent. In the Elliott Trophy rifle team match, Parris Island finished second and fourth, each team scoring one point less than those first and third. The other teams listed show the total number of members. Lieutenant William W. McMillan, Jr., Weapons Battalion, won the Marine Corps Rifle Match, the David S. McDougal Memorial Trophy, the Lauchheimer Trophy (combined rifle and pistol, setting a new record), and an Inter-Division Pistol Team medal. The Marine Corps Matches, which have been scheduled since 1916, were fired at Parris Island in 1955 for the first time in history.

Getting our job done takes hard work and long hours. We start as early as we can in the morning hoping that those on their third week can finish before the heat of the day. Not infrequently we have fired from six in the morning until five in the evening. Then when we had an easy stretch with a light training load, Jim Young was forced to hassle with Bill Card, Provost Marshal, because his MPs sent our marines back from the main gate for attempting to go on liberty during Depot Working Hours. The Depot declares leave periods or an occasional extra holiday with no consideration for extending the training period to compensate for time lost. November and December are particularly bad. We have the double holiday for Marine Corps Birthday and Veterans Day, Thanksgiving, Christmas, and New Year's. New platoons arrive each Saturday even though during these two months we lose a week of training. It invariably shows up in the scores. The pressure was so heavy last December that I had to get General Pollock's permission to violate an order he had issued. Then I published the following memorandum:

B-A-D N-E-W-S!
(Read It and Weep)

Depot Memorandum 136-55 concerns the Christmas and New Year's leave periods. It prescribes holiday routine on Saturdays 24 and 31 December and suspends ALL BUT ESSENTIAL WORK. This has been carelessly read or misinterpreted by some Weapons Battalion marines.

Here is the official scoop:

(1) We'll continue to give leave to all those who can be spared.

(2) We'll be as generous as possible with special liberty passes for those two Saturdays.

BUT:

(1) We MUST fire on both of those days. Otherwise, platoons firing record between Christmas and New Year's would lose

two days. Those of the following week would lose four days, since there is a parade Wednesday 28 December.

(2) We SHALL keep on board a minimum of one coach per target and one School Range instructor per platoon.

Depending on the weather and the progress we make, record days are planned for:

Thursday 22 December
Friday 30 December
Friday 6 January

Both Battalion Chaplains are available on call.

McKean
Ebenezer Scrooge of Weapons Battalion

Any drill or refresher training we conduct for Weapons marines must be scheduled after Cease Firing. In fact, we stood the last Inspector General's inspection after Depot Working Hours—and served supper three hours late. But the troops were commended and did well in the IG's proficiency test. This is how their average marks stacked up:

	Weapons	Others
Private First Class	61.0	55.2
Corporal	68.6	66.7
Sergeant	69.6	62.9
Staff NCO	72.8	69.3

"Others" includes DIs and all of Mainside's technical specialists; the test was in general military subjects. In addition to that Weapons marines find time to excel in intramural sports in the evening. My theory is that if you'll feed them well and work their duffs off they don't have time or energy to get into trouble.

My troops must be alert for wounds self-inflicted by frustrated Boots. We watch them on the line and shake down every man before he leaves the Range. Not too long ago one recruit told his coach that if he didn't qualify he'd put the last round through his head. The coach thought the recruit was joking. Then toward the end of his string at the 500-yard line the lad put a round in the chamber and started to crawl toward the muzzle. The coach stopped that with a flying tackle; the boy didn't finish the course; we sent him to the talking doctors. We had a different case in Platoon 195. Early one day when a Boot came off the line the coach discovered he had kept one round in his possession, of which the coach relieved him. Later, after he had again been on the line to fire and had left with his piece "cleared and locked," he was sitting on the bench in rear of the firing line. There was a muffled explosion; he cried, "My God, I'm shot." He had wounded himself in the foot with his own rifle and the damage would require long hospitalization, future surgery.

May second the right-hand column of the front page New York *Times* carried the story of the appearance of Randolph McC. Pate, Commandant of the Marine Corps, before the House Armed Services Committee the previous day. Pate announced this action: "The reassignment of Colonel William B. McKean, Commanding Officer of Weapons Battalion at the Boot Camp." He gave no reason. Scuttlebutt news traveled fast. On May third I published the following memorandum:

TO: All Hands
FROM: Commanding Officer
SUBJ: Departure

I have completely trustworthy but strictly unofficial information that I am to be relieved of the command of Weapons Training Battalion as a punitive administrative measure for my responsibility in the Ribbon Creek incident.

My relief will be Colonel Glenn C. Funk (05345). His date of arrival is unknown to me.

My last charge to each and every one of you follows:

(1) Give my relief the same enthusiastic co-operation and support you have given me.
(2) Keep getting the best marksmanship training results you possibly can *with complete honesty.*
(3) Win that Elliott Trophy Team Match.
(4) Take the Commanding General's Intramural Sports Trophy for the seventh year running.

It has been an honor to serve with you. There shall always be a warm spot in my heart for this my last command.

McKean

6

Weekend Duty

MATTHEW MCKEON'S alarm rang at four-twenty Saturday morning. He shut it off quickly to avoid rousing the two children, who would be romping at daylight anyway. His wife stirred and mumbled something not quite intelligible. Matt knew it was useless to try to engage her in conversation at this hour. She knew he had the weekend duty. She would have a neighbor drive her from Port Royal to Parris Island Sunday afternoon to get the car so that she could keep her appointment Monday with Dr. Huston. She was five months pregnant. Matt lighted a cigarette, then shaved and dressed quickly. He would get breakfast at Messhall 766. He arrived there at five. When Matt sat down at the DI table Sergeant Richard King, who had brought Platoon 71 to breakfast, was just leaving.

"Hi, King."

"Hi, Mac. I'm going back to see that the squadbay's policed up. I'll see you on Dog Range."

"No; I'll be down to the room before you leave. I've got to change uniform and I got some clean laundry to stow."

"Okay. I'll see you there."

There wasn't much conversation at the DI table. McKeon ate quickly and smoked another cigarette with his second cup of coffee. Then he drove down to Barracks 761 and parked out in front. He put away his laundry, straightened his share of the three-man room, dressed in starched and ironed utilities, buckled his duty belt around his waist, and drove out to D-Range, where he parked to the right of the 500-yard line.

Two relays had already marched to the butts. Targets were appearing in the frames through the haze of a chilly dawn. McKeon could see the other six relays in clusters at the 200-yard line. Huff and Scarborough drove up in Scarborough's car and parked. The three walked together slowly down the road talking about the prospects for Platoon 71's making a good qualification percentage next Thursday.

CWO Vernard Grunder was in charge of D-Range. He assembled Block NCOs and DIs near the center of the line and gave them a fight talk. This was the first day these recruits would fire the full course, fifty rounds. Grunder wanted them to make each shot good. While Grunder lectured the supervisors, Technical Sergeant Mattola held the microphone and over the portable public-address system gave his standard pep talk to the coaches. While Mattola stopped for breath, those on the line could hear Technical Sergeant Woodrow O'Neal on his loudspeaker in the butts. O'Neal was laying down the law. At five after six, one minute past sunrise, the first relay on D-Range cranked off. Over on C-Range CWO Leonard Oderman and Technical Sergeant Johnny Taylor had difficulties with their telephone system. They didn't commence firing for another fifteen minutes.

Scarborough, Huff, McKeon, and King kept their eyes on the twelve targets assigned Platoon 71. Each time a recruit finished a string of ten shots he would report his score to Huff, who noted it on his roster thumbtacked to the top of an ammunition box. Periodically a coach—there was one at each firing point—would talk over a particular problem with Scarborough. Mr. Grunder wandered up and down the line; when he noticed erratic firing he would stop and offer advice based on experience accumulated since he was a Boot at Parris Island twenty-eight years ago.

Six relays fired slow-fire standing at 200 yards. Then came rapid-fire sitting. The group shifted to the 300-yard line. There the recruits fired slow-fire sitting and kneeling; rapid-fire prone.

On to the 500-yard line they went for ten shots slow-fire prone. Two relays were designated to relieve the butt detail, which in turn fired the whole course while the four relays left over were engaged in cutting grass, sorting brass, and unloading ammunition off a truck into the ready-service magazine. Shortly after eleven the last two relays finished at the 500-yard line. They moved like skirmishers down the range picking up empty clips and cartridge cases. When this was completed and the whole area looked shipshape for the coming weekend Sergeant King assembled Platoon 71 and marched it to the cleaning racks behind Building 765. It was forty minutes before all rifles were cleaned and the platoon returned to Barracks 761. Meanwhile Huff and McKeon drove back and went into their DI room.

"What do you have lined up for the weekend, Huff?"

"Have them wash their clothes and fix their gear. They should work on their rifles, but see that those knuckleheads don't knock the dope off them. Shoeshine drill. That's about all. Take them to the movie tonight, if you can get in. If you can't, take them tomorrow night."

"How about item pool?"

"No. We'll have about two weeks before the 45-day test back in the Battalion area after they finish mess duty. What they learn now they'd forget before then. Don't let's worry about tests until they finish on the Range."

"Okay."

"Guess I'll shove off. See you Monday."

"Okay, Huff. See you Monday."

Not long after Huff left the DI headquarters in Barracks 761 McKeon yelled for Private Gerald C. Langone, Jr., one of the two recruit Section Leaders. Langone ran to the door of the DI room and stood at attention.

"Have the platoon fall out for chow."

"Aye, aye, sir."

Within seconds after Langone returned to the squadroom door, only fifteen feet from McKeon's room, the Boots came pouring out in a mad scramble. A few seconds more and they were standing rigidly in ranks on the sidewalk in front of the barracks. Langone snapped the padlock on the squadroom door and ran to his place. McKeon was in no hurry. He snubbed out his cigarette, put on his utility cap and duty belt, sauntered out to his position in front of Platoon 71.

"Right, face! Forward, march!" McKeon chanted the cadence.

On the way to Messhall 766, 300 yards down Wake Boulevard to the northeast, McKeon exercised his platoon in foot drill. The troops would mark time, march to the rear, halt, resume march. McKeon was convinced platoon drill had deteriorated since they left the Parade Ground and came to the Rifle Range. But now it was his turn to enter the messhall. He ordered column right, separation into two columns of files, halt.

"March into chow!"

The response was a lusty chorus: "AYE, AYE, SIR!"

McKeon watched over his troops while they were in the two mess lines being served cafeteria style. He signed Mess Sergeant Harry McCarty's logbook to indicate that his platoon had been fed. Then he paid forty-five cents to the chief messman for his own meal and joined other duty DIs at their separate, family-style table.

Members of Platoon 71 left the messhall individually when they finished eating and strolled back to barracks in small groups. On the way they passed recruit sentries guarding piles of seabags for those platoons leaving or coming out to the Range that day. Back at the barracks they stood around in clusters talking and enjoying a smoking break. Marksmanship was their principal topic.

After lingering over his coffee and talking shop with fellow DIs, Matthew McKeon reurned to the barracks. When his recruits saw him approach they scrambled into their squadroom. He followed them as the chorus shouted, "ATTENTION!" He announced that they would wash clothes, shine shoes, and spend at least an hour working on their rifles. After that Private Langone would take all who had made a score below 190 that morning across the street to the School Range. This group would snap-in for two hours. The others could write letters or study the *Marine's Guidebook*.

McKeon went back to his own room, took off his shirt, stretched out on his bunk, started to read, and fell asleep. He awakened about three when Langone knocked on the door. Langone reported that a heavy windstorm was carrying clouds of sand across the School Range. The troops were still trying to snap-in but weren't getting much out of it. McKeon gave him permission to secure.

At five-twenty Matthew McKeon marched his platoon to supper. The wind was still high and so he made no effort to hold foot drill. At seven-fifteen he marched the troops over to Weapons Battalion Lyceum, 150 yards from his barracks in the opposite direction from the messhall. The movie ended at nine-thirty. Back in the barracks McKeon inspected shoes. He required several recruits to shine them again. He gave the platoon time for a head call while he smoked a cigarette in his room.

As McKeon sat on his bunk smoking he heard the customary noise in the washroom. With seventy-eight men trying to get a bath under twelve shower-heads in ten minutes there is bound to be confusion. But this irritated the DI. He believed that quiet and orderly conduct were indicative of proper discipline.

Langone appeared at McKeon's door clothed just in underwear. He reported the platoon standing by to turn in. He preceded his DI back to the squadbay and called, "Attention!" The door led to the middle of the long room. Extending to the right and left with their ends close to the walls were two lines of double-decked iron bunks. Standing barefooted at the head and foot of each bunk was a recruit in his underwear. McKeon stood in the center of the room and eyed his charges. "Hit the rack!"

In a single movement, too fast for one to see the details but something like a back dive, the troops landed on their bunks and the springs bounced momentarily. But some of the boys were giggling and not lying at attention.

"Hit the deck!"

In a similar but reverse movement the troops were standing beside their bunks.

"You guys think it's a big deal getting in the sack. You're supposed to lay at attention. Instead of that you make a lot of noise. Instead of picking up something of value you guys are picking up these goof-offs: how to sneak a smoke, how to stay longer in the chow-hall. You guys are picking up bad habits."

McKeon exercised the platoon with a few push-ups. Then back in their bunks and out again. A few more push-ups. Back in their bunks. Bunk drill: lying on back, stomach, and each side. Finally they were lying at attention in absolute silence.

"You guys understand what I mean?"

Chorus: "YES, SIR!"

"Don't forget it! Carry on! Good night."

Chorus: "GOOD NIGHT, SIR!"

McKeon turned off the lights and went to his room. Sergeant King was there undressing. McKeon was aggravated. "This platoon isn't working as a unit. They're working in groups. It's a buddy-buddy system. Tell them to fall out and they will fall out, but their manner is slow and when they get out there maybe a quarter will be scratching their asses or looking up at airplanes when they know they have to fall in at attention. When Sergeant Arriva took us through in forty-eight Platoon 82 had real discipline. But Arriva wasn't any better than DIs we have now. The recruiters are just sending us punk material."

King commiserated. He didn't know about Parris Island in forty-eight, but there was taut disciplinc in his platoon when he came through San Diego in fifty-two. Maybe that was because most Boots, after combat conditioning at Camp Pendleton and Pickle Meadows, could expect to hit a replacement draft for Korea. They were more serious.

On this note Matt McKeon summoned the Fire Watch, gave him instructions for a morning call, and headed for the shower.

Sunday, April 8, the fading crescent of the moon in its last quarter broke over the horizon east of Parris Island at 4:16 A.M.

One hour later the recruit Fire Watch awakened McKeon and was secured. Platoon 71 had already been called. While it would be another hour before the field music sounded Reveille at the Liaison Hut, McKeon was going to Mass. Moreover, all those Harps in the platoon were going with him. They couldn't use him as an excuse for missing Mass. Those PBs—clerical euphemism for "Protestant Bastards"—could police the squad-room while the Catholics were gone.

Sergeant McKeon slipped into a pair of trousers, lighted a cigarette, and checked the daily schedule in his platoon logbook. Chow was scheduled for seven-thirty, which meant he couldn't stay until Mass was over. While services would begin at six-thirty, Father Bielski was sure to preach, and then there would be all of those Communions. It seems like Catholic recruits go to Communion every week, particularly at the Rifle Range—they are sure it gives them the breaks in their shooting.

It was still dark outside when McKeon walked into the squadbay. Some recruits were in the shower, others shaving, others making up their bunks. Private Langone would march the church party to Mass. McKeon returned to his room, shaved leisurely, and finished dressing. No need to wake King, Butler would call him if there was any trouble. Let's have Matthew McKeon tell it:

> Sunday morning, sir, the Catholic detail left around twenty after six to attend Mass at the Lyceum, which is under Weapons Training Battalion out there. I attended those services myself. I left around five after seven—services weren't over—the reason I left early was the simple reason I had to get back to take the non-Catholics to chow. We had to leave for chow at quarter past seven. I took them to chow that morning—that's non-Catholics. I checked in at the messhall, where they have a little piece of paper. You check the number of the platoon, the time you arrived, the Drill Instructor, then you initial that. They have another slip of paper alongside of it to tell them how many Catholics will be eating chow after services and we had—I believe—twenty-five or twenty-six. We ate chow—they ate chow that morning and straggled back from the messhall. I had a talk with Drill Instructors—I don't know how long I sat there—but I shot the breeze with the Drill Instructors.

Sunrise on Parris Island was at 6:03. It was a clear, windy day, rather cool for April. At 6:36 the tide in Ribbon Creek stood at high water slack, 6.7 feet above mean low water.

> Yes, sir. I got back to Building 761. Next, the Protestant

detail has to get out—the non-Catholic detail. They usually attend services Mainside if they don't have it at the Lyceum. I put a private—another recruit—in charge of the church detail to see that they all got back. They shoved off about a quarter to nine.

Chaplain Truman D. Twait, Baptist, Assistant Chaplain for Weapons Battalion, held divine services for Protestants in the Lyceum at nine o'clock. Twait served as an enlisted man in submarines during World War II and wears the submariners' distinguished service device under a chestful of ribbons. He is close to the troops, a fine counselor, a good preacher, quiet, modest, conscientious.

While Chaplain Twait supervised arrangement of the altar and gave last-minute instructions to his organist, Heddie Chambers, self-appointed usher, sheparded the recruits to seats, insisting that those in front be filled first. After the services she took the flowers from the altar and left them on top of the refrigerator on the back porch of our quarters. I was cleaning up the beach while my family went to Mass over at Mainside, and so we all missed Heddie's Sunday morning visit.

By the time they shoved off, the Catholic detail was usually back—down at the messhall and back to Barracks 761. Usually if I give the non-Catholics a smoke after eating chow, I'll give the Catholics a smoke. After they finished smoking, I told them to get the squadbay squared away. Sunday morning the Catholics get up and wash up, shave and get ready for church services. They do not do any police work. They don't have time to do police unless you get them up a little earlier. While they are gone, the Protestants—non-Catholics—they will do the police work. Then when the Catholics come back, what they haven't finished the Catholics take up.

I went topside that morning just after the non-Catholic detail left. I was talking to another Drill Instructor who had his platoon billeted on topside but at the other end of the building. Well, during the conversation with Sergeant Muckler, I told him I would go get the mail with him, seeing that he didn't have a vehicle—that I would drive him down to the Mail Room. I came back after talking to him and called Private Langone into the room.

"Langone, are all the church details back?"

"Yes, sir; they are."

"I don't want to see any dirty laundry in those laundry bags come Monday morning. Get them out there and wash up all the gear that they have in their laundry bags."

"We did that yesterday, sir."

"Well, I notice some laundry bags in there with dirty gear in them. Get them out and get them washed. When we don't have any dirty gear, they can take a break or have a smoke or turn to on their personal gear or clean their weapons."

"Aye, aye, sir." Langone left the DI room.

> Then I laid down in the rack there and picked up a newspaper. I don't recall anything that was in it of value. I laid down there for about fifteen or twenty minutes, just reading a newspaper. Then I got up, walked out the Drill Instructors' room, took a right, went down the passageway there and about, oh, fifteen feet, maybe—possibly twenty feet down the passageway —there's a passageway over to the left, which is a back entrance to Building 761. I took that passageway and I looked out the door—I didn't go out, I just looked out. I seen people down around the wash racks and I seen Private Butler and another group was sitting on the steps writing a letter, him and a couple more colored boys. I don't recall who the other colored boys were, but everything looked normal to me out there. In the squadbay—there was some troops in the squadbay shining their shoes. I went back to the Drill Instructors' room and laid down.
>
> The leg was bothering me quite bad that day. It's a severe pain, all the way from the foot all the way up to the hip. I'd had it roughly three weeks, maybe longer. I couldn't bend the toes. Seemed when I bend the toes the ligament running up behind the heel, it wouldn't stretch—I don't know much about the terminology. I walked with a limp, sir. When I walked, I supported myself with a squeegee handle.
>
> I laid down, sir, and I dozed off. I don't know how long I dozed off, but the next thing I remembered was Sergeant Scarborough—I heard him talking. I was facing the bulkhead and I rolled over.

"How come you're racked out this time of day, Mac?"

"It's Sunday, ain't it, Gunny?"

"Yeah. Say, one of your boys asked me to hold his watch yesterday. I forgot to give it back when he shoved off the line. I brought it over."

"Who was it?"

"Damned if I remember his name."

"Okay, I'll give it to the Section Leader."

"Mac, what did you think of the shooting yesterday?"

"I don't know what to think. I haven't watched Boots fire since I went through here in forty-eight. What do you think?"

"Well, I've been on the School Range since last fall and I've taken a platoon through every three weeks since. Like I told Huff, this platoon is really piss poor. It's the worst I've seen."

"Yeah. I'm getting more pee'd off with them all the time. Since they've been out here they've lost all their team spirit."

Sergeant Charles Muckler came in. "Whose platoon is that back there crapped out on the lawn?"

McKeon said, "It can't be mine; impossible!"

Muckler grinned. "I believe it is yours."

> So I went out that same passageway—you know—the back door. Sergeant Scarborough was behind me. I opened the door and there they were laying on the grass out there, some was laying on their elbows in this manner [demonstrating]. Some were crapped out on their back. Others were laying face down with their arms underneath their head. That's a cardinal sin; they never should do it. I can't explain, but they should never.
>
> I opened the door and yelled out for everybody to get inside. Private Butler, who was writing a letter, asked me if it was all right if him and the other few colored boys sitting there with him—all right for them to stay out there and finish writing a letter. I told Private Butler, who was assistant Section Leader, "What kind of nonsense is this, you being a Section Leader and letting this go on? Don't you see those people out there laying around?" I told everybody to go inside.
>
> They all got inside the squadbay, sir, and I walked down to the door leading to the platoon squadbay. I was going to give them "up and on shoulders," numerous counts with the rifle, the right arm first, right hand first, numerous counts, have people count one, two, three, one two, three, but I thought

different of it for the simple reason that usually when you give them "up and on shoulders" with that rifle—in the dark—in the squadbay, they do get a little tired going up and down. Then the rifle could accidentally hit the sacks—hit the racks—and I figured if I gave them "up and on shoulders" the rifles would hit the racks and knock the dope off—that's the information they have got in firing—that's their data. The next thing that came to my mind was a field day.

Was it my practice, sir? No, sir. It wasn't my usual practice; it wasn't, sir, I'll be frank with you. But the Sunday before, this church detail fell out and here come four or five straggling to the church detail. Well, I latched onto them and told them after they attended service, "I want to see you." The same way with the non-Catholic detail. I'm telling you, sir, if I see a reason for holding a field day, I hold it. I'm not being fresh or anything else—I'm not being wise or anything else, sir—the barracks is never clean enough for me, sir. So I had these people come back. When they came back from their respective services, I threw them all in the head and they scrubbed out that head for a couple of hours. That was the Sunday previous: I had the duty the weekend before. It was the ones I could corral—just the ones that had done wrong—the ones I actually could corral.

When Matthew McKeon was sure his troops were all in the squadbay he told Gerald Langone to follow him to the DI room. "Langone, some of the men were laying down on the grass outside. Where were you?"

"Sir, I was inside."

"If you don't get squared away, you're liable to go into combat some day and come home in a pine coffin. Your friends will mourn for you. Do you understand that?"

"Yes, sir. But I didn't see those guys, I was inside."

"You're Section Leader. It's your job to see them. Get that?"

"Yes, sir."

"Now I want to see those people turning to—holding a field day—and I don't want to see any of them goofing off."

"Aye, aye, sir."

Langone went back to the squadroom and ordered a field

day. This ended interruption of the conversation between McKeon and Scarborough.

"Mac, do you have a drink? I feel pretty rough."

"No, Gunny; we don't keep any here."

"Well, I kind of need one. We had a party yesterday. I know where one is, if you don't mind taking me to get it."

"Okay. This turned out to be a bad day for me, though I don't think I look as bad as you. Maybe a shot will perk me up. Let's go."

The two walked out to McKeon's car and drove 300 yards down Wake Boulevard to Building 700, where Weapons Battalion has its offices and barracks. While McKeon turned his car around Scarborough went over to his own car and removed a brown paper bag from the glove compartment. Then they both returned to the DI room with Scarborough carrying the bag and placing it on the table after McKeon closed the door.

"I can't take it straight, Gunny. I'll be back in a minute."

"Okay."

McKeon went up to Sergeant Charles J. Muckler's room to borrow a Coke. When he returned Scarborough took a bottle from the bag. It was a fifth of Hiram Walker's vodka, 80-proof, half-full. Each washed out a dirty coffee cup and fixed himself a drink. Scarborough mixed his with water.

Sergeant King, the other Junior DI of Platoon 71, now enters the picture. We'll let him speak for himself:

> I'm not positive of the time I got up. But after I awakened, I showered and shaved and got some uniforms out. I went in the recruits' squadbay to get them ready to wear when we got back to Mainside. I was in the squadbay for a short time when Sergeant McKeon ordered a field day to be held. I finished what I was pressing. Then I picked up all my gear and went in the Drill Instructors' room. Sergeant Scarborough was in the room when I got there. There was a short bit of conversation being held, I didn't pay too much attention to it. I was worried about my gear more than anything else. There was a bottle of vodka sitting on the table when I walked into the room. I sat down, not paying any attention to it. Sergeant Scarborough and him-

self, Sergeant McKeon, had a drink, maybe two, I'm not positive of the exact amount. After that someone offered me a drink and I took it. I took a swig right out of the bottle.

After noon chow, I came back and saw the bottle where it was left on the table. I put the cork on it and put it down on the deck next to the bulkhead. Then I just carried on where I left off with my gear.

King, Scarborough, and McKeon all testified they put the stopper on the bottle—a typical marine safety precaution.

McKeon continues:

Sergeant Scarborough wanted to run down to the Staff NCO Club and I told him I would take him down there. That's the first time I remember the time for the simple reason that I asked Sergeant Scarborough what time it was and he said it was ten minutes after twelve. I asked Sergeant King if he would take the troops to chow if I took Sergeant Scarborough down to the Staff Club. Sergeant King said he would. After that there was just general talk there and I went in and washed up.

"Here's your bottle, Gunny. Take it with you."

"Leave it here. I'll pick it up later."

I told Sergeant King I would pick up the mail and Sergeant King said, "All right; get the mail and be back by two o'clock because I want to go on liberty." That was around ten minutes to one. So, come one o'clock I knew the Mail Room would be open. I was going to call to Sergeant Muckler but I seen his platoon falling in outside. I got in the car with Sergeant Scarborough. Sergeant Muckler was getting his platoon over to the Supply Building to draw their shooting jackets for the morning. I went over there and asked Sergeant Muckler did he want to go down to get his mail at that time. Sergeant Muckler said, "I can't go down at this time; I've got to draw shooting jackets." I'd pulled up in the driveway between those two buildings where he was drawing his shooting jackets. I got back in the car and I was backing out. I recall the MPs being there, posting reliefs.

At 1:06 P.M. the tide in Ribbon Creek was at low water slack. Corporal Bukowski was on duty in Quonset Hut 164, Recruit Post Office.

Well, after I backed out of there I went down to the Post Office, went in and drew the mail, came back out and threw the mail in the trunk of the car and took Sergeant Scarborough down to the Staff NCO Club. Sergeant Scarborough and I both went inside the club. I believe I was a little ahead of Sergeant Scarborough. I heard someone yell to Sergeant Scarborough from the other side of the bar. I went in where the entrance is there and I pulled up and went to the bar. I didn't see Sergeant Scarborough at all after we went in the club.

I ordered Schlitz. It was served in a can, with a glass. I poured the beer in the glass. While I was in the club I took a few swallows of beer. I was casually talking to some people—I don't recall the names, who they were—just in general it was—and on the other side of the bar I noticed this guy I was on duty with before in Quantico. I left the beer at the bar and walked over on the other side of the bar.

I went over to him and shook hands and we just chewed the fat in general. I will call the name "Shoup." It may be the wrong pronunciation of it—I am very poor at pronouncing names. We talked just in general and I told him I heard he had made Master and he laughed and said he did—just general talk on it. He said, "Let me buy a drink." He said, "I will buy you a drink for every stripe I have made since the last time I have seen you." The last time I seen him he was a buck sergeant—and he bought me a triple shot of whiskey. I wasn't leaning up against the bar—we were talking away from the bar—I don't know if I am making myself clear or not.

We were talking away from the bar and I know he bought the whiskey. I reached over and took the glass and—just out of gratitude—took a sip of it and put it down. At that time the conversation got around about his vehicle. He said he had bought a new car and to come on out and see it. We walked outside the Staff Club and he had one of these—I don't know, one of these sports cars—looked like a sport car, something like a Jaguar, sir. We talked about the car, the speed he could get, the speed he done in it, the economy of it, and all that stuff. We walked back into the Staff NCO Club.

There was a gang—a bunch of fellows around that corner where we were standing before we went out. And I went over to get my beer for the simple reason to chase this whiskey with. I got back there, I didn't see the whiskey—didn't see the glass or anything else. Instead of making an issue of it—I didn't know any of the men standing there—instead of making an issue of it, I just overlooked it. Didn't say anything about it. At that time I noticed the clock on the bulkhead and it was twenty minutes of two. Then all of a sudden it hit me that Sergeant King had liberty and was to go at two o'clock. That is when I left the Staff NCO Club—and I finished that glass of beer. No, sir; I didn't finish the entire can.

No, sir. I am not customarily a drinker of hard liquor. I like beer. Yes, sir. Several occasions I've been tipsy. As far as I can remember, the last time I consumed any amount was around New Year's Eve. Then there was my brother's wedding, which was in November. There may have been times afterward or before that. When I drink, I drink beer.

Well, I went back to Building 761. I went inside. Sergeant King was in there and we talked in general. I told him the mail was in the trunk of the car and send some recruit out after it. It is customary that the recruit get it; Drill Instructors don't carry recruits' mail. We talked in general. To tell you the truth, I don't know what we did talk about. But I remember telling him to hold mail call—and I told him I was going to lay down a while. I remember laying down there—half dozing off—and Sergeant King was around there. Sergeant King was in and out of the Drill Instructors' room and I dozed off.

I remember Sergeant King waking me up. Sergeant King woke me up for the keys. He woke me up for the keys to my car. My wife wanted the car for the simple reason she had to go to the hospital the next morning and I wouldn't be home that evening. I wouldn't be home the next morning either. One of her girl friends carried her out to pick up the car, which she usually done when I had duty on the weekend. I told Sergeant King the keys were on the desk or in my trousers. I forget what I did tell him. I just rolled over and dozed off again, sir. I usually left a call for Private Langone to wake me up. He woke me up around ten after five.

Sergeant King testified he called McKeon at five. Private Langone testified he called McKeon at five-ten. Both could be right.

While Matthew McKeon slept the moon set over Broad River at 4:48 P.M. The sun was too close to the horizon for anyone to notice it. Several witnesses insisted the moon was shining four hours later.

When McKeon flaked out on his bunk King went to the squadroom and held mail call. As he entered he was greeted with the usual chorus: "ATTENTION!" Each recruit stood rigidly at the foot of his bunk, turned out in utility clothing, hopeful. King glanced at the envelopes and called out names: Lawless, Rambo, Delgado, Maloof, Serantes, Ferkel, Acker, Geckle, Nobles, Truitt, Baratta, Keaton, Wilkinson, Clariborne, O'Rourke. Upon hearing his name each recruit doubled-timed to the center of the room, clicked his heels at attention, took the letter, thanked the Sergeant, and ran back to his place. If he were lucky enough to have more than one letter he repeated the performance.

King announced that the rest of the afternoon would be devoted to working on gear and writing letters. No one would leave the squadbay except a relief for the watch at the clothesline. The troops would keep off their bunks. If anyone wanted to sit down, he had a locker-box. King went back to the DI room and read a book. After he called McKeon he went to Messhall 766 for supper and then continued to the Quonset hut area where he spent the next three hours playing cards with Corporal Barney.

Matthew McKeon awakened and lay on his bunk a few minutes preoccupied with his problem. If Platoon 71 wound up with a sour record, Sergeant Baker, Battalion Field Striper, certainly wouldn't give him a platoon of his own on the next cycle. Huff didn't seem worried. But Huff was getting that short-timer's attitude. It wouldn't be long before he was transferred from Parris Island, or at least designated as Special Subjects Instructor. Moreover, Huff had moved up and down. He had worked up to Senior DI and then later had been Junior DI again. McKeon thought that was degrading the prestige of a Staff NCO. He wanted a platoon of his own—a command. Then he would make *real* marines out of those yardbirds.

Huff didn't seem to be bearing down on them hard enough. Yet perhaps Huff hadn't reached his limit of tolerance. McKeon remembered Huff threatening the platoon some weeks ago. Earlier that day, sometime after Sergeant Muckler left the DI room, McKeon was reminded of Huff's threat: To march Platoon 71 into the swamps. Just glancing out the window toward the butts was enough to refresh McKeon on that idea.

This is what Huff said at the Inquiry:

Q. How did you know that platoons had been taken into the swamp, then?

A. Well, I guess I heard it.

Q. Did you ever tell Sergeant McKeon that such a procedure was an acceptable thing?

A. I said a lot of Drill Instructors do it.

Q. Did you ever tell Sergeant McKeon that that was an accepted thing if the platoon was goofing off?

A. No, sir.

Q. You're sure you never indicated to him that a platoon could be disciplined by being taken down to the water?

A. I never said the platoon could be disciplined, but I chewed their tails one day and I told them if they don't snap out of their hockey I would take them in the swamps.

Matthew McKeon recalled when his DI marched him into the swamp eight years before. His plan crystallized. He wouldn't wait for Huff to take action—that might be too late. He would do it now. Tonight. Though the swamps behind Third Battalion were more popular, there was plenty of similar marshland down beyond the butts. Maybe a night march would put some fear of God in the boys. He would take them out after dark.

Langone knocked and reported the platoon was formed for chow. McKeon dressed hurriedly, left the room, and marched Platoon 71 to the messhall. This was a tight spot in the schedule: His troops would enter the mess line at 5:35, ten minutes later a bus would leave Nissen Hut 299 for religious services at Mainside. While marching along Wake Boulevard he issued his instructions. Catholics had a novena in the New Depot Chapel at six-thirty. Private Porter was in charge of the detail; with him were McGuire, Grabowski, Brennan. At the same time in the Old Depot Chapel there was a Protestant hymn-sing. Private

Pool was in charge of that detail; with him were Brewer, Bruner, Drown, Barber, *Thompson,* Keaton, Veney. (Others might have attended; testimony was incomplete.)

On working days anyone driving along Wake Boulevard will usually see recruits on the Rifle Range walking to or from Mainside. Some have emergency dental appointments, others must see the optometrist. Those getting insured packages from home walk two and one-half miles to the Post Office to sign for them. Most officers and senior NCOs driving by will stop and pick them up. This isn't pure sympathy: it conserves training time. And also it is a useful leadership tool: it gives an officer the opportunity to ask pertinent but anonymous questions. It would be a fine time to determine whether or not the Boot is getting enough to eat—except he won't tell the truth. Conversations run something like this:

"How long have you been on the Rifle Range, son?"

"This is my third week, sir."

"How are you getting along?"

"All right, I guess, sir."

"Are you going to qualify?"

"Yes, sir; I got two twelve today, sir."

"How's the chow?"

"It's lots better than we get at Mainside, sir."

"Are you getting enough to eat?"

"Yes, sir."

"Do you get seconds when you want them?"

"Yes, sir."

Unfortunately the last two answers are not wholly true. A Boot never has enough to eat. Of course, with a Mess Sergeant like Harry McCarty, who makes a habit of keeping several loaves of bread and a few gallons of gravy on the table and who does the same with all the jam and peanut butter he can wrangle from Food Service, no recruit leaves the table hungry. But we still must reckon with his Drill Instructor. DIs habitually limit their troops on the time they will spend in the messhall. Moreover, going through the serving line a second time is ordinarily a myth.

While Platoon 71 was at the Rifle Range it was only one among twenty-eight. These were scheduled into the messhall at the rate of two every five minutes. The first platoon in line will have been out of the messhall an hour before the last platoon enters. Seconds are not served until everyone has been fed. Moreover, DIs take a dim view of recruits eating sweets or taking seconds, particularly when they are on the Rifle Range. Let's let Staff Sergeant Edward A. Huff, Senior DI of Platoon 71, express his feelings:

Q. Had you, prior to April 8, 1956, and after the platoon had established itself at the Weapons Training Battalion area for training on the Range, issued any orders to the platoon regarding seconds at chow and, if so, what were those orders?

A. I don't know if I had issued it exactly as an order, sir, but many of the Drill Instructors at Parris Island realize that if men are fat and if they go back for seconds they cannot get in proper position to fire a rifle, sir.

Q. With that in mind, what, if anything, had you said to the platoon regarding seconds at chow?

A. I think I said that they would not go back for seconds while they were firing, sir.

And so Matthew McKeon led his charges into the messhall and watched them go through the serving line. He then took his place at the DI table in the center, where he could observe most of what was going on. In his mind there was no question about second helpings; he said, "The recruits down here, they know they weren't supposed to have seconds, yet they ignored the order and went in and had seconds."

Platoon 71 was lucky Sunday evening in being last into the messhall. The call went for seconds. Gerald Langone got up to get some and passed Matthew McKeon. "Langone, where are you going?"

"I'm going up for seconds, sir."

"Why?"

"I'm hungry, sir."

"What did you do to be hungry?"

"What do I have to do to be hungry, sir?"

Langone walked away and got his seconds. McKeon was powerless there. Captain Patrick, Officer of the Day, was observing the mess line. If McKeon tried to interfere with Langone, Patrick would intercede and countermand his order. McKeon would only lose face, accomplish nothing. The hostility he felt must be contained. This served to increase the pressure that had been building up for a whole weekend.

7

Dragging

ABOUT NINE Monday morning I decide to make a run back to the barracks. Ragley drives me to the office. I telephone the Chief of Staff my negative report and tell him about the shrimper. He advises me that the Inspector General, Carson Roberts, whom I succeeded as Adjutant of Second Marines in Port-au-Prince, will arrive Parris Island by air about three this afternoon. Also, two helicopters on a training flight from Jacksonville, Florida, to New River, North Carolina, are being diverted. We can expect them shortly after noon. I gather up a few other loose ends and walk into our Personnel Office with the intention of getting Ragley to drive me back. Standing there beautifully turned out in his best liberty greens is a familiar master sergeant, John Clement.

"What are you doing here, boy?"

"Reporting for duty, Colonel."

"Toss your goddam orders to James, we can do the paper work later. I've got a job for you."

"I know. I heard about it in G-1."

"Where are your working clothes? If they're not handy, we'll draw you some—you can pay for them later."

"Down in the car."

"Get into 'em. How long will it take? Meet me in C-Butts."

"You won't have to wait for me, Colonel."

"Say. We're getting a shrimper. I want you to work with him. Maybe you know him, Rutledge Elliott?"

"Rut Elliott? We've been friends for years."

"Good. Get going. I'll see you in a few minutes."

"Aye, aye, sir."

When I was thinking about Sparks last night my mind was on Clement; he must have been emerging from my unconscious. He's not a typical marine, he's what we would like them all to be: tall, husky, ruddy, alert, utterly capable—and with a sense of humor. Give him a job and you can leave him alone. He has been a repeater at Weapons Battalion; in fact I doubt that he remembers how many tours he's had here. He's a topnotch demolitions man, which requires guts if anything does. Willie Tate, our previous Demolitions Officer, says when you see an armed hand grenade with its hung striker staring at you with a fishy eye, you sort of baby up to it, pamper it a bit.

John Clement worked with ammunition and explosive ordnance disposal in our battalion before he left us for Japan. At other times he has been in charge of the butts, managed a firing line, been Police Sergeant, rifle coach, marksmanship instructor on the School Range. He's had about every detail except Mess Sergeant—and I know he could handle that. But his long suit is water: boats, tackle, engines, tides, currents, rivers, and beaches. His knowledge and ability are legend here in the Low Country. Occasionally someone else may catch more or larger fish, but that is where the element of chance takes over.

A few weeks ago Clement was in to see me en route from Japan to Quantico. He wanted his orders changed for Parris Island so he could make more frequent visits to his wife in Columbia. She has been hospitalized with TB for more than five of the past eight years. He came home from the Orient early on a humanitarian transfer. The medicos say his wife hasn't much longer to live; she just doesn't respond to treatment. That makes it pretty rough for Clement. The two older children are with relatives in Texas; the baby is in North Carolina. Stationed at Parris Island, Clement could receive help from the two families and bring the children together.

CWO Walter Lawrence Tate, known to us as "Little Willie" because of his Gargantuan dimensions, used his influence in Washington to have Clement join him in Quantico. But when Clement arrived there and Willie heard his story, he used the same influence to get him back on Parris Island.

Ragley drives me back to C-Butts. This time I look at my watch; it is ten-fifteen. We figure the next low water for about two. When I get out of the truck, I can see the trawler at the mouth of Ribbon Creek. About that time a primitive-looking helicopter lands. Someone gets out; it is my boy Clark.

"We had to go to Savannah for fuel. Major Stith tried to talk the Air Force out of a chopper, but he wasn't having much luck. I gave the National Guard people a real snow job. This major volunteered to come over. His name's Clark, too."

"Good, Clark; you're always a fast talker. But now I'm going to break your heart and ground you. I want Clement to cover the area."

John Clement has just arrived; I call him over. "Want a ride in that eggbeater?"

"It's just what we need; I'm on my way."

"Not just yet. Let me give you a quick rundown." I do, though Clement doesn't really need it. He goes over, introduces himself to the Major, who is staying with his ship, and they take off.

The trawler keeps feeling his way up Ribbon Creek with nets hoisted to the gaff. He needs four and a half feet of water and the ebbing tide puts him in close quarters. She is a trim little boat. As she heaves in range of my bifocals, I can read her name: *Duty*. What could be more appropriate? He keeps inching her along, giving her not much more than steerageway, when she grounds directly in front of us. With consummate seamanship, he backs her off, brings her about in that narrowing ditch, and stands out to await next high water.

Technical Sergeant Gail Brock appears on the scene. Some months ago he and Mrs. Brock were both tech sergeants, but she's since been paid off. Brock is Chief Lifeguard for Special Services pools during his working time and Neighborhood Commissioner for the Boy Scouts while he is resting. He and I have worked together with the Scouts all the time I've been here. Brock's efforts have ben appreciated even at the level of the Coastal Carolina Council. But at the moment he is indignant. "Colonel, why didn't you send for me? I just heard about this."

"It's out of your line, Sergeant."

"Out of my line? Why this is just what me and my boys are trained for! We can dive in there with face masks and search the bottom. Or we can join hands and wade that whole creek. If there's anybody in there, we'll find them."

"Now take it easy. That water's cold and it's muddy and it's plenty dirty and there're oyster shells all over. There's nothing infects worse than an oyster-shell wound. I'm not going to have any skin divers in there, even if you wear shoes."

"We could sure do it, if the Colonel would just let us."

"Maybe you could, but the answer's still negative."

"Do you want a grapnel?"

"We got a good one from the Sheriff and Maintenance turned out two homemade jobs. Know where there're any more?"

"I've got one of my own with plenty of new Manila line that you're welcome to use."

"Go get it."

I stand alone and watch our boats dragging. Staff Sergeant Ernest Whitlow is out there as he has been since daylight. Whitlow, in contrast to many others, is a good family man. He is clean, sincere, quiet, industrious. He's our Assistant Police Sergeant. Among other things he supervises care of the lawns and getting odd jobs done around our quarters. He's our Maggie's special friend, had his arm across her shoulders looking at our flowers the day we brought our new Claire home from the hospital. Their first was born soon after that, their second a couple of weeks ago. Last summer Whitlow shipped over for three. He debated a long time before deciding. But there were payments to make on the new car and he knew he was again an expectant father—which we found out later. Could he have predicted the future, he would have gone back to the farm.

He's the eldest child in a large family and has two brothers in the service. He senses his responsibility. His father had a stroke followed by long hospitalization; right now his dad is relearning to talk. His mother and the younger children are attempting to run the farm. Whitlow wants to be near enough to help. We wangled him a transfer: For once Headquarters came right back with approval. Whitlow's due to leave for Yorktown in about three weeks—we allowed time for the new baby. Up there he'll be able to spend alternate weekends at home.

A fine handyman, Whitlow. Being raised in the Virginia foothills put him in good stead. There's never a job too complicated or difficult for him; he seems to know just what to do. He left Korea with a reputation as a crackerjack rocketman. We use him on the 3.5 bazooka in our weapons demonstrations.

While the helicopter covers the area meticulously from an altitude of 200 feet, Weapons Battalion boatmen continue to drag. They seem to be getting more bites as the tide recedes. It is tiring work and calls for infinite patience. One man sits in the stern with the motor throttled down to minimum speed. The other stands in the bow with the line played out through his hands; it doesn't take long to raise blisters even on hands long toughened by work in our Police Gang. Someone hooks an oyster bed or other hidden obstruction; then he carefully sets the line taut and heaves in. It is to no avail. We are in one of our periods of endless waiting. I stand to one side with Father Anthony Bielski, our Battalion Chaplain.

"You know, if there is someone drowned, this is going to be hard to explain."

"There's no doubt of that. They'll crucify the DI, but he'll have it coming to him."

"That's not what I'm thinking about. We have too many people who sit at desks and shuffle papers; they're always interested in written orders. Some nit-picker is going to want to know what order Weapons Battalion has which would prohibit an act like this."

"You can't have orders covering every contingency."

"I know that. We could have a volume—one heavier than you could lift—but no one would get through reading it. Besides, before you get one item written and published, the DIs would think of something else. You can't keep ahead of them, nor any other marine."

"Doesn't everyone know that? What are you worrying about?"

"Actually, I'm not worrying—it's too late to worry. I'm going to try to stay limber. But you wait and see. It'll probably happen during an investigation. Professional Staffmen think you can accomplish miracles with a piece of paper."

"But you couldn't have written an order saying: 'Thou shalt not march thy platoon through Ribbon Creek on a dark Sunday night without prior approval of the Commanding Officer.' "

"Sure I couldn't, but that's what they'll be looking for. It's going to be particularly bad under my system. I've rewritten all the orders to keep them general, brief, flexible, and few. My safety order for handling ammunition merely lists the governing references."

We watched the dragging in silence. After a long wait I broke it. "I've got the answer, but no one is ever going to make me do it. I could issue an order: 'Every member of this command will, at all times, use sound judgment in everything he does.' "

"Yes. You could publish that but you couldn't enforce it."

"That's just the point."

The helicopter lands within a few yards of us. Sergeant Clement and Major Clark come over to report. Their search has been thorough. They can swear that there are no exposed bodies, horizontal or vertical, in that entire marshy area. Major Clark advises me he has adequate fuel and will be happy to stand by for a while. As we turn to look at the boats in the creek, there is a low whistle. Gooch, Whitlow, and Hughes have hooked one. They have him in the boat. Well, this is it. The whole Marine Corps has had it, too! Cautioning the idlers to stand well clear,

I go over to the dilapidated little pier beyond the other end of C-Butts to meet them. "Get Dr. Sullivan out here on the double!" Having a Navy medical officer pronounce the man dead will keep us in the clear with the coroner and permit us to move him right away.

Ready hands, which are always to include those of Ragley, lift him onto the head of the pier and carry him to its foot where they place the body on a stretcher which has simultaneously been taken from the waiting ambulance. His face has been covered with a field jacket. It is the Section Leader, a tall, husky, Negro boy. He is in grotesque *rigor mortis*. Surprisingly, there are no apparent wounds from the grapnel. His arms and legs are in positions similar to a boxer's stance: there had obviously been a struggle; he went down fighting.

There is a feeling more intensely personal about this recruit than about a combat casualty. In combat we expect someone to get hurt. Marines die in aircraft, in field maneuvers; the highways take a horrible toll. But this seems so unnecessary. Hard-bitten old-timers, rough as they come, turn their heads as if they have found something more interesting on the horizon. The ambulance corpsman is standing by. "What are your orders?"

"Nothing definite, Colonel, but I plan to take him to West End Infirmary first."

"Why?"

"The Medical Manual says you put the fingerprints on Form N at the station where the man dies."

"We'll skip the regulations this time. West End is full of impressionable recruits. Take him directly to the morgue at the Naval Hospital." I turn to Sergeant Major Langston. "Call the hospital and tell them there's one on the way."

Lieutenant Robert F. Sullivan, Medical Corps, whom the entire Battalion virtually worships as they did his predecessor, Dr. Ernest H. Ferrell, arrives and makes his examination. He doesn't need the stethoscope. Hats come off while Tony Bielski blesses the body. The Provost Marshal's photographers take necessary pictures. The corpse is wrapped in a hospital blanket. We are about to load him into the meat wagon when there is another whistle from Ribbon Creek. "Put a tag on the litter. Mark it 'No. 1' so we can keep track of pictures and times. Take him over to the hospital and come right back. Call another ambulance."

It has been twenty minutes since we recovered the first one. By now we have established a routine. They place him on a litter at the head of the pier, cover him with a hospital blanket, and carry him to the spot where we had the first one. Our scuttlebutt indicated only one of the recruits was Negro, but there is no question about this second boy; he is Negro, too. Number Two is much like the first, but blood is oozing from a grapnel wound. He is frozen in nearly the same position; he, too, went down fighting. Doctor, pronounce him dead. Hats off. Tony, bless the body. Photographers, get your pictures, mark him "No. 2," put him in the ambulance. It is all reflex action, something like close-order drill.

Another whistle from Ribbon Creek. "Hold it! Don't take him away yet. You've room for two in that wagon."

They seem to be coming from the same spot. It took fifteen minutes this time. Number Three is a white boy. As our routine is completed, a relief ambulance drives up.

"Take them to the morgue."

We have Number Four in twelve minutes.

"Take him away."

Father Tony blesses all the bodies though just one is wearing a Catholic medal. But we are sure the folks at home—regardless of their religion—will get some consolation from knowing someone thought to say a little prayer.

Major Clark has to get back to Savannah. I express our sincere thanks for his assistance. His 'copter is away with a vertical take-off.

We have another hour yet before low water slack. At this rate the job will soon be washed up. Three or four boats concentrate on the hole, which they have located by sounding with boathooks. Occasionally a motor conks out. It's pretty rough on an outboard when it's revving at minimum speed. We bring the boat in by towing, change or repair the motor, and he stands out again. Upstream and down they go, tending the line with hands now raw. But we don't get a bite.

John Clement comes over and gives me his report. From the air, in spite of the murky surface appearance of the water, he has been able to see all of the creek bottom except for two holes. The other one, about 300 yards away and around the loop, has been dragged carefully. But since we dragged many times before making our first recovery from the near hole, we'd better try again. My boys do that, long and patiently.

Our two marine helicopters are due and they land close to their ETA. We had expected them to come into Page Field for instructions but they apparently got the word from the Beaufort tower and settle down behind C-Butts near the same spot Major Clark has so recently left. One of my boys who had previously worked with helicopters steps out of the group to signal them in.

It's common knowledge you can find any kind of trade you need among a bunch of marines. Getting someone to signal helicopters isn't even a strain. Out in Guam in the twenties Walter Stuart, then a marine lieutenant and Chief of Police at Agaña, needed a hangman to execute a convicted Chamorro murderer: Walter found a marine in his own outfit who admitted he had the requisite skill and demonstrated it with a tidy job.

Since it is near low water, another search might prove useful. The pilots are briefed and we load Clement aboard for another ride. Again the entire area is thoroughly covered: results negative.

Number Five seems to appear without warning. The boat carrying him stands up to the dock rather quietly before we notice its cargo. The crew told me later they must have hooked him several times. He looks much the same as the others and receives the same ceremony. As usual, Ragley is there to hand him up from the boat.

This boat crew consists of Gooch, Hughes, and Whitlow; they stay on the beach a while to take a breather. Gooch is standing a few yards away with his back turned toward us. I want to question him about the hole from which all recoveries have been made, four by his crew. I call. He must hear me, but there is no answer. I call—unthinking—the second time, before I notice the movement of his shoulders and ribs. Gooch won't be able to talk for a few minutes.

Boats keep breaking down, the tide keeps flowing in, and for another two and a half hours Weapons Battalion marines keep the grapnels dragging. There is always a relief crew waiting to go out. Back and forth they go, slowly and patiently, changing places occasionally with one another on line or motor. It won't be long before the trawler can go to work. While our hopes rest heavily on him, we can't play him for a sure thing. We'd better prepare for the next low water.

Maintenance sends out a battery of lights with portable generator. I talk the problem over with Tom Peck, the Fire Chief. One searchlight pointed cross-stream near our hole and another along the axis of the channel will give us adequate illumination. We have the lights set in place and arrange to telephone if they are going to be needed.

I look at Captain Patrick; he is completely bushed. Though I know Pat wants to continue as Officer of the Day until our work is finished, this is too much. CWO Alvin Emmerson Johnson, known to us as "Goober," who for the past twenty-nine years seems to have had but two duty stations, Parris Island and overseas, is wearing his duty belt and standing by. I call Patrick and Johnson over.

"Sir, I report as old Officer of the Day."

"Have you anything unusual to report?"

"Only what I've written and am going to write in the Guard Report Book, Colonel."

"You're relieved, Pat. If you take my advice, you'll break that seven-year abstinence and have a big shot of whiskey."

"Sir, I report as new Officer of the Day."

"Take the duty, Goober. There are no special instructions —you'll just have to help us play this by ear."

About four-thirty the trawler begins dragging. When we notice him standing up Ribbon Creek we call in our boats and send John Clement out aboard. Rutledge Elliott takes the whole stretch from A-Butts to the bend immediately to our right front. His small net is on the bottom. At the end of a run he hoists the net while he turns around. Even though we know that Rut's crewman, hand on the hoisting wire, can tell if they make a pickup, each time he brings the net to gaff our eyes are glued on it.

"Colonel! Here comes an official car. Four stars flying."

It is the Commandant. It is my duty to meet him. I hurry over to the high-numbered end of C-Butts, which is the closest parking place available to our new CP. From our small pier he could get the best view of the whole scene. The chauffeur gives me a wave-off and the car goes right on by. I am too flustered to salute. A second staff car whizzes in the wake of the first one. The Commandant's party debarks at the site of our old CP, some 250 yards away. Convention would require my getting there at double-time. After that wave-off, I walk. When I join the group there is an exchange of salutes and handshakes.

"Hello, Bill. Bill, what orders do you have or what Depot Order do you recall which specifically forbids a thing like this?"

"General, to the best of my knowledge there isn't any. This sort of thing just isn't done—but I can't recall any order that would apply."

"There has to be something to cover this."

"There may be—I hope so—but I haven't had much time since last night to read orders. I'm going to study them when I get this job finished. Right now I'm talking off the cuff but I can't stand here and lie to you: To the best of my recollection we have no order which covers a deal like this."

Of course the Commandant knows that we have always had a "General article" in our Code: Disorders and neglects to the prejudice of good order and discipline, conduct of a nature to bring discredit upon the Armed Forces, and unspecified crimes and offenses not capital.

General Burger points out details of the terrain to General Pate. I exchange a few semi-pleasantries with Carson Roberts, the recently appointed Inspector General. The whole group watches Rut Elliott's *Duty* make two or three passes. Eventually chauffeurs, aides, and generals mount up. I salute all the brass as their cars pull off. That is the last I see of our visitors.

Later I learn the Commandant held a press conference shortly after his arrival. That seemed to be the main purpose of his visit. Since it took newsmen hours to dig up enough facts to write a coherent story, the next morning's papers carry little more than a bulletin on the drownings. But Public Information Officers are on the ball: The Commandant's biography is available to stretch out reporter's copy.

Back to our rickety dock. Elliott continues to use the smaller net—without success. We had heard he would use the larger net as a last resort. If that doesn't bring up the body, it isn't there.

Captain Carl H. McMillan, Bull Surgeon at Parris Island, comes out and stands at the foot of the pier with his assistant, Captain James S. Brown, Jr. This is a good chance to get some information about physiology. "Surgeon, how long will *rigor mortis* stay in a body?"

"I guess it depends a great deal upon conditions. I was a young officer when they raised *S-4*. She had been down in cold sea-water about four months—as I remember. They brought in fifty-one bodies at one time for me to post. That first day they were all rigid, but then they began to deteriorate rapidly."

Meanwhile the helicopters take off for a dusk patrol. They hover close to the ground and scrutinize the edges of the stream. We hope that a porpoise might come in and nose him out. Suddenly one chopper hovers over our hole. It is obvious he has found something. Without voice-radio we can only guess. We wait while he comes in for a landing. One of the crew runs over and tells us they discovered a cap. They will mark it while we send a boat to retrieve it. Our boat goes out and bring back the cap. It is of a civilian style commonly worn by mariners. Anyway, it shows that we have good observation. But in due course the eggbeaters secure. Results negative.

Shortly afterward, during a turn at our end of the channel, Clement comes up over the dock while his boat goes back to the *Duty*. It returns the civilian cap. The 'copter lifted it from the head of the shrimper's crewman. John Clement explains that Rutledge Elliott has to clear the channel before dark. He couldn't use the big net because the stream is so narrow it would cause extensive damage. Shrimp nets are valuable. We have no way to reimburse his loss.

The boats are hauled out of the water. Motors are carried to our temporary shop set up in the nearest target shed. Goober Johnson checks the tide table and we decide to resume dragging at midnight. Our only immediate problem is making our outboard motors operational. Clement is the best man I know—anywhere—to get the job done. "Can you have them all running at midnight?"

"Yes, sir."

"Will you handle the show tonight while Sparks gets some sleep?"

"Yes, sir."

"Sparks, get out to Trailer Park and turn in. I don't believe even those kids can keep you awake now. John will call the shots tonight. We'll send for you if we need you. If we don't have any luck, I'm planning to use you about noon tomorrow."

"Aye, aye, sir." For once Sparks doesn't argue.

"Gooch, Edwards, Clark, Hughes, O'Neal, the rest of you characters, get back to the barracks; have some chow; rack out. You'll get a call for the midwatch."

Edwards takes me to one side. He wants to go home. He'll be back in plenty of time. I tell him that I won't refuse but I think he has holes in his head. He would lose time on the road that he could spend in the rack. He agrees.

Goober Johnson can carry on from here. He's had some sleep. Ragley drives me over to the quarters. "Pick me up at eleven-thirty. Bring me a sheepskin coat—it's going to be cold tonight. There'll be a cup of coffee when you get over. And *you* get some sleep, son."

"But I've got to gas the truck. The pump at Motor Transport is open until eleven."

"Okay. Gas up and get some sleep." He does and he doesn't.

Mom meets me at the door and starts to kiss me. "Go 'way. I want to be alone."

I go to the den and collapse in my chair. She brings me a

drink and sits there quietly. Finally I am able to talk. Rumors on the Depot are legion—even in the Children's School. The radio is humming.

"The truth is we've pulled out five of them. Five fine-looking men, all stiff and grotesque—just because of some goddam knucklehead."

"You couldn't help it."

"But I'm Commanding Officer—I'm responsible."

"But you haven't done anything wrong."

"No. But when the bureaucrats start passing the buck, I've had it. Why, Ran Pate was out there. All he asked me about was some order we might have which prohibits drowning recruits. I don't think we have any. I thought lots of other people would ask that question, but I didn't think it of him."

There is another spell when I can't indulge in idle chatter. Then Mom wants to fix me some food; there is beef and kidney stew ready to warm up. But I am afraid of solid food now. We finally agree on an eggnog—to which I add three ounces of whiskey. Shivering still I go up to Page's room and turn down the twin bed by the window. That will be farthest from the noise of the children. I set the alarm nearby and break out the Hudson's Bay blanket. It is eight-fifteen, I can have three hours. But I lose the first of those tossing and turning.

Mom calls me at eleven Monday night just before the alarm rings. Since summer uniform is prescribed I revive an old sea-going ruse: wearing long-handled underwear. When I'm dressed I go downstairs for a slug of coffee. Les Veigel is waiting for me at the kitchen table. First I bring him up to date and then tell him to get some sleep so that he'll have a clear head in the morning. I want him to do some research in Depot Orders so that I won't have to study them myself. At the Inquiry I want to have the same memories and bias I had when this rat-race started.

Major Lester Eugene Veigel has been Weapons Battalion Executive Officer two months since I promised the Chief of Staff that Veigel's "primary duty" would remain baseball coach.

I first met Les on the NROTC staff of the University of Michigan, where we served together two years. There I discovered him one of the most capable officers among his contemporaries. Les had just come from a night game when he meets me at the table. (Parris Island won). During this whole affair he works quietly in the background. The organization he arranges and the details he cares for are a mystery to me. What I do know is that we are operating at capacity around the clock and it takes first-rate administrative insight to keep up a full head of steam.

Corporal Thomas J. Ragley comes in while Les Veigel and I are co-ordinating our plans. Ragley had the Guard truck fueled and checked; a sheepskin coat for me is over his arm. We give him time to gulp some coffee before we head for the butts.

My official car is the Guard truck, a pickup. It is also used for Message Center runs, laundry, posting reliefs of the Guard, inspecting the Guard, and hauling recruits to or from Mainside. I have always had a good driver. McHale, who preceded Ragley, left for Japan a few months ago when Sergeant Major Langston arranged for the transfer for which McHale yearned. Ragley is a youngster of fine character, willing, polite, accommodating. He prefers staying around the barracks to making a liberty. It is quite apparent he's saving his money so he can go back to school. Ragley spent some time in the seminary until he finally decided he hadn't found his vocation.

It isn't yet midnight when Ragley and I reach the dock behind C-Butts. Though low water isn't due until two-twenty my boys have already started dragging. Chaplain Twait is on station and all four of the Catholic chaplains are here. Two or three newspapermen appear as we receive word the Commandant has directed they be given free rein: we have nothing to hide; we are to answer any question put to us. Fortunately, the better stories are back in Barracks 761 among recruit survivors.

As he promised, John Clement has all outboard motors operational. His perseverance keeps them going until the wind-up. But I wait to find out through the grapevine tomorrow that John Clement in spite of his calm outward appearance is under severe emotional strain. His wife is scheduled for a major operation at nine in the morning. During our evening break Clement tried to get a long-distance line to Columbia. By that time a task force of newsmen wanted out and thousands of parents with sons at Parris Island wanted in. Clement couldn't get through. Yet he asks no favors and keeps at work as if he has not a care in the world.

Gooch is a marine who thinks problems through. He drifts over to relay some of his ideas. "Colonel, there're going to be too many of us dragging that hole. I want to work down behind A-Butts. I was down there this afternoon and we got quite a number of bites."

"Okay, Gooch. Take your crew down there."

"We'll need a light."

The Fire Chief is beside me. "Can you fix it?"

"No strain, Colonel. I'll send a man down to spot it where he wants it."

Gooch still worries. "Another thing, Colonel; I'm afraid that boy may drift with the tide out into Broad River. If that happens we'll never find him."

"What do you recommend?"

"I'd like at low tide to build a fence across the mouth of the creek."

"Sheriff McTeer says that a body is invariably found right where it went down."

"But that shrimp net may have dragged him."

"It could have, but Elliott only used the net in one section of the creek. We'll drag the entire stretch the shrimper did. One more thing, Gooch; have you thought of material and labor? You'd need a fence perhaps 400 feet long and—in the middle—at least twelve feet high. I believe you'll see that it's impractical to build a fence. We'll have to take a chance."

"Aye, aye, sir." Gooch leaves, unhappy.

Gooch is a Georgia boy who doesn't impress you on first appearance. He's always well turned out—since he's tall, this helps in wearing the uniform—but he looks frail. Don't let appearance mislead you; his skeletal system is bound together with steel muscles. Gooch has eight years' service and was eight months a DI before he came to Weapons Battalion. He joined us from a Recruit Battalion after the training load dropped. Gooch was an outstanding DI and brought with him a letter of appreciation for his success in Reserve Training. (His assignment to us must have been an oversight on the part of Staff. The Sergeant Major took an inventory for me last month and found that of our 193 NCOs, 74 went to DI School; we received 21 that failed, 16 found psychiatrically unsuited for training recruits, and 4 who weren't assigned as DIs because they were Negroes—unwritten "policy" keeps them off the field.) Gooch operates our Coaches' School quietly but effectively. He has a fine record for his work in amtracs in Korea when the situation was hot. He has been on the promotion list three years. He married a widow; has one adopted child and one of his own. He is the kind who can really appreciate family life. But his wife has been away three months now—Gooch has a bunk in the barracks with the bachelors—his mother-in-law is slowly dying of cancer.

Dragging continues for more than four hours. Time after time the boats crews think they have a bite, but to no avail. Boats break down and motors are replaced. Only outboards and searchlight generator break the silence. Conversation is at a minimum. Those on the bank merely stare with the lights at the surface of the creek. There is no one around who is not dead-tired.

The Mess Gang is doing nobly; there have been sandwiches and coffee out on the creek since it became apparent this was going to be a prolonged operation. That roast beef left from the picnic is still holding out. When supplies run low Ragley drives back to the barracks and returns with another issue. But if Food Service ever finds out we sent chow to the trawler they'll want to collect for it.

Edwards is still working on the creek but he isn't good for much longer. With Richards and McClure in his crew, Edwards recovered the second body. One of our few Negro Staff NCOs, Edwards is a good marine: He keeps his mouth shut, gets the work done—and it's done right. Last summer we thought we'd rigged everything the Marine Corps Rifle Team wanted; at least

Lieutenant Colonel Walter R. Walsh, captain, and Major George Kross, coach, indicated we had. Then Captain Remes Delahunt, who was handling the international squad, wanted cubicles for his small-bore shooters. Hudson, the Police Sergeant, had gone to Bethesda for his baby's operation; Whitlow, his first assistant, was escorting Wixson's body to Arlington; that left Edwards managing the Police Gang. I sent for him and described what was needed. His responses were so brief and he was so quiet that I wasn't sure my message got through. A couple of hours later I walked over to Special Weapons Range to see if he had started the job; he was doing the finishing touches when I arrived. A few months ago Edwards was being sent temporarily to Camp LeJeune for Engineer School. Just before he left, an automobile salesman—hot under the collar—came to see me. Edwards had been out at the shop and told them he was being transferred. The dealer wanted to stop Edwards' monthly payments and close his account before he got out of town. There was an offer to give him an older car in trade, but obviously Edwards was getting the short end of the deal. I sent the salesman back with word that while I couldn't legally guarantee Edwards' payments I would personally vouch for him. Edwards sent a telegram; that evening he went out to Beaufort and paid off the balance in cash. News of this gave me a real lift. Had Edwards been white, there would have been no questions.

About four Tuesday morning I secure the operation. I order O'Neal, Hughes, Whitlow, and Edwards not to show up for the rest of the day; they are to go home and sleep.

While Ragley is driving me to the barracks I notice the street lights have peculiar rays projecting from them. Once in the office I discover I'd worn reading instead of distance glasses all through the night operation. I telephone Bill Buse at his quarters; the ringing signal sounds many times; his wife's sleepy voice answers; then I get Bill: "Nothing but a negative report. I expect to have the helicopters clear of the Range and open fire at six. We'll resume dragging at twelve-thirty. We'll suspend firing during the recovery operation, then crank off again and keep going until dark."

"I'll report it to the Old Man."

On the way out I go through the messhall. George Davey is at the galley range frying eggs. He's been on the job forty hours, more than twenty-four continuously. Before I realize that he would have been there preparing breakfast anyway, I ask him if we are keeping him up. "Many's the time I've told you I don't give a damn if cooks never sleep. This just goes to prove it. Keep the boys fed, George, I'm working their tails off."

"No marine leaves here hungry, Colonel."

I go over to the table where the boat crews are eating. Gooch has six or seven eggs on his plate—I don't count them, but it is all the plate will hold. The troops look really worn out. Their only conversation is that necessary to get food served.

I drag myself across the field to my quarters. The phone rings as I enter the house. It is Mr. Johnson, Officer of the Day:

"Goober, Colonel. The Chief just called and told me not to open fire. He told me it would be poor public relations if just by chance we recovered that body with a bullet hole in it."

"Okay. If that's the pitch, delay Reveille one hour. Better get going, it's nearly time for First Call. Don't forget to tell Davey about it in the galley."

"One hour. Aye, aye, sir."

I can't see it. We have to keep the show on the road. We've lost one day's firing and have a schedule to meet. If that body is there, it is well under water. Bullets would ricochet over the surface of the creek; besides, the beaten zone is beyond it. Oh, well; the Old Man calls the shots.

I planned to stay in the rack until about ten Tuesday morning. Les Veigel has agreed to take the helm. While it is easy to get to sleep this time, I just can't stay in bed. Before nine I am back at the office after shave, shower, clean clothes.

Les brings me up to date. We didn't have to call the helicopter crews early to clear the Range so we could open fire. They made a final search of the area just before this last high tide and then cleared for New River. The newspapers used our incident for their lead story. The Commandant is having another press conference. Reporters and photographers are covering Parris Island like a blanket. A Court of Inquiry has convened, visited the scene, and is now taking evidence. I don't realize it now, but Sergeant Major Langston is keeping my paper work in his "hold basket." While there is little to do yet out on Ribbon Creek, I go back to the CP early.

Before long there is a message from Bill Buse. We are to muster and account for every recruit; we are to search each building in the area as well as every place a man could be hiding out. I put Goober Johnson to work on that, knowing negative information is inconclusive—recruits have been able to hide out for days on Parris Island—and not knowing who had such an asinine inspiration. Eventually the report comes back: There is one recruit still missing, just as reported Sunday night; his name is *Hardeman;* he is a good swimmer; his mother is on the Depot.

My team is warming up; ambulance standing by; boats are being fitted with motors and shoved into the water. That resuscitator is on hand again with the explanation it might be needed for one of my boys. The searchlight battery is checked over for use tonight. While I had been told the Commandant would be back out on Ribbon Creek, an MP advises me his flag was lowered from the Administration Building an hour or so ago.

Sparks is back on the job. Motors are all operational. Clement says he had some sleep, but I doubt it. No need to start until the tide is a little lower, but we can talk it over. Both Gooch and Clement have ideas. The Sergeant Major interrupts:

"Colonel, could we use a frogman out here? He has all his gear."

"What in hell did they do—fly some recon people down from LeJeune?"

"I don't know where he came from, but he's here."

"Have them send him out; we'll talk to him."

It seems only seconds before a really squared-away sergeant salutes and reports. I can read the name on his utility jacket: "Seybold." Questions can be answered later. Major McLeod suggests we give Seybold detailed instructions. I veto that forthwith:

"He knows a lot more about his job than we do. Let's give him a free hand." I turn to Seybold: "Sergeant, come over here and meet Master Sergeant John Clement, the best goddam waterman in this area. You two work it out."

Clement briefs him and then Seybold changes into his rubber suit to get accustomed to the cold air.

Today I'm worrying about exposure, yet at this time of the year it could just as well be heat exhaustion. That will be an acute problem in another month. Even though our "system" has heat exhaustion under control you must constantly be vigilant. The last heat death occurred the day I reported: The lad was rather obese and became overexerted on the Elliott's Beach hike. A few weeks later out at Weapons Battalion some Junior DI reported with his platoon at the Police Shed only to discover that he should have been on the School Range. He took his men over there at double-time. Quite a number of the boys passed out—but with recruits you can always suspect a degree of mass hysteria. They were treated at the Rifle Range Infirmary and were all back to duty next morning. The DI was duly punished for use of poor judgment. Here in the butts we must be particularly alert: Recruits pulling targets are shielded from the wind. The last case we had here CWO José Llera, then in charge of D-Range, had packed in ice before the ambulance arrived.

Our boats drag unsuccessfully half an hour, then about one o'clock I stop them. We want the water to be as clear as possible. Clement tells me he will give Seybold a boatride over the area to familiarize him with it. When they leave the dock I spot O'Neal: that skulker! He knows I ordered him to rack out and that I would have sent him back to barracks if I'd caught him. Oh, well; I'll get him in a few minutes when the boat comes back in.

But in a few minutes our frogman is over the side. He starts well downstream from the hole. Back and forth he goes, pace by pace, feeling every inch with his feet. As he reaches each side of the creek he marks a line in the mud to guide him on the next crossing. Clement and O'Neal anchor below him and coach him on how the current sets. Every few crossings they move upstream and anchor again. This process is to continue two and a quarter hours. Sergeant John Price, member of the Depot

Rifle Team, makes periodic reports as he holds his telescope on the group—a team shooter will 'scope anything.

We are now dependent on the endurance of one man. I regret not asking for a whole recon platoon airmail from New River. I am cold in my sheepskin coat but Seybold is in water with the temperature at fifty. He claimed he was good for four or five hours, though I remain skeptical. After all, he hasn't been conditioned for this job.

Lieutenant Colonel Robert Thompson, Third Battalion Commander, brings over two civilians. One he introduces as Hardeman, brother of the recruit we are seeking. I don't learn the identity of the other until they have gone—it was the stepfather. We talk nearly an hour, though periodically I have to leave them a few minutes to get my eyes back in focus and my voice under control. It is apparent they are plain Georgia country folks. Chaplain Twait notices their shirtsleeves and promotes sheepskins for them. I tell the brother I won't prevent his viewing the body—if we recover it— but I recommend against it. I describe how the others looked after some nibbling by crabs—in this case the crabs have had another twenty-four hours to nibble. I explain that we have a ten-minute supply of oxygen for the frogman to use in the hole. There isn't much else to say except that we shall work every low tide until Friday at least. The two eventually leave with the older man making the only kind remark I hear: "May the good Lord be with you and help you, Colonel. We know you're doing everything you can."

Seybold reported to my office the following morning with his suntan uniform looking sharp enough to pass inspection anywhere. I asked him about his background.

With less than four years' service he decided to make the Marine Corps a career and shipped over two months ago. After Boot Training at Parris Island and a short hitch in the Fleet Marine Force at Camp LeJeune he was given reconnaissance training. Then he served a tour in Korea, where one of his more interesting jobs was mine disposal. He remembers Korean waters as much colder than Ribbon Creek. He finished DI School a few weeks ago and is now assigned to Third Battalion, the same as Platoon 71. Since this is his first trip to the Rifle Range, he is attending our Coaches' School.

Monday he tried to get down to the creek but MPs stopped him. He got a brush-off several times when he offered his services "through channels." Finally he was able to grab our Sergeant Major by the stacking swivel and plead his case. The frogman clothing? Confidentially, he embezzled it. He had an old, tattered suit which he wasn't required to turn in. He took that around to the storeroom of a Navy Underwater Demolition Team and "surveyed" it for a new one.

The Old Man comes out, looking grim. There isn't much we can talk about. All we can do is stand and wait while Seybold plods steadily back and forth. We are all depending on him. I will ask for a whole reconnaissance platoon tomorrow.

Two photographers appear shortly before the boat goes out. We describe the operation and tell them we still expect to find the last body in the same hole. Each wants to go in the boat or be furnished with one of his own. There isn't room in Clement's boat and I don't feel that I can risk stirring up the mud with another boat I know I can't control. I indicate a point overlooking the hole from the edge of the marsh. Both men are dressed in city clothes. One is chicken but the other doesn't hesitate. Sparks is waiting to go with Clement. "Come over here, Sparks. I want you to take this photographer out to that point. You'll probably have to approach it from B-Butts."

"It's not accessible, Colonel. We couldn't possibly make it. Besides, he'd ruin his clothes."

"What do you mean, not accessible?"

"It's full of brush, the mud is deep, there might even be quicksand."

"What you're telling me is that you want to go with Clement."

"Yes, sir. Fatback John needs me out there with that frogman."

"Sparks, I'm keeping you on the beach regardless. You've

got to run the operation during tonight's low tide. Just yesterday you were telling me that you're a good tracker. You were bragging to the Sheriff and went with him over the flats. This is much easier. Where the hell's your Indian blood? Get this man out there!"

"Aye, aye, sir." Sparks doesn't like it.

After more than two hours' stalking, the venturous photographer gets his picture.

Meanwhile Gooch is playing a hunch. He has a boat and crew dragging down behind A-Butts. He returns by foot, disconsolate: He lost the Sheriff's grapnel—the grapnel which recovered four out of five.

"Don't let that bother you, use another one. You may pull up the lost grapnel with it. If you don't, we'll get Maintenance to make a better one for the Sheriff to Clement's specifications."

Sergeant Price from his telescope reports the frogman looks tired. A short while ago Seybold climbed out on the muddy slope just long enough to take a few drags from a cigarette which O'Neal handed him. Now he is back in the water and making progress. But low water slack was forty-five minutes ago; the current is flowing in the opposite direction; Seybold is still to seaward of where we think we have the hole located. Frankly, I am becoming discouraged. I am afraid he started too far downstream; I don't think he can hold out much longer. I am worried about permitting him to use the oxygen mask now that he might be approaching a state of exhaustion. These youngsters often have more ambition than strength. Sergeant Price sounds off with no advance warning:

"He's got him! He's in the boat."

Clement and O'Neal come upstream with their burden as a standby boat with Fortner at the tiller goes down to retrieve our frogman. Clark and Ragley lift the corpse to the waiting stretcher and carry it to the foot of the dock. We change standard procedure:

"Uncover him. I'll declare him dead. Hats off. Tony, bless the body. Photographers, get your pictures. Take him to the morgue." Just time to catch a breath, then: "Tell Dr. Sullivan we have an exposure case on the way. Get that frogman over there. Now! They've got enough pictures. Get some hot coffee over to Sick Bay; they may not have any ready. Get Mr. Oderman out here on the double."

The Old Man walks some distance wearily, then turns. "Bill, you can open fire in the morning."

CWO Leonard Oderman, who this morning relieved Goober Johnson as Officer of the Day, drives up to the dock. "Leonard, get this place policed up with people who haven't been working out here. Tell Maintenance to secure the searchlight battery, we don't want it in the line of fire tomorrow morning. Secure the butts! Sound Liberty Call!"

I look for Clement. He has disappeared.

Ragley drops me off at Sick Bay and then goes around to my quarters to get a bottle of whiskey. Seybold is stripped and stretched out on a table under a heating lamp with a couple of blankets over him. Doctor and corpsmen are standing around attentively. Seybold puffs on a cigarette, obviously amused at getting so much attention. Ragley brings the whiskey. This Seybold regards as an unnecessary luxury, which he accepts and puts in his coffee.

Dr. Sullivan has in his hand a medical journal with an article on exposure. "What was the temperature of the water?"

"We didn't measure it—thought it might make Seybold feel too cold—but our guess is that it was between forty-five and fifty."

"This article says that when the temperature has been below fifty degrees hot drinks and alcoholic stimulants are contraindicated."

"That's a guesstimate, not a scientific measure. We'll change the temperature to fifty-one degrees."

I look for John Clement in the Staff Quarters; he isn't there; no one has seen him. I locate the Commander of the Guard, Sergeant Tolar, and tell him to find Clement and have him report to me. Father Tony and I go over to my quarters. I call the Staff NCO Club. Clement's brother-in-law, the steward, doesn't know where he is. The phone rings. It is a relayed message from Columbia: Clement's wife has been operated on schedule this morning and is doing satisfactorily. Then Tolar calls and reports Clement in the shower; he will be over in a few minutes. We get his story.

As he describes it, the corpse belched in Clement's face as they lifted it from the water. When he got on the dock Sergeant Major Langston offered Clement a cup of coffee. "That ain't strong enough!" Clement took off at high port.

Now we see the marks of a squared-away marine. John Clement did not have a bottle in his car nor in his locker. He headed for the Staff Club where he could get a legal drink. But he was in utility clothing, not a proper uniform there. And so he went through the back door into the galley, where friends served him. His own brother-in-law didn't know Clement was in the club. Not until his job was finished, not until all gear was secured, did Clement request permission to go to Columbia.

The Sergeant Major calls. O'Neal wants tomorrow morning off—he intends to get drunk. Mr. Grunder refused his request. I overrule Mr. Grunder.

The turn of events a few days later wouldn't get by in a novel. The surgeons discovered that Mrs. Clement wasn't responding to treatment for TB because some nonmalignant growths were disrupting certain body functions. The doctors took care of that. Prognosis: slow but complete recovery.

Weapons marines spent forty-three hours on Ribbon Creek. The situation was not of their own making. They exercised patience, imagination, initiative. They drove themselves to the limit of human endurance. To this day no command echelon above Weapons Battalion has given recognition to a job well done; instead, Colonel Glen Charles Funk was imported from Camp LeJeune to get the Battalion squared away.

I published the following memorandum on the bulletin board:

TO: ALL HANDS 11 Apr 56
FROM: COMMANDING OFFICER
SUBJ: APPRECIATION

My heartfelt appreciation and sincere thanks for a tough

job well done. Never before have I been blessed with a crew such as you. The credit is all yours. Should there be a rap to take, I'll be happy to take it.

McKEAN

May 7, about noon, Glen Funk took over my last command. Before the next daylight some misguided character acquired green paint and in large letters on the concrete in the Commanding Officer's parking space inscribed Funk's name twice. The first time, he misspelled it.

8

Sunday Evening

THE COURT-MARTIAL RECORD shows McKeon's emotional tension was high Sunday evening:

Q. What was the second field day you ordered? Why did you order that?

A. Sir. it was regarding seconds down at the messhall. Not only that, sir, when I come back there was four or five colored boys rassling—you know—fooling around. The main purpose of it, though, was regarding seconds. I can't say how many went back for seconds, but it was quite a few—they knew better. When I got back to Building 761, I ordered a field day. I myself personally ordered a field day. Private Langone, I told him I wanted to see him in my room.

"Langone, when you step across that threshold you had better start swinging."

McKeon opened the door. Langone came in, closed the door, backed up against it, and put his hands behind his back.

"Start swinging!"

"No, sir."

"Did you ever hit your father?"

"No, sir. I never did."

"Did you ever hit your mother?"

"No, sir."

McKeon slapped Langone twice. As Langone described it, "Sergeant McKeon sort of pushed my face one time and just gave me a very light slap the next time."

McKeon was questioned:

Q. Was it a hard slap or was it with a closed fist? Were you out to hurt him? What was the circumstance?

A. Sir, I wasn't out to hurt him, sir. I slapped my kid—to be frank with you—harder than I slapped him.

Q. Which kid?

A. My five-year-old daughter.

Q. Is that the way you teach respect, by slapping people?

A. I respect my superiors, sir. Ever since I was able to know right from wrong I was slapped many a time—and I respected them.

Q. By that you mean your folks?

A. The nuns in school.

Q. That's the way you were going to teach discipline here to these men in the Marine Corps?

A. A guy—slapping him and banging him around—it wasn't the idea of hurting him, sir. It was slapping him to show that I disapproved of what they were doing. It was to prove that we are trying to learn them something and we are the superiors and it wasn't to hurt them.

Q. Did you slap them to make them mad?

A. To make them mad?

Q. Yes.

A. No, sir; not to make them mad. To make them understand.

"Langone, why haven't you hit your father or mother?"

"Because I respect them, sir."

"Don't you respect your superiors?"

"Yes, sir."

"Was that any respect in the messhall this evening?"

"Sir, I'm sorry the way I sounded off in the messhall."

"Sit down and have a cigarette." McKeon crossed the room, took off his shirt, and sat on his bunk. "Langone, do you realize the responsibility you have in that platoon? Do you know the reason of a Section Leader—the duties of a Section Leader? You are liaison between the platoon and the Drill Instructor. Here you are as a Section Leader—and you are goofing off as much as those other kids. Naturally, they are going to follow you. The platoon doesn't have any discipline. The main thing of the marines is discipline. Without discipline you have nothing. The purpose of recruit training—the purpose of training here is not to go out of here with being an honor student—more or less—but to go out of here with good discipline. Some day they may call upon you to defend this country of ours—and if you don't have discipline you will have nothing. If you ever carry this discipline throughout the Marine Corps with you—and God forbid—if you do get into combat, you will be shipped home in a pine box. They will send you home so your Guinea friends can mourn over you."

"Sir, they're not Guineas, they're my Italian friends."

"You ought to get to know them better."

"Sir, I'll admit I've been goofing off. I will get the platoon squared away. I will square myself and square away the platoon."

"All right. Now get back there and keep the men busy with that field day. When you get back, send in Maloof and *Wood*."

"Aye, aye, sir." Langone left the DI room.

The sun set on Parris Island at 6:48. Sixteen minutes later high tide in Ribbon Creek stood at 7.3 feet.

McKeon sent for Maloof and *Wood*—he would send for McPherson next—because they were big men. McKeon explains: "Well, I believe I talked to the bigger men. They usually set the example and usually I called the big man in. If he spoke to a little guy, the little guy would shake, whereas if I called a little man in and told him to go up and square away a big man, it wouldn't do."

Matthew McKeon was practicing good leadership psychology which he learned in the school of hard knocks. There are many other traits necessary in a leader, certainly, but sheer height has a significant correlation with dominance. Walter Dill Scott, pioneer in applied psychology and later President of Northwestern University, learned that forty years before Ribbon Creek when he studied the attributes of effective salesmen. Something about tall men engenders respect while short men, on the contrary, usually have ingrained inferiority and in compensation carry a chip on their shoulders.

Wood entered the DI room first and was sitting on a locker-box when Maloof arrived. Maloof says, "I stood at the door and I was kind of flustered, pretty nervous. I didn't know what the score was and I wasn't standing at attention."

"Maloof, don't you know how to stand at attention."

"Yes, sir."

"Snap to."

As Maloof describes the scene, "Sergeant McKeon came toward me, raised his hand, turned in a disgusted manner, and the open hand glanced off the side of my face. And he talked to us about—"

McKeon was questioned:

Q. Did you hurt him?
A. No, sir.
Q. Was it your intention to hurt him?
A. No, sir.
Q. Was this your way of showing your disapproval?
A. It was my way, sir, of showing them that I didn't approve of the things that he did. That was the only reason I did it when I ever slapped a kid.

McKeon said to *Wood* and Maloof, "Why don't you two kaboshes slam each other? Why don't you bash each other?" Neither one of them wanted to fight.

Then he turned to *Wood*. "Just because you are colored, *Wood,* there's no difference between you and the other people in your platoon. You people are equal until you prove yourselves different. You and Maloof are goofing off as much as those little guys in there and when you people goof off, those little guys are going to goof off. What you get away with they will get away with. *Wood,* you square those other colored boys away—but not slamming them or beating them to a pulp. If you see them goofing off, go up and talk to them, ask what they are doing that for."

Next: "Maloof, I don't want you to go out there and beat those kids, but on the other hand, what those little guys are doing, they are only following your example. Whatever they do, it not only throws reflection on themselves, but on the whole platoon."

McKeon continues: "Yes, sir; I explained to them that being

a marine was not just wearing a uniform and getting their pay every two weeks and going on liberty and having a gay time. I says a marine, basically, has one primary job and that is as regarding fighting and learning to fight and learning to put themselves in condition both physically and mentally. Preparing themselves for some day—who knows when—preparing themselves for the day of combat, not just putting on a uniform and getting paid every two weeks."

Maloof remembers more of the conversation, which with him, *Wood,* Langone, and McPherson, took at least two hours: "We were told that it was up to us to square the platoon away—and the rest of the men that were Squad Leaders—and that we should try our best to get it squared away because Sergeant McKeon was at the end of his rope. I would say he had tried hard, very hard, and he got no results. I think Sergeant McKeon took it on himself as a pretty hard blow when he found out he couldn't do much with us. There was a general disorganization. He wanted an honor platoon out of us—and he also told us that—and it just got him mad when he found out. In combat, sir, an undisciplined man could mean death to the whole platoon—and not just one man. Whoever it was that was goofing off could cause the whole platoon to get knocked off."

Maloof was questioned further:

Q. Do you know whether Private *Wood* had been slapped?

A. No, sir.

Q. What was Private *Wood* doing the time you were in this room?

A. Sitting on the locker-box and listening to the conversation, sir.

Q. Did you notice his condition, if any?

A. Well, sir; he seemed—he seemed a little scared—as I was, too—and that was about it.

Q. Speak up.

A. He seemed a wee bit scared, sir.

Q. Was he crying?

A. There was a tear, sir.

Q. Speak up.

A. There was a tear, sir, in one of his eyes—his eyes were sort of swimming.

Q. All right. Now when you were in the room were you told that you were going out later on?

A. Yes, sir.

Q. What was said?

A. Sergeant McKeon said, "I am going to take you out in the boondocks," and we laughed—we thought it was pretty funny. And then he started talking about general conversation—about what the marines are like on the West Coast and what our training would be like further on.

Q. Did he say about what time he was going to take you out there?

A. He didn't say anything to me, sir.

Q. Did he ever tell you why he was waiting a while to take you out there?

A. I don't think so, sir.

Q. All right, Maloof; you were there in the room! What happened next? Tell us in as much detail as you can the happenings the rest of the evening.

A. Well, sir; Sergeant McKeon was talking to us about what life was like—what it would be like after we left Boot Camp. Then he told us about the West Coast marines and a little about his life and what he had done. He was talking in a joking manner all the way through—it was his natural manner to be very cordial—and then he said, "All right, get out of here and send me somebody else, so—"

Q. So he said, "somebody else." What kind of "somebody else" did he ask for?

A. The next biggest man.

Q. Biggest?

A. Yes, sir; and then we left and Private *Wood* sent in Private McPherson. We went back and started working on the field day. Then generally the word had gotten out that we were going to the boondocks and everybody was feeling pretty good and happy and thought it was a great idea. It was just a general feeling of joy, I guess—I mean, more or less it was something like that.

Matthew McKeon explained what he expected to accomplish by his night march: "Well, as I said before, sir, we tried several different varieties of teaching these people discipline and nothing seemed to work. It was just a mess—a big cycle over and over and over—and I figured we would take them down to the swamps and show them that way. If they went down and got a little wet and muddy it may put a little more spirit in the platoon. Also, I believed it would build up the morale of the platoon if they did something different. The main thing though was take them down there—and the next time I would tell them to do something—or anyone told them to do something—they would have done it."

Private Donald Hanson McPherson, No. 1, Front Rank, 1st Squad, stands six feet three, weighs 175 pounds. He is good-natured and was well-liked by his platoon mates. As McKeon says, "I observed McPherson; he was a pretty good boy, had good common sense. As a matter of fact, we got him on the finances of the platoon—what we got in the laundry and cobbler shop, either one. The money is held aside and I put him in charge of it because Sergeant Huff didn't want anything to do with it when it came to money. I guess he was just a little leery."

McKeon was standing out in the hallway when McPherson arrived. The latter entered the DI room and stood at attention. McKeon followed and closed the door.

"McPherson, you're acting like an individual out there. So is the rest of the platoon. Why aren't you doing something to help the platoon have better discipline—be a better platoon?" McKeon slapped McPherson on the face twice with the back of his hand. "What's wrong with you? Sit down on that locker-box!" McPherson sat while McKeon paced the room. "I've been in combat. I've seen platoons like this which lack spirit and discipline—they don't come through. I've seen platoons with a great deal of discipline and a great deal of spirit. I've seen how they do come through. Platoon 71 wouldn't come through in combat. Why does it lack spirit? What's wrong with it? What can be done to help it?"

"Sir, I felt the platoon had it too easy right from the beginning."

McKeon was called to the telephone. It was Elwyn Scarborough at the Staff NCO Club. Being on a dial system, only those two know the gist of their conversation. Within thirty minutes, however, long enough for another drink while he was seeking a different solution to his problem, Scarborough called Huff and asked for a ride home. McKeon returned to the DI room, spotted the vodka bottle, crossed the room, picked up the bottle from the floor near the table, raised it to his mouth, lowered it.

"Have you ever had a drink of vodka?"

"Yes, sir."

"Do you think it's good stuff?"

"Yes, sir."

"Would you like some of this?"

"That's up to you, sir. It doesn't matter."

"You can't have it anyway. When you prove to me that you are a man, then you can take a drink." There was a period of silence before McKeon continued: "You're right, McPherson. The trouble with the platoon—it's too easy here. We tried everything on you people regarding teaching you people discipline. Tonight we are going to try something different. I'm going to take you people to the boondocks, take you people to the swamps. I'm going to take you down in there and let the sharks nibble on you. What do you think about that?"

McPherson told the Inquiry: "I laughed to myself when he said it." To McKeon he replied, "Sir, I think it would be a good idea to take the platoon to the swamp area."

"All right. Get out of here! Tell the men to stand by to fall out."

"Aye, aye, sir." McPherson got up, clicked his heels, and closed the door when he left.

About eight-twenty Matthew McKeon followed David McPherson into the squadroom. A second field day was still in progress. The chorus called, "ATTENTION!"

"You people can secure that field day. I'm going to take you swimming. Those that can't swim will drown, those that can will be eaten by sharks. Fall out!"

McKeon describes this: "They secured their swabs and brooms and et cetera—what they had in the field day—secured those and fell out in front of Building 761, sir, on that sidewalk. I came out the front door. I went diagonally—I didn't walk up the sidewalk. As they were falling out I told them I wanted the big end up the road. When I got about fifteen or twenty feet from them I gave them a right face, forward march, column half right. It was two parked cars there—I remember—it was only room enough to have a column half right in order to maneuver through there. I gave column half right and across the road we went, onto Baker Range, and the platoon—"

Ten minutes later Sergeant Richard J. King walked past Barracks 761 on his way to Weapons Battalion Tavern, familiarly known as the "Slop Chute," which is a more realistic description. As he passed his platoon's billet, he noticed that the lights in the squadroom were out. For more than an hour King sat in the dingy, untidy basement in the northeast wing of Building 700 enjoying a few quiet beers. He returned to the DI room about 9:45.

By this time of evening Technical Sergeant Elwyn Scarborough, School Range Instructor for Platoon 71, was well anesthetized. This is what he said at the Inquiry:

Q. Are you sure about the time you returned from the Staff Club?

A. Well, it was not too late, Major. I can't say definitely, but I am pretty positive it was between seven and seven-thirty, sir. Staff Sergeant Edward A. Huff, Senior DI of Platoon 71, is the better witness.

Q. What was Sergeant Scarborough's condition?

A. He had been drinking. He was at the club.

Huff is a master of understatement. Let's have him take it from here:

> It was close to nine o'clock, sir. I couldn't say exactly. It was about twenty minutes to nine when my wife woke me to answer the phone. I had on my shorts and undershirt—was lying on the couch and watching TV. Tech Sergeant Scarborough called me up and asked me if I would run him back to Weapons Training Battalion, Building 700. I said, "Yes, I will. Where are you at?" He said he was over at the Staff NCO Club. I said I'd be over there in about five minutes. I dressed, got in the car, went over to the Staff Club, picked up Tech Sergeant Scarborough, drove him out to Building 700, pulled up in

front of Building 700 and he said, "Let's go over and see Staff Sergeant McKeon." I immediately said, "Well, Staff Sergeant McKeon may not be there." He said, "Why?" And I said, "Because I told Staff Sergeant McKeon to take the troops to the movie Saturday night and if too many platoons were there before him and he could not get in, he could take them to the movie Sunday night." He said, "Let's go over and check and see." I turned the car around, drove back just in front of Barracks 761, backed the car into the parking spot, turned around. I looked up to the squadroom. All the lights were out. I looked at the Drill Instructors' room and all their lights were out. So I said to Tech Sergeant Scarborough that he must have taken them to the movie. So, I again started the car, took him back to Building 700, turned about, went right back to my quarters.

Huff wouldn't be there long. He continues:

Then I returned home—lay back on the couch again. I got the phone call from Captain Patrick. It was either twenty minutes to ten or nineteen minutes to ten. I thought it was one of my buddies just trying to play a joke. As soon as I hung up, I called the Provost Marshal Office, who as soon as they got my phone call told me to get right up to the Range—there was trouble with the platoon. As soon as I put my clothes back on again—and I was doing about fifty miles an hour until I got back there—I went to Weapons Battalion. I walked in the Drill Instructors' room and I seen Sergeant McKeon sitting down. And as I walked in I just said, "Hi, Mac," and he just said, "Hi, Huff." I walked right straight into the washroom that we have there and got a cup of water, took a drink of it, dumped the rest out and came right back down, sat on the foot of my bed.

Technical Sergeant Johnny B. Taylor is a hulk of a man, ruddy, bald with a slight fringe of blonde hair. His speech and mannerisms are abrupt. Taylor's appearance and bearing command respect—any private who dared talk back to him would be taken automatically to the talking doctors. Johnny Taylor joined Weapons Battalion after a hitch with State Department, which he spent in the Middle East. He brought back a wife from either Lebanon or Syria. While she's had some difficulty adjusting to Taylor and this new world, her husband is always at home on the Rifle Range. His job is managing the C-Range firing line. The night of Platoon 71's march into Ribbon Creek, Johnny Taylor was Commander of the Guard, agent and deputy of Weapons Battalion's Officer of the Day. Sergeant Taylor told his version of the story both at the Inquiry and Court-Martial. The impressions were fresher in his mind during the first telling and, since the Inquiry met in closed session, Taylor was less inhibited. Everyone interested in the Ribbon Creek tragedy must listen to him:

> Between eight forty-five and nine o'clock the night of June 8—as you were, April 8—my sentry at the Ammunition Shed, Post 4, called the Corporal of the Guard. He heard a lot of hollering and loud talking going on down behind the butts. So the Corporal of the Guard relayed the message on to me and I got in my car and drove down to Dog-Range pits. I couldn't see anyone at the time I got there, so I stopped and got out and listened and cut the motor off. The noise was much further on down from where I had first stopped, so I drove on down behind Charlie Butts and cut my motor off again. I could hear talking going on out in the boondocks, but I couldn't see them out there at that time. So I turned, cranked my car, backed up, and turned it around so the lights would shine out on the water and I had my lights on so that I could see them then. The boys were coming out of the water. There was a couple on the far side and they were just coming up out of the water. I asked them what was going on. They were partly dressed and I tried to talk to them. The recruits wouldn't say anything, the first two that got by me. The next three were two white boys carrying a little colored boy. So, about that time, somebody hollered that the lights were blinding them—to cut them out. So, I run back and cut my lights off real quick and walked back toward the creek.
>
> In a few minutes, I imagine, the majority of the platoon had passed me by. I kept standing around there and the boys kept coming by me and I kept asking them what was going on and who was in charge. I kept inquiring where the Drill Instructor was. In a few minutes Sergeant McKeon came up to me and I asked him, "What the hell is going on?" And he just made this statement: "Sergeant, I'm responsible for this." I said, "Well, are you missing any men?" At that time he said he

thought he was missing about three. I said, "Well, get a count on your men. Get a check on them and get them in the barracks quickly. Get them in some dry clothes." The two white boys, I told them to put the little nigger boy in my car and I took off then to Sick Bay. On the way up the sentry stopped me at Charlie Ammunition Shed. While I was stopped there I got out and made a phone call.

I called the Corporal of the Guard, told him to go over to the movie and get the Officer of the Day and get him back down to Charlie Butts on the double. I tried to dial—and this is a dark place, sir, we have a little cubbyhole inside the bulkhead in the Charlie Ammunition Shed where the phone sits in there and there's no lights in there. I wanted to call Colonel McKean, but I couldn't think of his number and my cigarette lighter give out of fluid about that time. I was backing my car around to try to get light in on the telephone in there when Captain Patrick, Officer of the Day, drove up. I explained to him what had happened and by that time some of the platoon was getting almost up to us. He give me instructions to get the people in my car to Sick Bay. So I took off for Sick Bay with the little colored boy and the two white boys in the car.

I drove up to Sick Bay. The two white boys was—they was navigatable, they could move around. So I told them, "Get this little colored boy in." So I went on in and got the corpsman and told him what was happening and what to expect: That there would be more men coming in, to be ready for them. So, I went on and made an attempt to call Colonel McKean. I had already dialed his number and his phone was ringing when Captain Patrick, the Officer of the Day, walked in. So, I just handed him the phone and I went on down to the barracks at that time—down to Barracks 761.

I stood by Sergeant McKeon's room until the Captain came down. The Captain either called the MPs or the Provost Marshal or had someone else do it. I'm not positive about that part, sir.

Then I ran around and went back down to the butts and the MPs came along. After the MPs got there with their spotlights we spotted another man over across the creek. I believe his name was Private Cox. When we got him close to the bank, where I could talk to him, I asked him if he was all right. He said he was; he was just cold. I asked him if he could swim and he said he could. Then I said, "Well, come on across then." That's before we got a boat down. About that time the Captain and them came up and the Captain dispatched me to the boat docks at Weapons Training Battalion with a truck and some members of Guard Company to get a boat. We went down there and brought the boat back and got in the water.

A few minutes after we got in the water we put some of the men from Guard Company across the river—across the stream—to go out on patrols. The man came up on this side of the bank towards us, so the boat pulled down there and picked him up and brought him up. That was Private Cox. He made the statement that he got lost from the rest of the men.

Major Holben asked Sergeant Taylor if there was a moon that night. Taylor replied: "Not that I remember, sir. Things were happening so fast there and I was busy at the time I didn't pay any attention to whether there was a moon or not. But it was dark; yes, sir."

Captain Charles Erwen Patrick, raised in Kentucky, enlisted in the Marine Corps in 1939, completed his Boot Training at Parris Island, and became a professional soldier. He served in the Gilberts, at Eniwetok, in the Marshalls, at Tinian, on Iwo Jima, at Okinawa, and in Korea. Patrick is one of those marines on whom the Corps banks so heavily while treating so inconsiderately. Let him tell it:

"I was commissioned the first time June 2, 1944. I was reduced to master sergeant for budgetary reasons—I was a temporary officer—on June 19, 1946. I was recommissioned—to warrant officer—in November 1946. I was reduced to master sergeant—for budgetary reasons, I guess—again in February or March, 1948. I was recommissioned to second lieutenant in August of 1948."

He might have added when he testified at the Inquiry that he was still a temporary captain only recently selected for permanent warrant officer status. Mrs. Patrick is one of our better teachers in the Depot Children's School and they have two children. Captain Patrick came to Parris Island from Korea in October 1953. He served in Recruit Training Battalions about eighteen months. Then, against his will, he was ordered to Supply

School at Camp LeJeune and given a two-year quartermaster detail. Patrick was transferred out to Weapons Battalion last August as Supply Officer, a job he accomplished effectively, without friction. Eight o'clock the morning of April 8, he took over as Officer of the Day. Let him take it from there:

Q. I'd like to inform the Captain that it appears that you have a direct interest in this subject of inquiry and that the findings or opinions of this Court may relate to a matter over which you had a duty or right to exercise official control. In view of that fact, you may, upon request, be designated a Party to this Court. Do you understand that?

A. I understand that, sir.

Q. Do you desire to be made a Party to this Court?

A. No, sir; I do not.

Q. Do you expressly waive any right that you may have in that regard?

A. I waive my rights to be made Party in this Inquiry.

Q. Now, in the course of your duty as Officer of the Day, do you inspect the recruit areas in Weapons Training Battalion?

A. I do.

Q. And how is this inspection accomplished?

A. Well, the—while touring through the area, either driving through and walking around some of the buildings—watching the activities of the recruits. The routine is a little different on holidays than just on working days because of the working schedules and things of that nature. Patrolling through the area—

Q. How often do you as a normal rule inspect the recruit areas?

A. Well, I'd say on a Sunday when I have duty—or a holiday—that I drive around and inspect about once in the morning and once in the afternoon, once before midnight and once after midnight, as far as the Guard is concerned. In the area, I'm continually going around. That's about right—as my average.

Q. Well, are the functions that you carry out the same as the Commander of the Guard? I mean, he's under you, isn't he?

A. He's under me; he's my assistant.

Q. Now, do you do these things together or do you do them separately?

A. No, we do them separately—as a rule.

Q. So that if you went three or four times during the course of the day, would he have gone three or four times, so that in the course of the day it would have been between six and eight times that someone with authority would have been in that area?

A. Well, someone with authority is in the area all the time.

Q. Well, on this April 8, you inspected three or four times that day; is that right?

A. Well, I don't recall exactly; I would say about three or four times.

Q. Do you recall the last time you made one before the incident occurred?

A. I was inspecting the area just prior to the movie. When I drove back to the movie it was between seven and seven-thirty.

Q. At that time—when you drove by the area—did you see the men outside lined up in any type of formation?

A. I saw about ten platoons that were lined up—all up and down the street. That's where they line up to go to the movies. I didn't know any of the platoons by number—but I know that a lot of recruits were going to the movie that night.

Q. Now, did you have occasion to notice this particular platoon that was involved in the incident, before you were called—as to what occurred that particular night?

A. No; not that I recall. Not any particular platoon.

Q. Did you in particular inspect Platoon 71's billeting area?

A. I did not—as I recall. I drove back in the rear of the barracks and just looked around in the general area. I didn't go into their living quarters or anything of that sort.

Q. Do you ever inspect in the recruit living quarters?

A. Occasionally on my tour of duty I'll get out and go through looking for Fire Watches and to see if everybody is on their toes. In other words, just looking for anything unusual.

Q. Now, you mentioned Fire Watches. What are these Fire Watches?

A. Each platoon establishes a man out of their platoon—when they have a fire watch—to walk around the area and watch for any fires.

Q. Now, while you were at the movie, was your Commander of the Guard with you?

A. No, sir. He was at the Guard House.

Q. Now, directing your attention to the evening specifically of Sunday, April 8; where were you during the course of the early evening?

A. I remember that I drove around the area. I was inspecting the area on my way back to the movie. The movie was scheduled to start at 1945. The lights were all out in the theater, so I stopped at the movie and talked to the theater operator. He said that the electricity was off, that he called the electrician. The electrician was slow getting there. I called Major Schumaker and reported that I thought he should be there. The electrician was taking too long to get there because at this particular movie we had a larger amount of recruits attending the movie than normally does. It was a good movie and it was a Sunday evening and eight to ten platoons were waiting to get in the movie. The electrician arrived and they got the electricity on and the movie was about a half hour late getting started. We got all the recruits in—all the people that were going to the movie—and they started the movie, I think, about 2015 or somewhere around there. I was watching the movie from then on till I got the call.

Q. Is it included in your duties to inspect the movie and are you responsible for its operation and conduct?

A. Yes, it is.

Q. And what call was that you were referring to?

A. The Commander of the Guard called and told me—one of the sentries called the movie—a sentry was on the phone at the movie—and informed me that the Commander of the Guard wanted me immediately in Charlie Butts.

Q. Did you see Sergeant McKeon at any time on Sunday, April 8, 1956?

A. Yes, sir. I did.

Q. Will you please describe to the Court your meeting with Sergeant McKeon.

A. At about—the time I think was about 2115 when I received the call to go to Charlie Butts. I got in the car and at the Ammunition Shed on the 600-yard line on Charlie Range I met this platoon coming up the road in various different formations—groups—and the lights of the car were shining toward them. I talked to Sergeant McKeon very briefly. I asked him if anybody was missing or left. He said he thought they were missing. Then I told Sergeant McKeon and the recruit platoon to go on to the barracks. That was the discussion that I had with him. I saw him again in the barracks a few minutes later and placed him under arrest.

Q. What was the condition of the platoon?

A. The platoon was straggling along the road—in groups, to

some extent—partially undressed—some of them were. They were all wet. Men had on skivvy shirts. Some were barefooted, wet, and bedraggled. That was their general condition.

Q. What was the report to you at that time?

A. The report to me was that they had been into the swamps and were just returning. I asked them if there was anybody missing and they said that they thought there were some men missing in the swamp.

Q. What did you do then?

A. At that time there were two men being carried. I ordered the Commander of the Guard to take one and I took the other in my car and took them to the Dispensary. I told the platoon to go immediately to the barracks. After going to the Dispensary I called the Commanding Officer and then I rushed to the barracks and placed Staff Sergeant McKeon under arrest. I had the Commander of the Guard watching him. I had the Section Leader of the platoon hold a fast head check—line them up by their bunks and give me the number of men missing. At that time I called the Officer of the Day down here and told the Fire Department and the other people. Then I rushed on back down to C-Butts.

Q. Was the muster completed while you were there?

A. It was hastily completed—I'll put it—while I was there in the squadbay.

Q. Was the report given to you?

A. Yes. The report was given to me there were seven men missing. They counted the three men that were in Sick Bay.

Q. What did you do then?

A. After I called these people I went on to Charlie Butts to assist in the possible rescue.

Q. Was there anyone there when you arrived?

A. Yes. The fire truck and the Depot Officer of the Day had just arrived there and the Commander of the Guard and some members of the Guard were there. They had lights going—searching the area. Some members of the Guard Company had arrived or were arriving during that time.

Q. Was any search organized?

A. Yes. The patrols had already started out at that time.

Q. Can you give us any details of this search that was organized?

A. No, not particularly—except there were groups of men, as I recall, which started out down over through the swamps—down the left side of the creek itself. I immediately sent the Commander of the Guard to get a boat and when that came back we put a boat crew in, and went across the stream in groups of four or five people and, in some cases, two or three. They split out and went across the stream in the area while searchlights were beaming up and down the area.

Q. Was anyone located as a result of this search?

A. There was one lad who was found in the general area there on the bank of the stream.

9

Eyewitnesses

PRIVATE GERALD CHARLES LANGONE, JR., New Hyde Park, New York, erroneously listed as "Joe C." in the Court-Martial record, was the dominant of two Section Leaders in Platoon 71. He made a high score on the classification test and achieved a perfect mark on his 15-day examination. Slightly rebellious, somewhat a buffer between Drill Instructors and his fellow recruits, Langone appears frequently in the Ribbon Creek story. In the late afternoon of April 9 when Parris Island was in administrative turmoil and the body of *Thomas Hardeman* was still resting in the mud, Gerald Langone and Reginald Butler, the other Section Leader, were driven to the Beaufort Naval Hospital and escorted to the morgue. This is how Langone describes the scene: "Sir, there were only five down there at the time, sir. Someone lifted up the blanket and I looked, sir, and I knew who is was, sir. Then I told somebody their names."

Private Langone's conversation and activities before the fatal march appears in other chapters. Here we are interested in his account of the tragedy:

> About eight o'clock Sergeant McKeon walked in and told us to fall out, that we were going to the boondocks or to the woods. We fell out and went between A- and B-Ranges, went behind the butts on B-Range and made a right and went down to the middle of C-Range behind the butts. Then we made a left

and went into the water, sir. I was marching in the middle of the platoon. When we hit the bank I was the last one in. I was just making sure that no one took off to either side, sir. I was told to close ranks. Then once we got in the water I started working my way up towards the front again. They had went along the bank, sir, and a little ways up they went left and started a semi-circle out a little ways. They didn't keep together; they split it up. I started cutting across to get where I was before.

Well, sir; just as I reached that position some one cried out for help and then there was a lot of confusion. Someone yelled, "Form a chain," and nobody moved. So I took a couple of guys and put them in that opening and then everyone started moving over. We started to take off some clothes, but by the time I got my boots off—and sweat shirt and jacket—it was all over. It was quiet then. I swam along the edge of the platoon—their right-hand edge—and tried to help. When I reached what I thought would be the front of the platoon, I went further out in the stream—just a couple of feet, sir. I told the platoon to go up on shore. They went up on the shore then, sir. And as I started, I guess I was almost the last one out. But then when I got up to the shore—then some men were helping Sergeant McKeon out of the water. He was too tired to get up on the shore by himself.

Well, sir; Staff Sergeant McKeon didn't order us into the water. Sir, we just walked in. He just walked in and we all followed. Everyone followed him. When we came out Staff Sergeant McKeon was the last one out—except for a couple who assisted him up on the shore, sir. But Sergeant McKeon was out there—I think he must have went after five or six men, sir—himself. He didn't stop at all, sir. I know that, sir, and I imagine if we had all turned around and walked out, I don't think we would have been ordered in, sir. We just walked in. Nobody asked any questions. We just walked right in, sir.

Private Carmac Michael Brennan, 137 East 122 Street, New York City, six feet two, high-scorer on written tests, was in the Second Squad. He wrote this statement, under supervision of investigators from the Provost Marshal's Office, during the forenoon of April 9:

On the morning of 8th April 1956, after our platoon had returned from morning chow, the smoking lamp was lit, at about 1030 hrs. we were split up into two groups, one group was sitting around inside, the others were sitting outside & smoking, it was in this latter group that several recruits were caught sacking out on the grass. This caused us to have a Field Day. We then went to noon chow, the afternoon was spent sitting around writting letter, shinning shoes & fixing gear. We went to even chow at about 1730 hrs. and after chow I went mainside with the other Catholic boys to attend Novena services. I returned with the group to our barracks at about 1930 hrs in time to get into another "Field Day" which was kept going until about 2100. During this time it was rumored around the barracks that we were going swimming. At about 2100 hrs. we were told to fall out in front of the barracks in squad formation, S/Sgt. McKeon then gave us a right face & marched us down the street until we were opposite the Lyceum, he then gave us a column right and we marched straight out across Baker range, when we reached Baker range butts we marched down behind them towards Charlie Butts, when we were halfway behind Charlie butts we turned and head left into the swamp. S/Sgt. McKeon was at our head, we marched about 100 yds until we reached water & S/Sgt McKeon went in and we all slowly followed him. When we were all in we started upstream and worked our way out until the water was about 5 feet deep, most of the group were enjoying it at first until we turned and started down-stream and out, there was about 10 guys between me and S/Sgt McKeon who was still at the head of the group, which was slowly moving into deeper water & into a good current, it was about this time that someone call for "help", most of the guys in the head of the column could not swim to well & the current carried them out and then nearly all of them were crying for help. I saw two guys going out to try & get some of them, then the word came to get out of the water, which we did, we were in the water about 1/2 hr. We then saw the lights of the car, which had heard us & pulled up behind the butts, after about 10 minutes of milling around, we head back to our barracks where we took showers & hit the rack the time was about 2300. This statement is true to the best of my knowledge.

July 24, Brennan was called to the witness stand. During pretrial interview he had obviously told different stories to Prosecution and Defense. Their legal bickering developed nothing of advantage to either party, but Brennan's testimony gives some insight to his own attitudes and behavior:

Q. Did you hear the Accused make any statement as you entered the water?

A. Yes, sir. I did.

Q. What statement was that?

A. Well, he asked if everybody was all right and the reply came back, "No," and he said—there was some nonswimmers—he said, "Let them do the best they can," sir.

Q. What was the deepest the water got while you were in the water?

A. It went over my head at one point.

Q. Would you describe to the Court at what point it went over your head?

A. About two minutes or—about two minutes before the actual happenings, before the actual chaos happened.

Q. Was this before you heard any screams for help?

A. Yes, sir.

Q. What did you do when this panic ensued?

A. I stood still.

Q. Did you remain standing still for any appreciable length of time?

A. About three or four minutes.

Q. Then what did you do?

A. I went up on the shore.

Q. Are you a swimmer?

A. Yes, sir.

Recruits in Platoon 71 were squadded by height. Even though a six-footer, Private Walter Ford Nehrenz, Akron, Ohio, found himself in the Third Squad. He didn't seem to think quickly but there is no doubt that impressions once fixed in his mind are there to stay. His story is interesting because it is so objective:

> The platoon fell out behind the barracks and marched across the field. We were talking amongst ourselves—I mean—just talking to the guy next to you. A lot of guys were asking

each other whether we actually were going in the water. There was a lot of wisecracking. We got behind the butts, did a column movement, and then we marched out into the water. When we first went out from the bank the water was up to my hips, I would imagine. It was gradually getting deeper, I would say about up to my chest. As we were going downstream it gradually got over my head. I swam a little ways until I could touch bottom and then started back. Just when I started swimming—had to swim—everything happened all at once. I heard screaming.

It was difficult to move around in the water with boots on—and water in your boots. After the screaming it was just mass confusion. Everybody was trying to figure out what to do. Part of the platoon formed a human chain and tried to pull the guys out . . . the other guys who were drowning—trying to save them. I don't recall seeing any of the people that drowned.

Sergeant McKeon had a lot of patience for everybody. He took his time. If you didn't pick up something right away, he would go over it again and again to be sure you knew it. He never hit anybody—that I recall—but we've done calisthenics—physical exercise—and stuff like that. He was well liked by the platoon.

Richard Boyd Drown, Huntington, West Virginia, was listed as "Richard D. Brown" at the Inquiry but correctly identified at McKeon's trial. There was a Brown in Platoon 71, Bert Boyd Brown, Jr. Private Drown's narrative fills in some detail concerning the threat of sharks and march discipline:

Q. Did you hear Sergeant McKeon say anything about people that could swim?

A. Yes, sir. When we were fairly close to the swamp, sir. He said in a joking way, "Anyone of those who can't swim will be drowned and those who can swim will be eaten by the sharks," sir.

Q. Did you ever hear him holler, "Shark," while in the water?

A. Yes, sir.

Q. What were the circumstances?

A. Well, sir; the men were in high spirits and were joking around with each other. To the best of my recollection Sergeant McKeon hit somebody on the leg under the water and said, "Shark," in a joking way.

Q. Could you see the stick?

A. No, sir. I just heard his voice. We couldn't see him at all.

Q. How do you know it was Sergeant McKeon?

A. Well, sir; after you have been with a man for seven or eight weeks you get to know his voice pretty well.

Private John Michael Maloof, 5 Whitson Street, Forest Hills, Queens, New York, 6 feet 1½ inches tall, was in the First Squad. That position placed him only three or four men behind McKeon in the column. Maloof is a bright young fellow. At the Court-Martial he told a lucid, consistent story. Let's listen to his version:

> We walked across the Range and we broke into column of twos. There was a water sprinkler. Sergeant McKeon stumbled and fell toward it. He said, "All right; everybody walk through this water." I don't know whether everybody followed or not because it was pretty much of confusion. It wasn't column of twos any longer, it was a mass of bunches. We went by one range and got to another one. We did a column left and went across a very marshy boondocks. The mud was slippery and it was pretty slimy. We got down to the water and there was a small bank. We got in the water and went straight out. Then we turned right and went upstream. Sergeant McKeon told everybody to get in the water.
>
> The bottom was very mucky and slimy—it seemed that you slipped over the top of it. There was a faint light on the water and a reflection. Sergeant McKeon told us to stay out of this when the enemy was around—to stay close to the shore. Everybody was laughing and joking. They thought it was all pretty funny. I wasn't paying attention to Sergeant McKeon then, I was following along. It seemed to me like the stream was miles wide. I couldn't see the other side. We made a turn and started going downstream. The water was graduated from, I would say, waist to chest. Then almost at the end—before we dropped off that cliff—it was approximately up to here. [Maloof indicated his mouth.] I could taste salt water.
>
> Then there seemed to be a panic. The next thing I knew I was off that cliff, in deep water, floundering. There was a strong current pulling me down. I heard cries for help and I knew there was danger. It was pretty hard to swim with all

the clothes we had on. I tried to get back to shore and some guys grabbed me—I don't know what happened—I went down and came up again. It seemed to be a bottomless ditch—whatever it was—because when I went down I tried to touch. I kept trying to touch and I tried to get up as fast as possible. I didn't want to stay around and see how deep it was. I went down and came up again. Then I came back to where the water was about chest high. I took off what clothes I had on, except for a pair of skivvies, and handed them to somebody. I went downstream. We tried to pull out some of the fellows who were further downstream. I didn't see Sergeant McKeon again until after we got out of the water.

I said, "Sir, do you need any help?"

He said, "No."

I said, "Are you sure?"

Then he mumbled something about how we lost a lot of men in there.

I said, "Yes, sir. Shall we go back and get them?"

He said, "No. We will never find them. There's not enough light."

Private William Eugene Ervin, Bridgeport, Connecticut, whose name is variously spelled "Irvin" and "Erwin" in court records, was Right Guide of Platoon 71. In that position it was his duty to march alongside Matthew McKeon, but Ervin was unqualified in swimming and, as he said, "apprehensive." At the Inquiry, Ervin merely explained he dropped back to the rear of the column to tell the other men to get in the water. At the Court-Martial, Ervin indicated McKeon appointed him to assist Section Leader Langone, then he added he didn't want McKeon to be made angry. (Young marines are loath to admit fear; older ones brag about it.)

But Ervin's most important contribution to analysis and reconstruction of the Ribbon Creek tragedy was overlooked at both Inquiry and Court-Martial: that Platoon 71 marched parallel to a deep ditch before entering the water. Ervin was at the head of the column where he had the vantage of good observation. He was well oriented, as his testimony shows, and he appears to have superior night vision. His perceptions show no major conflict with those of any other witness, but they would locate the point of entry into the water anywhere from twenty-five to 250 feet left of those points assumed by others. More important, Platoon 71's direction of march would lie thirty degrees to the left of that hypothesized at the Court-Martial. This agrees quite neatly with the location of the trout hole and the area from which bodies of the six victims were recovered. It is a pity that neither Major Holben nor Major Sevier pressed Private Ervin for more detail. Despite this, Court records are quite suggestive:

Q. Did you cross a ditch before you went into the water?

A. To my knowledge, sir, we were marching alongside of a ditch, but I don't recall crossing a ditch. I don't recall crossing a ditch but I know we were marching beside one.

Q. On which side of you was the ditch?

A. My left side.

Q. How big a ditch was it?

A. Well, it was at nighttime sir, and—If I can remember—it looked to be about seven feet across, sir. That's what it seemed to be, I couldn't tell the exact dimensions.

Ervin said at the Court-Martial: "We marched on back of Charlie Butts and did a column left and walked over to what sort of looked to be something like a ditch and continued on until we got to the line between the marshland and the water."

The drainage ditch between B- and C-Ranges, except for two swales on the opposite side, is about twenty-five feet wide where it begins at the culvert in rear of the butts until it ends in Ribbon Creek. When the tide is at the stage it was as Platoon 71 entered Ribbon Creek, the water surface would be seven feet wide!

Recruit Melvin Barber is a six-footer from 818 West 146 Street, Manhattan. While he admitted having been in New York swimming pools, he made no decided effort to learn how to swim. Nor did the training at Weapons Battalion do him any good. During that experience Matthew McKeon said to *Wood* and Barber, "Big as you two are, you should be able to swim." Barber was No. 1, Rear Rank, First Squad. Had he kept his assigned position during the Ribbon Creek march he would have been right behind Private Ervin, who should have remained abreast of Sergeant McKeon. This is what Barber had to say at the Court-Martial:

> After evening chow most of us went to a religious—some of us went to religious services. I was one of them. Private *Thompson* and Private Keaton went with me. When we came back from the Protestant service we discovered that there was another field day. So we pitched in and after the field day Private *Wood* told me to take my cigarettes and everything I had out of my pocket and put them into my hat. After that Sergeant McKeon came in and told us we were going to the swamp—told us that the ones that couldn't swim would drown and the ones that could would be eaten by sharks. I took it as rather a joke.
>
> About eight-thirty—I think it was—he told us to fall outside for platoon formation. He marched us behind the butts, he marched us close to the banks, and then he led us into the creek. When we first started stepping into the creek it was very soft mud and most of us were slipping and holding on to each other. I believe the mud came as far as my ankles. When we got into the water Sergeant McKeon said, "Let's go downstream where there was a tide." So we went down the stream and some of us slowed down. I did, for one, because I couldn't swim and I was quite nervous and I didn't know how deep the water was. I knew I couldn't swim—so—it was a group that went and there was another group that stayed behind.
>
> Like I said before, I was getting quite nervous because I couldn't swim. If I had went a little further it might have been too high for me. I stopped in the water and a little while afterwards I heard some fellows yelling for help. But I couldn't do anything myself because I knew I couldn't swim. So I yelled out to form a chain. There was about ten of us. We tried to form—had formed a chain but nothing become of it. So after a while in the water Sergeant McKeon—I believe—ordered us out.

Private Richard Wesley Acker's name heads the roster of Platoon 71, but he led only alphabetically. He joined February 29, just as Platoon 71 was "going on the schedule," from Platoon 59-E, a "slow learners" platoon. When Recruit Acker got to

Parris Island he couldn't read well enough to take the usual written tests and so he was classified as "illiterate." While that classification is not always justified—a recruit may actually suffer a "reading block"—it is sufficient to give him an extra four weeks' training. This brought Acker above the fifth-grade reading level, which he demonstrated by getting ninety-six per cent on his 15-day achievement test in March. Acker shares with Martinez the claim of having encountered *Charles Reilly.*

Q. What squad are you in?

A. The 9th Squad, sir. I was in the 10th—but not any more, sir.

Q. Did the platoon enter into the water?

A. Yes, sir.

Q. At any time while you were—or just prior to entering the water—or in the water, did you see Private *Reilly?*

A. Yes, sir. He was right next to me all the time, sir.

Q. All the time you were in the water?

A. Yes, sir.

Q. When was the last time you saw him?

A. Just after the panic first started. He got scared and the current was pulling us out, sir. He started grabbing for me and was hanging onto my belt and my collar and was pulling me under and trying to keep himself up. I was trying to help him, but it was too much for me because I don't know very much about life-saving. I had to break away from him because he was almost drowning me. That was the last I saw of him.

Private Soren Thurstensen Daniel was third high in Platoon 71 on the GCT, a measure of intelligence despite official obfuscation. Only McPherson and Delahunty surpassed him, and Delahunty was not called at either Inquiry or Court-Martial. Daniel had little opportunity to talk at the Inquiry, but he did observe two victims and the conditions of Ribbon Creek. Here's the important part of his story:

> I'm in the Sixth Squad, sir. I saw Sergeant McKeon just after we fell out. After we had gotten into the water, sir, he asked the entire platoon at least once, possibly twice, if everybody was all right. I think the formation stayed together well until we

got into where it was very muddy and some of us got stuck. Then, between people being stuck and others trying to help them out, it broke up and got jumbled around a bit, sir.

I saw Private *Thomas* just after I had entered the water; he was just about alongside of me. At that time the water was just about waist deep. Private *Thomas* was headed back up toward the butts—that was before we turned around. After we turned around, sir, and headed out toward the deeper part, I saw Private *Wood;* he was headed toward the deeper part, too, sir.

Well, I went out where it was over my head—I stepped in a hole and I had to tread water for a minute. I moved back when I found I couldn't stand up. I went back where I could stand up a little bit. This was before the trouble started, sir.

Recruit Ronald William Geckle, five feet eight, nonswimmer, was a witness at both Courts. But neither time did he receive detailed examination. This leaves a hiatus in the Ribbon Creek story because Geckle was apparently the last recruit who saw *Jerry Lamonte Thomas* alive. Unfortunately Geckle's testimony is contradictory. This is what he said at the Inquiry:

Q. Did you see anyone in trouble?

A. I did once, sir. I had hold of a boy but he drug me under twice and I couldn't swim so I dug out where the shallow water was and I got into the chain and I got on the bank.

Q. Who was it you had hold of?

A. *Thomas,* sir.

Q. Would you go over that again? He had hold of you?

A. Yes, sir. He dragged me under twice and I couldn't swim. I could swim somewhat—that I learned in swimming class, but—so, I got him loose and I got out of the deep water and where the chain was.

In contrast, this is how Private Geckle recalled his experience at the Court-Martial:

Q. Did you ever get into deeper water than you indicated by the height of one inch below the top of your pocket?

A. Just once, sir. That was when I was with *Jerry Thomas,* sir.

Q. When you were doing what?

A. When I was with *Jerry Thomas*. Private Poole and I, neither one of us could swim, so I had hold of Private *Thomas* and Poole had hold of me. And when Poole let go of me, *Jerry Thomas* and I went under the water and I came back up and couldn't find *Jerry* and I went on toward the bank, sir.

Q. When you went under water did you do that because you slipped or because it was over your head?

A. Because I slipped, sir.

Private Jerome Daszo, five feet ten, Fourth Squad, was a reluctant witness before each Court and contributed little to our knowledge of the tragedy. He confirmed McKeon's statement about being drowned or eaten by sharks, but added "it was in the form of a joke." He told about recruits playing the shark game with sticks under water. He claimed that he was in water over his head before the panic. But his important testimony concerns *Donald Francis O'Shea:*

> Well, sir, he was about fifteen feet away from me and he was splashing around in the water with his hands and yelling for help. About two or three times I heard him yell for help. Then I saw a couple of guys diving towards him, sir. That was about all, sir.

Recruit Earl Thomas Grabowski, Kearney, New Jersey, was called to the Inquiry. Weeks later, after he had read the newspapers, talked to the folks at home, and been interviewed by numerous investigators, he appeared as first recruit witness in the Court-Martial. We meet him elsewhere as middleman during courtroom fireworks and also as important narrator of the *Hardeman*-Leake story. Right now we're interested in his observations of the Ribbon Creek incident:

Q. During any time on that march did you hear Sergeant McKeon say anything about men that could swim or men that could not swim?

A. Yes, sir. He said was there any nonswimmers and some of the boys yelled out, "Here we are, sir." I don't recall anything else.

Q. Now, where did he call out, "Are there any nonswimmers?"

A. Well, sir; that was when we were about all in, sir—in the water—and we were about waist deep. He was in front leading us and he turned around and most of the nonswimmers—I believe—were in the back.

Q. Did you ever enter any deep water?

A. Yes, sir.

Q. How deep?

A. I went over my head, sir. I dropped off the ledge.

Q. Were you still following Sergeant McKeon at this time?

A. No, sir. I started back. I started to swim back. I was coming back and I thought I had reached the level ground and when I did, I stood up. That's when some of the boys gave me some of their clothing. They wanted to swim out there.

Q. Did you ever see Private *Hardeman* while you were in the water?

A. I don't think so, sir. Yes, sir; I do recall now, sir. He was next to Myers and Myers was with me. That's the last I saw of him, sir.

Q. Grabowski, you are privileged to make any further statement covering anything related to the subject matter of this Inquiry which you think should be a matter of record and which has not been fully brought out by previous questioning.

A. Well, sir; later on, I heard Sergeant McKeon say, "Everybody out." Well, he said something like that and we were coming out. I noticed Sergeant McKeon was in the water and he was helping most of the boys and he was trying his best to get the other boys out. I helped someone out but I don't know what happened to him then. I helped someone else after that—that someone handed to me—and I had him out of the water and I know he was safe, but I couldn't see their faces. The first one I had, I thought was *O'Shea,* but he seemed all right. I don't know how he might have gotten back into the water. There were a few other boys. *O'Shea,* someone like—handed him to me. I had him. Then I had someone's clothing in my hands also. Somehow, I got someone else and I was helping him out. He was shaky and scared. I remember I was calling Private Maloof, "Here is your boots." When I went to give them to him I just fell into some mud and I was going down to about waist deep and Private Ferkel pulled me out. Right then he must have got mad at me and thought I could get out. I knew if I moved more I would have gone down faster. That's when I saw Sergeant McKeon ahead of me and he was looking around—I guess to see if I was all right. Then when I got out I saw Sergeant McKeon and he went up the embankment and I think it was him that pulled me out with someone else. We pulled the rest of the boys in back of us out. I know Sergeant McKeon was the last one out because that's when I saw him coming by.

Thomas Grabowski's bias changed between April and July. This is what he told in his later version:

> We went to the Novena and on the way back about six or seven of us come back from where we got off the bus. We come to the rear door of the barracks and Sergeant McKeon asked us who was there. I answered, "The detail from church, sir," and that's when I smelled a little liquor on him. I was about as close to him as this mike. I went to work on the field day and a little while later Sergeant McKeon told us to fall outside in the back.
>
> So we went outside and he come out and told us we were going out to have a swim, go swimming. So we were laughing. Then when we were on the Range we passed by one of those small buildings—to the left of it—and we came to a water sprinkler and he told us to through it. So most of us went through the sprinkler. Sergeant McKeon was leading us and used the stick to feel around in the grass and he said a few words—watch out for snakes or sharks, or something like that.
>
> So we were going down more and we were falling in mud—slipping in the mud—and then we were getting near the water and he told us, "Follow me." So we all got in the water and then he asked us where the nonswimmers were and most of them answered. Then we started to move out—and Sergeant McKeon was ahead of me—and that's when I dropped. I tried to swim back and I heard that panic. I dropped like you would be walking along and you slip somewhere. The water was over my head there. I tried to swim back.
>
> That's where the panic struck out amongst the boys. They started yelling and I started to swim back and that's when I found *O'Shea.* He was trying to grab on top of me and I was taking him and someone said, "I'll take him." So I was swimming back and the current was strong and we formed this chain gang. Some boys gave me their clothes and I lost them—their boots. We pulled most of them into the low water and someone called, "Everybody out."

Private Stephen Henry McGuire was the first witness called at the afternoon session of the Inquiry April 10. While his story is somewhat disoriented—and neither Major Holben nor Colonel Heles were particularly successful in leading him out—it is important: McGuire shares claim with Mulligan and Grabowski for having seen *Donald Francis O'Shea* in the act of drowning. Moreover, McGuire contends he tried to assist *Leroy Thompson,* whom Porter and Moran thought they rescued. We're listening to McGuire:

> In the evening, right after chow, I went to the Novena. When I arrived back at the barracks they were doing a little field day there—scrubbing the floors. I don't remember who, but somebody said, "Stand by to fall out for a while." Everybody fell out and went down to the boondockers—the swamps. Going in, sir, that's where I get mixed up 'cause when we were coming out, we were all over the place.
>
> Well, sir; we were where the water was. I just followed the man in front of me—we just went into the water. We got just a few feet—just maybe, just about the waist—and went upstream to the right a little. Then Sergeant McKeon asked if everybody was all right—two or three times—and everybody would say, "Yes, sir." He was showing us how, if we were in combat and the moon was shining on the water, how to keep from letting the enemy see you—the light on the water from the moon, how to hold your rifle over your head. Then he asked again if everyone was all right and everybody said, "Yes, sir." I'd say I was fifteen feet from Sergeant McKeon—about from here to the bulkhead, sir.
>
> Well, sir; when we hit the water, everybody just once we got in there—I just started fooling around in the water. I wasn't nervous or nothing. There wasn't nothing right then to be excited about. I don't think anybody was nervous—just swimming around in there. No, not exactly swimming, sir; just doing the dog paddle around.
>
> Was there a moon out? Well, sir; yes there was. Because, sir, how I remember was when he was telling us this. I could see the glare from the moon on the water. I tried to keep out. I get it mixed up—I get it mixed up what he said, how to keep out of the moonlight—the glare of it on the water—showing how to keep out of the moonlight—but that's how I remember there was moonlight on the water.

Just before we doubled back, Sergeant McKeon asked if everybody was all right. I remember that distinctly. Just before we went back, he asked if everybody was all right. Maybe ten of them that were up there with Sergeant McKeon when they hit the drop off—in other words, everybody was probably just up to their chest or their neck. Well, about the third time he did ask if everybody was all right—maybe fifteen seconds to a minute later—somebody yelled, "help." That's when I was about from here to the bulkhead away—my side was turned toward him—then I heard "help."

I looked over and everybody was just jumping—just jumping. So I started to go over there and I seen Sergeant McKeon trying—trying to help out as best he could. Just about everybody was jumping on him there. I guess the ones that were there didn't know how to swim—some of them. Well, sir; the current when I got there—the current was constantly pulling them out, sir. 'Cause I myself, I went back. I myself had a hard time getting over in that current—to get back. That's the way I could think of, sir—to figure out what happened. 'Cause when I heard "help," I swam over there—I didn't walk over.

Yes, sir; I think I did see Private *O'Shea,* sir. I thought I seen him. He had the reddest face in the platoon, sir. It was just —his face was just actually like a tomato. Like I say, when I was going over to see what I could do, I seen Private *Thompson* and Private *O'Shea* were fighting among themselves as to who was going to stay on top of the water. They were struggling there. I got over there and I tried to help one of them—and I don't know what happened to *O'Shea,* sir. The last time I seen him, sir, he was above water a little. That's the last time I seen him. *Thompson?* Sir, he was a big boy and I tried to do the best I could. He was bringing me under all the time. He didn't say a word—didn't even yell or scream or nothing. He was just moving in the water, you know, jumping around, trying to stay on top of the water. I tried to help him, sir, and he just slipped and he went under, sir. I couldn't see him. I'm almost positive it was *Thompson,* sir.

Yes, sir; Sergeant McKeon was his normal self. I didn't notice anything, sir, as far as going into the—and everything. To tell you the truth, before we went down there—and we heard we were going down there—it didn't scare me a bit because I figured thousands of people had been down there. So it didn't bother me a bit. The only time I was scared was when I came out of the water. I thought—right then I started to get a little nervous.

Recruit Hugh Gene Mulligan, Third Squad Leader, is another member of Platoon 71 whose test scores will give him an opportunity to try for an officer's commission. Along with platoon mates McGuire and Grabowski, Mulligan talks of *Donald O'Shea.*

Q. What happened after you went into the water?

A. Well, sir; here was a little confusion. The bottom just seemed to drop out at certain spots. After five or ten minutes—around that time—the bottom just didn't seem to be there any more. There was a strong current a little further up by the front, sir, and a couple of men—everything was dark and there was a lot of shouting when we first went in—and they got caught in the current, sir. Everybody was in the form of a chain, sir. I believe the Section Leader, Private Langone, got us into a reasonable chain. I was swimming, sir.

Q. Did you see Private *O'Shea* at any time while you were in the water?

A. I couldn't say positively, sir. I thought I had *O'Shea* one time.

Q. What caused you to go to his assistance?

A. Well, sir; there was a man out there splashing around. I couldn't say if it was *O'Shea,* but there was a man out there and he was splashing around and there was another man alongside of him. He seemed to be having a little trouble and I grabbed this man and we got him into walking ground, sir.

Q. Was he apparently all right when you left him?

A. Yes, sir. He was standing up. I didn't bother to actually tell who I was talking to. It was hard to distinguish. I just said, "Keep your head," and took him over and left him, sir.

10

Inquiry

PRIVATE GERALD LANGONE, Section Leader, gained a semblance of control over sixty-six members of Platoon 71 before the muddy, wet, half-clothed rabble entered the squadbay in Barracks 761. When they arrived about nine-thirty, three MPs were waiting. They told the recruits to take a shower and put on dry clothing. One unidentified Boot answered Sick Call at six that evening and the corpsman kept him in the Infirmary. Leake, Whitmore, and Brower were delivered at Sick Bay after they emerged from Ribbon Creek; the corpsman waited for instructions until midnight and then decided to turn them in. Seven were missing.

Matthew McKeon entered the squadbay and started to inquire about those. Captain Patrick, Officer of the Day, called him back to the DI room and placed him under arrest. Patrick then telephoned Staff Sergeant Huff, Senior DI of the platoon, and ordered him out to the Rifle Range.

Huff went directly to the squadbay. "What's the matter with you bastards? You chicken? You got no guts?"

An MP called Huff from the squadbay and told him he was under arrest and to get in the DI room, which Huff entered. McKeon was sitting on his bunk. "How are they going, Mac?"

McKeon said, "Hi, Huff," and just shook his head.

Huff went into the washroom and got a cup of water. McKeon walked toward the door of the washroom. An MP barged in and drew his pistol. Huff turned and saw him: "Who you pointing that thing at?"

"You people sit down!"

After a time Huff was able to convince the MPs he wasn't supposed to be under arrest. He was permitted to go into the squadbay, take a muster, and put the troops to bed. But whispering continued long after lights out. There was plenty of time to compare experiences.

The only routine for Platoon 71 until Thursday morning would be marching to meals. Still the boys were not idle. Early Monday each was required to write a statement; then before dark a horde of newsmen descended on their barracks and kept appearing off and on for more than two days. Monday evening Langone and Butler were driven to the morgue at the Naval Hospital to identify five bodies. Wires and telephone calls came from home. And then there was the Inquiry.

After Joe Burger, Commanding Parris Island, telephoned Randy Pate, Corps Commandant, when the latter reached his office the morning of April 9, Burger instructed Bill Buse, Chief of Staff, to convene a Court of Inquiry. Nelson Reeve, G-1, (Personnel), named the members after hurried conversations over his squawk-box. Duane Faw, Legal Officer, drafted the appointing order which instructed the Inquiry to meet at one that afternoon. The group was called to order Tuesday morning.

A Court of Inquiry is a fact-finding body. Ideally it is strictly impartial. Generally it follows court-martial procedure, is guided by Rules of Evidence, and affords named "Parties"—those whose behavior might be in question—their legal rights, particularly to counsel. When it receives sworn testimony, as it did in the Ribbon Creek investigation, that testimony can be introduced at a later court-martial subject to ruling there on the admissibility of any challenged item. However, an Inquiry may be liberal in accepting hearsay and opinion evidence by duly noting it to be such—this frequently discloses truth that might not otherwise appear.

The task assigned the Ribbon Creek Inquiry we must read verbatim:

> The court shall make a thorough investigation into all of the circumstances connected with the marching of Platoon 71 into the swamp and the disappearance of subject-named men. [*Thomas Hardeman, Donald O'Shea, Charles Reilly, Jerry Thomas, Leroy Thompson, Norman Wood.*] The court shall report its findings of fact, opinions and recommendations with respect to the circumstances surrounding the marching of Platoon 71 into the swamps, and the deaths, injuries or disappearance of naval personnel and their line of duty and misconduct status, and responsibility for the incident, including recommended disciplinary action.

It was directed that Staff Sergeant Matthew C. McKeon be made a Party to the Inquiry and be accorded his rights under the law.

The goal outlined in Burger's appointing order seems perfectly clear: to limit investigation to the Ribbon Creek incident and to synthesize a clear, logical picture of that event. But none who dealt with the Inquiry during the course of the following month felt constrained to follow the script.

This Inquiry consisted of Colonel John B. Heles, U. S. Marine Corps, President; Major Gerald B. McIntyre, U. S. Marine Corps Reserve, and Lieutenant William J. Spann, Medical Corps, U. S. Naval Reserve, members; and Major Donald E. Holben, Counsel for the Court. Heles, rounding out twenty years' commissioned service, was regularly G-2 (Intelligence) and Depot Inspector. McIntyre came to Parris Island for the summer Reserve Training Program and was assigned to the office of G-3 (Training). Spann had been with the Depot Medical Department for fifteen months fulfilling his obligated service. Holben was from the Depot Legal Office. It is noteworthy that the whole Court was Staff.

Counsel at an inquiry is master of ceremonies. Donald Eugene Holben, age thirty-three, fourteen years' service, permanent first lieutenant but three months' temporary major, was qualified both as an infantry and legal officer. Holben lived at Mainside in Quarters 237 on Saipan Street off Nicaragua. He was last overseas in 1951 and had been on Parris Island twenty-one months. During that time he had been Legal Officer for Headquarters and Service Battalion, S-3 (Training Officer) in First

Recruit Training Battalion, and just a few weeks in his new job. Holben was under pressure: In Court it came through channels from the President; out of Court it came through channels from the Depot Legal Officer; and then he must cope with chary witnesses and elusive documents all over the Depot, never knowing whom he might offend from Commandant to new recruit.

In the circumstances Holben's performance was quite adequate. Where interesting facts were overlooked, Holben is not accountable. The Court was responsible for guiding questioning to develop a clear and complete picture. Reviewing authorities both at Parris Island and in Washington were ultimately responsible and might return the report with instructions to inquire further. In such light our critique of the Inquiry follows. Should the reader find he needs a scapegoat, he may choose between politics and the system.

Time was needed to sift relevant details from a mass of extraneous data; adequate time was not available. Each survivor wrote a statement describing the Ribbon Creek incident, but these half-legible papers were just fragments of the recruits' observations. Full stories could only be developed through prolonged interrogation by someone highly trained in that art. Major Holben was never provided an adequate staff of investigators and legmen. Instead, to keep evidence flowing into the courtroom, he was forced to rely on those statements.

This resulted in Holben's introducing witnesses who made no substantial contribution. Recruit William Pool repeated some of McKeon's remarks which had already been verified. Recruit Reginald Butler merely told that he identified five bodies—a matter about which there was no question and evidence which was only cumulative. Recruit Carl Whitmore testified that he saw *Thomas Hardeman* at the beginning of the march.

Yet who wouldn't like to hear from Private Edward Clarence Cox, Jr.? Cox was the lad discovered on the far side of Ribbon Creek who got back more than an hour after the drownings. His story about getting lost from the platoon might have afforded valuable clues to the behavior of the victims. It is reasonable to assume Cox was mixed up in the panic, but obviously his written statement was noncommittal. Survivors of panic don't like to talk about it. What man escaping a burning theater wants to admit he trampled women and children? What rational man will confess himself a criminal, to have violated custom law, or to have disregarded cultural tradition while in the midst of panic? In order to get the truth from him he must be guaranteed immunity to prosecution—and complete privacy. We have no evidence, of course, that Private Cox was involved in the melee. Since he was young he should be more prone to recite his experience than a mature man. Still it was a good lead: Cox might have undergone rigid interrogation.

Another good lead was that sentry, from another recruit platoon, who reported hearing noises down behind the butts. That youngster could have been identified by the Guard Report Book. Calling him might also have avoided an error in the record: The telephonic report to the Corporal of the Guard came from Post No. 4, the sentry at D-Range Ammunition Shed. The wind was blowing from the west; sounds traveled in the direction of his post. The testimony of Technical Sergeant Johnny Taylor was clear: He answered the call from D-Range and then returned via the road between B- and C-Ranges. But the Inquiry found that the report came from Post No. 3, where Taylor made his first phone call. After the Inquiry closed, Brigadier Greene, second President, asked me to give the wrong sentry a letter of appreciation for carrying out his orders.

Another silent but available witness leaves a most important fact in perpetual mystery: Is it really true that Matthew McKeon was first in and last out of Ribbon Creek? Private Lew Brewer testified that there was a calling for help, the human chain was ineffective, and he stripped off his clothes. Then he saw Private Michael Connell holding Sergeant McKeon and helping him out of the water. Brewer, according to his version, assisted Connell in taking McKeon to knee-deep water. They turned him loose there because men were still calling for help. Brewer said he went back into deep water but failed in his effort to rescue *Norman Wood*. Wouldn't you like to hear what Connell had to say when the incident was but thirty-six hours old; before the slogans "follow me" and "first in, last out" were broadcast?

Then there were maps. Every marine lieutenant in Basic School finds his course emphasizes hydrography and terrain. He is taught to read maps and aerial photographs, to draw road and position sketches. He learns that less than one-quarter of the United States is adequately mapped for military purposes. More important, he learns that Nature is continually ahead of cartographers, maps are out of date even before they are published, and that there is no substitute for reconnaissance. Yet it took Attorney Emile Berman, Defense Counsel at the Court-Martial, to remind the Marine Corps of its lessons. One of his confidants told me Berman spent $1,000 apiece for four aerial photographs of Ribbon Creek and even then "promoted" a five-man survey team to come down from New River and spend ten days on that creek. During the Court-Martial, Mr. Volle, chief surveyor, testified that our Public Works map, introduced as evidence at the Inquiry, was sadly out of date with respect to the course of the creekbed. A telephone call to Commander Joseph J. Smisek, Public Works Officer, by any of us would have provided a timely hydrographic record and eliminated subsequent controversy and speculation.

Why the Inquiry didn't subpoena more official records is another mystery. The Guard Report Book in the Marine Corps is a cherished institution comparable with the Ship's Log in the Navy. At Weapons Battalion that and the Liaison Duty NCO Log were both books of original entry with virtually on-the-spot notations. Times of different events were accurately recorded. Entries were made when memories were fresh. But these records were never called for. Peculiarly, when Parris Island quieted down we were instructed by Staff to open a third and duplicating book, an "Operations Journal."

But the Inquiry didn't neglect official documents altogether: Not numbered that way, there were thirty-five exhibits of which twenty-one were schedules, lesson plans, and orders. Court Exhibit 10a, for example, was the lesson plan for combat swimming. Unfortunately any similarity between that plan and the way we taught recruits at Weapons Battalion was sheer coincidence: The plan was completely unrealistic in light of space available, time allotted, and the usual progress made by recruits. Apparently the Court assumed that an order issued is habitually carried out. Leaders who rely on that assumption are disillusioned invariably.

One other aspect of documents appeared at the Inquiry as it did recurrently on Parris Island: How can Administrators handle those unsigned? Their general rule is: "A writing that is not authenticated may not properly be received in evidence." Many are the unwary who fail to turn six pages in the book to learn that a business entry made in regular course need not be signed: nor do they consider offering the document as real evidence, like a knife or pistol. I was responsible for two of these papers appearing at the Inquiry. One was the schedule for recruits, issued daily. Both Inquiry and Court-Martial solved that difficulty by calling Sergeant Huff to tell that he pasted it in his Platoon Log. But then the Inquiry wished to determine for record which of the dead marines were qualified swimmers. The "best evidence" was a roster of Platoon 71, kept by Staff Sergeant Alfred J. Halliwell, head swimming coach, which indicated each second-class swimmer by a pencil checkmark and a notation at the foot of the roster indicating that. But Administrators can't be persuaded a crumpled, dirty sheet of paper is evidence. The roster was taken to the administrative office of Third Recruit Training Battalion where a clerk entered on Form NAVMC 118 (1)-PD, the first page of the individual's Service Record Book, "Class of swimmer 2d" in the case of *Hardeman* and *Wood*. Lack of such entry was accepted as indicating "unqualified." But this page, a sort of index, is never signed.

Some double questions at the Inquiry that stand on the record without elaboration make for confusion to anyone attempting to reconstruct the case. Here is a sample:

Q. Was this the colored boy that you saw and were helping out or was this someone else?

A. Yes, sir.

Q. You were following in back of the man in front of you and went into deep water?

A. Yes, sir. The darkness right there—we couldn't tell which way we were going—just following the man in front of you.
Q. What was his manner then? Was he happy or otherwise?
A. I couldn't actually say. I believe he was, sir.
Q. Was it up to your chest or up to your neck?
A. I'd say it was around my chest or neck, sir.
Q. This was after the hymn-sing? This was after the platoon was falling in outside the barracks?
A. I thought you meant inside the barracks, sir.

But this did less to contaminate the record than did leading questions, questions which put answers in the witnesses' mouths. These were recruits, highly suggestible and desiring to please. They were surrounded by more officers than they had ever seen together at one time. They wanted to agree with the questioner and certainly didn't want to contradict an officer. Above all, they wished to give the "right" answers. This encouraged substantiating narratives of early witnesses when we might like to weigh shades of difference in individual observations.

It is also evident from the transcript that recruit witnesses were handled occasionally with undue brusqueness. These recruits had been through a terrifying experience and were still recovering from shock. While it is impossible to reconstruct the intonations and mannerisms of the questioners (though personal acquaintance with them makes lifelike reading for me), I believe these recruits might have been treated with less formality and more sympathy so that they would have yielded clearer stories.

Still it wasn't just recruits who got worked over. Captain Charles Patrick, Weapons Battalion Officer of the Day, was recalled after he had testified four days previously. Patrick was warned that the Inquiry might develop findings which related to his manner of performing official duty. He was then confronted with more than a hundred questions regarding that duty. A few of these indicate the trend:

Q. As Officer of the Day do you have any written orders?
Q. Are you familiar with the orders for the Officer of the Day?
Q. Is there any order relating to recruits?
Q. Do you recall how that is stated in the order?

Q. Do you inspect the recruit areas in Weapons Battalion?
Q. How often, as a normal rule, do you inspect these areas?
Q. How many sentry posts do you have?

Patrick did his job conscientiously and he proved it. Then he worried for weeks about punitive measures against him.

Nor did Sergeant Huff leave the Inquiry unscathed:

Q. Sergeant, is it customary for the Drill Instructors to drink while on duty?
A. I wouldn't say it is authorized. No, sir. Definitely not.
Q. Answer my question!
A. No, sir.
Q. Would you say that this taking of the platoons in the swamps is common?
A. Can you phrase the question a little better, sir?
Q. I don't think that Counsel has to rephrase that question. The question asks for your opinion as a result of experience. Can you answer it 'yes' or 'no'?
A. Well, sir; for me myself, the question is what?
Q. I'm asking you for your opinion, based upon your life as a Drill Instructor, whether or not it's common for platoons to be taken into the swamp.
A. Not any of my platoons.

When professional military lawyers hear of an impending inquiry they reach for the Naval Supplement because inquiries are not frequent. But Donald Holben had just returned to the trade after long absence and was given no time for homework. This resulted:

PRESIDENT: "Before the Exhibit is received in evidence we should look at it and examine it. The entry in the record is that a document is submitted to Counsel and to the Court. I believe it is. It used to be."

COUNSEL: "It is not current procedure."

PRESIDENT: "The President will continue to sight each Exhibit in order to pass on its admissibility."

It is true that new-style professional military lawyers usually exercise a monopoly over matters legal; many consider it beneath their dignity to bow to a mere line officer. Yet an inquiry is old-fashioned procedure grafted on the new Book. While in this case Counsel does advise the Court about law, it is the Court that makes judicial determinations.

Tuesday all day and Wednesday morning there was a parade of twenty-three survivors across the witness stand at the Court of Inquiry on the first floor of Building 154 at Mainside. A bus transferred batches of recruits from the Rifle Range to the Administration Building, where they huddled in small groups in the hallway waiting to testify or to get a ride back. Many took the stand and told coherent, pertinent stories. Others made no contribution.

Under direction of Colonel John Baptist Heles, Depot Inspector, the Inquiry gathered evidence about the Ribbon Creek tragedy from Tuesday morning until Thursday noon. Total meeting time, including a view of the scene, was less than fifteen hours. Wednesday's session ran overtime seventy-five minutes, otherwise meetings conformed to Depot Working Hours in the true spirit of Staff. John Heles had guidance, of course, right from the top: Commandant Pate was looking for some local order Sergeant McKeon had violated. Heles would concentrate on reconnaissance, planning, control. Even the violation of petty orders would be important to him. His line of questioning demonstrates this clearly:

HELES: Did Sergeant McKeon, as far as you know, explain to the platoon the procedure for getting into the water, going a certain distance, then turning right and going parallel to the bank and turning right back into the bank?

PORTER: Not that I recall, sir.

HELES: Had you ever had a night march before?

RAMBO: Sir, we marched at night. But we never went to the boondocks, sir.

HELES: Did Sergeant McKeon indicate to you in his room on April 8, before the platoon marched away from the barracks—did he indicate any plan as to what would be done after you got in the water?

MCPHERSON: No, sir.

HELES: There were no commands given? You heard no commands at all?

McGuire: No, sir. I just followed the one in front of me.

Heles: Was there some struggling and breaking of formation?

Daniel: Well, I think the formation stayed together pretty well until we got into where it was very muddy and some of us got stuck. Then between people being stuck and others trying to help them out, it broke up and got jumbled around a bit, sir.

Heles: There was conversation going on between recruits?

Daniel: Yes, sir.

Heles: Were there any lights of any kind with the platoon? Did Sergeant McKeon take any lights along, going from the barracks to the water?

Porter: A light?

Heles: A flashlight or anything?

Porter: No, sir. I didn't see any flashlight, sir.

Hence the Inquiry found as an "opinion" that: "Staff Sergeant McKeon violated Depot Order 1510.11 in that he marched Platoon 71 in formation in the darkness without the white towels and lights." (A flashlight at each end of the column and a white towel around each neck is a traffic safety precaution.)

Yet this emphasis on planning and control would later afford a good argument for McKeon's defense: If the recruits had been well-disciplined and had followed in the trace of their leader, none would have been in danger.

But as the situation developed, it proved that planning in minute detail breeds inflexibility. Such planning had to be unlearned after marines were in trench warfare in France. It needs to be unlearned since their experience in the Korean stalemate. In open warfare, especially with modern weapons, we must put our trust in the small-unit leader—give him maximum initiative—tell him "what," not "how." No longer can Staff write voluminous plans filled with minutiae and expect them to work.

Wednesday at 2:50 P.M. Colonel Heles announced in open court that Matthew McKeon would be charged with murder. Proceedings continued for another ninety minutes that day and for a similar period the next morning, but long-distance wires from Parris Island to New York managed to sandwich McKeon's urgent calls between those of newsmen. Lieutenant Jeremiah Collins, Counsel for the "Party" who with Heles' announcement was technically "Defendant," realized that McKeon needed the finest legal skill obtainable. Matt McKeon realized that, too. Though still completely shaken emotionally, he was comforted by the thought that his brother-in-law, Thomas P. Costello, had a good practice in New York and was man of the hour. Collins upset Holben and even worried Heles, who was afraid he might prejudice McKeon's legal rights, by requesting a recess. This Heles granted with misgivings, since he had been instructed to complete the Inquiry with dispatch.

This delay gave Holben time to study his books and take another reading on presentation of the case. He now saw that he couldn't avoid calling me as a witness. This would induce complications because I was next in succession to command at Parris Island and only Colonel Bob McDowell, G-4 (Quartermaster), limited to supply duty, stood between General Joe Burger and me in seniority. Burger didn't want to appoint a naval officer as President, though several were available. He wouldn't ask for Colonel Frank June, who commanded the Air Station at Beaufort. He didn't want to reach over to Charleston and request Colonel Jim Hester from the Marine Barracks there. While he weighed these courses of action he was still afraid some legal trifle might disqualify McDowell. But he appointed McDowell anyway and set him to studying the record.

When I learned the situation through scuttlebutt, I went in to see Major Duane Faw, Depot Legal Officer. There were two factors in my motivation. First, I was afraid that Joe Burger faced professional ruin on account of the incident. Joe had been Major General four years, he was well liked. He hadn't had command long enough to learn the ways of Parris Island, while Staff filtered much of the information he should have received. Punishing Joe Burger would be rank injustice. Second, with press and Congress keeping the Marine Corps in a state of siege, it was to our advantage the Inquiry move fast. There was no doubt in my mind we could afford delay: We had to keep the show on the road.

Faw and I went up to the Old Man's office after we thoroughly talked over the situation. I recommended to Burger that the Inquiry continue and promised to waive my rights in being named a Party and in having the President senior to me. I urged that I already intended to retire July 1 and that I had nothing to lose. As I sized up this situation, the worst I could get would be a letter of admonition. There were tears in Joe Burger's eyes. "No, Bill. I'm not going to let you do it. You do have something to lose: your fine military reputation. I'm appointing Bob McDowell and he's already studying the record."

April 18 my fitness report for six weeks ending February 29—and ostensibly filled out by Joe Burger in March—was delivered to me by the Staff Secretary. It was next to the worst I received in twenty-six years. Another, somewhat poorer, came from Burger when he was relieved of command early in May.

Meanwhile Pate was calling from Washington several times a day issuing detailed instructions to Burger. Not many hours after I left the Old Man's office word came that Bob McDowell could rest on his oars: My classmate, Brigadier General Wallace Martin Greene, Jr., was en route to Parris Island as trouble shooter.

Wallie Greene, a Vermont boy, graduated from the Naval Academy in 1930 standing 119 in a class of 402. When we were originally commissioned Fred Beans and Glen Herndon were both senior to Wallie and junior to me. Glen died in an airplane crash, which his parents out in Colorado witnessed, in 1937. Fred retired as brigadier in 1948. From then until six months ago I had been one number senior to Wallie. But the selection board liked his record and I was passed over.

Wallie didn't have the build to be a star athlete at Annapolis, so he swam for exercise and worked assiduously over his books. His career from second lieutenant to major was in line with that of his surviving classmates. Like all of us he was at sea, in school, on foreign service, in the Fleet Marine Force. Then he latched on to Thomas E. Watson, now lieutenant general, retired, known by many as the "screaming midget" and by a few as "T. Easy." As an operations officer Greene was with Watson during the reinforcement of Samoa, the landing at Eniwetok, and then with the gallant 2d Marine Division at Saipan, Tinian, and Okinawa. Their record speaks for itself.

With usual persistence and attentiveness through long hours, Wallie Greene absorbed the Inquiry record to date. He came out to Weapons Battalion and I escorted him over the scene of the tragedy. On Saturday, April 14, having been on Parris Island some thirty-six hours, Wallie assumed Presidency of the Inquiry. The record bears the following entries after he had been sworn:

> "PRESIDENT: I would like to ask the guidance of Almighty God."
> "The President offered a prayer."

Still under oath "faithfully to perform his duties," four days later Greene was about to declare the Inquiry closed. We find this in the record:

> "PRESIDENT: The President desires to make a statement.
> With my hand on the Holy Scripture and in the presence of Staff Sergeant McKeon and these witnesses, I swear before God that this Court has arrived at what it considers to be the truth, the whole truth and nothing but the truth in this case, and it makes its recommendations seeking only justice for all parties concerned."

Wallie returned to Parris Island following Pate's hearing before the House Armed Services Committee. He would set up the Recruit Training Command, operationally responsible to the Commandant himself. Greene brought with him a hand-picked Staff, an open-ended personnel requisition, an unlimited expense account. After landing at Page Field he received his ruffle and flourish, guard of honor, and gun salute. For one day, between Burger's departure and Litzenberg's arrival, he was in command of Parris Island. Eleven months later he displaced Litzenberg.

Greene lost no time in briefing his Battalion Commanders. Since Glen Funk hadn't yet relieved me, I was summoned to the conference. When that was dismissed I went into Wallie's new but temporary office. He reminded me his Inquiry found that recruits were adequately supervised while stationed at Weapons Battalion. He hinted, remotely, that he was sorry I was to be relieved. Then he concluded, "Bill, you know me. If there had been the least evidence that you either neglected or failed in your duty, I would have clobbered you!"

11

Screening

PARENTS WHO REALLY CARE dream their sons will associate at Parris Island with Eagle Scouts, high-school class presidents, winners of Sunday School Bibles. If they could only see some of the riffraff that gets off the train at Yemassee, fond parents would be heartbroken. What we do get is a cross-section of the adolescent American population heavily biased toward the lower extreme of our socio-economic scale. It's our job to make men and marines of all we can while sorting out rejects so that at the end of ten weeks we can graduate a platoon which will make every parent feel proud. We locate these rejects by "screening," but it's a damn coarse mesh.

Applicants at our Recruiting Stations are given a simple written test of intelligence known as the "Armed Forces Qualification Test." If they fail that, they stop right there. But the recruiting sergeant is cursed with his "quota"; ineffective salesmen go back to the line. Time after time we meet youngsters at Parris Island who admit the sergeant helped them with their test. Many others pass by *copying the x*'s a brighter neighboring applicant makes on his answer sheet. Some do the rounds of different offices until they learn the pattern of correct *x*-marks or manage to pass through sheer trial and error. *Thomas Hardeman*'s brother Eugene told a New York *Times* reporter April 10: "He kept taking tests and he finally got into the Marines." This is confirmed by *Hardeman*'s score on the GCT, which was 55 and sent him to "Slow Learners' Platoon."

Next the youngster goes to an Armed Forces Examining Station for a physical. Standards there have been set by joint boards and Selective Service to insure that any ambulatory warm body is accepted. Even then it is charitable understatement to say that in a high percentage of cases these medical examinations are perfunctory. But once our boy passes the local doctors, he's sworn in and shipped to Parris Island.

Here screening begins anew with assembly-line techniques and all their weakness in grading human beings. Every recruit upon arrival gets checked physically, mentally, and psychologically—those broad terms are confusing but we'll have better understanding when we examine them more closely. These lines skim off a good deal of scum while the DIs' observation and a steady flow of paperwork gets more. To deal with potential rejects we have five committees which make a study of each individual case: Physical Survey Board, Aptitude Board, Hardship Board, Under-Age Discharge Board, and Undesirable Discharge Board. Each case forms a separate record and must be approved personally by the Commanding General; every new marine marked for separation has the privilege of seeing the Commanding General—alone—and making an appeal. All those recommended for separation by the first four boards receive "good" discharges. Then the Government furnishes clothing for these rejects and pays their way home—if they go home.

The Physical Survey Board is composed of medical officers. They examine the individual carefully and write up a long case history. Often the recruit goes to Beaufort Naval Hospital for special laboratory work and observation. He may be sent to another hospital, such as Charleston, for clinical examination by medical specialists. What do they find? One common defect is otitis media—pus running out of the ears—youngsters admit they've had that condition for months. Many have old injuries to legs that won't support them, yet a marine is fundamentally a gravel-cruncher. Epileptics are provided with a supply of dilantin by their family physicians, then the DI catches them taking pills and runs them over to Sick Bay. A few real psychotics appear, and the Navy must furnish an attendant to get them home. Hernias can be repaired without much strain and so we often keep those. Teeth are dreadful—many an eighteen-year-old requires upper and lower full plates—but our dentists work shifts, when they have to, and the dental cripples stay unless rejected for something else—and even then unfinished prosthetic work is done by the Veterans Administration. Eyes are a terrific headache: West End Infirmary sends out to Weapons Battalion weekly a list of those having adequately corrected vision in the left eye while the right eye is beyond all hope. It is our job to teach these recruits to shoot left-handed, yet before the war I never saw a left-handed marine rifleman nor do I remember any youngsters who couldn't see the bull's eye. There were old-timers, of course, who hadn't seen it for years at the 1000-yard range—but they learned to square the target. Peculiarly, we require 20/20 vision of our officer candidates, who will always have field glasses on their person and never be required to fire a rifle in combat.

Under-Age Discharges are not particularly trying, though they do increase our taxes. If the recruiter has any question about a lad he demands a birth certificate. But Federal law permits the boy of eighteen to enlist without parental consent and many sixteen-year-olds support a heavy growth of stubble. If the youngster signs up when motivated by patriotism or desire for adventure, we're naturally quite sympathetic—many a marine has served in combat and then a few years later submitted a birth certificate with request to correct his record—though when we find these youngsters we send them home until they've had another birthday or two. The nasty case is the apparent seventeen-year-old with an affidavit stating his date of birth and giving his mother's consent. A couple of weeks on the Parade Ground and this character changes his mind; he admits that his mother connived with him and signed a phony. Then she, with no obvious shame, forwards a birth certificate and admits she's guilty of perjury. Unfortunately her case is never tried.

The next, more interesting, category is Hardship. What do parents expect of their children? Through their own pleasure they bring them into the world—too often unwanted, neglect them in childhood, and then expect them to become a source of income long before they're grown. Typically it's the mother who is so eager for money. Soon after her boy arrives at Parris Island for training she gets a long letter from the Commanding Officer offering information and assistance. By return mail she sends the Old Man a plea for a share of his pay. falsely thinking that any mother with a boy in service is entitled to Government support. Some imagine that mere claim of dependency will force Uncle to shell out; others believe a private's stipend is real money. None seem to realize the youngster has expenses during his period of training: Seventy-eight dollars a month won't go far when the recruit pays his own transportation costs for Boot Leave. Besides, we try to sell him a suit of blues, which the Government won't provide within his clothing allowance.

When the application for unjustified Dependent's Allowance is refused and his kinfolk aren't satisfied with a small voluntary allotment the marine might register—though many absolutely refuse that—we get a sheaf of affidavits requesting Hardship Discharge. Many of those from doctors, lawyers, or elected officials are verbosely noncommittal. But eventually the boy acquires enough documents on the second or third round so that the Board may judge his case. Grandfather can no longer manage the farm—he has been hospitalized these last two years. Our family doctor advises mother to give up her job because her health is failing—as it has been for a long time. Father died eighteen months ago and there is no one else at home to attend several (flourishing) businesses. Nearly always the situation existed when the lad, acting through some compulsion to get away from home, having written permission, joined the Marine Corps—but now he's decided he doesn't like it. These requests are most frequently refused, though when the marine through sheer stupidity has neglected a difficult situation at home we send him back to meet his obligations.

Recruits with police records, which they denied upon enlistment, are certain to meet the Undesirable Discharge Board. These cases develop late in training after there has been time for the FBI to check their fingerprints. Many sneak through with their denial because law enforcement agencies out in the provinces have no system of perpetual records. If you want to find out whether a man was arrested in Jackson, Michigan, for example, you must read through the blotter over the years. Others with police records get absolution from some misguided judge provided they do penance by joining the Marine Corps—though it might be a good idea, we don't operate a reform school. But there is a reform school in Pennsylvania where graduates find a marine recruiting sergeant waiting just outside the gate—nor has this practice been effectively suppressed. Still, we usually locate the real criminals.

Not long ago I turned over to the FBI one of my marines who seemed a fine potential soldier, but he had escaped from reform school in one state, the penitentiary in another, and was wanted by G-men as a member of a stolen-car gang that specialized stealing Lincolns up in Michigan and running them down to Georgia. Just two or three months ago an ex-Boot, apprehended while firing at Weapons Battalion, was electrocuted at Sing Sing. He and the girl-friend, both teen-agers, murdered her mother because they didn't like her interference with their lovemaking; then they went on a five-day binge right in the mother's flat while her body remained in the bathtub. The girl got twenty years—we still have a double standard.

The fifth and most interesting committee on screening recruits is the Aptitude Board, which consists of a line officer, medical officer, psychiatrist, and psychologist. Before recruits meet this Board they spend ten days or longer at POU—our Psychiatric Observation Unit—where they are observed and tested. Some get to POU through the psychological screening which takes place during their first few days at Parris Island, when they take a short written test and then get a five-minute interview with a psychiatrist or clinical psychologist. Because of limited time, this procedure obviously sorts out only those whose abnormal symptoms are quite apparent.

Others get to POU after making a low score on the GCT—General Classification Test—or being unable to undergo this test because of supposed illiteracy. Before a good share of these get to POU, however, they spend four weeks in a Slow Learners' Platoon—known locally as E-Platoons with *E* meaning *educational*—operated by Second Recruit Training Battalion, where experienced teachers attempt to teach them to read and write. But most of those at POU were sent there directly or through Sick Bay by their DI after he observed their aberrant behavior. Our E-Platoon system, which has a rather amazing record of success, is the only facility at Parris Island that contributes to society at large. Other categories of deviant behavior are simply returned to society.

Robert Hamilton Beezer, with a two-year-old Ph.D. in psychology from Ohio State, then a research scientist at the Human Resources Research Office, an organization at George Washington University operated under contract with the Army, questioned our Aptitude Boards in his letter published in the *American Psychologist* of December 1953. Dr. Beezer talked with a Navy noncommissioned [sic] officer and then became disturbed at our dumping back into the lap of civilian society individuals who were "undesirable" for military service. He described this riffraff as "chronic malingerers, thieves, sexual deviates, and neurotics." Beezer was concerned that our rejects hadn't received therapeutic measures the social service professions can offer; he felt that if these unfortunates couldn't be salvaged for the Armed Forces, at least they shouldn't be returned as a threat to the civil community. Since we do screen and observe a large number of men and women, Beezer figures this a golden opportunity to provide treatment for social deviates.

Robert Beezer had a good point, though he did err in lumping together those whose cases should be handled by court-martial with those whose social ailments lead to a general discharge under honorable conditions. We actually could make an important contribution to the mental health of our nation by doing something for these troops. I argued with Dr. William A. Butcher when he was Depot Psychiatrist and proposed forming a whole battalion of bed-wetters. They would sleep in bunks rigged to give them an electric shock when salt water closed the circuit. My solution calls for an experiment in special training (which Butcher doesn't believe would work) rather than psychotherapy. With electric shock and food pellets we train Norway rats in the laboratory over a period of minutes; why not human beings over the months? There is just one compelling negative answer to this challenge: money. We have been assigned neither the mission nor funds to conduct sociological experiments.

By the time the youngster appears before the Aptitude Board his case has been studied and written up. His appearance is more for giving him his day in court than anything else, though the Board does send a small percentage back for duty for further trial. Then a large portion of these return to the Board. There is one major weakness in our aptitude screening: The program has never been validated. We have no means of knowing how many rejects might with careful training have adjusted to military life; we never know how many fail to adjust to their civilian environment. When our psychiatrists—as they often do—state dogmatically that within five years a particular recruit will be committed to an institution, no one can challenge this prediction: There has never been a follow-up. We do, however, apply the best knowledge of psychological science while the Red Cross—though we're not permitted to quote that organization in the record—comes through with a report on the social situation whenever it helps us to render judgment.

The first time I attended an Aptitude Board meeting, to learn my job as alternate Senior Member, I had already heard of this case through my chaplain, Ed Hartz, whose finger was continually on the pulse of our Recruit Area. A little colored boy from western Pennsylvania was here on the Rifle Range before they discovered him. His platoon was making a head call in one of the Butler buildings just before turning in. While he was standing at the urinal, his father appeared: "Boy, yo' ain't doin' what yo' DI tells yo'."

Did he take off? The platoon—all in their underwear—chased him nearly 800 yards down toward C-Butts before they caught him and brought him back. All night he lay curled up in his bunk with his head under the covers. Next morning his DI sent him to POU. At the Aptitude Board a single question from Dr. Bowen, medical member, brought out the whole story. His descriptions were so vivid they were almost convincing. His father told him to join the Marine Corps and even went down to the railroad station to see him off. His father had appeared to him frequently during his training. But now he was getting afraid of these visits. He only saw that part of his father's body above the thighs; he indicated: "Musta been dats whe' dey was cut off in da accident."

Dr. Bowen prodded, "Boy, wasn't your father a good Christian man?"

"Yassuh, but ah's still sca'd."

This lad actually wanted to remain in the Marine Corps—if we could protect him from his hallucinations. Dr. Bowen's probing was only to give us a clearer picture of this case; he knows it is useless to argue with a psychotic.

Bed-wetters may ask for a private hearing but usually they come to the Aptitude Board in groups. They've been together under observation on the ward and there is the usual social history. As some less compassionate corpsmen say, "They've been over at POU urinating on one another for a couple of weeks." Each answers to his name while the Senior Member riffles through a stack of records.

"At ease, men. Each of you—through no fault of his own—suffers from a condition which would make it unreasonable to keep you in the Marine Corps. Do you all know what condition I'm speaking of?"

Chorus: "Yes, sir."

"Do you understand why we can't keep you in the Marine Corps?"

CHORUS: "Yes, sir."

"Now, I spoke to you before the Board met. I told you that you would get a general discharge under honorable conditions. That is a good discharge, not a bad discharge. It will let you go home, go to school, get a job, or do anything you want except come back in the service. Do you understand that?"

CHORUS: "Yes, sir."

"Are there any questions?"

Invariably one comes to a slovenly position of attention, shuffles his feet, and stammers: "Sir, if I get cured of this can I come back in thc Marine Corps?"

"Yes, but it will be necessary that you go to your family doctor and do what he tells you to do. You will have to have a statement from him saying you've been cured for several months. Then go to the Recruiting Station, tell the sergeant about your case, and he'll refer it to the Commandant of the Marine Corps." (Beyond that it is theory—I don't know if any return.) Back to the whole group: "One final word. Unless you see fit to tell someone about it, the reason you were discharged will remain a matter of confidence between you and the Marine Corps. Do you understand that?"

CHORUS: "YES, SIR!" The mass sigh of relief is quite audible.

Each year hundreds of grown-up men go back home because they're enuretic. Quite naturally this is an intolerable affliction in barracks, at sea, or in the field. We might cure some, perhaps, if we were in that business. Most, of course, have underlying behavior disorders. A few come from an environment where they are not even noticed. The case history of one youngster showed that he was married. Dr. Bowen questioned him:

"Son, is it true that you are married?"

"Yes, sir."

"Doesn't your wife say anything about your wetting the bed?"

"No, sir. She wets the bed, too."

More pitiful are illiterates. Quite a few are not even good risks for E-Platoons. The Aptitude Board sees both these and those who fail after their additional four weeks' training. Some appear in small groups, others individually.

"At ease, son. The Board understands you've been having some difficulty at Parris Island. What seems to be the trouble?"

"Ah jist caint get the hang a readin', suh."

"How did you do in your E-Platoon?"

"Ah tried, but ah jist couldn't ketch on."

"You understand that in the Marine Corps you need to be able to read orders? You might be on patrol and have to send back a written message? You have to read to pass a promotion exam? You wouldn't want to be a private all your life, would you?"

"No, suh."

"Good luck, son. We're sorry we can't keep you in the Marine Corps. We hope you do well on the outside."

So you think all our illiterates come from Mississippi or Georgia? That is far from the truth. We see them from Massachusetts—or from Ohio—or with a high school diploma from commuting distance of Philadelphia. Many of our school systems give "social promotions" to the boy whether he learns anything or not. A good number of these lads suffer from a psychological reading "block" and could have been trained to overcome their deficiency. Yet I'm not sure we do right in screening out illiterates; perhaps there's a place for them.

Our Aptitude Board gets its share of mamma's boys, too. Most of them are really disgusting, a few actually pathetic. How well I recall that tall, husky lad from western Virginia. Trembling, tears in eyes, he was completely shaken:

"What are you going to do when you get out of the Marine Corps, son?"

"I'm going straight home to my mother and I'm never going to leave her again." She was a widow.

"You mean you're going to let her take care of you and support you?"

"Yes, sir."

"That's not being much of a man, is it?" He was twenty-two and had been forced to enlist through pressure from his Draft Board.

"No, sir. But I don't care. I just want to be with my mother." He began sobbing.

"All right, son. We'll get you home as soon as we can. The Marine Corps needs men, not you. Somebody else can fight your country's battles. Are you going to be proud of that?"

"No, sir."

"You're excused."

The boy with hallucinations about his dead father probably suffered from an incipient functional psychosis. He was the only one I saw fitting that particular pattern, though occasionally we see some with convincing, yet mild schizophrenia. More typical are the psycho-neurotic disorders, conversion hysteria and anxiety reaction. These appear frequently. We saw a woman marine, divorcee, who became paralyzed from the waist down without organic basis. Men quite often develop a psychosomatic paralysis of legs or arms and this seems to appear about the time they begin to fire the rifle. But the Aptitude Board never meets without seeing anxiety reactions; in the jargon of Parris Island, they're "shook." It's extremely difficult to pass judgment on these cases because we always feel they "lack guts" or they've heard about POU and are just plain malingerers. Unquestionably malingerers get screened out, we don't know how many. The anxiety reaction claims he's nervous, he can't stand the DI yelling at him. Often he breaks down in tears while being interviewed by the Board, particularly if a member needles him with mild cruelty or threatens to send him back to duty. One character showed up who was "shook" when he got to Yemassee. He wasn't with his platoon long enough to get a haircut. When we decreed he get a trial "on the schedule," it took two strong corpsmen to get him through the door. When taken forcibly to a platoon, he ran away as soon as unhanded. This man finally left Parris Island in his original civilian clothes and without ever being shorn.

One category gets separated from the Corps either through Aptitude Board or Undesirable Discharge Board: homosexuals. If their condition is latent—they don't realize they're queer—the talking doctors discover them and they leave under honorable conditions. That naked line at Hygienic is enough to disturb these people—the dynamics must be similar to a burlesque show I saw at the Haymarket in Chicago thirty years ago. Eating, sleeping, marching closely together lead to anxiety. The DI sends the lad to POU and he's on his way out. Those who proposition or make passes at fellow recruits are active homosexuals without question, though astute DIs seem able to earmark others who later break down under questioning. All of the active type have their choice of court-martial or undesirable discharge; they invariably select the latter. Apparently homos, men and women, anticipate the lush fields in the Armed Forces; when they're discovered, they're abruptly disappointed. Probably they're all cases for the medical profession, but we have neither room nor time for them in the service.

The GCT—General Classification Test—is the third of our primary screening instruments. This test we get from the Army. It was developed through two wars by experts, is based on our most modern learning, was standardized on a gigantic population to insure reliability. Yet the GCT forms a hazard to effective leadership. First, we try to disguise its significance: We claim it measures something different from intelligence. Let me quote from Historical Division, Department of the Army's *Procurement and Training of Ground Combat Troops:*

> Classification by intellectual capacity was more precise. For this purpose inductees were given an Army General Classification Test (AGCT) designed to measure ability to learn. The confusion of AGCT scores with concepts of "I.Q." or "mental age" was forbidden by the War Department. The AGCT measured a compound of native endowments and of the effects of schooling and social experience, amounting to "intelligence" in the popular and practical sense in which it was useful to the Army.

We call ours a "classification test;" Wonderlic calls his a "personnel test;" the Thurstones named theirs a "psychological test." It's all quite subtle, but it doesn't fool the troops: They know we're trying to measure "intelligence"—whatever that is. And to top it off, every man knows his own score. Without hesitation the DI will recite his platoon average. This false claim we're measuring "learning ability" or "military aptitude" only serves to make the troops question our integrity in other matters.

But the second hazard is more real: We mark a human being with his score as if it were a micromeasure; he carries it through his military life. We require minimum scores for admission to each specialist school, though these requirements were concocted at a desk in Washington and based on "educated guessing." Only Electronics Staff did anything to validate their specifications—and they knew mathematics thoroughly, test theory negligibly. When a man with low GCT comes to the Aptitude Board, the psychiatrist doesn't even smile as he substitutes a standard score for an IQ and tells the Board that man might legally be committed to an asylum. More often than not, he doesn't even check a low GCT score against a Kent or Army Beta.

Just the other day one of my marines was up for Office Hours and I noted his GCT score was sixty-eight, yet it was apparent from his conversation he couldn't be that dull—assuming the score had any significance. Upon my questioning he told me that during testing he had missed the numbering sequence in one whole column on his answer sheet. For example, his answer to Item 30 was marked in the space designated for No. 31. He was instructed by the test monitor to make a notation on his answer sheet and let it go. Unfortunately the test-scoring machine couldn't read that notation.

If we'd had the GCT twenty-five years ago Calvin Watters and José Llera couldn't have finished their first cruise in the Marine Corps—they would have been given early discharges. But they turned out to be good officers—Cal made captain, Joe CWO, were a big help in the management of Weapons Battalion, and served fifty-nine years between them. Both were middle-aged when tested, which isn't too good. Cal went only to the first few grades in school and Joe couldn't speak English when he enlisted —he nearly starved in the beginning. But no one considers that. Then we had PFC Ball in the outfit. He had a low GCT and was also married. We had to promote him meritoriously to sergeant and wangle him a re-test from Headquarters just to keep him in the Corps—and here was a good marine who wanted to make it a career. Fortunately, a man usually does better on a re-test. Admittedly with large groups of men we need these numbers. But they don't tell much about an individual marine even though they're effective if we consider a group. When we're working with individuals more should be left to the Commanding Officer's judgment.

Yes, we let these numbers carry us away. We tack them on human beings as a measure—not like those on the quarterback's jersey. Our numbers tell whether a marine can go to school, or be an officer, or even stay in the Corps. Even the Congress failed to understand. In the Selective Service Act of 1948 (at the Army's behest) they wrote that the GCT "passing score" is 70. How can we set a passing mark in intelligence? I guess I'm old-fashioned, but I feel that our drive for high GCTs is robbing the Corps of the professional soldier. I would look for an optimum band of scores and refuse to enlist a man if his GCT were too high. The potential Ph.D. isn't going to be happy spending twelve to fifteen years working himself up to master sergeant, and we can make a good rifleman or mortar section leader from a man who is something less than college material. Instead of rejecting the slow learner who is emotionally sound, we need merely tailor our training to fit his needs. Then we have a career man: satisfied, loyal, grateful.

Despite three formal screening devices and the DI's observation which sends our rejects back to civilian life routed through one of five Boards, everyone at Parris Island must be continually vigilant. Don't leave your keys in the car—which is normal at many posts—some eloping recruit may run the gate hidden behind your tags. One trusting chaplain had his car stolen twice. This injunction, through somebody's carelessness, disappeared from Post Regulations; after a rash of recruit joy-riding, it was restored. A few years ago a recruit attacked and killed a small child—and those officers' quarters at West End are in the midst of the Recruit Area. A few months before I reported, a recruit bivouacked in the quarters of my predecessor, Colonel Ralph

King, who was away on temporary duty. Each day the Executive Officer, Jim Young, or the Adjutant, Sam Brogli, inspected, but the maid's room was locked and they didn't bother it. Ralph King was fond of cigars and left behind a good supply; the recruit liked Ralph's cigars, too. The Colonel had a deep freeze loaded with his favorite foods, which the recruit also appreciated. This skulker threw his garbage and left-overs into the maid's closet—eventually the stench drove him out. When he was found hiding in the marsh he was wearing King's white flannel trousers, soiled beyond hope.

Though we screen out rejects, we pay the penalty in poor public relations: Few men hold good will toward an organization that refuses to accept them. Imaginations work overtime, especially among the paranoids. More than 200 years ago some old Admiral of the Blue coined an expression: "Tell it to the Marines." It seems that any unusual tale might be endowed with credibility only if a marine would accept it. Marines had been everywhere and seen everything. That test may have a degree of reliability, but be on your guard when a marine tells it to you. They seem to follow the advice of my old seagoing roommate, Rear Admiral John Daniel Hayes, now retired: "Don't adhere so closely to the facts that you ruin a good story."

Newcomers to any tropical post, for years have heard of the native with elephantiasis: "He's not very close to camp, but you'll see him one of these days when we're out in the hills. His gonads are so big he has to carry them in a wheelbarrow." That story was told in the Philippines, Samoa, Santo Domingo, Haiti, Nicaragua. Nor did it matter that wheelbarrows were unknown to the culture or economy. I suspect a marine of imposing on the credulity of James Michener, who in one of his tales located that same native on the Island of Bougainville.

Another classic—I've heard sworn testimony that it happened both in Shanghai and Port-au-Prince—is the court-martial story. It seems the Accused was on trial for conduct unbecoming an officer and gentleman. After receiving adequate stimulation in a nearby pub, he had field-stripped a popular cat house. The Madam was sworn in as star witness:

"State your name, residence and occupation."

She managed that question.

"If you recognize the Accused, state as whom."

With blank expression the Witness was mute.

"Do you know that man over there?" The Judge Advocate pointed to the Accused.

"No, but I know several of these other gentlemen." The Witness smiled at the Court.

Now the Parris Island recruit gets no formal instruction in story-telling, but during his first week or two he seems to absorb that skill. Not yet a master—like the old-timers—he's at least a journeyman. By the time he gets home on Boot Leave many's the civilian about to be taken. If this new marine limited his adventure stories to the old gang, they'd know him well enough to understand. Real trouble begins when he romanticizes to Mamma, or the minister, or the editor of Hometown *Clarion*. When they're taken in the Marine Corps gets it; angry letters go to Congressmen, recruiters, the Commandant. We hear of indignities, brutality, inhumanity, bestiality. The DI becomes Belial. Marines in general make Hitler's *Gestapo* mere pantywaists. Invariably—and this is the catch—the complainant remains anonymous or refuses to give adequate information to permit an investigation.

Some of our more able story-tellers are those sent home by the Aptitude Board. Often they've never even been on the training schedule, they've not had time to master the obscene language in which they're so proficient, all they know about Parris Island they've learned at POU. Most are resentful about not making the grade; seldom do they want their friends to learn the true reason for their separation. Their stories become utterly fantastic—and their flight from reality is too often aided by mild psychosis.

We have an occupational disease at Weapons Battalion. Dr. Robert Sullivan calls it "rifle sling palsy." During Dr. Ernest Ferrell's tenure we studied the incidence rate and found that one recruit in 8,000 might be seriously affected. This disability has been written up in an Army medical journal. We keep alert for it and exercise close medical supervision, but every now and then a case turns up. To support the rifle, the left arm is placed in a loop of the sling, which in turn is tightened in position close to the armpit. This tightening is done gradually over several days, slings are loosened frequently, the arm is exercised. Occasionally a recruit feels a numbness in his fingers or loses control of his left hand; he is immediately sent to Sick Bay for treatment. Most of these cases recover in short order. We can't pin it on bodily conformation; we can't predict its occurrence; we have no positive antidote; we just live with it. At times I suspect overeager marksmanship instructors or DIs through suggestion give us patterns of group hysteria. But what a story this makes back home! They tightened our slings until they cut off all circulation. (The injury occurs to a syndrome of nerves.) They made us keep them that way all day. Half of my platoon went to the hospital and got medical surveys, but look at me, boy: I'm rugged; I could take it.

Rugged combat marines are a sinful lot. Lieutenant Colonel Harvey Curtis (Joe) Tschirgi, from Iowa and once famous Naval Academy football player, talked about this when we were together at Headquarters: "Until I got to China after the war and watched some of the troops behave, I didn't realize what a gang of cutthroats, thugs, thieves, and scoundrels we had in the Marine Corps." Perhaps we can generalize from Joe Tschirgi's observation: Marines are no damn good—in peacetime. While they're in the field we want them to be tough, callous to human suffering, willing to hazard risks, phlegmatic about death. When they're home we want them to be proper gentlemen, considerate of their fellow man, adherent to rules of safety, striving for longevity. This forced ambivalence—or double standard—is certain to generate conflict in the individual. Perhaps we should reexamine our standards.

Before World War II a good portion of our recruiting was done at the freight yards. Our sergeants found vagrants there who were tired of riding the rods or blind baggage; they were ready to do most anything for regular meals, clean bunks, whole clothing. We also enlisted foreigners without question: One recruiting sergeant changed an applicant's name from "Propik" to "Tracy" because he thought it would be easier to pronounce and look better on the muster roll. First Sergeant Charlie Hess, with the 10th Marines at Camp Perry in 1931, complained to me: "Lieutenant, we're getting nothing putt a punch of gottam foreigners now—Hunkies, Vops, Pollaks. Vy, Schwartz and me are the only vuns in the whole tam battery that can speak Cherman!" We also had po' whites who thought $20.80 and a horse-blanket was high living. The Marine Corps was a home for misfits in other walks of life—and it was effective.

12

Survivors

PRIVATE JOHN EDWARD MARTINEZ of Brooklyn testified at the Court of Inquiry during the forenoon session of April 11. From Sunday night until this Wednesday morning he had been discussing the Ribbon Creek tragedy with newspaper reporters as well as his platoon mates. Latin character lends flavor to his version:

Q. Where were you when the platoon entered the water?

A. When the formation broke up, we were then in front.

Q. Where was Sergeant McKeon in relation to you?

A. At the lead, sir; to my left.

Q. How far?

A. Just about ten feet.

Q. Did you hear him say anything after the platoon entered the water?

A. He said we'd walk around awhile. Then I guess we went in a little too deep and that's when the trouble started.

Q. Did you see Private *Wood* while you were in the water?

A. At first I thought it was Private *Thompson* or *Wood,* but now I'm practically sure it was Private *Wood,* sir.

Q. Where did you see him?

A. He was a few feet away from me. When I got to him, he was practically finished already. He had so much water in his lungs he couldn't cry for help. All I heard was like when you gargle your throat. There was water in his lungs, sir. I latched onto him and started pulling him in. He grabbed the cord around my neck, sir—with the keys—and he pulled me down and I went down once. I had to let go and he came back up with me and I grabbed onto him again. Some of the boys that were drowning right next to him grabbed onto me also and I had to push him away and they took me down again. I had to let go of Private *Wood,* sir. I couldn't hold on because I had my boots on—and all my clothes—and I was going down. I don't think I would have come up if I went down again.

Q. How deep was the water?

A. I couldn't tell you, sir. It was over my head—that's for sure.

Q. Did you recognize any of the other people in the area right then?

A. Yes, sir. I pulled in Private *Reilly* just before *Wood,* sir. When I left him, he was standing. I couldn't understand when we got back to the barracks why he was gone. I thought he was all right.

Q. You say you pulled him in?

A. Yes, sir.

Q. Where did you take him?

A. Well, I didn't have time to put him on land because there were a lot of boys out there that needed help—that were drowning. So I pulled him as far as he could stand. He was standing about chest-high in water and I thought he was okay. He seemed okay. He talked awhile. Then it was just a matter of seconds and I had to leave him. I went out after *Wood.*

Q. That was the last time you saw Private *Reilly?*

A. Yes, sir.

Q. You could not recognize any other men that were in the area right then?

A. No, sir. I know I pulled one of the little fellows out, but I don't know who it was. I grabbed him by the back of his shirt. He was standing and he was okay, but I didn't know who it was, sir.

Q. At any time did you see anyone cross this stream to the opposite bank from where the platoon entered?

A. No, sir.

Q. Were you out about as far as anyone?

A. I think I was, sir—one of the farthest out. Because I took off my clothes and boots and went back out to see if I could find Private *Wood*—and at that time another boy was missing. I went out to see if I could find him. Most of the boys were already out of the water and some were near the banks. I swam out without my clothes on and I didn't realize the tide was so fast. I was going downstream pretty fast and I was pretty far out. When I turned around I could hardly see the boys any more—I was traveling too fast. So I started yelling to them to come out there and help me dive for them to see if there was a little chance of grabbing somebody. I was out there and while I was going under I couldn't feel anything.

Q. Were you diving?

A. Yes, sir. I was out there trying my best to see if I could feel somebody under water. Then the boys yelled to me Sergeant McKeon gave the order to get out of the water—everybody yelled to me. But I wouldn't leave because I felt that there was still a little chance that we might get one and I was calling them to come out and help me. They wanted to come out, but then somebody yelled, "Everybody's okay; everybody's out of the water." I didn't hear any splashing or anything or any cries for help. For some reason it was hard to believe, but I believed it and I swam in.

Q. You didn't see anyone on the opposite bank?

A. No, sir. It was very dark.

Q. Did you ever get over to the opposite bank?

A. No, sir. I got pretty close to it. I was practically halfway across, if not more than that.

Neither Counsel for the Court, the Court, nor the Party desired to further examine this witness. The witness made the following statement: "I can't remember anything else, sir, except that everybody tried their best and it was very hard under the conditions—under the circumstances. I guess somebody had to go down."

That John Martinez really persisted in attempting rescue had been confirmed by Joseph Moran, first witness at the Inquiry:

> Well, sir, I helped out with that—I believe it was Private Myers—and I got on shore. Now everybody was by the banks. So I was yelling to be quiet so we could see if there was anyone in the water. Private Martinez was making a little noise—he wanted to go and get everybody—dive for them, or something. And he started to swim out toward the middle, at more or less an angle, and he was pretty far out. I was tired, so I told him that everybody was all right because I was afraid he was going to drown, too, sir.

There were seventy-seven, seventy-eight, or seventy-nine marines in Platoon 71 on April 8, depending upon whether you accept my figures, those of the Inquiry, or those of the Court-Martial. Eleven of their names began with *B*. Brewer, Bruner, Brower, and Butler testified at the Inquiry. Barber and Brennan appeared at the Court-Martial. Banashefski, Barata, Blair, Brooks, and Brown, whose names are not so easy to confuse, stayed behind the scenes.

Private Mims Brower joined Platoon 71 after the forming period from Platoon 59, a slow learners' group. Brower went first to an E-Platoon because his classification score placed him in the lowest four per cent of the male population eligible for military service. Under terms of the Selective Service Act of 1948, he "failed"—the Army could have rejected him. Mims Brower was in the Ninth Squad with *Thomas Hardeman*. It is for that reason his few words are valuable:

Q. During the time the platoon was in the water did you at any time see Private *Hardeman?*

A. Yes, sir.

Q. Where?

A. Sir, he marches right in front of me and I was holding on to his belt.

Q. Then what happened afterwards?

A. Sir, someone up front went to holler for help, sir, and he could swim pretty good, sir, and I turned his belt loose and he said he was going up there. He took off and that's the last I saw of him, sir.

Recruit Lew Ray Brewer, Jackson, Mississippi, was one of twenty-seven reservists in Platoon 71; *Donald O'Shea* had been in the Reserve but integrated. Brewer's rating on the General Classification Test marks him as potential officer material. On the 15-day achievement examination he made a perfect score. Since he was in the Fourth Squad, Brewer began the Ribbon Creek march near the middle of the column. He, Bruner, and Martinez claimed they encountered *Norman Alfred Wood* in deep water. This is Brewer's story:

Q. What happened when the platoon went into the swamps?

A. We marched right straight out into the water until it was about chest-deep on me, sir, and then we started—we moved to our left. We made a left—you know—just marched around to the left.

Q. The whole column went to the left?

A. Yes, sir. And we walked down into the water. We walked on down—I don't know how far it was, sir; it wasn't very far. And some of the men started calling for help. I don't know who the men were. I don't know exactly how many there were, sir. But this one man—

Q. How deep was the water where you were standing?

A. About chest-deep. And one of our men yelled for the men to join hands like that and I yelled this myself, too. There weren't too many joined in this chain, so I started to take off my utility shirt and my trousers and my boots, sir, and handed them to the man behind me and I went out into the water. Sergeant McKeon, here, sir —with another man alongside of Sergeant McKeon—had ahold of him—and I started out through the water and I helped this man bring Sergeant—well I—after I had stripped off my clothes, sir, me and this other boy that was in the platoon, we helped Sergeant McKeon out to the—it was about knee-deep when I let go of him and some of the men were still calling out there, "Can't you help me get out of this deep water?"

Q. Do you recall seeing Private *Wood* in the water?

A. Yes, sir. When I turned loose Sergeant McKeon—me and this other boy helped him in closer to the bank—and these men were still hollering for help. I had already stripped out of my clothes and I went back toward the call of these men that were calling for help and I don't know if this was Private *Wood,* sir. I couldn't say for sure it was Private *Wood,* but I think it was.

Q. What makes you think it was Private *Wood?*

A. Because of his size—for one thing—and the sound of his voice.

Q. What was so distinctive about his size?

A. He's a very large man, sir, and very strong. He's about the biggest man we have in our platoon.

Q. Was he white?

A. No. He's a colored man, sir.

Q. How many other colored people were up near the front of the column where Private *Wood* was?

A. I don't know, sir. I know Private *Wood* was up there. When I was up front with Sergeant McKeon, Private *Wood* was up there, too. As far as the other colored boys—I don't know if they were up there or not.

Q. Could Private *Wood* swim?

A. He couldn't well, sir. He was afraid of the water.

Q. All right; continue. What did you do?

A. I tried to get my hand across Private *Wood's* body, sir, and he wouldn't let me. So I tried to get around behind him. That's when I cupped my hand under his chin and he was panicky and he carried me under with him and he tried to climb up on me, sir. And he carried me under and after he got under he got me by the legs. And when I got loose from Private *Wood*—I'm saying Private *Wood* because, although I'm not too sure it was Private *Wood*—when he turned loose of me, when I came up, I didn't see him any more, sir.

Q. What did you do then?

A. Well, after I got through coughing, sir, I went to the bank, and Sergeant McKeon and this other boy that helped him out—I started back toward the boys that were driven in there, sir.

Q. Who was the other man that helped you?

A. Private Connell, sir.

Q. When you brought the Sergeant back to the bank, did you have any clothes on then?

A. No, sir. I did not.

Q. Now, you said you pulled the Sergeant into a place where he could stand; is that correct?

A. I said I helped pull him. Now, he could stand, sir. He could stand.

Q. Well, why did you help him?

A. This other boy was helping me. I don't know whether the Sergeant was hurt or not and this other boy said, "Help me get him out of the water." So I helped him.

Q. Well, what was your impression: that he needed help or didn't he need help?

A. He seemed exhausted, sir. Yes, sir. He was having trouble, sir.

Q. Did this happen right at the beginning of the panic?

A. No, sir. It didn't. Not right at the beginning, sir, because these men were calling for help and I stripped my clothes and swam a little piece and then walked, too. I wasn't out in the water too deep then—and like I started out—and then this boy called me to help him and I went back and helped him. So it wasn't at the beginning. No, sir.

Private Clarence Robert Bruner, Jr., who scored poorly on written tests, must have been frightened, reluctant, or merely taciturn at the Inquiry. Yet we must hear him because he is one of three who claimed to have struggled with *Norman Wood:*

> I was in the rear, sir, of my same squad, the Tenth Squad. I just followed. We were out about fifteen, eighteen foot, and we started going back downstream a little bit. I don't mean downstream; I mean back down the way we came up. Guys started hollering, "Help!" and everybody just got scared. When the guys were screaming—there were some guys out there that were going under and I swam out to try and help them. I was trying to get hold of them and they pulled me under once and I came back up. He had hold of my feet—by my legs—then he let loose of my legs and then I never did see him any more. I couldn't be for sure, sir; I think it was Private *Wood*. The best I could see was the back of his hair and it was kinda like a colored guy's hair. After that, sir, I swam back as far as I could and then the other guys helped me out.

Eugene Ervin said: "When I went back there I saw a man in the water and he looked like he was crying. So I went back to help him. It was Private Bruner, one of the men that just was in here. I recall him saying he tried to help somebody. But he couldn't hold onto the man and that's the reason for his crying."

Recruit Dewin Delwyn Leonard, Roselle Park, New Jersey, testified at both Inquiry and Court-Martial. (Major Holben's record of the former calls him "Edward" Leonard.) Leonard is a six-footer and was in the Second Squad. He believes he saw either *Thompson* or *Wood*. Considering both victims, Leonard shares this claim with six platoon mates. Minor variations in his testimony between April and July demonstrate fallibility in human memory. We quote only the Inquiry:

> Q. Describe what happened as the platoon started into the water.
>
> A. Well, sir; we started towards the water and Sergeant McKeon was the first one in. We went in the water and we started parallel toward the shore. When the entire platoon was in, we started to form a circle.
>
> Q. Continue.
>
> A. As we then did a circle, sir, and first of all nothing happened.

One boy got a little scared, but he got over it. As we were marching along, Sergeant McKeon was teaching us what we'd do in case we were in combat or anything, to stick close to the shore. And he was describing, sir, how the moonlight—and everything.

Q. Well, was anyone behind him?

A. Well, sir; we were all huddled in a group and Sergeant McKeon was still talking to us, but he was starting to tread water and he wasn't actually leading anyone into deep water. Some of us followed, though.

Q. Did other men follow?

A. Yes, sir. Some of us did follow and some of the ones that couldn't swim stayed on in the low water, where you could touch ground.

Q. What was the condition of the current?

A. The undercurrent was rough, sir.

Q. What happened then?

A. Well, sir; some of the boys couldn't hold on, I guess the current got them. A few of them started to be carried away.

Q. Did you have reason to notice this Private *Thompson* about this time?

A. I'm not sure which it was, sir. It was either Private *Thompson* or Private *Wood*. I was ten feet of them before they went down.

Q. What was this person doing?

A. He was trying to stay above water, sir.

Q. Why do you say it was Private *Thompson* or Private *Wood?*

A. That's the only two colored boys that were at the head of the line and that were big.

Q. Did you say that you attempted to reach this person?

A. Yes, sir.

Q. Did you fail to reach him or did you reach him?

A. Yes, sir. I had my clothes on and my boondockers and I just couldn't reach him in time.

Q. When was the last time that you saw this person?

A. You mean Private *Wood,* sir?

Q. Well, whoever it was.

A. Well, I was within about ten feet of him and I seen him sink under water and I kept swimming towards him but that's the last I saw of him.

Q. What did you do then?

A. I looked around, sir, and I saw them trying to help one boy on shore, sir. So I couldn't do any good out there so I came back and I took Private Porter's clothes from him because he was going to try and swim out further and help out. Then I went in and helped the boys on shore.

Private William Earl Rambo had this story to tell at the Inquiry during the morning of April 10:

> Sergeant McKeon hollered at us, "Is everybody all right?" And everybody said they was. He asked them afterwards—a few minutes after he asked them a last time if they was all right—some of them started hollering. And I guess they got—they got panicky. Myself, I thought they were just goofing off and fooling.
>
> Sir, the water was up around my chest, sir. Where I was at there was no current. I wasn't too far out then. Gradually we all kept going out.
>
> Well, most of the men were over there hollering for help and most of us that could swim saved them. We thought we would go over and help them out. But I didn't hear any commands to go into deep water.
>
> Well, sir; I saw Private *Wood* or Private *Thompson*—I couldn't tell which one it was. It was dark—a little too dark for me to tell which one it was, sir. I could tell that they were colored guys—neither one of them could swim, I don't think. I took it for granted it was Private *Wood* or Private *Thompson,* either one.
>
> They were out in front of me a little ways—out towards the deeper water. Yes, sir; he was out in deeper water; he was out a little bit further. He was batting water with his hands. He was striking the top of the water and he was hollering for help. Me and another boy had—I don't know which one it was. We were all trying to help each other, sir. I don't know which one it was I had. We tried. We had one of them—we were making towards the bank. That's when he was hollering and some of the guys started towards him and we took this boy out on the bank. There was some other guys way over there towards him, so I thought they were going to help him out. So we took this other boy and took him back to shore.

Recruit Joseph Anthony Moran, Forest Hills, Queens, New York, son of Thelma Ritter, actress, was lead-off Boot witness at the Inquiry. His testimony is important because it confused rather than clarified a murky picture and because it leaves us an unsolved mystery, confirmed by Private Porter, buried in the slimy waters of Ribbon Creek. Moran confused the evidence by insisting at both Inquiry and Court-Martial that Platoon 71 went upstream, circled and came down, then circled again and went back up. His was the only story to describe that additional circling movement. Then Moran insisted he and Porter "saved" *Leroy Thompson.* Despite the probability of some aberration, Moran was a fine witness; his version of the incident is brutally condensed here to avoid repetition: We held Moran in reserve while his platoon mates talked and we need yet preserve a fragment of the story for Porter.

> A lot of men broke ranks and went up alongside their friends and so we weren't too well formed by the time we got down to the river. While it was all right up front, the men in back got in some sort of mud, quicksand, or bog, I don't know what it was. I was with Private Langone and one of the last ones in the river. Close to the bank the water was up to your thigh and then in some parts it was at your waist. There was a lot of joking; things seemed to be pretty funny. Nobody was scared at first. Then all of a sudden there was a slight undertow—I imagine it got deeper—I started to get carried way off, where it was over my head.
>
> I noticed Private *Thompson,* who was fairly near me. I was drifting away from him while he kept going under. I thought at first he was fooling. Then I swam back to him. Private Porter was already there. We took *Thompson* toward the ground where it was good enough for him to stand—it was up to his shoulders, maybe. We couldn't take him to shore because by now a lot of the men were hollering for help. Since I wanted to get my clothes off, we just stood Private *Thompson* right there. He seemed all right. We stood him up and he didn't go limp. He was standing there when I turned around.
>
> I gave my shirt and boots to Private Ferkel. Today I found out that there was a man around my neck; a lot of people were trying to drag me under—Private Truitt was on my back all the time. Well, sir, I helped out with that—I believe it was Private Myers—and then I got on shore. It was very dark—that's what hindered a lot. There was a private—I can't think of his name now—he was shocked; he didn't have any clothes on; he was

all shaking. So I put him on my back and started to carry him toward where the rest of the group were going.

After we left the second group of cars I was walking back with Sergeant McKeon. He was pretty shook up. He was talking about the men out there—we left men out there—just more or less talking to himself, sir. I asked him if he wanted a cigarette and he said, "No." He didn't seem to be paying much attention to anything or where he was going either.

Private Donald Joseph Porter was in charge of those Platoon 71 Boots who attended the Novena. Porter was in the Second Squad, which made him one of the taller men in Platoon 71; low average on his written tests, he was among the more observant and physically capable. His story is notable because it is well-oriented, shows objectivity, and was told thirty-six hours after the incident:

> I saw Private *Thompson* and he was in need of help. He seemed to be going down and splashing there a bit. He wasn't making too much of a commotion. I grabbed him with Private Moran and together we brought him in. We brought him in a ways until we could stand—where the water came up to about our shoulders—and we stopped. To us, to myself, he looked all right. If he had been faint or weak or something he would have fell right back into that water. So I just turned around and started to help the others.
>
> I tried to get some of the other boys and take them out, but I found this to be very hard because of my clothing. And I took off my boots, my utility shirt, and skivvie shirt and I swam out. I grabbed one of the boys that were in the water and I carried him to shore. I found out that this was Private Myers.

Swimming instruction is given during the first week recruits are on the Rifle Range. This is scheduled at night so that maximum daylight will be available for marksmanship. After a training film, changing into trunks, and a shower, each platoon is divided into groups of swimmers and nonswimmers according to the recruits' individual statements. Those in doubt are urged to attempt the test.

Boots who can swim one hundred meters, tread water thirty

seconds, and float on their backs, are classified as second-class swimmers. Almost nightly there are the overambitious who try the 100-meter swim and fail. These usually take a lane near the side of the pool and get out of the water under their own power or with the assistance of other failures. Rather frequently we see some character whose determination exceeds his good judgment. He struggles until he "passes out." Lifeguards anticipate frequent rescues.

Self-confessed nonswimmers remain at the shallow end of the pool and begin rudimentary instruction. The first stage of this is overcoming fear of the water. But about once in 800 cases our instructors encounter a true hydrophobe: a recruit with abject, morbid terror of water. What would you do with him?

Robert Seashore, then chairman of Northwestern University's psychology department, told us a story which gives the clue. His friend, let's call him Joe Clancy, was a successful businessman. Joe still followed the market and kept abreast of his professional reading. But Joe had spent the past two years in the psychopathic ward. There was just one thing wrong with him: He thought he was pregnant. Seashore believed he could do something about this and so he went to visit Clancy. After small talk "establishing rapport," Seashore was ready to score his point:

"Joe, how long have you been here in the hospital?"

"Two years the twenty-fifth of last March."

"Joe, what's the period of gestation in the human being?"

"Well, Robert, in women it's nine months but with men it takes longer."

Seashore learned his lesson: It's fruitless to argue with a psychotic. And so our swimming instructors respect the individuality of the hydrophobe: no use to persuade, no cause for an aptitude survey. Forcing the man into the water might unbalance him completely. He is required only to observe.

Louis Curtis Leake, in Platoon 71, while not a true hydrophobe was strongly inclined in that direction. In the swimming pool he did what he was told—after a fashion. When the ten-hour course was complete, Leake had made no improvement. His fear of water was unabated.

Leake was Negro, had no high school, came from Newark, New Jersey. Except for swimming, his performance was about average. Leake was in the Tenth Squad, which placed him near the rear of the column going into Ribbon Creek. When he had barely entered the water, not more than ankle-deep, his knees buckled under him. For a time *Leroy Thompson* stayed beside Leake. Then *Thomas Hardeman,* the Georgia country boy, supported him. The water got beyond knee depth. Leake slipped in the mud and went all the way under. *Hardeman* grabbed Leake by the belt and placed him on Walter Sygman's back. Sygman was a six-footer. About this time McKeon called out, "Where are the nonswimmers?"

There was a discouraged, weak chorus, scattered through the column which replied, "Here we are, sir."

McKeon called again, "Where's Leake?"

Sygman carried Leake piggy-back toward McKeon, who came from the head of the column to meet them. "Leake, are you scared?"

"Yes, sir!"

Sygman then carried Leake to the rear of the column near Thomas Doorhy and set him down. It was not long before Carl Whitmore, somewhat forward in the column, heard Leake cry for assistance. Again Leake slipped, this time from Sygman's grasp, and went under. Sygman pulled him up, passed him to Doorhy, and told Doorhy to take him to shallow water. Eventually Leake was assisted by the human chain. Once on the bank of Ribbon Creek he had chills which he readily admitted at the Court-Martial were caused both from cold and fright. In the butts he vomited. Sergeant Taylor took Leake in his car to Sick Bay. When the corpsman took his temperature it was 93.

Sociologists devoted to the study of prejudice toward minority groups might note how the American citizen reacts in crisis. Here we had a Northern Negro, Southern farm boy, Jewish lad, and Irish Catholic working together.

When we repatriated a few marine officer prisoners of war at In'chon, Korea, in September 1945 I was able to get a lucid description of panic in No. 2 Hold of *Oryoku Maru.* But it was a different sort of panic and these survivors perceived themselves in spectators' roles because they didn't get mixed up in the melee; besides, there were nine months for impressions to crystallize. Trying to dovetail observations of the Ribbon Creek panic is a different matter: Ultimate truth washed out on the ebbing tide that very night. Yet here is a summary, confused as it may be, of what survivors say happened to the six casualties:

Thomas Hardeman was last seen by Mims Brower going to assist those in trouble.

Donald O'Shea was "rescued" by the individual efforts of Hugh Mulligan and Earl Grabowski. Stephen McGuire saw *O'Shea* disappear while struggling with *Thompson.* Jerome Daszo saw two unidentified recruits diving for *O'Shea.*

Charles Reilly was "rescued" by John Martinez. Richard Acker struggled with *Reilly,* broke loose, saw him disappear.

Jerry Thomas was seen in the water by Soren Daniel. Ronald Geckle broke loose from *Thomas* and saw him no more.

Leroy Thompson was "rescued" by the joint effort of Joseph Moran and Donald Porter. Stephen McGuire tried but failed to save *Thompson* as he struggled with *O'Shea.* Dewin Leonard swam toward either *Wood* or *Thompson,* who disappeared. William Rambo saw one Negro recruit struggling and crying for help.

Norman Wood was seen in the water by Soren Daniel. Lew Brewer and John Martinez individually attempted to rescue *Wood* but failed. Clarence Bruner and Matthew McKeon individually struggled with Wood, broke loose, saw him disappear.

13

Findings

WHEN PRESIDENT GREENE took charge of the Inquiry it had accomplished its mission: to make a thorough investigation into all of the circumstances connected with the marching of Platoon 71 into the swamp and the resulting death of six marines. The Court heard all principals that would be called: recruits, fellow DIs, School Range Instructor, Officer of the Day, Commander of the Guard, Provost Marshal. The bodies were adequately identified and no one doubted the cause of death. Even the Depot Psychiatrist had testified that McKeon was sufficiently free of medical defect and psychological disturbance on April 8 to distinguish right from wrong.

Just when the Inquiry could have been buttoned up, Thomas P. Costello and James P. McGarry were introduced as additional Counsel for the Defendant. They might have asked to recall previous witnesses. Greene might have asked to recall previous witnesses. Instead, the whole issue was changed. The Inquiry was no longer directed toward McKeon and Platoon 71, toward the death of *Thomas Hardeman, Donald O'Shea, Charles Reilly, Jerry Thomas, Leroy Thompson, Norman Wood*. The Inquiry was directed toward Parris Island: regulations, procedures, training, customs, practices, and command relations—responsibility. The Inquiry was oriented toward passing the buck —up.

Unquestionably Commandant Pate instructed Brigadier Greene in conference or by telephone to do just that. Later he even criticized the Court for not going further:

> I do not agree with the action of the Court in confining its finding of fact and opinions to the relatively narrow issue of the degree of culpability attributable to Sergeant McKeon. The Court was not so confined by its appointing order. It is obvious that the Court was not confined by a paucity of evidence or information. In a very real sense the Marine Corps is on trial for the tragedy of Ribbon Creek just as surely as is Sergeant McKeon.

But in my opinion Pate was just acting heroic, magnanimous. He didn't really mean what he said. He was writing for the New York *Times* and the nation's wire services. Had the Court been so negligent after he personally selected and instructed Greene, why did Pate with his next breath send Greene back to Parris Island as his personal representative?

Anyway, the Inquiry continued five more days sailing on a different tack. With helmsman Greene at the wheel Office Hours were disregarded. The Court worked all day Saturday, Sunday afternoon, Monday until ten. By mid-afternoon Tuesday the Court was closed; Costello and McGarry could leave. At seven-thirty Wednesday, April 18, nearly ten days to the hour since the tragedy, the Inquiry delivered its findings. During this crash program we learn a great deal about Parris Island despite the fact we learn nothing more about Ribbon Creek.

Wallie Greene had but one criticism of the record to date: It neglected to describe McKeon's state of sobriety. Greene directed Holben to call Dr. Robert J. Atcheson to the stand as first witness under the new regime. Atcheson admitted he didn't understand the Bogens test for intoxication and even suggested that a layman, perhaps the Provost Marshal, should interpret this medical finding. Atcheson denied clinical evidence of McKeon's being intoxicated but didn't bother to repudiate his written report—already on record—to the contrary.

Next up were Sergeant Nolan, master of tide tables, and Captain Weddel, custodian of Depot Orders. Weddel brought in seven documents on his first appearance and was later called to introduce two more. Then the Inquiry was forced to recess thirteen minutes: Colonel David Wray Silvey was unable to waste valuable time in Counsel's office, adjacent to the courtroom, merely standing by. Even though two officers senior to him were members of the Court, there was no protest.

Following Dave Silvey was Captain Donald Anthony Chiapetti, thirty-one, twelve years an officer, brilliant, industrious. Don Chiapetti was in charge of Drill Instructors' School. His quotation of facts and figures led Attorney Costello to conclude Chiapetti had spent hours memorizing his testimony. But it was not so. Don knows every facet of his job; he does pertinent applied research in selection and training; he is satisfied with nothing short of perfection.

After a five-minute recess, while Thomas Costello still expressed admiration for Captain Chiapetti's intimate grasp of the problem in training Drill Instructors, I finally had my day in Court. Right after Counsel Holben administered the oath, I took him by surprise:

WITNESS: I would like, if I might, to make an opening statement which may be of assistance to the Court.

PRESIDENT: Go ahead, Colonel.

WITNESS: I am the Commanding Officer of Weapons Training Battalion. I had jurisdiction over the area and the people who were involved in this incident. A Commanding Officer is responsible for everything that his unit does or fails to do. I am fully aware of my rights under the Constitution and the Revised Statutes of the United States. I wish to waive my right to be named as a Party to this Inquiry. I wish to waive any rights subsidiary thereto, such as: being present, having Counsel, calling and examining witnesses, or any restriction that there might be on my own testimony. It is not my intention during this Inquiry to claim the personal privilege of refusing to answer any question which I feel may be incriminating. I am ready to go ahead. May I add that my sole interest is to see the truth developed by this Inquiry as expeditiously as possible?

That testimony fills twenty jampacked pages of the record. You will find it retold throughout this volume. Mr. Costello was most considerate in his cross-examination. Major Holben behaved with politeness. Brigadier Greene, as he did with several other witnesses, had me conclude with a synopsis of my military history. After the findings were delivered to his office, General Burger and Staff made a determined effort to repudiate some of the things I had said. I'll stand on the record.

Technical Sergeant John D. Perdeus, Weapons Battalion Liaison NCO, followed me to the stand. Perdeus' job is to supervise housekeeping in the Recruit Area and see that all DIs get the word. He testified about his organization and his relation with recruit platoons while they are on the Rifle Range. Costello, during cross-examination, revealed a story about embezzlement of Special Service funds which irked Holben:

Q. When Drill Instructors take their platoons to the movies, do they report to you?

A. Yes, sir.

Q. All movies?

A. Yes, sir. For a couple of reasons. One, when they go to the movies they check out with us; in fact, any time throughout the morning or afternoon they stop by and pick up a chit that explains how many men are going to the movie, what platoon, and who is the duty Drill Instructor taking them.

Q. Do they not give you that after they come back from the movies?

A. No. We take it prior. I'll tell you why. This system has been followed for a considerable length of time. There are more reasons than one behind this. Currently we use a turnstile system where a man turns in his own dime. But heretofore we used ticket sales. You bought a ticket as you went in. It was one of these little chits—actually, as I was given to understand—that helped to hang a man who pocketed some of the money.

HOLBEN: To explain for the record, I wish to explain that term *hang* which you have just said.

PERDEUS: Well, I use it—he did not have as much money in the till as he used to. Currently he uses a turnstile.

Perdeus was the last witness Saturday, April 14, President Greene's first day in Court.

After lunch Sunday, Captain Charles E. Patrick was recalled and harassed by Major Holben as we previously noted. Lieutenant Colonel Robert Thompson, Commanding Officer Third Recruit Training Battalion, followed Patrick. Then Thompson's assistants appeared: Captain Richard P. Grey, McKeon's Company Commander; Master Sergeant Hershel L. Baker, Battalion Field Striper; and Master Sergeant Hans C. Manthey, Chief Drill Instructor, whose name Major Holben omitted from the index to the Inquiry proceedings. Thompson and his crew testified that Matthew McKeon was a first-rate DI, that he had been warned about maltreatment and extortion, and that they had never heard about night marches into swamps.

After that it took four witnesses to get the vodka bottle into evidence. PFC Fred A. Magruder, stationed as guard over McKeon, saw him hide the bottle and confiscated it. Magruder gave the bottle to Staff Sergeant Malcom G. Overpeck, Depot Sergeant of the Guard. Overpeck gave the bottle to First Lieutenant Oral K. Newman, Jr., Depot Officer of the Day. Newman gave the bottle to Sergeant Loren A. Raddatz, an investigator in the Provost Marshal's Office, who had enough foresight to mark and seal the bottle, lock it up, and produce it in court.

Two more witnesses, mentioned elsewhere, then it was time for Lieutenant Lowell J. Smythe, Medical Corps, U. S. Navy, pathologist responsible for the autopsies. Smythe spent twenty-six hours on post-mortem examinations and now, a week later, was still engaged in laboratory work. He could make a "preliminary diagnosis," however. It is interesting to observe this triumph in medical science and failure in human relations:

> The cause of death in each of the above-named cases, from the information we have at present, is regarded as being drowning. We really have two bases for arriving at that conclusion. The first of them is the findings on the bodies themselves. In most instances of drowning, the specific findings at the autopsy table are not one hundred per cent conclusive. In other words, the findings are essentially those of asphyxia. They die from a lack of air and the findings are quite similar to what we find in cases of asphyxiation by strangulation, for example. However, in addition to these findings, we have examined the blood from

the heart of these six men, the right side and the left side of the heart, and—may I add a little background here for this particular test?

When a man dies from drowning he respires into his lungs the water which he is drowned by. In this particular, of course, it was salt water he respired into his lungs. This salt water has a much higher concentration of salt in it than do the body tissues. So the salt diffuses out from the lungs into the blood stream which is in intimate contact with the lungs. It is then carried back to the heart. The blood from the lungs returns to the left side of the heart. And so when we examine the blood from the right and left side of the heart in cases of drowning in salt water, we find a normal salt content on the right side of the heart, from which the blood from the rest of the body returns, and we find a greatly increased amount of salt content in the left side of the heart, which returns the blood from the lungs.

We examined these specimens of whole blood from these two parts of the heart, the right and left side. In each instance we found essentially the normal amount of salt in the right side of the heart of each of these men and a greatly increased amount of salt content on the left side of the heart of each of these men. Therefore, I feel quite definitely that this test, plus the clinical findings—or the autopsy findings—of asphyxiation, indicate that these men died from drowning in salt water.

No, we have not as yet completed the final study. We have, of course, completed the examination of the bodies themselves. But the tissues which we removed to test, at the time of the autopsy, have not yet been processed. We have not made the microscopic slides which eventually we will make and so the autopsy is not as yet completed. It will be approximately three or four weeks before they will be through.

At 1:50 P.M., Monday, April 16, Major Holben rested his case. In the event Matthew McKeon or his three counselors wished to make any statement or call witnesses in rebuttal, it was time to go ahead. Attorney Costello rose from counsel table and revealed his surprise maneuver:

Well, we have a problem, General. I do not know whether you have been made aware of it or not. We have made a request through Major Faw to get immunity for any witnesses whom we would call to testify at this hearing. In this investigation I have been trying to seek witnesses who may throw some light on the issues this Court has before it. We found that men who might aid in bringing to the Court the true facts—that they felt they were afraid to come forth. They were afraid because they felt if they came and testified and their testimony was in any way critical of the methods used here at Parris Island their careers as marines would be finished and so they refuse to come and testify because of this fear even though they themselves may not be involved. For example, the individual himself would not necessarily have to be guilty of any offense or the breaking of any regulations but he might be an individual who had knowledge that something wrong was going on around the base and even that individual was afraid to come forth to testify.

Some of these people we talked to told us they would only testify if they got immunity and they got that immunity in writing. Major Faw gave us an answer this afternoon at one o'clock. Certain conditions were laid down for the granting of this immunity by the Commanding General and we have at this time in our possession the conditions which were laid down by the Commanding General for the granting of this immunity. Even though we feel these conditions are somewhat stringent and will not be acceptable to these men, we will at least present to them what the conditions of the immunity are. If they agree to come in here and testify, we will bring them in. So I would like for that reason, and also because we would like to go through these statements, to have an adjournment at this time before we decide to call any witnesses.

Brigadier Greene recessed the court to meet again at his call, which was six hours later, well after dinner that evening. Attorney Costello had lobbed a mortar shell right into General Burger's lap. Even though he had been aboard only three months the Old Man knew of many skeletons in the Parris Island closet. Costello's hinting in general rather than specific terms aroused in Burger intense emotional conflict. There were many Depot sins protected by inviolateness of the confessional: secret files. Were these revealed under oath at the Inquiry, they might become public record.

Costello, on the one hand, was on sound ground psychologically: He knew that every organization has both a public and a private life. His insinuations were bound to inflict deep wounds. But Costello, on the other hand, was in legal quicksand: He knew that, under an ancient rule of law, no one can be convicted upon his uncorroborated confession or admission. It is necessary to prove the corpus delicti. He might feasibly bring in a battalion of witnesses to swear that they had marched or been marched through swamps, that they had maltreated recruits or been maltreated. So long as these witnesses were adequately vague about dates, were uncertain in identifying others, General Burger could never sustain a conviction. Without such conviction, it would be extremely difficult—if not impossible—to endanger any enlisted marine's career.

Greene's Court of Inquiry came to order at 7:40 P.M. Costello was again on his feet:

> Well, I would like to advise the Court that we presented to the witnesses we had hoped to call the conditions of immunity that were set forth this afternoon and these men were not willing to come forth under these conditions. They advised us that the only conditions that they would come here and testify under would be if they had the guarantee of immunity in writing before they came before this Court. So at this time we do not attempt to call any witnesses. If there is no further relevant testimony to be offered, we would just like to make a statement to close the proceedings as far as the Defense is concerned.

Cautious, Greene wanted to consider that statement. He closed the court sixty-eight minutes. Then he read into the record the following statement:

> The Convening Authority has notified the Court that his reasons for not granting blanket immunity are as follows: (1) Blanket immunity might permit someone now under suspicion or investigation to escape punishment. (2) If the Party has knowledge of an offense against the Code, he has a duty to report the matter to proper authorities and if this is done Government investigators may be able to obtain admissible evidence of the offense, without permitting the guilty person to escape without punishment.

> However, the Convening Authority has stated that he will consider requests for immunity under the following circumstances: (1) The person for whom the immunity is requested must have been called as a witness. (2) He must have failed to answer a question upon the basis of Article 31, Uniform Code of Military Justice. (3) The answer to the question must be material or relevant to the subject of the investigation. (4) The essence of the expected testimony must be conveyed to the Convening Authority. (5) The evidence is not otherwise obtainable.

Greene offered to subpoena anyone Costello wished to call. Costello explained that it would be useless. It was time for arguments.

Major Holben rated leading off:

> If it please the Court: Many issues have presented themselves to the Inquiry these past several days. Without burdening the Court with all ramifications, I would like to point out what I consider to be the primary issue: responsibility for this march. I will deal first with what I consider to be the responsibility of the Party.
>
> I have not been able to find any evidence that would authorize this as a training march. Regulations grant certain discretion to a person who has to carry them out. But no regulation covers all circumstances; discretion has to be tempered with common sense.
>
> We know that the Party had no authority to punish troops under his control because that authority is well set out by the law and rests with the Commanding Officer in every case.
>
> There has been some issue raised about drinking by the Party prior to the act in question. I have explored it through testimony. None of the witnesses we have been able to find who were familiar with the Party have been able to testify, in honesty, that he was drunk. So I do not see that drunkenness is any excuse for this act.
>
> Take the other approach: What was the command's responsibility? Sergeant McKeon was selected and sent to this Depot to go to Drill Instructors' School. There he was screened for this very exacting duty which he would be required to do. There were quite a few people in the class with which he started

who did not complete the course for psychiatric reasons or because they could not pass their tests. This shows that the Marine Corps has set up certain standards for Drill Instructors—and they are high. We intend to keep them high.

When Sergeant McKeon was sent to the Third Recruit Training Battalion, his Battalion Commander related certain information to him concerning maltreatment. The same procedure took place when he met his Company Commander for the first time. There he was issued a copy of the SOP for Drill Instructors. The Chief Drill Instructor has testified that when questions arise concerning the Drill Instructor's relation with recruits, if he cannot furnish the answer, he will find it out.

Now this incident occurred at Weapons Training Battalion. There has been ample evidence to show that operational control was in the Commanding Officer of Weapons Training Battalion. As far as Staff Sergeant McKeon's Battalion Commander, Colonel Thompson, is concerned, he had no supervisory authority over the platoon.

Now what supervision was exercised at Weapons Training Battalion? I think you gentlemen of the Court, being in military service and realizing what problems of supervision there are in a large command, can sympathize with Colonel McKean's problems. Also you realize that he took steps to see that his command was properly supervised. The supervision was what—I would say—would be normal in my experience for a military command. I feel that I have shown the Court through competent evidence that the man who has a definite responsibility for the acts of persons in that command has taken adequate steps to supervise and see that the personnel in that command carry out the regulations.

I feel that the command is exonerated entirely for anything that happened on Sunday, April 8. Thank you.

Don Holben missed the boat. To begin with, he had the wrong attitude. He forgot that his job was to determine facts, not to prosecute or defend. He said that McKeon lacked authority for what he did and that McKeon couldn't plead drunkenness as an excuse, but he failed to specify any offense. Then he went ahead to defend Parris Island, which had had no charges preferred against it—unless you consider an abundance of fantastic newspaper stories. Finally, Don Holben made no recommendations to guide the Court in its findings. This was an opportunity for a man of courage—an opportunity to suggest that Ribbon Creek was a horrible accident, that Matthew McKeon had failed to meet the exacting requirements of a Staff NCO, and that he should be discharged administratively from the Marine Corps forthwith. In that way the Corps would appear magnanimous.

Don Holben's assuming the attitude of Defense Counsel for Parris Island is not surprising. Unimaginative lawyers accustomed to taking sides in a case often forget their prescribed role when confronted with an inquiry, an infrequent occurrence. Sometimes the Court itself forgets its mission of developing facts and behaves as if it were hearing a court-martial trial.

It was time for Thomas P. Costello, professional lawyer, to have the floor. Though he had been on Parris Island only seventy-eight hours, he gained remarkable insight to the whole situation. Let's hear him:

> I would like to begin my remarks by making a request to the Court: That General Burger disqualify himself as the officer who will review the recommendations and the evidence presented by this Court. We make this request on two grounds. First, General Burger since April 8 and up to the present has on many occasions expressed judgment of the issues. As a matter of fact, there is conclusive evidence to prove he has prejudged the issues here. He has stated in effect that Staff Sergeant Matthew McKeon is the responsible party and that the Marine Corps has no responsibility whatsoever. We submit that General Burger, under these circumstances, cannot possibly fairly judge the issues. He only could have fairly judged these issues if he had kept an open mind until this Board of Inquiry had concluded its findings, the evidence was presented to him, and he read every word of this testimony. He has failed to do this.
>
> Another reason or consideration why it might be well for General Burger to disqualify himself is that as the commander of this post he has the ultimate responsibility for what goes on. He is responsible for every single individual in the United States Marine Corps on this post, and in a sense he would be sitting in judgment of himself. It might be a little bit difficult for

General Burger to find himself a disinterested party. So I think if General Burger views the issues that are before him, he might voluntarily disqualify himself to judge these issues.

Now concerning the facts of the case, we have had a most unfortunate accident. The Court should take into consideration the fact that Sergeant McKeon was the first one into the water and the last one out. These men who testified here—the survivors—almost to a man have sung his praises despite the tragic incident which took place. That brings us to one of the chief issues of the case: whether or not there was any maltreatment. I feel in my heart and soul that if these men had followed in the same line that Sergeant McKeon had walked, this unfortunate tragedy would not have taken place. It might be well to take into consideration the fact that no one, beforehand, had knowledge these waters were dangerous.

I am very happy that Major Holben—a great deal was made of the fact that Sergeant McKeon had taken one or two drinks early in the evening—considers drinking not an issue in this case. As a matter of fact, the doctor who was called here testified that his examination of Sergeant McKeon shortly after the accident found him to be sober. As far as the Bogens test was concerned, he just dropped it outside the window and let the wind blow it away.

It seems to me since so much evidence has been produced here to the effect that Staff Sergeant Matthew McKeon was informed about maltreatment there must be an awful lot of it. Else why the necessity of so much warning concerning maltreatment? The manual on maltreatment states as the test a Drill Instructor is to consider in determining what is maltreatment and what isn't maltreatment, "If it hurts, it's hurt." In other words, to determine—it seems to me—to determine whether or not a punch in the jaw is maltreatment, you should punch yourself first. If it doesn't hurt, you can go right ahead and punch the recruit in the jaw. That is exactly—that is exactly what that means. There is no other meaning that we can derive from it.

The issue here set forth by Major Holben went, "Where does the responsibility lie?" If there is responsibility, it lies either on the shoulders of Staff Sergeant McKeon, it lies on the shoulders of the United States Marine Corps at this base, or both may be responsible; or, as a fourth alternative, neither one may be responsible for what took place.

Let us consider the first issue: whether or not Staff Sergeant McKeon has any responsibility for what took place. We submit that since there was no specific prohibition for the use of that area for night training exercises or for the teaching of discipline to the troops, no order was violated. We further submit that Sergeant McKeon had authority, both written and implied, for what he did on the evening of April 8. He had authority in Depot Order 348 to conduct extra activities, to bring out the best in his platoon. There were examples given of what these extra activities should be, but these were not all-inclusive. Captain Grey, the Company Commander, testified very clearly that the Drill Instructor is left with a great deal of discretion in deciding what these extra activities are. So here we have unquestionably, in the Standard Operating Procedure of Parris Island, written authority for Staff Sergeant McKeon to do exactly what he did on the night in question.

As far as implied authority is concerned, that is written even more clearly in the facts of this case. I need only to point out Staff Sergeant Huff's testimony here, which is one of the key items that has been offered in this entire trial. We have Staff Sergeant McKeon, who is junior to Sergeant Huff who—perhaps—was standing alongside of Sergeant Huff when Huff said to his men, "If you don't get off your hockey, I am going to take you out into the swamps." Here is a superior to Staff Sergeant McKeon telling him, in effect, that this is what we do here. This is how we train our men. Is there any reason then why Staff Sergeant McKeon thought this was not customary procedure here on Parris Island? The conclusion reached on the first issue is that this was not the responsibility in any way whatsoever of Staff Sergeant McKeon.

Colonel McKean testified there was a rash of training exercises in the swamps—that was the exact expression he used. Now a *rash* must mean quite a few training exercises in the swamps. It seems to me that this post was on notice of this condition and still they only prohibited the Elliott's Beach area. In law we have a relationship known as a principal-agent relationship. Generally the principal is liable for the acts of his agent. The principal is liable for the acts of his agent because he has vested that agent with a certain authority. When that agent acts in furtherance of the principal's business, then the principal is liable. There is no getting away from the fact that the Marine Corps here is the principal and that Staff Sergeant Matthew McKeon was their agent, that Staff Sergeant McKeon was furthering the best interests of the Marine Corps in trying to teach his men discipline at the time of this unfortunate accident.

Now here we come to the crux of the case. Here is the question I am going to put to this Court: Are you men going to separate the United States Marine Corps from Staff Sergeant Matthew McKeon? Are you men, who trained this man, who took him as one of you, who trained him over the course of years—this man who fought in the Korean War under the Marine banner, this man who went to the Drill Instructors' School here for five weeks—are you suddenly going to disassociate yourself from Staff Sergeant McKeon and put him over on an island by himself and say, "It is all your fault, it is none of ours"? I don't think the Marine Corps is going to do that. I don't think so because I think there is unity here: If one falls, both must fall; if one stands, I think that both will stand.

That brings me to the third and final point that I would like to raise here tonight. As far as this case has been developed it appears to me that we have here a pure accident. The mere happening of an accident—be it tragic or otherwise—is no proof that some human agency is responsible for it. We have many examples of that. My wife—the very day that this happened, as a matter of fact—was driving my car and she went through a large puddle. Half a block away she applied her brakes, they failed and she ran into another car. Now she might well have killed six people when those brakes failed. That was an accident, but certainly no responsibility could be placed upon her shoulders for that accident. She did not reasonably anticipate that the water had destroyed the condition of the brakes.

From all the evidence that has been introduced—it would seem to me—what we have here is a pure accident. Now for the Marine Corps—in this instance the officers of this Court—to come to that conclusion and to submit such a recommendation, I would say, would require a great deal of courage, because of some public opinion involved, because of some Congressmen

> who have expressed an interest in the proceedings here. But I would like to submit this suggestion: That that be the determination and conclusion of this body, that they have the courage to make that their determination. I feel that this Court and this Corps—that has proved itself in battle not to be afraid of foreign enemies such as Japs, Krauts, or Chinese—certainly should not be afraid of any segment of public opinion. So I would discount that element of the case.
>
> I now would request that this Court judge the case on its merits. I might say that General Greene began the proceedings here asking God to bless these proceedings. I would like to complete my statement at this time with a request that God may give courage to this Court to decide this case on its merits, to let the chips fall where they may. And I feel in all honesty, and in all sincerity, the conviction that the facts of this case call for a determination this was an unfortunate accident and that no human agency was responsible for it. Thank you.

Attorney Costello's argument was convincing. But it would convince neither Major Holben nor the Court. It was recognized procedure for Holben to have the last word. Most of his remarks were reiteration, but two points are intriguing:

> I feel that Counsel's statement as to the Convening Authority's action should best be brought to his attention in some official correspondence and not in argument. I am sure that the Court will take this up with the Convening Authority with that in mind without having him read it as part of the argument.
>
> Some reference has been made to an accident. I wish that this could be written off as an accident. There is nothing that I could wish more. But I am afraid that when a man takes people who he knows cannot swim into water up to his neck—and I refer to testimony of the recruits that they followed Staff Sergeant McKeon into water up to his neck and their necks—and that he knew that they could not swim—some of them—and that they subsequently drown—at least four of the six that drowned could not swim sufficiently to pass their second-class test—I feel that that is evidence of gross and willful disregard of probable consequences under those circumstances. The probable consequence being, under those conditions, someone would drown. This is not an accident. I have nothing further.

The Court of Inquiry closed at 9:40 P.M., Monday, April 16. It met for one minute the following morning. That afternoon it was open thirteen minutes to receive a roster of Platoon 71 and take judicial notice of moonrise and moonset—from the book which Sergeant Nolan, three days before, said didn't contain that information. Wednesday at 7:35 P.M. the Court opened long enough for President Greene to "swear by the Holy Scripture." The Court was then cleared and its findings were read into the record.

Findings of fact—which later analysis proves not entirely fact—are contained in thirty paragraphs. Findings of opinion take twenty more. These were quoted verbatim in major newspapers on May 2, 1956. Many are rcproduced in other parts of this narrative and it would be boring to review them here. One opinion, however, was unfortunate: It ricocheted. That opinion was: "that Staff Sergeant McKeon at the time he marched his Platoon into Ribbon Creek was under the influence of alcohol to an unknown degree."

Recommendations were that Matthew McKeon be brought to trial by general court-martial under four charges while Elwyn B. Scarborough and Richard J. King receive appropriate disciplinary action. We'll review those trials later. Right now it is more interesting to see what Joe Burger, star football and lacrosse player, Maryland '25, did when the ball was passed to him.

Major General Joseph Charles Burger, Commanding General, Marine Corps Recruit Depot, Parris Island, as Convening Authority of the Ribbon Creek Court of Inquiry had but one obligation: to endorse the record of proceedings and forward it to the Judge Advocate General of the Navy via the Commandant of the Marine Corps. This was Burger's opportunity to take positive action (granting always that Commandant Pate wasn't issuing private, oral instructions to the contrary). But the 9,000-word comment attached to the record merely proposed action. These involved Parris Island:

> As a result of the foregoing investigation, this Headquar-

ters proposes to take the following action: (a) Issue an order at Depot level placing all marshes, tidal streams, beaches and waters out-of-bounds for recruit training; (b) Initiate a study to revise the language and approach of certain lesson plans in Drill Instructors' School; (c) Initiate an independent investigation into the conduct of recruits of Platoon 71 while in the waters of Ribbon Creek to explore more fully the possibility of meritorious conduct on the part of individual recruits, with particular reference to Private Thomas C. Hardeman, 1587021, U. S. Marine Corps (deceased).

Burger proceeded at length to rationalize and deny the custom of night marches in Parris Island swampland. He developed in April a weak and overextended salient in argumentation which Emile Berman's superb generalship—with little effort—would pinch out and annihilate in July. Burger's tactic was so vital to the denouement of the Ribbon Creek incident that we must examine it carefully. This is what Joe Burger said on the record of Inquiry:

> Knowing that the marching of recruits into marshlands is prohibited, is there a practice to do so that is known and condoned at this command? The answer is found in the testimony of thirteen witnesses who were queried on the point. Of the thirteen, eleven had no knowledge of a platoon being taken into marsh areas, and two had hearsay testimony of something of that nature in the remote past. Staff Sergeant Huff stated he had "heard" of platoons being taken in the swamps when he first came here in 1954. Upon further examination he testified that it had never been done in a platoon of which he had been a Drill Instructor, nor had it been done in a Battalion to which he belonged. He stated he had never heard of it being done with platoons of the Second, Third, or Fourth Recruit Training Battalions, but had heard of platoons of the First Battalion being "out there." Queried further, he revealed he had never seen a platoon in the marshes, but at some time last summer, while drinking at the Staff NCO Club, he heard a man whom he did not know remark he (the man) had seen a platoon "in the boondocks in the First Battalion." The only other witness who had heard of a platoon in the "swamps" was Colonel William B. McKean who testified he heard of a "rash of marching" in the

"swamps" in Elliott's Beach area which motivated the prohibition of it at some earlier date. Court Exhibit 10 shows the prohibition existed in March 1955. It is believed Colonel McKean referred to the wandering into the marsh of recruits who were on night marches in 1954 when scouting and patrolling was taught as part of the recruit training program. However, the point is immaterial, since the record shows that entries into the marshes in that area were halted over a year ago. The eleven witnesses who had no knowledge of marching or training in marsh areas (before 8 April, 1956) were: Sergeant Richard J. King, Junior Drill Instructor of Platoon 71; Colonel David W. Silvey, Assistant Chief of Staff, G-3, since September 1953; Technical Sergeant John D. Perdeus, Liaison NCO, Weapons Training Battalion since November 1955; Captain Charles E. Patrick, Officer of the Day, Weapons Training Battalion; Lieutenant Colonel Robert A. Thompson, Commanding Officer of Third Recruit Training Battalion; First Sergeant Herschel L. Baker, Field Sergeant Major; Master Sergeant Hans C. Manthey, Chief Drill Instructor; Captain J. D. Green, Assistant Depot Adjutant and former Adjutant of Third Recruit Training Battalion; and, with respect to Platoon 71, three recruits: Privates Moran, Porter, and Rambo. These thirteen witnesses represent a cross-section of personnel at this Depot from recruits to Colonels with three years of local duty. Assuming that one or two platoons may have been marched in the marshes during the past year, the record proves that it is not a practice, and that isolated instances (if any) are not known to the command. It therefore could not be condoned.

Burger's effort to deny existence of the practice of night marches into swamps becomes ludicrous when we analyze the argument of Major Duane Faw, his ghost writer. Faw relied on the record of Inquiry even though its Counsel, Major Holben, didn't probe too deeply. Faw also gave weight to negative information, which isn't information at all: Just because a host of people haven't heard of a practice doesn't prove that practice fails to exist. Then Depot Legal Officer Faw lifted the remarks of his eleven witnesses out of context to sustain his proof; let's evaluate these: Sergeant King, who did his Boot Training at San Diego, said he had thought about night marches into swamps and had idle conversation with different people which brought the idea into his mind that they could have happened. Colonel Silvey's questioning concerned the use of marshes for training; he said that he didn't know whether they had actually been used, but if they had he contended it was unauthorized. Sergeant Perdeus' questioning was limited to the time he had been Liaison NCO at Weapons Battalion, and in context to the Weapons area. Captain Patrick was similarly restricted to his eight months in Weapons Battalion and the "area behind the rifle butts along Ribbon Creek or in Ribbon Creek;" Patrick went through Boot Training at Parris Island and also spent eighteen months in Recruit Battalions during his current tour. Colonel Thompson limited his remarks to authorized training and was champion of strict adherence to schedules. Sergeant Baker had never been a DI and admitted: "In past performances of any incident that's ever happened in one of my Battalions, I have been the last one to know about it." Sergeant Manthey denied knowledge of any misconduct by DIs except what he read in the newspapers—and doubted—or saw in court-martial orders; Manthey is an old member of the DI Clan. Captain Green is an administrator who seldom gets out of the office. The three recruits hadn't been around long enough to know much of anything. More important, Major Faw knew full well that we don't weigh evidence by tallying the number of witnesses pro and con.

Tuesday, April 10, shortly after noon, we were preparing for another drag of Ribbon Creek. *Thomas Hardeman* was still missing. Fifteen to twenty Weapons Battalions marines were standing near our shaky pier behind the butts. No outsiders, particularly reporters, were in sight. I was curious about the custom of swamp marches and took an informal poll. First I asked how many went through Boot Camp at Parris Island. That eliminated two; one was my Sergeant Major, John Langston, who became a marine the easy way at San Diego. I asked of the remainder how many as recruits had been marched at night into swamps. The show of hands was a clear majority. Then I asked how many, of their own knowledge, could testify that fellow recruits had been marched through swamps during Boot Training.

The show of hands was unanimous. Staff Sergeant Fortner claimed he had had that experience virtually every night.

Master Sergeant John Clement, a sound Texas gentleman in whom I have the utmost confidence, told me that many times on his previous tour at Weapons Battalion he found in the Dredge Cut evidence, such as tracks, clothing, and equipment, indicating some outfit had marched through.

My curiosity was satisfied. The poll was a fair sampling of different enlisted ranks over a considerable period of time.

General Burger came out to Ribbon Creek about two o'clock that afternoon and stayed until our frogman, Sergeant Seybold, recovered the body. During our anxiety and waiting, I told Burger about the poll. He listened attentively but made no comment. The following week he preferred to listen to his training expert, Dave Silvey.

When it came time to comment on night swamp marches, this is what Faw wrote for Burger's signature:

> It is believed Colonel McKean referred to the wandering into the marsh of recruits on night marches in 1954 when scouting and partrolling was taught.

Faw didn't need to gaze into his crystal ball, he only had to dial 6216 to find out what I knew. He wasn't reluctant to talk with Silvey and then write for Burger:

> Recruits have no occasion to enter a marsh except on the trip to Elliott's Beach. Although it was not shown in the record, the prohibition in that area was not made as a safety factor. I am advised that the restriction was imposed to prevent recruits who were off course on a night compass march from being unduly muddy.

Except that swamp marching was not condoned, Joe Burger's argument is specious. Though he didn't write it himself, Joe shouldn't have signed it: He knows the value of negative information. Joe Burger was senior member of the last full-length Junior Class at the Marine Corps Schools, Quantico, before World War II. He completed the course in May 1940. Since

I was a student in the same course the previous year and an instructor while Joe was there, I know that he listened many times to the hazards of negative information. For instance, take a large woods. You may have it scouted by aircraft, a tank section, or a cavalry patrol. Reports of the enemy are negative. That still doesn't preclude an enemy regiment concealed in those same woods looking down your throat.

Faw's belittling Huff's testimony by saying: "Some time last summer, while drinking at the Staff NCO Club, he heard a man he did not know remark he (the man) had seen a platoon in the boondocks" demonstrated either that Faw was not interested in sifting information to find truth, or that he was slanting his analysis as directed by Burger. Huff wanted to assist McKeon, but at the same time he wasn't about to incriminate himself while testifying under oath nor to squeal on any fellow DI. Huff's shrewdness proved its merit when Burger denied immunity to witnesses for McKeon.

General Burger's endorsement of the Inquiry record mentioned the scope of investigation. This is what he had to say:

> It is pointed out that my appointing order does not in any way limit the scope of the investigation, but permits the Court of Inquiry to delve into any act or omission that may have contributed either directly or indirectly to the incident. The record has been reviewed not only to determine if the facts and opinions found by the Court are supported by the record, but also to determine if the scope of the Inquiry was broad enough to answer certain peripheral questions raised by the occurrence of such an incident. It is my conclusion that the investigation, itself, was sufficiently broad in scope, but that the findings and opinions do not fully reflect the scope of the Inquiry. This may be explained by the observation that the Court did not make findings of the obvious facts—those things well known to the Convening Authority because of his familiarity with and proximity to them, but which are not so obvious to Reviewing Authorities.

While Burger was satisfied, Commandant Pate wasn't:

> I do not agree with the action of the Court in confining its

finding of fact and opinions to the relatively narrow issue of the degree of culpability attributable to Sergeant McKeon.

Burger and Pate might have done well to read all of the testimony carefully. They would have found that Holben's thesis was: If it isn't authorized, it isn't legal. The Court obviously had the same attitude. It has been traditional for marines to read their orders carefully and execute them to the letter: "Not for them to reason why." For years the Navy has taunted marines because they did this—and then called for marines to enforce compliance when strict obedience was mandatory. While both may lay the blame on Staff, Burger and Pate should be more familiar with marine psychology.

Though Joe Burger disregarded marine psychology, he was not reluctant to get involved in legal psychology. Thomas Costello's request for immunity of witnesses failed to impress the Old Man. This is Burger's analysis:

> At the conclusion of the proceedings, Counsel for the Party requested immunity for certain unnamed prospective witnesses. Conditions under which immunity would be considered were announced to Counsel and no witnesses were produced. The Court offered to produce any witnesses desired by the Party, but no witnesses were requested. A close examination of the remarks of Counsel indicates they were made for effect, only, and they are not considered as evidence. It is considered that if there was any witness who could testify to any matter favorably affecting the interests of the Party, the witness would have been requested. But assuming that the Party knew of one or two individuals who at some time may have taken a platoon into the marshlands, and who would testify if granted immunity, it is obvious from the manifestations of guilty knowledge that such conduct was undertaken surreptitiously, and is not known to any responsible person at the command. The acts could not therefore be condoned. The fact that others, unknown to this command or its subordinate units, had on rare occasions taken a platoon into the marshes would in no way explain or excuse the conduct of the Party; particularly since the act of the Party involves marching into a tidal stream, and not into a marsh.

This argument shows Burger's (or Attorney-Major Faw's)

refusal to face reality. Costello knew what he was doing. It wouldn't be sound judgment to reveal plans for his defense when McKeon was not yet on trial. If Parris Island wanted to play ostrich, Costello could do nothing about it—except bide his time. But Costello's calling on Burger to disqualify himself did make an impression.

Burger might have convened a general court-martial forthwith. There would have been no obstacle in "importing" officer members and lawyers from other posts to avoid bias. That is what eventually happened. But Burger lacked confidence:

> Counsel for the Party raised the question, in his argument, of the competency of the undersigned to act upon the record of proceedings of this Court of Inquiry. In view of the administrative nature of the proceedings I do not consider myself in any way disqualified to act on the basic record. The position and objections of Counsel for the Party were not directed to my qualifications to convene a general court-martial; however, the rationale is more nearly appropriate to such action. The incident has had a profound effect upon all members of this command and it is doubtful if a court could be assembled of personnel from this command who have not formed an opinion on some material issue. Although I do not consider myself disqualified to convene a court-martial to try the charges and specifications appended, I consider that my refraining from doing so will avoid the issue and prevent any breath of suspicion with regard to the trial. The charges and specifications are therefore forwarded herewith with the recommendation that they be referred for trial to a general court-martial convened by higher authority.

There is a law of gravity peculiar to the military: When you pass the buck upward, an ax falls.

14

Leadership

Brigadier General Francis Ivan (Ike) Fenton, Sr., highly decorated, professionally skillful, socially popular retired veteran of the two World Wars now in Atlanta supplementing his pension distributing liquor to military installations in the Southeast, made his routine call at Parris Island while the Marine Corps Commandant was fretting over the record of the Ribbon Creek Inquiry. Ike's observation was concise: 'There's nothing wrong with the Marine Corps that a few years of peace won't cure." And Ike's diagnosis is implicit: The Corps needs marked reduction in size leading to stability in manning its combat units which over time will enable its return to a professional basis. That professionalism may readily be summarized: sound leadership.

If marines of the future are to serve their nation and meet past standards they must regenerate a solid core of professional leaders, officer and NCO. Lieutenant Commander W. Winter, Naval Reserve, in a 1949 issue of *Naval Institute Proceedings,* viewing the Navy in retrospect during postwar reaction evaluated professional officers as competent and self-sacrificing. Herman Wouk, whose *Caine Mutiny* is too frequently quoted for opposite purposes, recognized in Navy procedures a master plan fragmentized by excellent brains for effective execution by the inexperienced surge manning the Fleet on mobilization. Wouk also paid tribute to professionals—including his villain, Queeg—who kept the Fleet at sea while the Navy could be expanded.

There is no question that leadership ability of both officers and NCOs has degenerated to the danger point over the past seventeen years. One major cause is dilution. We started with 1,350 officers in 1939 and reached a World War II peak of 37,660. Most of our early losses at Pearl Harbor, Tientsin, Guam, Wake and Corregidor were taken by our hard core of professionals. Postwar demobilization dropped our officer strength below 7,000; then expansion for the Korean police action bounced it back to more than 20,000. Strength in Staff NCOs fluctuated proportionately. Ten years after V-J Day the second lieutenants who finished Basic School in 1941 were in the upper quarter of the lieutenant colonels' roster and even then the list between them and the Commandant was spiked fifty per cent with ex-Reserve officers—all too many of whom integrated because the salary was attractive—who turned professional during demobilization. During both expansions *ersatz* officers filled blank files after brief training and virtually no practical leadership experience. Hundreds of NCOs fleeted up—but we frequently lost good sergeants and gained incompetent lieutenants in the exchange—and this further diluted our once hard core of Staff NCOs.

When the prewar officer competed for an appointment it was clearly understood he was making the service his vocation. He was free to resign any time he decided he had made the wrong choice. One lieutenant, after involved politics which obtained him a commission from the ranks, married, finished Basic School in Philadelphia, and went to Quantico, where he was assigned to four-in-a-box living quarters. His wife was unhappy because she was accustomed to more refined circumstances; moreover, she noted that Smedley Darlington Butler, then Commanding General, had comparatively lavish accommodations. Father-in-law, who worked so hard previously to get the lieutenant his appointment, again visited the Major General Commandant, Wendell Cushing (Buck) Neville. "How much does it cost to buy a second lieutenant out of the Marine Corps?" The reply was immediate. "Two cents. Tell him to mail his resignation directly to me." In a matter of hours the unhappy youngster was a civilian—he became more unhappy later, but the process wasn't reversible.

Now we have a large, completely different influx: those fulfilling obligated service. Rather than be drafted into the Army as a private, these characters do the minimum work necessary for a commission because they think life as an officer easier than that in the ranks, and also they wish to exercise some control over when they do their required service. A large share of these draft-evaders just mark time waiting for their release. This was pointed up by a Recruit Battalion Sergeant Major sitting on our Re-enlistment Board: "Well, sir. They go to Basic School and stay at Quantico until basketball season is over. Then they come down here for a season of football and basketball. After that they come into a Recruit Battalion for about three months to complete their active duty. What can we expect?"

Then we have our temporary officers, though they are professionals and hence attentive to duty. Many in this group have been both officer and enlisted man twice, some three times. For them the future is most uncertain. When they complete enough service for optional retirement, they want out.

Nor is our present-day American environment—or this stage of the pendulum swing in our culture—encouraging for military leadership. In July 1954, A. T. Lawson, writer of management articles, argued in *Military Review* that our leaders come from the people: Army leadership will be no better than its people. Discipline, courage, dependability, justice, accuracy, alertness, and integrity are qualities that have been forgotten. When in history men have turned from God to the unstable values of materialism, the soul of the nation—and the Army—has soon been lost. Our Government needs to adopt policies which will regain and maintain proper respect for authority.

Despite our astronomical budgets and gigantic mobilization base we're in the cycle traditional among English-speaking peoples expressed by Kipling's "Tommy this and Tommy that and Tommy wait outside." Armed power for peace is considered a necessary evil. Professional soldiering is viewed as a temporary occupation for second-class citizens. Civilian jobs for first-rate technicians and leaders are waiting for all. The youngster who completes professional training, such as engineering, doesn't even go job hunting: He relaxes on campus awaiting the most attractive offer.

But more insidious is the postwar trend toward derogation of the services which comes from press, classroom, and pulpit. One viewpoint was stated by H. G. Telsey in a 1949 issue of *Naval Institute Proceedings:* Those features of military society which are traditional yet objectionable ornaments to the structure of the military services must be separated from those other features which are the foundation stones, the beams and the girders of the military edifice. Americans require individual opportunity, a degree of individual importance, and self-respect. We need to revise court-martial procedures, eliminate "caste." The traditional powers, privileges, and distinctions of our commissioned officers exceed those which are due to their office. The officer corps must become a military aristocracy—founded upon merit alone—whose members will have powers, privileges, and distinctions conducive to the proper performance of their functions and assured to them through being necessary.

Lieutenant Colonel A. L. Wermuth, General Staff Corps, sees this problem from a different aspect in April 1955 *Military Review:* The spirit of mass man is depreciating the quality of our future soldiers. A highly developed society requires conformity, not individuality. Liberty means freedom to do what one ought to do. Mass man repudiates his obligation to defend his society. Mass man insists that only self-discipline is worth while—but military discipline must be imposed from without. The stereotype of World War II novels was the ruthless, callous, self-glorifying commander. None of the Doolittle Board was an ex-enlisted man; their recommendations were central to the career Army. But none would be living under the conditions he influenced. Legislative prescriptions favor militant minority groups—which have no responsibility for the security of the nation. The Uniform Code of Military Justice has interfered with the requirements of military discipline. Yet military man is among those few who regard it a privilege to serve their country.

Lieutenant Commander F. C. Dyer, Naval Reserve, agrees on one point with Colonel Wermuth but in December 1954 *Military Review* has a more altruistic objective. This is the gist of his reasoning: Recent war novels have amounted to a diatribe against the officer caste. The officer is usually the villain while the real enemy is seldom considered. An officer could read these, list the undesirable deeds and traits, use the list as a guide for proper officer conduct, and hope that time and good faith will bring him the qualities agreeable to the literary interpreters of the scene.

For more than ten years we've had a military stalking horse: caste system. In fact we've reached the point in the social sciences where Professor Cecil A. Gibb, an Australian who wrote the Leadership chapter in *Handbook of Social Psychology,* 1954, only considers that man a leader whose influence is voluntarily accepted by his followers—this would exclude the lieutenant assigned to command a platoon of reluctant draftees. Many social scientists plug for "democratic leadership" and refer to the basic experimental work done by Dr. Ronald Lippitt, but they neglect analyzing his description of the democratic atmosphere: Policies and goals are determined through group discussion, the leader merely offers technical advice when needed—and even then suggests alternative procedures, members of the group work with whomever they chose, tasks are apportioned by common consent. Under those rules could we ever again report, "The Marines have landed and have the situation well in hand"?

Mr. E. A. Gibson, who spent ten years before the mast in both the merchant marine and Navy deck service, in a 1949 issue of *Naval Institute Proceedings* defends the caste system as an essential. He shows that it engenders mutual respect between officer and sailor and points out that enlisted men do not feel inferior: They expect noninterference with their privacies. He calls newsmen of the day inadequately informed from biased samples.

This concerted drive against the officer caste—and that also includes the professional NCO—had a profound effect: It led to the Uniform Code of Military Justice, which in my opinion is not uniform, nor military, nor justice. Rear Admiral A. E. Jarrell pointed out in a 1954 issue of *Naval Institute Proceedings* that civilians now control the most important function of command—discipline—yet they assume none of the responsibilities of command. In different context, Army Brigadier General P. M. Robinett said in the April 1952 *Military Review:* "It is the duty of a military man to step down when his considered opinion is set aside by political superiors. To defer to superiors on the ground of civilian control is only base flattery unworthy of a soldier." That is one solution to the problem.

Yet for over 150 years we were governed by good old "Rocks and Shoals," legal code of the naval service. It served us well, though it had to change with the times. The 1800 version limited us to using a plain cat-of-nine-tails; it couldn't be made of wire nor could its lashes be knotted. But no longer in the Code is old Article 1, which legislators relegated to a different portion of the Revised Statutes:

> Commanders in the naval service are required to show in themselves a good example of virtue, honor, patriotism, and subordination; to be vigilant in inspecting the conduct of all persons who are placed under their command; to guard against and suppress all dissolute and immoral practices, and to correct, according to the laws and regulations of the Navy, all persons who are guilty of them; and any officer who offends against this article shall be punished as a court-martial may adjudge.

I believe this article was omitted from our new Code because our culture now demands curbing the prestige as well as the authority of the Commanding Officer. Through the long history of war the last thing any professional soldier expected to attain was wealth. His motto was taken from Richard Lovelace, who 300 years ago said: "I could not love thee, Dear, so much, Lov'd I not honour more." Or in the modern terms of British Major Reginald Hargreaves stated in October 1953 *Military Review:* "The vital spark is that single-minded devotion which places duty before all thoughts of self and counts the day well spent only when the self-same stern, unbending spirit of duty can find no cause for reproach." But the age of chivalry is dead!

No longer do we entrust our nation's destiny and the lives of our sons to the professional military leader; rather we watch over him with our democratic form of political commissar: the legal beagle. Our modern officer's commission is an anachronism: "Know ye, that reposing special trust and confidence in the patriotism, valor, fidelity and abilities of Joe Doakes, I have nominated and by and with the advice and consent of the Senate do appoint him . . ." Our modern administrators by their every act belie that trust and confidence. This problem was so well described by Lieutenant Colonel Robert D. Heinl in a 1956 issue of *Naval Institute Proceedings* that only a complete reprint of his text could do it justice here. Let me give a typical example from my own experience:

A Weapons Battalion junior officer was apprehended on Parris Island by MPs for speeding. In "traffic court" he stated to Major Horace William Card, Provost Marshal, that his speedometer was broken and so he just followed traffic in the 35-mile zone. Card demanded his keys and sent a corporal MP outside to drive the car and verify the lieutenant's story. He was excused when Card found it to be true. When I was a lieutenant that officer would have resigned at the instant his statement was questioned. But no longer is an officer's word his bond.

Another way our administrators dishonor every military leader from general to corporal is in their campaign to insure loyalty (Democrat, Missouri) or security (Republican, Pennsylvania). Every officer takes an oath to "support and defend the Constitution of the United States against all enemies, foreign or domestic, and to bear true faith and allegiance to the same." Every enlistment contract is sealed with an oath to "bear true faith and allegiance to the United States of America" and to "serve them honestly and faithfully against all their enemies whomsoever." When Mr. Truman issued his Executive Order No. 9835 he merely said he expected in the future the same loyalty from the Armed Forces he had received in the past. At that time among 90,000 active marines nine were under suspicion—and I believe all were later cleared. But eager-beaver file-builders—unfortunately they were military legal beagles—wanted more paper to process while their civilian gumshoe camp-followers, who now spend so much time spying on homosexuals that one suspects their own normality, wanted an increase in force. They got both. Now we are coerced into swearing that we were telling the truth when we took our oaths of office and that we aren't subversive and that we don't belong to an ever-increasing list of subversive organizations that we've never heard of. Naturally, any real subversive would be happy to subscribe to the same oath every Monday morning before breakfast.

In 1953 I managed to evade security clearance when the Classified Material Control Officer, one John M. Lietwiler, addressed an order from himself rather than "by direction of the Commandant." Lietwiler included a brief discussion: "So the question has been asked: 'Who clears the Commanding Officer?' The answer briefly is: 'His Commanding Officer.' Well, of course, how far does that go on? It goes up to the Chief of Naval Operations who is exempt from such clearance by the fact that he is a Presidential appointee." All officers are Presidential appointees, but some two-striper who wrote the regulation for the Bureau didn't think of that. I remembered at least three full years during the war when I was required to read dispatches and plans of such high secrecy that up to this very day I try to forget their contents. But last summer the bureaucrats finally caught up with me at Weapons. I thought of the oath under which I had served continuously for twenty-nine years and toyed with the idea of a subversive group to which I belong: It once did overthrow the lawfully established Government in this country by force and violence while another time it came rather close. That group is the McKean family. Thomas signed the Declaration of Independence and was active in the Revolution; his grandson, Franklin Buchanan, commanded the Confederate States Navy. Though McKeans don't advocate overthrowing the Government at present, I'm sure each one reserves his inherent right to fight against an intolerable situation. Then I thought of the paper work in which I'd be involved—reams of it—with no consideration for the bureaucrats who would generate, then process it. Also I tried to forecast the reaction of General Lemuel Shepherd, stanch offspring of Virginia Military Institute—still proud of the Yankees their cadets slaughtered—and then our Commandant. Certainly I'd be on Lem's you-know-what list just one number higher than Colonel Frank Schwable, USNA 1929 and son of a marine colonel, who was crucified by General Shepherd for alleged collaboration with Chinese Communists despite the Inquiry's recommendation no disciplinary action be taken. So I chickened out and signed at the cost of my self-respect.

I'm convinced this *Gestapo*-like operation expected to insure security or loyalty is ruining the dignity and prestige of the Armed Forces. Yet equally bad has been the effort of two administrations and four Congresses to put a price tag on service. Instead of reinforcing the tradition of an honorable career in the profession of arms, the man in uniform is now treated as hired help—part of the work force—a member of "plant security" so to speak. The old *prerogative* is now a *fringe benefit*. Soldiering seems to be a technical skill to be hired and fired rather than a way of life. Misguided military boards and legislative committees spend fruitless hours devising "career incentives," all of which contribute to increased taxes. Clarence Francis, retiring Chairman of General Foods, had his speech quoted in one of the American Management Association publications: "You can buy a man's time. You can buy a man's physical presence in a given place. You can even buy a measured number of skilled muscular motions per hour or day. But you cannot buy enthusiasm. You cannot buy initiative. You cannot buy loyalty. You have to *earn* those things." If that is true in civilian organization, can you buy a man's life in the profession of arms? Campbell Huxley Brown, retired marine major, says: "A good marine is always broke, always thirsty, and always wants to be where he ain't." The professional soldier or sailor's philosophy is that he gives service—which is its own reward; he receives just enough while active to live decently, and when retired to exist. I used to consider it a basic economic assumption that the man in uniform could live nicely on $50 a month more than he gets, but considering what happened to the old gold dollar with which we started building up life insurance equities thirty years ago, I'd like to raise the ante to $100.

Weakening the authority and prestige of military leaders by attempting to "democratize" our Armed Forces is a problem to be solved by legislators. Perhaps our culture is destined to the maturity attributed to China where the scholar is respected and the soldier is scum of the earth. (In that event—and in the interest of recruiting—our history books should be rewritten so they no longer belittle the mercenary Hessians.) But we also have some leadership weaknesses that need correction within the service. One of these is the postwar tendency toward rigid specialization. Younger officers are failing to realize they're general practitioners, they limit their endeavors to their Military Occupational Specialty. Major Richard H. Kern called attention to this in December 1955 *Marine Corps Gazette* through an article entitled "The Numbers Game." Business is experiencing the same difficulty. Peter Drucker in September 1955 *Offiice Equipment and Methods* said: "The specialist tends to make his craft or function an end in itself; the new technology will demand that functional managers see the business as a whole and understand what it requires of them." W. B. Given, Jr., in a 1956 issue of *Management Review* entitled his article "Must managers specialize? The case for executive versatility."

Concomitant with overspecialization is clock-watching. Suggest to a Recruit Company officer he do an administrative chore when the recruit is off the training schedule, that young officer is horrified. Major James Young had Captain John Jagoda understudying him as Executive Officer. "The Colonel expects his Exec to be present at breakfast in the Recruit Mess at least once a week." Breakfast was at four-thirty. Jagoda responded, "What the hell do we have an OD for?" Yet the officer who is really interested in his troops visits them at odd hours. If Saturday night supper and Sunday morning breakfast, for example, are both satisfactory, you can be confident the cooks are on the ball at other times. If the barracks heads are policed by Church Call on Sunday, you don't worry about them at weekly inspection. Officers used to be available for a 168-hour week and leave was a privilege. Now leave is an entitlement—a fringe benefit—and we're urged to take every day of it to save the Government a few dollars in terminal leave payments. Perhaps clock-watching and leave-taking among the juniors is the cause of increasing coronaries among the seniors, a problem now worrying Admiral Arleigh Burke, Chief of Naval Operations.

Just at the end of World War II I had a case which combined overspecialization and clock-watching. The surrender came on exactly the wrong day for us: the effective day for redistributing shipping among three Amphibious Forces. We had hundreds of vessels scattered all over the Pacific and now were forced to redistribute our redistribution. The situation was so bad that in each dispatch order we included "report present location." Operations was in a real snarl, working day and night, needing help. I held my fingers on a group of naval gunfire liaison officers who had no more gunfire to worry about. Those not missing in the redistribution—such as one I have yet to meet—were assigned to Operations. One lieutenant after a day or two protested this work was outside his specialty and—more important—he had completed his forty hours, so he intended to relax for the remainder of the week. McKean's short course in military courtesy took care of that situation.

Then right alongside overspecialization is oversupervision. This results both from lack of experience among the juniors and from lack of confidence in them. It used to take an officer ten or twelve years to make captain: the Officer Promotion Act of 1947 contemplates six years; today it takes three years. That former partnership under the wing of an older officer—the lieutenant worked while the captain observed—has been lost; the experience was invaluable; captains like John Halla and George Maynard knew how to break in a lieutenant the right way. Not only that, the sergeants expected to help; George Monteith, senior buck sergeant in 64th Company, most respectfully taught me the fine points of close-order drill and practical aspects of infantry weapons that had been glossed over at Basic School. This is a healthy attitude which is also recognized in business, where W. B. Given, Jr., and B. J. Muller-Thym note that in developing himself the executive learns through subordinates. Yet we have a fast-growing military group adhering to the opposite philosophy who make no allowance for error. Lieutenant

General R. S. McLain, Army, said in March 1947 *Military Review* that the basic factor of leadership is innate. He called the leaders of World War II "synthetic" and contended they had to be given orders following a definite pattern because they would have been found lacking in many leadership qualities if they had been called upon to exercise their own judgment.

Oversupervision is a common disease in our culture. Major M. M. Boatner, III, Infantry, gives a neat description in August 1955 *Military Review:* "Like ulcers and coronary thrombosis, oversupervision is an affliction that stems from the most admirable of personal traits. Energetic and conscientious people are the most likely victims of all three diseases. The big difference, however, is that ulcers and coronary thrombosis are not contagious; oversupervision is, and can spread from an individual source down through the chain of command to debilitate entire units." Captain William P. Mack, Navy, in April 1957 *Naval Institute Proceedings* says: "We must press for greater progress, particularly in the field of removing some of the multiple layers of oversupervision now imposed on ship and unit commanders in order to restore their freedom of command." Reverend Theodore V. Purcell, SJ, Loyola University professor who made a comprehensive study of CIO Packinghouse Workers Local 28 in Swift & Company's Chicago plant, said in December 1954 *Armed Forces Management:* "Supervision is obviously necessary, but oversupervision is definitely unnecessary."

What was the state of supervision at the time of the Ribbon Creek incident? Lieutenant Colonel Robert A. Thompson, Battalion Commander, was asked to compare his own recruit training in 1934 with that of 1956. This is what he said: "Actually, we have more supervision at this time than we did when I went through recruit training here—and I mean both Drill Instructor and officer supervision. As I recall, we had only two Drill Instructors with the platoon. I only recall having seen one officer during my tour here and that was Captain Hollenburg, who turned out for the final inspection—after which we departed. I saw other officers, sir, but that is the only one who had any relationship with the platoon." Asked if he had an adequate number of properly qualified personnel in his Battalion to carry out his assigned training mission, Thompson replied: "I figure that I do, sir. That—in my opinion, I do."

Joseph C. Burger, Commanding General, took four paragraphs to comment on supervision for the Inquiry record. He described supervision by the Commanding General, Depot G-3, Battalion Commander, Executive Officer, Battalion S-3, Instruction Monitors, Field Sergeant Major, Recruit Company Commander, Chief Drill Instructor, Officer of the Day, and Commander of the Guard. In summary he said:

> It should be emphasized here that no attempt is made to maintain a commissioned officer physically present with each platoon at all times. To the contrary, Drill Instructors have been selected with meticulous care, and are considered to be as reliable as younger, less experienced junior officers. The duty Drill Instructor is considered to be on a true duty status with his platoon. He should require no closer supervision than any other duty noncommissioned officer. Experience has taught that, with rare exception, the Drill Instructor is worthy of his trust. Even so, officer supervision is considered important, and for this reason all company administrative duties have been removed from Recruit Training Companies in order to permit the officers to spend more time with the troops. Additional officer supervision is not indicated by the record of proceedings.

The Court of Inquiry's opinions were: "That Staff Sergeant McKeon was carefully selected, properly instructed, and adequately supervised as a Drill Instructor. That the recruit platoons while stationed at the Rifle Range are adequately supervised by personnel of Weapons Training Battalion."

Then Randolph McC. Pate, Marine Corps Commandant, said: "I have established at Parris Island a separate recruit training command, commanded by a brigadier general especially selected by me, who will report to me directly in order that I may personally control and monitor steps which must be taken to insure more effective supervision of our recruit training." In his policy statement next day, Pate outlined his scheme:

> Recruit platoons will continue to be entrusted to the care

> of noncommissioned officer Drill Instructors. As a change from the practices of recent years there must be commissioned officer supervision of the manner in which each platoon is handled. This supervision is not to be such that it comes between the Drill Instructor and his platoon, but it is to be discerning enough that there is constant awareness of what is transpiring in the daily life of each platoon. This awareness must be such that discrepancies by the Drill Instructors in the handling of their platoons are noted. The correction of discrepancies must be handled by the appropriate responsible officers in such fashion that the recruits retain their perspective of the noncommissioned officer as their fountain of authority and knowledge.

Not described in either document was Pate's action setting up an inspection corps, outside Battalion organization and responsible only to his personally-selected brigadier, consisting of Lieutenant Colonel Richard L. Sullivan and ten eager young captains.

Up to this point we've examined the current Marine Corps deficiencies in that art without defining the word *leadership*. Dorwin Cartwright and Alvin Zander, University of Michigan professors, wrote the first textbook in Group Dynamics without defining the word yet admitting leadership is a most important element in their field. British General Sir William Slim says leadership is projection of the personality of the commander. An unidentified Irish writer in *An Cosantóir* of November 1945 points out that instances of good leadership are learned from each campaign while instances of poor leadership are not so well known because no one returns to tell of them or else they are not readily recognized. Brigadier General J. P. Holland, Army, in January 1956 *Military Review* says leadership is pride: pride in one's self, pride in one's fellow man, pride in perfection. Holland maintains that leadership is not taught, it is instilled. Lieutenant General Willard S. Paul, who was then Army G-1, noted in May 1949 *Military Review* that two groups of urges affect the mind of an individual in the service: what he wants to do and what he must do. Paul contends that effective leadership is the catalyst which fuses these two incompatible elements into a high state of morale. Lawrence A. Appley, President of American Management Association, in his many writings defines leadership as the art of getting things done through people.

Yet we emulate Cartwright and Zander by passing over the *what* and dealing with the *how*. Each marine leader has a job to do with troops and equipment available to him. It isn't customary, nor often practical, to stage a pep rally, hold a caucus, conduct an opinion poll, or resort to the Australian ballot. Napoleon said the two levers for moving soldiers are interest and fear. British Lieutenant Colonel G. O. N. Thompson points out in September 1947 *Royal Engineers Journal* that once a right decision has been made or an order given it must be pursued relentlessly to its uttermost conclusion—a leader must be able to drive those who are not willing to follow him. And that gets us into the subject of discipline.

Discipline holds the Marine Corps together. It assures us that when the quarterback calls the signal every member of the team will be following through on that play. Some define discipline as instant, willing, cheerful obedience. But it is much more than that. Discipline requires intelligent understanding of the Mission of the outfit—the job in hand. It requires that the small-unit leader use his initiative: When the situation changes from that predicted and he lacks time or opportunity to communicate with his superior, it may require that he actually disobey an order so that his efforts may contribute toward accomplishment of his mission. Discipline enables us to predict the behavior of team members. This was nicely illustrated when newsmen in the office of the Commandant, General Thomas Holcomb, were lauding the defense of Wake Island. Holcomb retorted, "What the hell did you expect, anyway?"

Fundamentally we obtain discipline through a system of rewards and punishments. This requires finesse. Overdoing either is harmful. Between these two extremes, of course, come exhortation, persuasion, and example set by the leader who expects his subordinates to imitate him.

Rewards come to the professional in form of promotion, important assignments, medals, commendatory letters, and occasional words of appreciation from a senior leader. Yet in the long run, all of these are vacuous symbols. Even the enjoyment of a fine professional reputation is a rather blank reward. What really counts is one's own self-satisfaction in knowing the job was well done: His plan worked; his objective was taken with little confusion and minimum casualties; his problem child is back in line.

Persuasion may be illustrated in the apt definition of discipline given to a group of midshipmen by a now-forgotten mustang aviator. His theme was flight discipline: "Gentlemen, discipline is merely the cumulative growth of other people's experience. If you will adhere faithfully to air discipline, you can expect to live to be ninety-nine and then be hanged for rape."

Example invariably reminds me of Colonel Archibald D. Abel, now dead, who bilged out of USNA 1926, did a short stint on the road selling women's apparel, then enlisted in the Marine Corps. Before Arch was commissioned in 1930, he had a DI cruise at the old East Wing of Parris Island. Boots in those days scrubbed their clothing after dinner each evening. Arch would station his platoon at the scrub rack, get them started, then he and his junior would go back to their room and reappear each with a bucket containing a change of clothing: trousers, shirt, drawers, undershirt, socks. They would sit on the wooden barracks steps patiently washing these articles while the recruits were doing their own laundry. This spotless DI clothing took its place at one end of the platoon clothesline and was in fact most exemplary. There was just one minor facet that didn't come to the platoon's attention: Arch and his junior kept one clothing outfit for the sole purpose of setting an example; the clothing they actually wore went to the laundry.

But at the negative end of the scale we still rely on punishment, too often considered a synonym for *discipline*. The basic rule is to administer punishment to the individual for a specific offense; unjudicious mass punishment destroys unit discipline. In fact, Lieutenant Colonel J. W. Hopkins, Jr., Armor, stated in August 1954 *Military Review* that even mass censure is inherently dangerous, and qualified leaders would agree.

British Lieutenant Colonel G. O. N. Thompson, to whom

we previously referred, gives some rules for administering punishment: Never punish if there is another way; limit severity to that needed; don't clutter records with minor punishment; make punishment fit the crime; never bring the man to the Commanding Officer until you have done your bit and failed; never be prejudiced by a man's apparent bad record. Thompson's rules are generally accepted by Marine Corps leaders. We note particularly he distinguishes between formal and informal punishment, that which goes on a man's record and that inflicted by those leaders who may rank from corporal to lieutenant colonel but have no legal authority to give formal punishment. Noting this, it would have served the Marine Corps better for our self-righteous Brass to have evaded the question of *who* administers punishment. The law is clear in its positive sense by limiting infliction of formal punishment to specified leaders and specific methods, but the law is silent in its negative sense because it makes no general prohibition. Every leader worthy of the title continually gives minor punishment by claiming his device is "extra instruction," "necessary work," or "voluntary action" of the recipient.

Aboard ship the Captain alone can punish—but the Executive Officer holds a preliminary investigation, invariably termed "Executive Officer's Mast," and awards penalties to minor offenders in accord with a private understanding between the Captain and him. In turn, division officers "impound" a sailor's liberty card until he gets a haircut or new pair of shoes. They schedule "necessary" chipping and painting during liberty hours. My Captains aboard ship let me know with certainty that they disfavored seeing a marine at Mast. It was up to me to see that my boys didn't get there unless they committed a serious crime—and after punishment for that we shanghaied them.

One scheme I used was arranging and making known a hierarchy of jobs ranking from most to least desirable. Captain's orderly was choice; brig sentry underway or brow sentry at the dock were torture. Fine Captain's orderlies became corporals. Others slipped one or more rungs down the ladder with a chance to work back up. But that wasn't enough. What could you do with the brig sentry? Or the corporal you didn't want to take to Mast and have reduced? Here we needed mutuality of understanding. The offending marine knew that I had no legal authority to punish. But in consideration for my not taking him to Mast, he was usually ready to negotiate some "voluntary" action with the First Sergeant. In this way he could show remorse for previous behavior and signify good intentions for the future. Liberty cards were deposited for "safekeeping"—say, two weeks. Marine compartments and cleaning stations were more spotless than the galley. We also had a thrift plan: The more a marine saved, the less likely was he to get in trouble ashore. While some bought War Bonds, it was more usual to make a "deposit." This money was impounded to the individual's account—at 4%—until he was discharged.

Washington hadn't been long in commission when the Disbursing Officer's Chief complained to Steve Adalac, my First Sergeant: "What the hell's the matter with you marines, Steve? I brought aboard a year's supply of deposit books. Enough for any battleship." (He had about twenty books for an original allowance of 1,800 enlisted men.) "Two paydays and I have just five books left."

"Your trouble, Chief, is you don't know our marine captain. You'd better get enough books for our whole detachment!"

There was a different system when Paul Drake and I were lieutenants in George Maynard's company at San Diego. Lieutenant Colonel Thomas S. Clarke, Battalion Commander, could punish legally. But our Company B had its "sunset parade." We held troop right after morning colors. Let's assume Private Mich failed to run a patch through his rifle. Lieutenant Drake need only say, "Three day's sunset parade," and move on to the next marine. The platoon sergeant took it from there. Liberty Call sounded at three-thirty. If marines weren't in town and well-established by five, there was no sense going ashore that day—so we scheduled sunset parade for six. It was strictly extra instruction. Our miscreants turned out in service uniform under arms, stood another troop inspection which had to satisfy our NCO-in-Charge-of-Quarters, and when he was pleased they might secure their rifles and take off on liberty. But they seldom did. By that time of day they could find more pleasure over a quiet beer at the Post Exchange than they would going downtown. Each marine in Company B, 6th Marines, understood that sunset parade was strictly "voluntary." Without offense to our comradeship, he could ask to see the Battalion Commander. But when he did, there was the stain on his Service Record Book required by any official appearance at Office Hours. Moreover, the Old Man habitually lowered the boom. No one asked to see the Battalion Commander during my two years in the company.

But when the Old Man is lax or inconsistent, unofficial punishment is a different matter. The troops watch the odds. In this situation they would prefer to chance Mast. *Texas* was like that when she first went into reduced commission. Our skipper, Captain Fred F. Rogers, had spent years as a Japanese language student and naval attaché. The kindest thing one might say: He was regaining the feel of command. During his first six months aboard, the maximum punishment awarded was three days' bread and water—to a mess attendant who ran berserk with a knife. Just before we left the Pacific Fleet, Roy Fowell came aboard as my Gunnery Sergeant. A few days at sea and he was down in my office: "Captain, if you was told by a couple of punks to commit a physical impossibility, would you make it official or would you take 'em up on the fantail and beat hell out of 'em?"

"I'd prefer direct action, Fowell, but we're in a peculiar situation. You'd better make it official."

When the two culprits didn't want to negotiate with me, I was on the spot. All I could do was inform them they would go to Mast and I would do my utmost to make it worth their while. Fortunately, this skipper particularly disliked seeing marines at Mast. I laid my case before the Executive, a type who would give three different officers permission to use the Ship's-Service station wagon to go three different places at the same time. All I got from him was permission to see the Captain. It took diplomatic persuasion with the latter, but I finally delivered my message: If he didn't want marines at Mast, he had better clobber them when they did show up. Our Captain tried the case in joinder. Two jaws dropped in unison at his sentence: five days' bread and water. Marine brig sentries and corporals of the guard insured that there was no supplementary ration. Rumors went through the Marine Detachment that the Old Man did what I told him to do. There were no marines at Mast for the rest of that cruise.

Unofficial punishment and hazing seem to overlap in a vague twilight zone. Commandant Pate in his appearance before Congress and statements to the press emphasized *hazing,* a word not in the Parris Island vernacular, though it is in Depot General Orders related to maltreatment. Pate may have dredged up that word from his unconscious where it had been dormant since his "rat" days at Virginia Military Institute; or it may have been contributed by his alleged ghost writer, Major General Merrill B. Twining, who then commanded First Marine Division but is habitually summoned to Washington in moments of crisis. Two points indicate the latter: Twining was a midshipman at the Naval Academy when hazing flourished; Pate's statements are written in Twining's style.

Hazing entered our Anglo-American culture in 1678, derived from the Old French word *haser* which appeared about 1450. Originally in English it meant to affright, scare, scold, or punish by blows. About 1840 *hazing* appeared in nautical English, where it remains to this day and means aboard ship to harass by exacting disagreeable or unnecessary work. About 1850 *hazing* appeared on campus, where it means to harass with abusive or ridiculous tricks, to subject to cruel horseplay.

Lieutenant (junior grade) Percival Eaton McDowell, called "Pete" and an accomplished boxer because of his Christian name, 4th Division Officer of *Oklahoma* in 1927 used mass punishment —or hazing—in a situation I believe warranted. When it was raining topside early in the cruise he inspected midshipmen's lockers only to find them stowed with filthy clothing and crawling with roaches. He ordered the compartment policed up. A few days later a midshipman sounded off, "It's raining topside again.

I guess that sonofabitch McDowell will hold another locker inspection." To our misfortune Pete was on the other side of the tier of lockers talking with his bosun's mate. We heard from him next morning at Quarters: "A few of you gentlemen may not know what I'm talking about—most of you should—the others will get the word fast. Some midshipman volunteered a description of my character. Let me say I'm going to be just that for the rest of the cruise."

When gun drill was secured in the morning those in other divisions flaked out on deck while midshipmen in McDowell's division kept right on working. We chipped all the paint off a compartment just above the double bottoms and then we chipped the trunk leading to it from the main deck and then we painted both spaces and then we started chipping again; it was hot, ventilation was barely adequate, but every moment of the working day not devoted to ship's drills was spent manicuring that compartment until the cruise ended. Pete McDowell's action was legal; it instilled some sorely needed discipline in student officers. His bluejackets had good discipline; had the incident happened among them, he would have ignored it unless he could positively identify the culprit.

Hazing of the inappropriate college variety got so bad at the Naval Academy that Congress saw fit to pass a law forbidding it. Still the practice continued for years. Plebes questioned by outsiders were taught to deny that hazing existed. I've denied it though some hefty crew man had me "assume the angle," elevated himself on a chair, and lifted my feet off the floor by swinging a broom across my buttocks, that very day. DIs teach recruits to deny hazing exists. My nephew wrote from San Diego in 1941, in response to a straightforward letter I sent him when I had word of his enlistment, cursing the DIs roundly and telling me they warned him not to write home about what was going on; since I was a member of the fraternity, he didn't sense any violation of confidence in describing the situation to me.

When a practice such as hazing gets established in the culture—and we see it has been in western Europe culture 500 years—it isn't going to be abruptly eliminated by legislation, administrative edict, or judicial decision. General Pate's boldness in claiming he eliminated hazing at Parris Island is autistic thinking.

During both Inquiry and Court-Martial Matthew McKeon's Counsel raised the issue of "shock treatment" and if it weren't for that we could omit the subject here even though it is an interesting training phenomenon which faces the marine leader. CWO Walter Lawrence (Willie) Tate, with twenty-eight years in the ranks from private to warrant officer and the mainstay of any artillery outfit—to say nothing of being near genius in demolitions—believes recruits are confused during their entire stay on Parris Island. Like Willie Tate, Donald Anthony Chiapetti was once himself a recruit, but World War II, a tour in China, and the Korean police action made Don a captain and he heads the DI School. Don calls it "shock" and thinks it wears off in the first two or three weeks of Boot Training. Both Willie and Don agree fundamentally on the process.

Mom hovers over our teen-ager at home—presses his clothes, makes his bed, urges him to eat, picks up after him. Then one day he visits a Marine recruiting station. He is asked to sit down. The sergeant may even call him "Mr. Sadowski." Soon Mom and Dad sign the consent papers and the youngster is sworn in. No longer is it "Mr. Sadowski." It's "Sadowski, get over here!"

During the ride by train and bus he falls in with other victims of our propaganda. They compare stories they've all heard from other marines. These get added power through strong imagination and repetition. A wondering group is facing the unknown. Rather much fear has developed before they debark at Yemassee. Here nothing is done to allay that fear. Our receptionist at Yemassee is invariably a martinet. He has learned to spot any new recruit on his visible horizon. He loses no time in making himself known and taking charge. There is no need for a hearing aid to make out his orders. He gets the rabble under control. Yemassee is a dry, forlorn railroad crossing, below the average one encounters on Southern roads. Even then the recruit doesn't see the better part of that small town. He is herded into a dinky, crowded barracks to await the next bus.

Now the sergeant at this receiving barracks has several jobs. One, as Marine Corps representative at this outpost, is to maintain our prestige. He keeps his modest principality looking like an oasis in the desert—without any permanent help assigned. And so he immediately puts these new marines to work: painting the fence, mowing grass, swabbing down. There is but little time—he learns to make the most of it. All too soon for the unofficial mayor of Yemassee, his draft boards a bus. Smaller groups have gradually merged into a larger one. Conversational interaction has increased. Being kept busy tended to subdue the talk at Yemassee. But this 35-mile ride operates to give it free rein. There comes a hush when the bus stops at Recruit Receiving on Parris Island.

Here an alert, practiced NCO takes the mob in hand. It becomes immediately known that he will be addressed only as "Sir." The crowd is herded into a dingy hut and seated on backless benches. Travel orders are turned in, rosters compiled, a platoon is tentatively formed. The NCO's talk is stereotyped. His answers to questions are curt, rarely satisfying or reassuring. Once he has formed a unit, the men are herded outside the shack and turned over to the tender mercies of their DI.

The DI loses no time in self-introduction. During the weeks to come, he is BOSS. The Marine Corps has certainly played a dirty trick on him this time. While the prospect is dim with such a misbegotten dredging of riffraff, he's going to try and make MEN out of these S-birds—men and MARINES. Two ranks, right face, the platoon straggles off. It is a long walk to Hygienic. When the sun isn't bearing down a cold wind whistles. Our DI isn't expected to keep these boys in step, though he does encourage silence.

Eventually, after time to build up severe mental pressure, the Boots are halted outside another dingy building. They may have some time to wait—quietly. Entering one room they shed all valuables and small personal effects, place them in a numbered canvas bag, accept a metal tag as receipt. Already attached to a cord, this tag is hung around the neck. The line moves slowly into the next room. Loud voices are here, too. Recruits strip and place all clothing in numbered bins. A naked line forms with a hospital corpsman at the head. He switches a flashlight over each body, with particular attention to pubic hair, and conducts a "short arm" inspection. This embarrassment alone is enough to cause a modest boy to have nightmares for a week. But it is impersonal and conducted with assembly-line precision. The line sets the pace for the workers.

We turn left and wait at the next door. Just inside is a straight, barracks chair behind which stands a Negro barber with power clippers. His hair is long and wavy, he usually needs a trim. Most of the recruits do, too—they get it. In a matter of seconds the recruit is virtually skinned. Above his shoulders he resembles a Mexican hairless dog. He moves to the right and goes through the showers. Here is plenty of soap—the last the Government will furnish—and also close supervision. He scrubs, washes off, goes through a foot bath, and dries down. The line forms by a counter. He draws socks and drawers, putting on a pair of each. While he is waiting, one of his fellow recruits measures his chest size and marks clothing data on his bare right arm with an indelible crayon.

As he passes through other stations he is fitted with shoes, ungainly utility uniforms, and other components of the first issue. Such as he doesn't wear goes into his brand-new seabag. Then he reclaims his small personal effects and forms a line at the adjacent hut. Here he sends home by mail or express all of those articles he left back in the bin. By the time the recruit shoulders his seabag and heads for the Recruit Battalion area, he is in a state of shock. Regardless of his former environment and status, he has gone through a great leveling process. He has been just another naked body without any hair. Now with a burden on his back, he is still heading toward the unknown. In Parris-Islandese, "he's shook."

If every American citizen could see with his own eyes the change we induce in our recruits, none would question our contribution to society. Two brief glimpses of the same platoon would suffice: The first is a view of that motley rabble straggling into Recruit Receiving; the second comes twelve weeks later when the platoon is marching in perfect cadence, heads held high in pride of achievement, beautifully turned out in the uniform of the season, en route to the bus station for departure on Boot Leave. You must see this to believe it. After months living with the system it is virtually impossible to comprehend. While there is no difficulty in becoming familiar with our procedures, understanding the psychological dynamics may some day be possible as progress in social science continues.

I believe the most difficult period in the life of the human male is in the late teens. He is in that twilight zone between childhood and adulthood. He is attempting to leave the one group and gain admission to the other. In the old environment his behavior was rather well specified and he had learned to conform. In the new environment he is given freedom of choice. But he becomes confused when he discovers that this is an area of conflict: conflict in ideologies, attitudes, values. At times he is shy and sensitive, at other times his inner conflict leads to outward aggression. He is entering a new world, the prospect is unclear, he is uncertain. This is a time of emotional instability .This is also the time he becomes a recruit. He has just left home and Mom's inevitable apron-strings. (Often he joins the Marines to get away from them.) Now he is on his own in a brutal world.

We teach him obedience first off. He may have had techniques for circumventing the will of parents and teachers; the DI will overcome those. Nor is it blind obedience: We try to teach him intelligent obedience, conformity with the accepted rules of the group. In due course he becomes imbued with discipline, discipline that originates from within but—it must be admitted—is policed from without. Now there are those people who contend that the only pure form of discipline comes voluntarily from within. These people view the military with alarm. They claim to achieve their goals through persuasion and teaching the individual to think for himself. They contend that Natural Law will take care of reward and punishment. Up to a point there can be no argument, but we continue to have our police forces and prisons. Thousands die on the highways because they are unwilling to conform with the considered judgment of their fellows. In our culture, discipline to be effective must be both positive and negative.

Our recruit learns responsibility—integrity, if you will. He learns that both his life and that of his teammates depend on him. He learns punctuality, often for the first time. He acquires dependability. Along with this he becomes imbued with patriotism. There are many on the outside who consider this misguided chauvinism. They believe strong feeling of nationalism is a taint. Despite that our Boot absorbs this attitude along with the glorious tradition of our Corps. Then he will be available to defend our shores and protect those internationally minded idealists in their reveries.

Of course we're simultaneously equipping the Boot with the tools of his trade: rifle and bayonet, their related tactics and technique. But we're also forced to review many things he should have learned at home. We insure that he knows how and does bathe, shave, take care of his feet, safeguard his health.

We had a Baltimore boy at the Naval Academy—and since he's now a disabled, retired rear admiral, I shan't identify him—who bathed once a week whether he needed it or not: He figured that bathing oftener would sap his strength. Five or six days each week he took a vigorous workout in the gym. Before his habits suffered an abrupt change—instigated by the upper-classmen at his table in the messhall—he went around all day smelling like the Navy goat.

Regular hours, substantial food, and hard work make a considerable difference in the health of the Boot. Jim Eiland, Food Service Officer, was once accused of not giving the troops enough to eat. He weighed one platoon upon arrival and again on completion of training. There was an average gain of eight pounds a man—and it must be noted overweight Boots reduced the average. Those needing it are fitted with glasses. Hernias are discovered and repaired. An appendix erupts and is removed. And the operation in the Dental Clinic is terrific. What impressed me more than anything while getting a new denture was learning the number of recruits who require a full set of false teeth.

Nor should we forget the chaplains. Without any proselyting, they struggle to get the boy in church. Baptisms and confirmations are numbered in the hundreds. Voluntary classes of religious instruction are continuous. Many a mother asks the chaplain to persuade her son to return to his church: a task in which she has failed. And this points up an observation not always pleasant to contemplate: While the sample is somewhat biased, our recruits are a cross-section of Young America.

The DI who accomplishes this metamorphosis is a Staff NCO—and we've had a rash of letters from the Commandant dealing with Staff NCOs. These suggest that those in the staff grades are not what they used to be and we're exhorted to train them in leadership, to give them authority and prestige. Yet as recently as February 1956 Captain Frederic Alvin Green noted in *Marine Corps Gazette:* Seldom does anyone in today's Marine Corps have sufficient authority to perform tasks commensurate with the responsibilities of his rank. The Corps is great today because, in the past, every marine regardless of rank could be counted upon to think and act in any situation. We must assign tasks rather than pre-outlined step-by-step solutions.

Our DI makes the Marine Corps. We select him carefully, using the best techniques we know. We train him conscientiously for the job—and have a truthfully uneconomical attrition in training. Then we turn over sixty to eighty long-haired civilian children to his care. He lives with them twelve weeks, ten on schedule. He teaches them how to wash behind their ears as well as the elements of destroying an enemy while remaining alive on the battlefield. So we hand him several pounds of paper containing step-by-step solutions. We keep him on the job while Special Subjects Instructors and junior officers punch the clock. All too often we display our lack of confidence in him. When his enlistment expires we hand him a sheaf of paper telling him how good things are in civilian life and then offer "fringe benefits" encouraging him to re-enlist.

At the Ribbon Creek Inquiry, Colonel Robert A. Thompson, Matthew McKeon's Battalion Commander, was questioned about a DI's discretion:

Q. Now, sir, does a Drill Instructor have any discretion above and beyond the actual orders that are written down in the Standing

Operating Procedure or Battalion Orders or Depot Orders as far as the training of the troops is concerned?

A. He has not as far as recruit training is concerned. I think it is rather a complete and thorough coverage in the recruit lesson plan which develops the training schedule itself and in the Standing Operating Procedure for the training of recruits and the additional orders which the Battalion publishes.

Q. Your testimony then is that the Drill Instructor can not go outside of these specific instructions as laid down. Is that right?

A. Not legally. That is correct, sir.

Q. And would you say the Drill Instructor has a great deal of discretion as to how his platoon is going to be disciplined?

A. Not as how they are going to be disciplined, no. As to how they are taught discipline, the training schedule specifies it, but as far as a Drill Instructor disciplining a platoon, he has no authority to do so.

Captain Richard P. Grey, McKeon's Company Commander, was more realistic:

Q. I believe you mentioned something about a Drill Instructor having the right to give the men extra activities, which might cover items not specifically covered in the SOP.

A. The Drill Instructor is encouraged to see that his platoon is gainfully occupied at all times.

Q. And it is his discretion to decide what these extra activities shall be?

A. It is.

Q. It is not set forth in any SOP specifically what it shall be?

A. Not that I recall—except the plan for physical drill.

Q. During the evening there are certain specific instructions as to how the men should spend their time. Isn't it a fact if a platoon falls behind in their schedule the Drill Instructor will use the evenings to bring his men up to par—or up to schedule?

A. It is to the Drill Instructor's advantage to do so.

Here we have the DI guided in the theory of his job by conflicting policy views of his leaders. On the field, in the practice of his job, he is ground between two millstones: recruits on the bottom, officers and the law on top. Almost every DI will crack if he stays on the field too long; there are individual differences in tolerance. But this is the most valuable leadership experience in the whole Marine Corps. Could I write policy and draft promotion plans again, every sergeant would prove his success as a DI before he was qualified for promotion to staff grade. This would include cooks and motor mechanics, stockmen and clerks, photographers and armorers, fly-boys and gravel-crunchers. It is our best practical test of leadership short of combat—and Parris Island could be made an experimental laboratory for the study of leadership.

Now if you're sure the millennium is approaching and there is no further need for the military, we can translate our sermon into civilian language. For more than thirty years the Harvard group, sparked by Mayo and Roethlisberger, has been preaching from one text: "While material efficiency has been increasing for two hundred years, human capacity for working together has in the same period continually diminished." So those lessons we learn in the military—usually the hard way—can be adapted to civilian application by social psychologists and professional managers in business and industry.

Douglas Freeman, deceased Richmond editor and historian of the Army of Northern Virginia, in one of his lectures summarized the leader's job most effectively: Know your stuff, be a man, look after your men. Major C. S. Glew in April 1954 *Canadian Army Journal* says: An officer imbued with high ideals, a complete and sympathetic understanding of his men, the iron hand in the velvet glove, a willingness to accept responsibility, a good turnout and a healthy attitude, ability to make decisions, a wholesome degree of humility for his own shortcomings, respect for his men, ability to take a crack in the shin, has the spark of leadership. Lieutenant Commander Malcolm W. Cagle notes in a 1949 issue of *Naval Institute Proceedings* that junior officers must get to know their men intimately, but without familiarity; personally, yet with dignity. Commander Charles S. Arthur in the same journal the previous year divides the method of leadership into three categories: by contract, the method of democracy; by compulsion, the method of dictatorship; and familistic. Arthur believes that paternalistic leadership is the fountainhead of military valor. Perhaps military leadership doesn't need to be paternalistic, but that's the way it is. The effective unit has the feeling of belonging to a family of which the leader is the authoritarian but normally benign head. The material which binds this group together is individual integrity, which generates the mutual respect of all members. (One can make a good thesis contending soldiers fight for a leader, not for an abstract cause. Soldiers in the *Guardia Nacional de Nicaragua,* for instance, fought for Lieutenant Puller or Lieutenant Beans—they didn't understand the concepts of nationalism, freedom, democracy.) Finally, this paternal leader deals with individuals—marines—and permanently eliminates from his vocabulary the term *personnel.*

Perhaps we're learning more as we go on, but our code of leadership behavior is not new. It was reduced to writing and published as a General Order by Major General John Archer LeJeune shortly after he became Commandant in 1920. Since then it has appeared in each edition of the *Marine Corps Manual.* Marine leaders who guide themselves by this doctrine are on their way to success:

> RELATIONS BETWEEN OFFICERS AND MEN
>
> *Comradeship and Brotherhood.* The spirit of comradeship and brotherhood in arms which has traditionally existed throughout the ranks of the Marine Corps is a vital characteristic of the Corps. It must be fostered and kept alive and made the moving force in all Marine Corps organizations.
>
> *Teacher and Scholar.* The relation between officers and enlisted men should in no sense be that of superior and inferior nor that of master and servant, but rather that of teacher and scholar. In fact, it should partake of the nature of the relation between father and son, to the extent that officers, especially commanding officers, are responsible for the physical, mental, and moral welfare, as well as the discipline and military training of the young men under their command who are serving the nation in the Marine Corps.
>
> The recognition of this responsibility on the part of officers is vital to the well-being of the Marine Corps. It is especially so, for the reason that so large a proportion of the men enlisting are under twenty-one years of age. These men are in the forma-

tive period of their lives, and officers owe it to them, to their parents, and to the nation, that when discharged from the service they should be far better men physically, mentally, and morally than they were when they enlisted.

To accomplish this task successfully a constant effort must be made by all officers to fill each day with useful and interesting instruction and wholesome recreation for the men. This effort must be intelligent and not perfunctory, the object being not only to eliminate idleness, but to train and cultivate the bodies, the minds, and the spirit of our men.

Love of Corps and Country. It will be necessary for officers not only to devote their close attention to the many questions affecting the comfort, health, morals, religious guidance, military training and discipline of the men under their command, but also actively to enlist the interest of their men in building up and maintaining their bodies in the finest physical condition; to encourage them to improve their professional knowledge and to make every effort by means of historical, educational and patriotic addresses to cultivate in their hearts a deep abiding love of the corps and country.

Leadership. Finally, it must be kept in mind that the young American responds quickly and readily to the exhibition of qualities of leadership on the part of his officers. Some of these qualities are industry, energy, initiative, determination, enthusiasm, firmness, kindness, justness, self-control, unselfishness, honor and courage. Every officer should endeavor by all means in his power to make himself the possessor of these qualities and thereby to fit himself to be a real leader of men.

May I add one footnote? The further an officer progresses in the military hierarchy, the more human lives he controls, hence the more personal humility he should feel.

15

Supervision

GENERAL BURGER'S REMARKS attached to the Inquiry record are dated April 24; multiple copies probably reached Washington next day. There Staff at both Headquarters Marine Corps and the Judge Advocate General's Office worked overtime to "process" the record—members of the Congress were impatient.

First reaction at the Seat of Government was this message from the Commandant to Parris Island on April 30:

> CONTINUED PRECAUTIONS ARE DIRECTED TO INSURE THAT INTEMPERATE USERS OF ALCOHOL ARE NOT ASSIGNED DUTY AS DRILL INSTRUCTORS X PARTICULAR VIGILANCE IS DIRECTED TOWARD THE ENFORCEMENT OF CURRENT PROHIBITORY REGULATIONS CONCERNING THE USE OF ALCOHOL IN ANY FORM WHILE PERSONNEL ARE IN A DUTY STATUS 301301Z

Only later did we learn how busy was that Monday on both sides of the Potomac: Commandant, Judge Advocate General, and Secretary of the Navy all signed their endorsements to the Inquiry proceedings while General Pate himself made arrangements to meet the House Armed Services Committee next day. Here are extracts from remarks Pate added to the record:

> The apparent cause of these deaths was the act of an assistant Drill Instructor who led his recruit platoon into a tidal

stream as an incident of a night march ordered by him on his own initiative for presumed disciplinary reasons. The convening authority approved a recommendation for trial by general court-martial and I agree that this is necessary. Accordingly, the charges are forwarded for action by the Secretary of the Navy.

The case of Sergeant McKeon is a matter for disposition in accordance with the Code, but other matters must be considered. The Marine Corps system of recruit training has been drawn into question. In a very real sense the Marine Corps is on trial for the tragedy of Ribbon Creek just as surely as is Sergeant McKeon. I will not blind myself to this fact, nor will I seek to disown the responsibility which is mine as Commandant of the Marine Corps.

Where other services have taken pride in West Point and Annapolis, the Marine Corps has formed somewhat the same attachment for its celebrated recruit training depot, rightfully regarding it as a unique and outstanding institution. It has provided hard and grueling training but has nevertheless taken a strong hold on the rank and file of those who have known its rigorous environment. Men who were destined to become cabinet officers, senators, congressmen, college professors, generals, admirals, and other outstanding personages are numbered among the legion of young men who have passed through it. Few of its graduates have ever condemned it.

Recruit training consists in preparing and conditioning mentally, physically, and emotionally a group of young and naturally well-disposed youths to meet the experience of violence and bloodshed which is war. It would be a poor rationalization to profess any other objective.

For the individual there is nothing logical in war, there is no reward for him save the satisfaction of fulfilling his duty to the nation, tempered by the bleak prospect of dismemberment or death. Men who face the ordeal of battle without flinching do so because of some loyalty, some abstract sense of dedication to cause or purpose, some natural or instilled pride in resolute behavior sufficient to override every natural instinct for survival.

The deliberate inculcation of this spirit has always been the supreme object of our recruit training. Parris Island over the years and through the wars has put forth a remarkable breed of hard, well-trained and fiercely loyal young men admirably trained to serve the nation's purpose of winning the wars in which it engages. These men form an elite group which is the envy of every general staff in the world. On the battlefield they have never given their nation a moment's cause for doubt or shame. They have done everything their country has ever asked them to do and usually much more.

These men are products of a system which also produced the tragedy of Ribbon Creek. This system is characterized by its exclusive employment of senior noncommissioned officers entrusted with the duty of teaching men to be marines. In a Corps which has been unique in regarding the noncommissioned officer as the backbone of its recruit training structure, an assignment as Drill Instructor carries with it the highest stamp of approval.

The only reward for such an assignment lies in pride of selection and sense of accomplishment. This duty is not shunned but it is not sought after. It means a lonely, withdrawn existence of constant surveillance, long hours of drill and instruction and intense concentration on the attainment of detailed perfection. I know of no harder life anywhere in the armed forces nor do I know of any finer or more dedicated group of men than the square-shouldered drill sergeants who perform this arduous task.

Since World War II some practices have crept into the handling of recruits which are not only unnecessary but do not comport with the dignity of the individual or his self-respect. Such practices were extremely rare in the past. While they are still relatively rare, I attribute their increasing appearance in recent years to the lack of mature judgment on the part of a certain few Drill Instructors. This has led occasionally to senseless acts in the nature of hazing and having no place in an ordered and responsible military institution. Hazing, indignities in any form, mass punishment or disciplinary marches to the point of exhaustion form no proper part of our recruit training system. The system has continued to engender loyalty and love of country and to produce hard-fighting marines in spite of any such abuses—certainly not because of them.

The Marine Corps is on trial in a moral sense just as is Sergeant McKeon. The supervision of our system of recruit training must therefore be reorganized.

Pate stated he had directed a reorganization which would increase supervision and also entail reassignment of certain officers. This would involve a separate Recruit Training Command responsible directly to him, an Inspector General of Recruit Training at his Headquarters, and staffing the Depots with selected officers to supervise and monitor the conduct of recruit training. Pate continued:

> A brigadier general will report to me directly in order that I may personally control and monitor the steps which must be taken to insure more effective supervision. I will continue this extraordinary organization under my direct and personal control until I am convinced there can be no cause for any American to offer reasonable objection to the program. I have issued instructions that any form of treatment incompatible with accepted American standards of human dignity be absolutely eliminated. While we have recognized the need for closer supervision, we are convinced that actual training of recruits must be conducted by the same men who give them orders in battle—the noncommissioned officers.

Next morning Randolph Pate went to Capitol Hill. The full text of his comments was released to the press, but none of Burger's 16-page analysis was made public. Burger pled that supervision at Parris Island was optimal, while the Inquiry reported McKeon in particular and recruit platoons on the Rifle Range in general received adequate supervision. We had to wait for another, more private statement from Pate to determine the basis for his contrary opinion.

Before that we should hear what he announced orally to the Committee. The New York *Times* stated that Pate transferred Burger "for viewing the case too narrowly as a manslaughter action against one man and failing to recognize also a moral issue involving the whole Corps." Yet Pate failed to describe or elaborate on the "moral issue."

But Pate did elaborate on the Inquiry findings: Besides the public scandal involving mass punishment, vodka, and those not drowning being eaten by sharks charged against Matthew McKeon, the Commandant added treatment incompatible with

American standards of human dignity and charged it against the Marine Corps. Later he would be plagued by his contention that these practices crept in since World War II; too many ex-marines would insist there had been no remarkable change in the system in forty years and that they still valued their experiences. This would induce an ambivalent reaction in Pate and handicap his later decisions. By May 10 newsmen forced Pate to announce that he transferred officers "not to punish them, but to speed the fresh approach to the problem of supervision."

Randy Pate, son of a naval constructor, was born on or near Parris Island, February 11, 1898. He entered Virginia Military Institute in the same year that his distant cousin and predecessor in office, Lemuel Cornick Shepherd, Jr., graduated. Both descend from the highly reputable Cornicks of tidewater Virginia. Pate was commissioned a second lieutenant in 1921. For twenty years he had duties characteristic for marine officers of that period, such as Santo Domingo, Haiti, Hawaii, and China. If Pate's experience deviated from the norm, it was in emphasis on Staff: His only combat command was the First Marine Division in Korea.

He began World War II as D-4 (Logistics Officer) of the First Marine Division, commanded by Major General Alexander A. Vandegrift. While Pate had "staff responsibility" for the confusion and waste on Red Beach at Guadalcanal, he is not accountable—this was the first time marines in amphibious operations faced reality. Neither organization nor training were designed to cope with the overwhelming logistic problem of supplying a division. Two experiences marked Randy's service at Guadalcanal: During an air raid one night he jumped into a slit trench—only to discover it was designed for something else. In mid-campaign he developed tropical ulcers and was evacuated. The flying boat which took him out was hung up on a coral reef several days before its occupants were rescued.

When Commandant Pate visited Parris Island immediately after the drownings his most important action was his statement—policy guidance for us all—that the Marine Corps had nothing to hide. Word passed that reporters and photographers should be extended all courtesies. Questions would be answered freely. Newsmen might interview recruits from Platoon 71.

The wisdom of this latter decision may be questioned. Those Boots were young, impressionable, generally inarticulate, emotionally shaken. Colonel Heles' Court of Inquiry wouldn't convene until the following morning. That Inquiry had the job of developing facts heavily cloaked in obscurity. Even in civilian life legal authorities find it necessary to confine material witnesses and for a time hold them incommunicado. Any cry of "censorship" from the press would have been counterbalanced by the needed quest for truth through normal, legal channels. Thus Pate encouraged trial by public opinion from the beginning. Evidence is bound to suffer contamination when witnesses' imaginations are stimulated by those seeking human interest stories in contrast to cold, hard, detailed facts. But the most important question about Pate's we-have-nothing-to-hide directive was: Did he mean it?

Wednesday the publisher of Beaufort *Gazette,* Howard Cooper, requested an interview with Sergeant Johnny Taylor, Weapons Battalion Commander of the Guard. It was evident he was capitalizing on Pate's invitation. Cooper's intimacy with Parris Island led him to Weapons Battalion, site of the incident, for an inside story. He selected Taylor both as a principal witness and enlisted marine: Cooper knew from experience that marine officers are usually reticent. I intercepted Mr. Cooper to protect Sergeant Taylor. By the time we were through talking, Cooper had the bulk of his story from me. I let him have it as I had seen it; he quoted me freely.

When that issue of Beaufort *Gazette* reached Washington a reporter from Washington *Post and Times Herald* telephoned me. This interview lasted about half an hour and the resulting story was essentially a rewrite of Cooper's. The reporter tried to get me to make admissions contrary to fact; for instance, that Parris Island officers encouraged and condoned night marches through swamps. It was a rough argument, but this newsman neither put words in my mouth nor misquoted me in any way. Pate read the story next morning. Scuttlebutt had it that he was unhappy. Then when Greene set up his Recruit Training Command, Staff superimposed upon Staff, he gave us the party line, something like this:

> The Commandant has said that you're all free to talk to newspaper reporters. You can tell them anything you want. I'm not about to change the Commandant's instructions. If you care to, go ahead and talk to reporters. What you say I'll read in the papers. And if I don't like what you say, goddammit, gentlemen, you'll leave Parris Island that same day! I have verbal authority to transfer any and all of you immediately. So when it comes to reporters you'd be much safer if you sent them to me. I'm ready to talk to any of them.

If the Marine Corps had nothing to hide, why did Pate so fear a Congressional investigation? This fear is apparent from the postscript to his policy statement of May 1:

> As a result of my statement of the action I am taking, the Committee has decided to hold any further action on their part until we have had a chance to demonstrate that we can set our house in order of our own accord. The Committee has given us ninety days to demonstrate that we can and will do what I have said we will do.
>
> Let there be no mistake about it. The House Committee has merely deferred the decision as to what action they will take until we have had a chance to show that they need take no further action. In an election year, they have shown a most generous confidence in our good intentions and in our ability to produce results.

That "Policy of the Commandant of the Marine Corps Governing Recruit Training," unsigned but dated May 1—Brigadier Greene carried a bundle of copies to Parris Island—was obviously intended for private distribution. But a copy did reach the hands of Emile Zola Berman and thus embarrass Trial Counsel at the Court-Martial. This twelve-page document, with a two-page postscript added when Pate descended from Capitol Hill, was based "upon what has been disclosed by the Court of Inquiry and by additional facts which have been developed outside the record of the Court." Those "additional facts" could only have been generated by letters, phone calls, conversation, and telegrams, none subject to Rules of Evidence or evaluated by scientific method—as lawyers describe them, all were ex parte. Against these charges Parris Island had no opportunity to offer defense. Here are some extracts:

> The picture which is forming shows our recruit depots as repeated scenes of callousness and brutality in an atmosphere of coarseness and verbal filth. I am not going into the details, but I must admit that those things are sufficiently prevalent to give an element of substance to the public picture of our training system.
>
> As a change from the practices of recent years there must be commissioned officer supervision of the manner in which each platoon is handled. Now I come to those things which we now clearly recognize as excrescences which, over the years, have grown upon the system. They had no part of the system of recruit training as it existed for many years.
>
> The first of these unhealthy practices to be removed is the tacit divorcement of the commissioned officer from the supervision over the conduct of training of the recruit. The practice has varied in degree from time to time and place to place. But it is true that in large measure the noncommissioned officers who are the Drill Instructors have been left to their own devices with hardly *pro forma* acceptance of responsibility by the responsible officers for the daily conduct of training. Never again must we find that officers in recruit training units cannot remember when they last made a visit of inspection—or that an officer of the day charged with inspection of recruit units believes his duty is satisfied by a whisk through the area in a vehicle.
>
> The next practice to be eliminated is that of a sustained attitude of vulgarity and coarseness—even filth—toward the recruit. I do not expect marines to be plaster saints, but we will no longer tolerate a Drill Instructor who must interlard his remarks to a recruit with a constant stream of vulgarity and verbal filth. In regard to this practice, I am not inclining in any way toward those persons who profess to believe that a recruit camp should be like a Sunday School.
>
> Next to be eradicated is the practice of hazing and maltreatment, ranging from senseless acts of the type indulged in by

> sophomores, to outright acts of brutality. The nature and number of them have no doubt varied. Acts of personal humiliation and indignity have no place in a system intended to produce a prideful and self-respecting marine. Acts of brutality are criminal acts—forbidden by law. I have received many letters from former marines, supporting our system but which mention these acts. It has come as a shock to me that these practices have become so common in recent years that there were few who had not seen or experienced them.
>
> The tragedy at Parris Island brought to light the use of liquor in circumstances which are outside the pale of conduct by men of probity.
>
> The complete conduct of affairs at the recruit depots must undergo a general improvement in their tone. A healthy, vigorous and alert organization for recruit training must not be made to suffer from being within an organization which takes a routine lackadaisical attitude toward its general conduct of affairs.
>
> We must have the whole course of events fully documented. We must know what we first find out as to the prevalence and nature of malpractices. The incidence of such things as forced marches to exhaustion, punishment duck-walks, and other physical maltreatment, the hazing and personal indignities of heads-in-buckets, verbal, filthy abuse, public ridicule for receipt of personal and private letters, all incidents of this nature must be known. We must know what we did about them.

The logical fallacy in accepting such evidence of questionable validity lies in generalizing from the specific. The inductive method can never establish generality as a certainty. During the previous three years marines serving at Parris Island were convicted of murder, larceny, extortion, perjury, drunkenness, burglary, forgery, assault, adultery, desertion. But should all Parris Island stand condemned? Here we see the Commandant preferring five charges against Parris Island, withholding the usual legal rights from those accused, and maintaining that "treatment incompatible with accepted American standards of human dignity must be absolutely eliminated"—all in one breath.

It's rather certain General Pate brought Major General Merrill B. Twining, brother of Nathan F. and Robert B., also capable professional officers, from California to ghost-write his Inquiry endorsement and his policy statement. Staff phone calls, Parris Island to Washington, confirmed this and the style is that of Bill Twining. (He claims to have invented *unilateral,* is fond of *excrescence,* and learned *pro forma* at law school.) But thirty-five miles south of Headquarters, at Quantico, was Lieutenant General Edwin A. Pollock, who five months previously was in command at Parris Island. Al Pollock had more intimate knowledge of Parris Island than any other general officer; if Bill Twining were ever there, it was as a lieutenant. Pollock's knowledge combined with his political acumen and gentlemanly moderation could have proved invaluable—and when a new Commandant was being selected late in 1955, it was touch and go between Pate and Pollock.

16

Court Meets

WHEN BRIGADIER GREENE'S Inquiry record got to Washington it stayed in the mill there for a week. What happened at the seat of Government is anybody's guess, though one point is certain: It wasn't processed through three offices in one day even though endorsements of the Commandant of the Marine Corps, Judge Advocate General of the Navy, and Secretary of the Navy are all dated April 30. It is most probable that following "crash" conferences all three endorsements were approved in the "rough" and then some junior officer "walked it through" for signature the day prior to Randolph Pate's appearance before the Congressional Committee.

Then on May 4 Charles S. Thomas, Secretary of the Navy, signed his appointing order for the Court-Martial, which was directed to convene ten days later. Just at this time Emile Zola Berman stepped in: He wasn't about to consent to summary procedure. Berman, of course, had his current schedule to meet and he used that to plead for postponement. Besides, he wanted to get a background check on each member of the Court, which would take more time. There was even another, more compassionate wrinkle: Betty McKeon was expecting late in July. It would be convenient psychologically to have the child born during the trial. Berman got his postponement for two months, until July 14. Apparently no one looked at the calendar in the Navy Department to see that this was Saturday.

By July 9 the Secretary had to modify his appointing order. Whether Berman's background investigation had anything to do with the change will remain a matter for speculation, but three members of the original Court were relieved: Lieutenant Colonel Robert D. Shaffer, Lieutenant Colonel Walter Gall, and Lieutenant Commander Hampton Hubbard. Simultaneously Captain William L. Otten, Jr., was appointed second assistant Trial Counsel.

Limitation on court membership is only that, where practicable, the senior should be an officer not below the rank of captain. Otherwise, "the convening authority shall appoint as members such persons as in his opinion are best qualified for the duty by reason of age, education, training, experience, length of service, and judicial temperament." There is no definition of *judicial temperament* nor any scale for measuring whether or not the officer has it in an adequate amount.

The average Marine Corps member was thirty-nine and had over twenty years' service. Age ranged from thirty-two to forty-six; length of service from fifteen to twenty-five years. Judging from data in the Marine Corps "lineal list," all marine members had served in enlisted status, though one may have been a Naval Aviation Cadet. Colonel Hutchinson and Major Demas were recruits at Parris Island, the former in 1931 and the latter in 1944. The seventh member was a Navy doctor. With that summary we can list the jury:

Colonel Edward Leigh Hutchinson
Lieutenant Colonel Nicholas August Sisak
Lieutenant Colonel Duane Fultz
Lieutenant Colonel Daniel Joseph Regan
Major Edwin Thomas Carlton
Major John Gust Demas
Lieutenant (Medical Corps) Bentley A. Nelson

Naval justice got a new look in 1950. Replacing the old law which did right well for a century and a half, the new Code gives permanent jobs to a whole legion of professional lawyers in uniform. This Code set up the demand for a great influx of attorneys, many of whom returned to the service because they considered it more rewarding than their practice on the outside.

Regulations—"administrative law"—based on the new Code created a new caste: legal beagles. These are the only officers who can disagree with their Commanding Officer and annex their remarks to the case on which he acts. Legal Specialists take pains to convince the Old Man that the whole system has been changed, that without their guidance his head would go on the block. Too often they are convincing.

Their strategic point of emphasis is Art. 37, Uniform Code of Military Justice, which says in part:

> No authority shall censure, reprimand, or admonish such court or any member, law officer, or counsel thereof, with respect to the findings or sentence adjudged by the court, or with respect to any other exercise of its or his functions in the conduct of the proceeding.

But this article doesn't prohibit that authority from offering his constructive criticism nor exercising his inherent duty of general supervision. Nonetheless our unofficial "Military Bar Association" has been so persuasive that most Commanding Officers have decided to keep their fingers on their numbers.

When the new Code had been effective less than two years I was in the wilderness of a university campus rather than "at home" in the refined culture of a military establishment. We had a clear case of unauthorized absence on the part of my quartermaster. In taking action on the record after the trial I had the audacity to comment on the factual evidence. My remarks were purely constructive and expressed in eleven lines. Our District Law Specialist took three legal-size pages to write me up. Completely unfamiliar with the geography and details of local relationships, he read between the lines many ideas that were not in evidence. Finally he remarked:

> While the action of the convening authority did not prejudice the rights of the accused, it is felt that it is so contrary to the spirit and letter of the Uniform Code of Military Justice that some comment should be made on it. It would seem probable that this action was taken because of ignorance of the requirements of the Code and inexperience in its administration.

Now that lawyer had never seen me, knew nothing about me. As a fact my experience with naval courts-martial encompassed more than twenty years. I had even trained at least one young law school graduate (Harvard) in military procedures. And so the situation boils down to this: Military lawyers are free to admonish or censure a Commanding Officer but the process is irreversible!

Some day the new law will boomerang. We can find precedent in court-martial orders. My friend Andy, a likable but rather carefree soul, was judge advocate of a permanent court-martial. Two Navy nurses were on trial for smuggling liquor into the States in a Government ship. Andy was sympathetic. They were women, he liked to be chivalrous. They liked a drink, so did Andy. Besides, he had done the same thing himself on more than one occasion without getting caught. Andy was a clever lawyer but this time he failed in his duty. He made sure the gals received a valid trial so they could not again be placed in jeopardy. Then he so loused up his case the Court had no alternative to acquittal. Andy was tried and convicted for neglect. Under the new Code it is improbable the Convening Authority would even write him a nasty letter.

Friday afternoon, July 13, we meet something new under the Code: a pretrial conference in the regular court-martial room of Parris Island's Administration Building. Present were opposing Counsel and the Law Officer. Precedent was obtained from the *Army Law Officer's Manual*, 1954, which Judge Klein cited to bless the meeting with authority, since the old Code frowned severely on Counsel "trying the case out of court." Irving Klein led off:

"It is the sense of the meeting—as expressed by Mr. Berman—that it is to be informal, that no ruling needs to be made upon any matter submitted, that the purpose is to endeavor to obtain stipulations and agreement as to the *modus operandi*. Does that cover it?"

Klein passed to Berman:

"Captain Klein, it has been my impression—although I may be misguided—that several witnesses will be produced by the Prosecution to prove identification of the deceased, as well as cause of death.

I am prepared now to enter into a stipulation on the record conceding that the death of members of Platoon 71, who may be enumerated by name, was the result of drowning in Ribbon Creek on the evening of April 8, 1956, when Platoon 71 was led into that creek by the Accused, Staff Sergeant McKeon."

KLEIN: May I have a copy of the charges and specifications?

SEVIER: We neglected to bring those over.

KLEIN: You did not mention that this happened at night.

BERMAN: I believe I said "evening."

KLEIN: Are you willing to concede it was night?

BERMAN: I am not prepared to concede to weather conditions. I am only conceding identification, cause of death, and place of occurrence. *(A messenger from the adjoining office entered and whispered.)* I have been advised that the Commandant of the Marine Corps is on the telephone and asks that I speak with him. Do I have your permission?

KLEIN: By all means.

Berman, returning after seventeen minutes: "I am trying to avoid the necessity for putting proof in of the fact of death or of the facts of identification."

KLEIN: Now I just want to say one thing. You will agree—I am sure—that the fact of death is an element which must be proved.

BERMAN: It must be proved, but it can be proved by concession.

KLEIN: I think the Court of Military Appeals has criticized that approach.

BERMAN: Well, I don't know—

KLEIN: The concession of an element—of course, I am not rendering any opinion—

BERMAN: What do you think about it, Major?

SEVIER: Well, I am a little bit skeptical. I am in accord with the desire that you expressed—that of expediting the trial. I feel that there is a stipulation there of at least two required elements. I am in doubt as to the propriety of the acceptance of that stipulation. I would have to study the stipulation and I am not prepared to give my answer at this time.

BERMAN: Sir, may I make this suggestion? If there is any objection to the wordage or the terminology, I am prepared to accept any suggestion from Major Sevier which meets what I am stipulating. I am not concerned with what words are used.

KLEIN: The aim is admirable. The only question I can see is

the question of propriety and wisdom in view of judicial decisions. That is a matter for Trial Counsel to decide. [But Judge Klein would have to rule on admissibility.]

SEVIER: I may add—in all fairness to the Defense—my present intention is not to accept the offer of stipulation.

Counselor Berman changed the subject by announcing his intent to offer some aerial photographs as fair and accurate representations of Ribbon Creek. Judge Klein conceded that once a witness so described the pictures, grounds for admissibility would be laid. Prosecutor Sevier questioned they could be a true representation and suggested that viewing the scene would better orient members of the Court; he concluded: "Mr. Berman, on that we would like to kick it around a little bit. We will give you an answer because I am sure you are anxious to know."

Third item on Defense agenda was notice to Law Officer and Prosecutor that before the Court was sworn and in the absence of members of the Court, Berman intended to move that Charges I and IV, which alleged illegal possession and consumption of alcohol, be stricken. He promised copies of his briefs, already drafted and now being typed, by Saturday noon for Klein and Sevier to study over the weekend. Sevier questioned the propriety of such a motion while Klein admitted he would need to check the book. Lengthy conversations did not result in any decision. The next topic was courtroom arrangements:

SEVIER: I have a few administrative details I would like to take up. First of all, as to the arrangement of the courtroom. It is a little bit different. Do you have any comments or suggestions concerning that? If you do, I would appreciate them.

BERMAN: Major, I have not been there today, but judging from the arrangements I saw yesterday—and which I do not believe can be altered substantially—I believe it will be almost a necessity to find out whether or not we can get microphones for the witness, Counsel, and Law Officer. The acoustics in that room are not very good. They are extremely poor.

KLEIN: They are?

BERMAN: Extremely so. Members of the Court may have to lean out of their chairs and Counsel hover over a witness, while he is talking, to hear. It is going to make it very uncomfortable. I am sure they must have some kind of a system here where they can set up mikes by these witnesses and for the various participants. You would only need one at the Counsel table, one at ours, and one at the witness, and perhaps one for the Law Officer—since he would be called upon to make rulings—and maybe one microphone that you can hold and walk around with.

KLEIN: To walk around with?

BERMAN: Yes, to walk around with.

SEVIER: If it is available, we will get it.

KLEIN: Well, with your permission, I would suggest that we call in Major Faw. He may have explored the question and he may have some information for us on that score. (Duane Faw, Depot Legal Officer, was in his office diagonally across the corridor waiting for demands from his brother legal beagles who had been harassing him nearly three months. He came over to the court-martial room in answer to their summons.) Major Faw, the question has been raised as to the adequacy of acoustics—the hearing—in the courtroom. It has been suggested that perhaps microphones can be placed at the Trial Counsel's table, the Defense Counsel's table, the Law Officer's bench, and at the Witness Stand—and perhaps, too, a roving sort of microphone arrangement could be arranged. I don't know whether that question has been explored, but are you prepared to tell us anything about that?

FAW: Frankly I do not think it has been explored because I did not think of this in that light. I assume we are having a trial for the Court members.

KLEIN: Not only for the Court members. The purpose we have in mind is that the Trial Counsel, Court members, Defense Counsel, and the Law Officer, and the witnesses hear questions asked and answered. The audience may be an auxiliary beneficiary.

Major Faw made a long speech outlining his problems: The room they were now in was originally designated for the trial until both the Defense and the Public Information Officer appealed for more space. Then a room topside with twice the space was reserved and five air conditioners installed. A week ago Defense claimed that room inadequate to present their case. Now a complete new courtroom had been built in the auditorium of the Depot Children's School. Faw agreed the acoustics were such that people in the rear of the auditorium would have a hard time hearing a witness and concluded: "No effort has been made—to my knowledge—to produce microphones to broadcast the hearing to spectators. My first concern is that I know of no such equipment at this Depot—it took me seven months to obtain a conference microphone. My second concern is that I have never been in a courtroom anywhere at any time where a microphone was used. It is completely a novel impression to me. I would like to think about that myself."

KLEIN: It has been used in hearings to my knowledge.

FAW: Yes, in Congressional hearings. It certainly has.

KLEIN: It is not my personal experience having seen one in a courtroom. Have you, Mr. Berman?

BERMAN: They have been used in courts throughout the states, Captain.

KLEIN: The request is made. I suggest that it be submitted for consideration.

SEVIER: Sir, I believe the proper method is that the request be submitted to me and I will take it up with the representative of the Convening Authority. The request is considered as made?

KLEIN: That is right.

FAW: I will take it upon myself to inform the Chief of Staff who in turn will inform the Acting Commanding General immediately. We do not wish to delay matters.

KLEIN: That is the reason we asked you to come in here—to see whether the question has been explored and consideration given to it and to inform you of the request which is now made.

FAW: I did not want to go ahead on my own. As soon as I have a chance to consult with Trial Counsel—

KLEIN: Yes, he may have some views on it that have not as yet been expressed.

FAW: I would like to have an opportunity to talk to him before I go to the Chief of Staff with the idea.

KLEIN: Certainly.

FAW: I would like to talk to him privately.

KLEIN: Go ahead.

FAW: As soon as you recess I will be available and as soon as I talk with you I will go without paper work of any kind to present your request.

When Faw left the room Klein questioned Berman about his satisfaction with members of the Court and his intention to request enlisted members. Berman was noncommittal on the first and to the second question answered, "Presently, no." Then Berman complained that he knew a revised appointing order had been issued, he had been assured copies addressed both to New York and Parris Island, he still hadn't received one.

SEVIER: The order has come to this base addressed to the President of the Court. I haven't received mine addressed to me. I purloined a copy of it.

KLEIN: Let us expedite it. If it is addressed to the President—you have seen it—know where it is—and in the absence of the President, I would suggest you give them copies.

SEVIER: A while ago I was trying to offer them copies of that and the charge sheet. I will give them to you.

BERMAN: Copies of the charge sheet?

SEVIER: No. Extra copies of the charges for your worksheets.

BERMAN: Please don't misunderstand me, Major. I am in no way suggesting that you have been derelict or anything like that. I just knew that such an order was signed. The mails here are a little peculiar and that may well account for it. But of course it is important for us to get that as soon as we can. We are concerned with the composition of what we consider to be a jury and we would like to find out what we can about these jurors.

KLEIN: There is nothing else that concerns me. If you have further information that is proper for the Law Officer to know at this time, I would appreciate it.

BERMAN: I want to thank you, Captain Klein, for this meeting. I hope we have accomplished something productive—something of productive value from it. In any event I think it is good for another reason: It is good for the parties in the presence of the Law Officer to sit down and get some view of their attitudes and desires for a lack of technicalities and a drawn-out trial—if it can be avoided. That was my major interest.

KLEIN: Is there anything else?

BERMAN: I think that about does it. I presume that on some major issues of admissibility of evidence and what constitutes legally a defense we will have adequate opportunity to take that up as the proofs are developed. I will say, however, that we have offenses here alleged under *oppression*—and I think that you as we are going to find this largely a matter of first impressions. We have worked very hard in whatever direction we could find legally to be of assistance to you as well as to our client. We are here with a case so wide open that it is essentially a case of first impressions and we will have to deal with the legal concept as a first impression.

KLEIN: I will need help from you then.

BERMAN: We are prepared to do the best we can.

KLEIN: There must have been occasions of oppression and maltreatment, though, that have been tried. Have there not? You say you have not found any?

BERMAN: I would suggest to you, Captain, there was not a single definition of *oppression* to be found in important cases under the Code or before the Code or as far back almost as to the early origin of the British Navy. So when I say "first impressions" I am telling you it is the first.

KLEIN: Does the Manual define it?

BERMAN: No, sir.

KLEIN: I will not take time now to reply.

BERMAN: I shall certainly offer you a brief on this matter long before it becomes necessary for you to pass on any motions. I am simply calling your attention generally to the fact that we will really have to get down to allegorizing legal principles wherever they originate from. There is nothing simple about this case, that is for sure. With that happy thought, gentlemen, I will leave you.

Though Court was expected to convene Saturday, Colonel Hutchinson, Captain Klein, and Major Sevier agreed privately it would be more convenient to get underway Monday. As Trial Counsel, Charles Sevier might be compared with a District Attorney or State's Prosecutor in civilian jurisdictions, but there are differences. Trial Counsel does prosecute in the name of the United States, yet he is also responsible for obtaining and equipping the courtroom, issuing subpoenas for all witnesses, keeping the record of proceedings, and acting as master of ceremonies. He is forbidden to suppress evidence favorable to the Defense or to voice his own belief as to guilt or innocence of the Accused. While it is his duty to reveal the whole truth, it is not his duty to assist or advise the Defense.

Court opened at nine Monday morning in the specially rigged—though not yet wired for sound—auditorium of the Depot Children's School. Miss Lou Hiers, school principal, and old John Gannt, janitor, both of whom had served the school twenty years, had supervised construction of the "new" building in 1943, and had safeguarded it since, were displeased with this intrusion.

Prosecutor Sevier read the appointing order and noted the Secretary made a clerical error in Sevier's own middle initial. He was then prepared for a dramatic announcement: "The Prosecution is ready to proceed with the trial in the case of the United States against Staff Sergeant Matthew C. McKeon, U. S. Marine Corps. The Accused is present in court."

Five reporters were sworn, though three would be added later. Sevier announced that legal qualifications of the Prosecution were correctly stated and that none of the three Prosecutors had acted as Investigating Officer, Law Officer, Court member, or member of the Defense in this case or as Counsel for the Accused at a pretrial investigation or other proceedings involving the same general matter.

SEVIER: By whom will the Accused be defended?

VALENTIN: The Accused will be defended by regularly appointed Defense Counsel, Lieutenant Colonel Alaric W. Valentin, U. S. Marine Corps, and Major John R. DeBarr, U. S. Marine Corps. The Accused will further be defended by specifically requested individual Counsel. I wish to allow them to introduce themselves and state their qualifications.

BERMAN: Mr. Law Officer, Mr. President, members of the Court: My name is Emile Z. Berman. I am a member of the Bar of the State of New York, admitted to practice in those courts since 1925. I am also admitted to the United States District Courts for the Eastern and Southern Districts of New York and I am admitted to practice before the United States Court of Appeals for the Second Circuit of the United States.

LESTER: I am Howard Lester. I am an attorney duly admitted to practice in the State of New York, Eastern and Southern Districts.

COLLINS: I am Lieutenant Collins. I am certified in accordance with paragraph 27b of the Code.

JANKLOW: I am Morton Janklow, duly admitted to licensed practice in the State of New York.

COSTELLO: I am Thomas P. Costello, duly admitted to practice in the State of New York.

Sevier questioned the Defense about legal qualifications of

the two appointed Counsel and about previous involvement of any Counsel as Accuser, Prosecutor, Investigator, Law Officer, or member of the Court in this case. After satisfactory procedural reply, Klein's observation, though also procedural, is humorous in understatement: "It appears that Counsel for both sides have the requisite qualifications."

KLEIN: Has the Accused made a request in writing that membership of this Court include enlisted persons?

SEVIER: The Accused has not made such a request.

KLEIN: Proceed to convene the Court.

Everyone in the courtroom stood while oaths were administered. Prosecutor Sevier swore in members of the Court and Law Officer Klein. Colonel Hutchinson then swore in the three Prosecutors and seven Defenders.

KLEIN: The Court is now convened.

It was time for Sevier to announce the nature of the charges in McKeon's case, but Berman was on his feet: "Mr. Law Officer: The Defense proposes at this point to make some motions regarding the charges and specifications thereunder. We ask that these motions be heard now and that the members of the Court be excused during argument upon such motions."

KLEIN: Has Trial Counsel anything to state concerning the hearing of such motions?

SEVIER: Yes, sir. Trial Counsel submits such proceedings are improper. Further, that it is not provided for in the Uniform Code of Military Justice. Further, there are now no charges before the Court. Until Trial Counsel, at the proper time—at the time indicated in the *Manual for Courts-Martial* under rules prescribed by the President of the United States—until it comes that time where I present the charges and specifications to the Court, the Court has nothing upon which to entertain a motion.

BERMAN: Mr. Law Officer: I propose to argue both the procedure and the merits of the motion in the absence of the Court. It is a matter of law upon which the Law Officer—as I understand the Code—is charged with exclusive responsibility for determining.

KLEIN: Without determining whether the motion, on its merits, shall be considered in the presence of the Court, but now making the determination that the motion to proceed with the motion at this particular time, prior to the service of the—not service of, the presentation of—the delivering of the charges and specifications to the Court and the members, I will excuse the Court only for the preliminary purpose of determining whether the motion should be heard before the specifications and charges are put before members of the Court. The members of the Court are excused.

Klein listened to the motion to hear the motion. Then he listened to the motion. After that there were further difficulties for him to resolve. These arguments lasted five hours, but with two and one half hours of recesses it was eleven o'clock Tuesday morning before members of the Court could again settle comfortably in their chairs. They did come back once Monday morning, just long enough for Colonel Hutchinson and Captain Klein to agree upon Working Hours.

Only jurors were absent from that crowded courtroom, but newsmen were not able to hear distinctly and as a result misinterpreted a portion of these crucial arguments. Let's see if in a few hundred words we can follow the chain of reasoning which took our lawyers thousands of words.

While the Uniform Code of Military Justice grafted a good deal of civilian procedure into courts-martial, Attorney Berman wanted to inject even more. His position is described by his own reference to the statement of Judge Learned Hand in the case of the United States vs. Lotsch, 307 US 622:

> . . . there is indeed always a danger when several crimes are tried together that the jury may use the evidence cumulatively; that is, that, although so much as would be admissible upon any one of the charges might not have persuaded them of the accused's guilt, the sum of it will convince them as to all. This possibility violates the doctrine that only direct evidence of the transaction charged will ordinarily be accepted, and that the accused is not to be convicted because of his criminal disposition . . .

Emile Berman moved to sever the liquor charges from those of oppression and manslaughter, holding the former minor offenses in comparison with the latter. His rationale went like this: McKeon's alleged possession and consumption of vodka had no relationship to the accusations of manslaughter and oppression beyond the fact they occurred on the same day. Should the Court learn of these minor offenses, however, they might be unduly prejudiced in their consideration of the major ones. Berman introduced into evidence the court-martial records of Elwyn Scarborough and Richard King, who drank from the same bottle at the same time with Matthew McKeon, to show that their cases had been tried by summary court-martial, the lowest type available, and that their sentences were rather light. The point Berman glossed over was that unlike Scarborough and King, McKeon was on duty. Mr. Berman gave weight to a few lines in the Manual:

> Ordinarily, charges for minor derelictions should not be joined with charges for serious offenses. For example, a charge of failure to report for a routine roll call should not be joined with a charge of burglary. If, however, the minor offense serves to explain the circumstances of the greater offense, it is permissible to charge both.

Defender Berman also found support in the case of the United States vs. Hines, 7 USCMA 75, where Chief Judge Quinn characterized the offenses of being drunk and disorderly in the orderly room and incapacitation for the performance of duty by reason of previous indulgence in intoxicating liquor as among the most minor offenses in military law. Quinn was also of the opinion that joining these charges with those of two assaults and offering violence to a superior officer was a reversible error.

Major Sevier answered with hundreds of words when a few would have been more powerful: First, Berman's reference to the Manual was taken out of context from instructions to Convening Authorities, who are responsible for joining charges. Second, the liquor charges might possibly explain circumstances of manslaughter and oppression charges, but even standing alone they were not minor: Illegal possession could lead to two years' confinement at hard labor, forfeiture of all pay and allowances, and dishonorable discharge, which sentence could only be awarded by general court-martial, the highest type in the system. McKeon's case was an aggravation of Scarborough's and King's offenses because only he was on duty. Penalty for the drinking charge was not specified—though Berman mentioned three months' confinement and Sevier unwittingly agreed—but could be determined by the Court. Third, the clincher: In the United States vs. Keith, 4 CMR 34, the Court of Military Appeals said:

> The joinder of entirely separate, distinct, and completely unrelated charges is not condemned by military procedure. Instead, for practical reasons of dispatch, it has come to be the customary practice to join all known offenses against an accused and to dispose of all at a single trial. However, in civilian practice it is unusual and often improper to join unrelated offenses in the same trial. See Rule 8(a), Federal Rules of Criminal Procedure. No such limitations exist in the sphere of military justice.

The Manual says, "Charges against the accused, if tried at all, should be tried at a single trial."

Near the end of this phase of argument Sevier reminded Klein that all members and the Law Officer were still subject to challenge. Berman insisted he had no challenge against the Law Officer and questioned Sevier, who replied: "The Government will indicate at the time set forth in the procedure." At this point Judge Klein faced two problems: Since the Secretary of the Navy had ordered the charges joined, would it be fitting for Klein to order them severed? Then, if this were an interlocutory question, he could rule; if it were a motion to dismiss, his ruling was subject to objection by any member of the Court. Berman inferred this might be a historic case and left to imagination its being quoted in the case books. Klein reserved decision for Tuesday.

Counselor Berman then unveiled a new topic: He wanted access to some 27,000 questionnaires at Headquarters Marine Corps. Let's hear a snatch of the discussion:

SEVIER: My position is still no showing of materiality.
KLEIN: Mr. Berman claims materiality.

SEVIER: Well, sir; I think that he suspicions materiality. I don't believe that he claims materiality because—as I understand—he hasn't seen them.

KLEIN: He believes that General Pate's inquiry concerning methods employed indicated materiality. Is it your intention to call General Pate? You needn't answer that.

BERMAN: I have no answer for that.

For the moment Judge Klein reserved decision on the second question while Defender Berman raised a third: He wanted a roster of Parris Island's 1956 separatees, people who would know that night exercises in marshland were a recognized practice.

KLEIN: Would they know it more than people who have not been discharged?

BERMAN: They would not know it more, but they would speak more freely. Since you asked me the question point-blank, I answered you without in the slightest making it difficult to see why I was compelled to make these requests.

KLEIN: You imply that someone sworn may not tell the truth?

BERMAN: Mr. Law Officer, I do not propose to say any more about this matter than I have already said.

Prosecutor Sevier insisted rightfully that Defender Berman's request for questionnaires and roster must come through him. Judge Klein agreed and adjourned Court for the day with his remark, "I consider that at the present time the two requests are not directed at me."

Monday evening Berman turned in his paper work while Sevier scouted around to learn that questionnaires and roster were both available should Klein determine them admissible. Tuesday morning Judge Klein ruled that Attorney Berman could have access to both sets of documents, yet at the same time Klein held secure a route of withdrawal by appending to the record pertinent correspondence between Counselor Berman and Secretary Thomas and by recording the remarks that he would decide later on admissibility of any evidence thus obtained. An hour recess followed while Berman and Sevier went to long-distance telephones.

After the recess Judge Klein denied Attorney Berman's motion to dismiss Charges I and IV, the liquor accusations.

Though by 10:15 A.M. Tuesday, July 17, Irving Klein had made three decisions, he couldn't yet summon members of the Court. Emile Berman had another motion: to dismiss Charge IV because the specification, drinking in the presence of a recruit, did not allege an offense. To understand this we'll be forced to review the "general article" in the Uniform Code of Military Justice.

Since the days of the Continental Congress when our first military law was adapted from that of the British, we have had two or three catch-all punitive articles generally described as: conduct to the prejudice of good order and discipline, scandalous conduct tending to the destruction of good morals, and conduct unbecoming an officer and gentleman. Specific offenses under these charges might be violation of Federal law not contained in the military code; breach of the written law of a state, territory, or foreign country; or mere nonconformance with recognized custom and usage of the service.

Now a Drill Instructor is expected to set his recruits a good example, a tradition in any leadership situation. Here Major Sevier might have referred to several passages in Depot Orders requiring that good example—had he considered it important—but on this issue Sevier was confident he could take for granted the attitude of the Court. Sevier relaxed.

Berman didn't. Despite the inevitability of his being overruled—all specifications had been thoroughly examined by bright young legal beagles in the Office of the Judge Advocate General, a reassuring situation for Irving Klein—Emile Berman's argument was powerful, intriguing, oratorical. It really hurts to abridge this one, but it was much longer than it was important to the Ribbon Creek trial:

> Disorders and neglects punishable under Article 134 are not acts prejudicial only in a remote or indirect sense. . . . Per-

sons in a position of authority might—if so moved by ulterior motives—characterize any act as being to the prejudice of good order and discipline. . . . This concept is so repugnant to American standards of justice and fair play that it was necessary to include the above-quoted language to protect persons subject to the Code from unwarranted prosecution . . . They were given legislative assurance that they need not fear prosecution arising out of each and every act committed by them—on duty or off—during the course of their enlistments.

Sir, nowhere is there any reference—even by implication—to prohibition of conduct of the type involved in the case at bar. . . . It is an ancient and a respected maxim of Anglo-Saxon law that in the construction and interpretation of statutes the expressed statement of one thing presumes the exclusion of others not so stated. . . . Penal statutes are to be strictly construed. . . . To do otherwise is to abrogate and render meaningless the most basic protections known to our law. . . . Where the liberty of men depends upon their ability to comprehend the behaviors which the statute is designed to prohibit, without a clear and specific application and enunciation of the act there can be no valid charge either in law or in morality.

Finally, sir, to grant the prosecuting authority the right to devise a new offense whenever it desires to obtain a conviction when the accused has never been put on notice of the possibility that his conduct could be the basis for a newly fabricated offense is to invest in the authorities a tyrannical and oppressive power. It is in effect an attempt to reinstate the power to make law ex post facto.

KLEIN: The motion is denied.

At eleven, Tuesday, members of the Court finally emerged from seclusion and resumed their seats. Prosecutor Sevier described the general nature of the charges against McKeon which we can simplify by tabulation:

Charge I. Disobedience: Possession and use of an alcoholic beverage in an unauthorized place.

Charge II. Oppression: Leading Platoon 71 into Ribbon Creek in mud and water over their heads.

Charge III. Manslaughter, two counts:
(1) By culpable negligence.

(2) While perpetrating the offense of oppression.

Charge IV. Conduct to the prejudice of good order and discipline: While on duty, drinking intoxicants in the presence of a recruit.

It was time for challenges.

SEVIER: The records in this case reveal no grounds for challenge. If any member of the Court or the Law Officer is aware of any facts which he believes may be grounds for challenge against him by either side, he should now state such facts. (*He paused.*) Let the record show that no member of the Court so indicated.

Trial Counsel then described the procedure he intended to follow in questioning the Court.

SEVIER: If it please the Court: This is the time in the procedure for challenges for cause. The Prosecution and Defense are both entitled to *voir dire* examination of the members of the Court. I understand that we may either ask the Court individually—without placing them under oath on the stand, or that we may, if we so desire, place them under oath on the stand—questions regarding fitness to sit as a member of this Court. I would prefer merely to address my questions to members individually without placing them on the stand.

KLEIN: That is perfectly all right. In other words, you prefer to follow the civil court procedure of having a jury—proposed jury—prospective jury—in the jury box and questioning them. Is that correct? Is that the course you desire to pursue?

SEVIER: Yes.

KLEIN: Permitted.

Judge Klein was playing to the grandstand. In this instance he lacked authority to permit or prohibit. The procedure Major Sevier described had been approved by ex-Artillery Captain Harry S. Truman on February 8, 1951, in Executive Order 10214, when in accordance with law he promulgated the *Manual for Courts-Martial*. Klein could have found that in his book on page 90.

Counsel Sevier polled the members one at a time asking four questions, which we abbreviate: What do you know about this case? Have you formed an opinion? Can you render fair and impartial judgment based upon the evidence presented here? Do you know the defendant? Sevier was satisfied with the answers he received. He announced that he had neither challenge for cause nor a peremptory challenge.

In his turn, Attorney Berman couldn't be brief, explicit, formal. From the very beginning he must induce in the jurors a psychological set, a sympathetic attitude toward the situation he wanted to portray. This point is of such crucial importance to our understanding of the trial and to our appreciation of the genius of Emile Zola Berman that we must take time out for a moment to review the dynamics of perceptual organization.

I am indebted to Professor Charles E. Osgood, Psychology Department, University of Illinois, and to the Oxford University Press, publishers of Osgood's *Method and Theory in Experimental Psychology,* for the illustration. Look at this diagram:

Does it have any meaning for you? No? But when you're told that it represents "A Washerwoman Cleaning the Floor" you instantly attach meaning to the diagram. Look at it again. You're now challenged to attempt to perceive this drawing in any other context.

Emile Berman is an eminent practitioner of courtroom psychology. Listen while he talks with members of the Court:

> Mr. President, officers of the Court: My name is Berman—Emile Z. Berman—and I am a civilian Counsel for the Accused here. What I want to do is talk with you about your views on some of the matters that have already been discussed with you.

I want to make it plain to you that it is neither my function nor my desire to cross-examine you—if I may use that word—so I hope that none of you get that impression. Some of you gentlemen have mentioned in the past that your only association in terms of hearing anything about this case was in its early days —I believe, to use the language used, early releases—meaning newspaper releases, perhaps—I don't recall whether there were radio or television stories. You have not, I presume, seen the charges and you have only had read to you a very general description of what these charges consist of. So I would like to ask you—to start with—a general proposition. I presume, Colonel Hutchinson, if I put this problem to you we will soon find out whether the views of the other members of the Court are the same or dissimilar to yours: Do you, as a matter of concepts, equate the taking of a few drinks with intoxication or drunkenness?

HUTCHINSON: No, I do not.

Sisak agreed with Hutchinson.

BERMAN: Incidentally, gentlemen, if I by any chance mispronounce your name, will you please do me the great courtesy of correcting me?

Fultz, Regan, and Carlton agreed with Hutchinson. Demas agreed after correcting the pronunciation of his name.

BERMAN: Lieutenant Nelson: I see that you are a doctor, a Navy doctor I presume. Is that so, sir?

NELSON: Yes.

BERMAN: Now, quite apart from any medical training of your own, just hearing this question as a concept in terms of living—could you hear the question that I asked Colonel Hutchinson and his response to me?

NELSON: Yes.

BERMAN: Do you have any view other than that which has been expressed on that subject?

NELSON: No, sir. My view is in agreement with the other members of the Court.

BERMAN: And are those views—that is to say the views that you hold—at all influenced by the fact that you are a doctor? In other words, that would not change your opinion in one way or the other on that question; is that correct?

NELSON: No, sir. I don't believe so.

BERMAN: All right. Thank you, sir.

Counselor Berman was ready for the second plateau. Psychologically it was reinforcement of the same set: creating objectivity, encouraging fair play, combating prejudice, instilling skepticism, engendering "reasonable doubt." Berman:

> Without asking you gentlemen specifically the nature of the stories you read, I might as well be brutally frank about those headlines in the early days—captions all over the country—"Drunk leads death march." The newspapers have their own ways of phrasing headlines—I say this in the presence of a large body of the press here. My question to you, Colonel, is—and it is only for you to say—I am sure that you know yourself—I have only had the pleasure of a casual meeting with you—but upon examination of yourself and what it has taken of your life to make you what you are today, is there the slightest doubt—should I, for example, who bears the weight of responsibility for the defense of this sergeant, have the slightest concern that headlines of any kind, recent or early, will interfere with your judgment in this matter one bit?

HUTCHINSON: It will not interfere one bit.

BERMAN: And would that be the same as to say that you believe you are so constituted that neither sympathy nor prejudice will interfere with your conclusions; you will accept the evidence, as you view it, with respect to what the truth is?

HUTCHINSON: Facts in the case will be the only things that affect my decision.

Mr. Berman didn't repeat the whole question to the others as he polled the Court on newspaper publicity given the Ribbon Creek tragedy, but he did rephrase and repeat some parts, reinforcing the concept that newspaper reports are not evidence. Sisak, Fultz, Carlton, Demas, and Nelson assured him they would weigh the facts in accordance with their oath.

Attorney Berman climbed to the third plateau: official sentiment. Berman knew that the law says "No person subject to this code shall attempt to coerce or, by any unauthorized means, influence the action of a court-martial of any member thereof in reaching the findings or sentence." But Randolph McCall Pate, Commandant of the Marine Corps, had severely condemned Matthew McKeon—and all Parris Island as well—publicly. Emile Berman could use that public condemnation as a counterpoise for shaping the Court's attiude:

> Now I want to make reference to some other matters which may or may not have come to your attention. I don't regard anything that I have to ask you or any answers which you may make to me to be of a delicate nature. My job here is to put my position plainly before you—honestly and with the self-respect that I hold myself in. My position here is simply to acknowledge that you are officers of the Marine Corps who have no reason you can consider that would interfere with your proper judgment of this case. It is in that context—and not because I am here to go into extraneous matters—that I want to ask you about this problem. I am not sure that it is a problem. I am not sure because I don't know enough about your reactions. That is why I ask you about them point-blank. On May 1, 1956, the Commandant of the Marine Corps, General Pate, testified publicly before a committee of a house of Congress called the "Armed Services Committee." That testimony, coming from a man of such high status, properly was fairly widely distributed and fairly widely covered by the press from one end of the country to the other. I repeat, properly so. This was the head of a very honored service in our nation's life. Judging from the Congressional transcript, there was a considerable amount of testimony and inquiries by Congressmen and others which may have appeared in various newspapers as a column or a half column or just a news item; I don't know. That is, I don't know what newspapers you might have read on the subject, if any. But the point that I am now asking you about, Colonel, did you read—as I recall this to your mind now—anything concerning the testimony of the Commandant before this committee to which I have made reference?

HUTCHINSON: No, I did not read anything on that testimony.

BERMAN: I presume that you do know that he was a witness before a Congressional committee?

HUTCHINSON: He was.

BERMAN: But that is all you know about it?

HUTCHINSON: I was under way from the West Indies at that time—coming back from maneuvers—so I didn't read the papers.

BERMAN: What I was trying to say—and what I am almost ready to believe—in the West Indies this did not make news?

HUTCHINSON: No; we didn't have access to news aboard ship.

The six other members of the Court admitted having read a synopsis of the Commandant's testimony or of having heard something about his appearance on Capitol Hill. All assured Defense Counsel that Pate's testimony would play no part in their deliberations or decisions in the case. The exchange with Lieutenant Colonel Daniel Regan is worth repeating:

REGAN: Yes, sir. I believe I did read something around May first—I can't be sure of the date—and—

BERMAN: That's pretty good; that's the date he testified. So it may have been May second that you read it.

REGAN: But to answer your question specifically: What I read in the paper, I do not know that is what he said. As you said before, what you read in the newspapers is not necessarily what happened. Being perfectly honest—but to answer your last question—you have my assurance that what he might have said would not influence me.

Berman's final plateau was counteracting prejudice that members of the Court may have acquired through familiarity with Parris Island. Fultz, Regan, and Nelson were making their first visit. Hutchinson had gone through Boot Training here in 1931 and then for six months in 1940 had been in command of an anti-aircraft group based on Parris Island (but probably situated on Hilton Head Island). Sisak served at the Recruit Depot as second lieutenant in 1940. Demas did his Boot Training here in 1944; came back for two weeks in 1953 as Inspector-Instructor of a Pennsylvania reserve unit. But Edwin Carlton had done a tour here ending in May 1955. In various Recruit Training Battalions he was Company Commander five months, Battalion Executive Officer eighteen months, and Battalion Commander four months. He would require more questioning.

Peculiarly, Carlton was Berman's stanchest juror: He is a

hard man to convince. For months we met together on the Exchange Council where Carlton demanded that our successive Exchange Officers prove everything to him. When he supervised an inventory, the results were perfect. If a pay raise were recommended for some employee, Carlton had to be convinced it was merited. His reputation on courts-martial was as prime "reasonable doubter."

BERMAN: Major Carlton, I should like to remind you that a very substantial element of the proof in this case involves recruit training practices on the part of Drill Instructors. Would you consider yourself an expert in that field?

CARLTON: I don't know about an expert, but I think I know as much about it as anyone else in the field.

BERMAN: Well, I certainly have no reason to assume differently. But if these training practices have to do with matters which are not specifically prescribed in the lesson plans, would you also be aware of those?

CARLTON: Yes, sir.

BERMAN: Well, this poses a problem to me. Since I don't know how to solve a problem except by putting it out on the line, I'll see whether you and I both can solve it, sir. Assuming that there would be witnesses in this case testify to certain practices, would you be in a position to divorce your experience at Parris Island and accept testimony from the stand if your own experience might hold to a different view?

SEVIER: If it please the Court: I consider this beyond the scope of *voir dire*. It seems to be getting into admissibility or inadmissibility of what might or might not come in as evidence.

KLEIN: I will allow it. I consider it proper *voir dire*.

BERMAN: Major, I will try to make myself plain—and please, sir, do me the courtesy of believing that my inquiry of you has no personal element at all. It is as though I, as a lawyer, were sitting on the jury and the problem is: Could I take the law from the judge against the background of the law as I have lived it and practiced it? Now, there is some kind of similarity to that situation in what I am asking of you. This Court will be required to make its decision and determination on the evidence admitted by the Law Officer—upon exhibits introduced and probabilities based on that evidence—but, as I understand it, no member can substitute his own recollection or judgment of facts over evidence that comes from the witness stand. Now here you sit, having been on this very base in a recruit training program for two years, the last of which antedates the tragic accident that produced this trial by only eight months. The problem—and I don't know whether you can help me, but I am asking you to give me your best views on it—the problem is whether or not you can completely shut your mind—it is a big job to ask of anyone—to shut your mind to whatever you conceive to have been the facts on Parris Island in connection with activities in recruit training—the activities of Drill Instructors—and to accept the evidence and decide the case exclusively on what comes from the witnesses. I don't know. I don't know even whether you do know.

CARLTON: I expected your question.

BERMAN: You expected it?

CARLTON: And I gave it a lot of thought.

BERMAN: Very good, sir. That makes it easier then.

CARLTON: And I felt—after analyzing the whole thing—that I could listen to the personnel on the witness stand and come up with a logical conclusion regardless of what it was. I could be wrong, but that is the way I figured it out.

BERMAN: I want to make one thing plain to you, Major. I do not doubt for one moment the integrity of your answer. My problem—if I have one—is to consider whatever I know in human life to find out whether such a thing can likely happen. I don't know. It comes to me fresh. I am glad that you have thought about it. I shall give great consideration to a considered opinion rather than one that you have been called upon to make at first impression. I thank you, sir, for your answer.

BERMAN (*to the Court*): I have seen defense lawyers, both civilian and military, put millions of questions—it seems to me—to prospective jurors—or members of the Court—and I have long ago learned that the best one can do is address himself to fundamental principles. So, I will ask you now a general question: In light of what has been asked of you by me, and the general implications of the questions—as well as the questions of Major Sevier—are there any members of this Court who would like to tell us anything about themselves or their attitudes which they think would be of some help in determining your ability to serve fairly and impartially and in the truest concept of a fair, free trial?

There was no response.

BERMAN: Well, I certainly thank you for the opportunity of chatting with you.

Lawyer Berman wasn't yet through with Carlton. At this point it was time for lunch. He requested a recess so that he and his associates might find out whether any member of the Court had signed orders which would later appear as exhibits. Then he suggested that the 75-minute luncheon recess agreed upon the previous day was too short. He had made an "experimental run." President Hutchinson extended it fifteen minutes.

After this recess Berman kept the floor: Mr. President, Law Officer, Major Carlton: I have been giving some thought to the last problem—or last question—we discussed with each other before the luncheon recess. I am going to ask you—since presumably you had given thought to it before I did—are you in a position to give me your assurance, without any reservation whatsoever. that you will decide this case on the evidence that comes before you in this courtroom, the law you are instructed on by the Court, and nothing else—and that nothing else, including either your belief as to what facts may be based on your own experience or any emotion arising out of your own experience, will sway you?

CARLTON: I have discussed this with myself—and myself only—and I believe I could do it.

BERMAN: Do I have your assurance that you can do this?

CARLTON: You have. I have none whatsoever. (*Carlton was talking about mental reservations.*)

BERMAN: I thank you, Major, and I accept your answer in the spirit in which you have given it to me. (*He turned to Klein.*) The Defense has no challenges.

Had Emile Berman doubted Carlton's integrity, he would have challenged him peremptorily without bothering to question him. Instead, he used this opportunity to mold in all jurors the attitudes he desired. Berman knew the court-martial "numbers racket," the requirement for two-thirds or three-quarters voting. With six members on the Court, four votes would convict or adjudge imprisonment less than ten years; with seven members it would take five votes. For a sentence exceeding ten years' confinement, it would require five votes from six members, six votes from seven. Arithmetically the Defense had nothing to lose. In fact Counsel knew that Major Carlton was a prospective dissenter who could easily swing the outcome.

Technically, Prosecutor Sevier was wrong in calling examination of the Court *"voir dire." Voir dire* requires a special oath. It is often used in the law before questioning a witness to ascertain his competency. It was used under the old Articles for the Government of the Navy for that purpose and also when the member of a court-martial raised the question of his competency to sit in a specific case. Under the old Code it was held that "members of a court-martial cannot be questioned on *voir dire* preliminary to challenge with a view to discovering possible grounds for challenge." But under the old Code officers were assumed to be gentlemen until proved otherwise.

This assumption of an officer's inherent honor and integrity isn't valid under the Uniform Code of Military Justice, Model 1951. When appointed, the officer swears to "support and defend the Constitution of the United States, to bear true faith and allegiance to the same, to well and faithfully discharge the duties of his office." Monday, first trial day in the case of United States vs. McKeon, seven officers took this oath:

> You do swear that you will faithfully perform all the duties incumbent upon you as a member of this court; that you will faithfully and impartially try, according to the evidence, your conscience, and the laws and regulations provided for trials by courts-martial, the case of the accused now before this court; and that if any doubt should arise not explained by the laws and regulations, then according to the best of your understanding and the custom of war in like cases. . . . So help you God.

Tuesday morning, Major Sevier instructed: "If any member of the Court (or the Law Officer) is aware of any facts which he believes may be a ground for challenge by either side against him, he should now state such facts." Then he and Berman spent the morning asking individual members if they would honor their oath! This procedure is authorized specifically in *Manual for Courts-Martial,* 1951, paragraph 62b. Questioning may be informal or on *voir dire*. It makes the old-time professional soldier squirm.

Defense Counsel Emile Zola Berman didn't require Trial Counsel to read aloud the charges and specifications. Each member of the Court would be handed his own copy anyway and even without this reading the allegations would automatically be incorporated in the record. Defense had no further motions to dismiss charges or grant relief; Judge Klein had quashed those earlier that morning.

SEVIER: We are ready to receive the plea. Staff Sergeant Matthew C. McKeon, U. S. Marine Corps, how do you plead?

Berman's Defense team and McKeon were all required to rise at this time, but Berman did the talking. His response is simplified by tabulation:

I.	Possession and use of alcoholic beverage:	Accused stands mute
II.	Oppression:	Not guilty
III.	Manslaughter by culpable negligence:	Not guilty
	Manslaughter while oppressing:	Not guilty
IV.	Drinking before a recruit:	Accused stands mute

This plea, "the accused stands mute," shook Judge Klein; we examine his reactions in different context. But Emile Berman was merely continuing his consummate trial psychology. He had previously argued that these two charges were trivial and served only to prejudice McKeon in consideration of the two serious charges. While Berman lost his argument, he wanted the Court to realize that such irrelevant, contemptible scandal only engendered unfair bias.

After the arraignment there was a short recess to permit Judge Klein to read his book while Prosecutor Sevier made arrangements to wire the courtroom for sound. Three minutes more and Court adjourned to permit installation of a public address system. The afternoon session was open fifteen minutes. Thus at the end of the second trial day members of the Court had occupied their seats little more than eighty minutes.

17

Counselor Berman

RIBBON CREEK provided news copy for ten days after the drownings, then following an equal period of quiet, General Pate's report to the House Armed Services Committee fanned the smoldering fire of public opinion into a nation-wide conflagration. Reaction was ambivalent: Thousands condemned Matthew McKeon as a wanton criminal; other thousands viewed him as the scapegoat of a too-powerful military hierarchy. Yet most agreed on one principle: He rated competent legal defense.

Such defense is afforded an accused in all courts, military and civilian—but the general public automatically depreciates appointed counsel. That might have been the reaction of Thomas P. Costello, McKeon's brother-in-law, skillful attorney, intimately familiar with the case and all its implications. Though not on record, it is obvious Costello sought legal aid for McKeon, whose family roots are in Massachusetts rather than New York. After the Soldiers and Sailors Relief Act, designed to protect the serviceman from mortgage foreclosures, lawsuits, unwanted divorce, lawyers throughout the country formed a habit of donating legal services to the man in uniform. Costello invoked that habit. May 8 came the announcement a committee of prominent New York judges and lawyers volunteered their services. Chief Counsel would be Emile Zola Berman, hardly known to the lay community but honored in professional circles as "a lawyer's lawyer."

French Major Ferdinand Walsin Esterhazy, who claimed descent from Hungarian nobility, in 1894 wrote an abstract of secret documents which he agreed to furnish German Major Schwartzkoppen, military attaché in Paris. This abstract was intercepted by French counterintelligence with no clue to its author. The military hierarchy needed a conviction to camouflage its own ineptness and infidelity. On the basis of handwriting, Captain Alfred Dreyfus was tried by court-martial; convicted of treason; sentenced to life imprisonment on Devil's Island. In 1896 Colonel Georges Picquart discovered Esterhazy's guilt but was silenced. The next year brother Mathieu Dreyfus made the same discovery and petitioned a new trial. In 1898 Emile Zola, French novelist and social reformer, wrote an article about the Dreyfus Affair entitled *"J'accuse."* Esterhazy was tried by court-martial and acquitted on forged evidence. Zola was convicted of libel but escaped to England. In 1899 Dreyfus was given a new trial, convicted again, then pardoned by the President of the Republic. Alfred Dreyfus took his case to civilian appellate courts and in 1906 was reinstated as a major. Esterhazy was dismissed from the French Army.

The Dreyfus affair had repercussions throughout the Western world. This victim of bigotry, intolerance, and prejudice was a Jew from a disputed border state, Alsace. The affair won the sympathy of a revolutionary couple in another disputed area, Brest-Litovsk, then part of Russia, later Eastern Poland. This couple immigrated to New York. Their first son, born shortly after arrival, was named Emile Zola Berman; their second, Alfred.

Emile Berman apparently considered McKeon's trial a modern Dreyfus case. He was quoted in *Life* as saying, "I thought the Marine Corps was using this boy to cover its own responsibility." Berman's organization of McKeon's defense, in spite of this, was schizoid: His artful suggestion out of court encouraged the press to draw comparisons between Matthew McKeon's trial and the Dreyfus Affair; his overt behavior and speech in court gave him the role of Marine Corps Protector. Peculiarly, encyclopedias fail to mention Dreyfus' lawyers.

An attorney's work in any legal action resembles an iceberg —less than a third of it is visible on the surface. His maneuvers outside the courtroom are as important as those of the military leader approaching the field of battle. Before the lawyer or captain makes contact with his opponent the issue is usually decided. Matthew McKeon's case was no exception, but there is an essential difference between the two campaigns: The captain's plans and preliminary actions became historical record; the lawyer conceals his own strategy under his hat.

We do know from the Court-Martial transcript that Emile Berman paid visits to Rear Admiral William Sheeley, Acting Judge Advocate General of the Navy, and to Lieutenant General Lewis Puller, retired. It is generally accepted that he visited General Randolph Pate, probably twice. Those intimate with the Defense admit Berman or his associates investigated the background of each member of the Court. But those acts of preparation could be only a sample of the whole project. It would be educational indeed to develop a full behind-the-scenes account of this phase and learn some of the political moves, some of the trade secrets, which influence an important law case. That goal is not attainable short of Berman's writing his memoirs and even those, obviously, would be subject neither to cross-examination nor Rules of Evidence.

Yet Emile Berman did reveal one trade secret, as it served his purpose the day before the trial opened, when he held a press conference on Parris Island. Berman released to newsmen texts of letters exchanged with the Secretary of the Navy.

Attorney Berman wrote Secretary Thomas requesting the latter issue an order insuring that no marine who told the truth in connection with the Court-Martial would be subject to reprisal. Berman claimed he and his associates found Parris Island NCOs "extremely reluctant to discuss matters and issues which would be particularly relevant to the Defense." These issues were "practices involving night exercises and marches into the boondocks and tidal waters at Parris Island." Berman contended he had "run into a barrier of silence" which was "motivated entirely by fear of reprisal and punitive action."

Psychologically Secretary Thomas was on the spot. Implicit in Mr. Berman's suggestion was a close parallel with the Dreyfus case. Also, he was reviving the thesis defended by his teammate, Attorney Costello, when he pled for immunity of witnesses at the Inquiry. But the unstated premise most disheartening to those who have faith in the law is that sworn witnesses violate their oath to "tell the truth, the whole truth, and nothing but the truth."

Thomas replied that he wanted to do everything possible to insure a fair trial, then added: "I am confident that no one in a position of authority in the Marine Corps would subject any person to reprisals or punitive measures as a result of his telling the truth at the trial." That was all Thomas could do, but he lost the engagement. In a court of public opinion conditioned by gossip columnists and scandalmongers the jury would come to a predicted verdict: "Where there's smoke, there's fire." Hundreds would rise to the cause.

Monday, July 9, with the McKeon trial scheduled to begin Saturday, Attorney Berman dispatched another letter to the Secretary of the Navy. This request was twofold. First, he wanted to review and evaluate a questionnaire which Commandant Pate submitted to 27,000 marines seeking their experiences and views concerning training methods. Second, he wanted a roster with civilian addresses of all marines, excluding psychiatric cases, discharged at Parris Island that year. Berman sent a carbon copy to Headquarters Marine Corps, enough to cause much squirming in the Seat of Government.

Secretary Thomas' reply, obviously prepared at Headquarters in the usual procedure, indicated Commandant Pate's inquiry was occasioned by his recent assignment to that office, was designed for his personal use, and sought ideas for improving training in order to achieve combat readiness. Thomas questioned that these documents were either material or relevant to McKeon's trial, but he did consent to make them available if the Law Officer so ruled. Thomas denied the request for the roster on the ground that "such names would be administratively extremely difficult to ascertain," and added the opinion that those ex-marines probably lacked information relevant to the case. Thomas did agree, however, to endeavor to supply addresses of any Berman might specifically name.

Lawyer Berman's campaign to try McKeon's case in the court of public opinion received powerful stimulation from this refusal. The implication was obvious: Military bureaucrats were concealing important information—the Marine Corps did have something to hide. Perversion of justice in McKeon's trial would be in striking parallel with the Dreyfus trial. Berman continued to wage his campaign immediately after the Court organized.

Prosecutor Sevier resisted Berman's moves unnecessarily and thus strengthened the Defense position. Sevier contended Berman must "go through channels," namely Trial Counsel, with a written request containing a synopsis of testimony expected and reasons it was needed. Sevier held that Berman failed to show relevancy and materiality. But how could Berman describe the contents of documents he had never seen? He couldn't show they were material and relevant, he merely proposed this probable. He offered to provide a four-man team to screen the questionnaires; he would send it to Washington if necessary. Sevier also urged that the roster would be difficult to compile and that witnesses selected from that list could offer nothing material. This long debate was in an open courtroom with just members of the Court excluded.

The second trial day Judge Klein ruled for the Defense. By that time Trial Counsel had arranged for the Defense team to screen the questionnaires and had also discovered that Parris Island's Machine Records Installation could provide the roster without strain. After that there was no mention of these in the trial, though Berman did refer to the questionnaires once in a press conference.

Emile Zola Berman is no exception to the general rule that any effective trial lawyer is a master showman. During fifteen courtroom days in the case of the United States vs. McKeon he continually pulled new, spectacular rabbits from his capacious hat. Berman charmed Court, witnesses, the working press, spectators, and his associates. Major Sevier and his Prosecution team suddenly found themselves playing the Broadway boards—and were probably the only observers who failed to appreciate Berman's histrionics. Here we take a few threads from the Ribbon Creek skein to appreciate them more fully than they would appear in day-to-day sequence.

First witness at the trial, Adjutant Charles R. Weddel, introduced Depot Orders on which Prosecutor Sevier would build his case.

SEVIER: You may inquire, sir. (*He turned Weddel over for cross-examination.*)

BERMAN: Do you have Depot Order 1746.2 with you? (*This hadn't been mentioned in Sevier's questioning.*)

WEDDEL: I don't believe so, sir. (*He answered before Sevier could object.*)

SEVIER: I believe that is outside the scope of direct examination.

BERMAN: Thc witness is here now. Surely we won't have to go through the procedure of on and off and on again.

SEVIER: Sir, I do not propose, without objection, to permit Defense to introduce direct evidence by way of cross-examination.

KLEIN: Inasmuch as Trial Counsel insists on that orderly procedure, I suggest that when you conduct your part of the case you recall the witness.

BERMAN: In considering everybody's desire to keep this trial short and crisp, I presume this order will prolong this case unnecessarily.

KLEIN: I'm inclined to agree.

Berman persisted, Sevier repeated his objection, Judge Klein made no further ruling. During a short recess Berman had Weddel procure a document not previously admitted. Then he sent him back to the Adjutant's Office to search his files and return after lunch.

The general rule, normally observed with care in the military, limits cross-examination to matters developed in direct examination. Such enables the Prosecution, without undue interruption, to present a clear, logical picture, controlling the scope and extent of its unfolding. In turn the Defense has this same opportunity. In a long trial it tends to limit confusion. Since the Court never reads the record—members rely on memories and a few rough notes—orderly presentation aids their mental organization of testimony. This might have psychological advantage to the Defense, whose rebuttal has the attribute of recency.

But Emile Berman was determined that both parties move abreast, not in tandem. He would fight from start to finish. Should the picture get confused, there would be more cause for reasonable doubt.

Second witness was Master Sergeant Hans C. Manthey, Chief Drill Instructor, who on direct examination testified that an order controlling alcoholic beverages was posted on an area bulletin board McKeon was obligated to examine.

BERMAN: Was it you who would make recommendations with regard to when a Junior Drill Instructor was given a platoon as Senior?

SEVIER: I object. This is outside the scope.

KLEIN: Objection sustained.

BERMAN: I would like to call the Court's attention to the fact I am making this witness my own for this purpose. Nothing is going to be served by a parade off and on the stand. Witnesses will have to be recalled to get the full scope of their testimony.

KLEIN: I agree with the observation and with that purpose I will permit you to go ahead.

SEVIER: Sir, I object. Is Defense allowed to place their case before the Court by cross-examination?

KLEIN: Hold it. In view of your objection, it will be sustained. We will recall the witness.

BERMAN: I understand. Sergeant, will you hold yourself available for call by Defense Counsel?

KLEIN: I want to say at this point that I shall, of course—naturally—spend every effort to expedite. But in view of the valid legal objection to the position of evidence, I shall be obliged—in view of my oath which was taken.

Klein continued by issuing erroneous instructions to the Court regarding questions put by members. That brought Manthey back to the stand after lunch.

BERMAN: I would like to put some other questions, unless the Law Officer adheres to the ruling that—despite the presence of the witness on the stand—I am barred from asking him questions concerning other matters which are material and relevant to this case. I know of no contrary provision either in the Code or the Manual, which I examined over the luncheon recess. In my view this Court would be governed by rules and procedures of United States District Courts. These would permit the interrogation of this man on a new matter. The archaic notion that a witness may not be cross-examined simply because he is called on one side or another has, in recent years, yielded to the notion of expediency. The notion that a case is a game has long ago been abandoned. We have the witness, he is available for testimony.

KLEIN: Perhaps as we go on Trial Counsel may come to a different view.

BERMAN: I take it, sir, that I am limited at this time with this witness?

KLEIN: So be it. I cannot perceive at this moment what Trial Counsel may have in mind pursuing the course that he does.

We have followed here only the main thread of argument, which was long and unusually verbose, even for the courtroom. Attorney Berman sailed close to the wind on a different tack: that in introducing Manthey to the stand Prosecutor Sevier broached the question of Manthey's supervisory position over McKeon.

BERMAN: I hoped not to have to pursue a technical position; but if that is the way it is, I pursue it.

SEVIER: I might like to mention the chip in the wall that you'd try to drive a freight train through. However, I believe that is outside the scope. This man had the orders; we have had the ruling. The limited scope is still my desire. It is my desire that the Defense present their case at that time provided by the rules in the Manual.

KLEIN: Will you read what you are referring to?

SEVIER: Sir, it is the custom of courts-martial which I have been practicing since the Code came into effect.

KLEIN: When you refer to a rule, point to the book. If you have the rule ready, let's read it.

This argument continued. Finally Berman agreed to abide by Klein's ruling—to avoid a barrage of objections—but with the reservation that he was free to renew the question as other witnesses appeared.

Berman did just that with the third witness, Lieutenant Colonel Robert A. Thompson, Battalion Commander. Defense Counsel asked Thompson for his definition of *maltreatment* and Trial Counsel imposed the usual objection. Berman introduced a new wrinkle by offering the testimony "subject to connection." Judge Klein acquiesced, with the result that Defense shouldered a commanding salient into the Prosecution stronghold.

Provost Marshal McLeod was fourth and last witness that afternoon, first up next morning. Berman had other difficulties with McLeod but he did use Parris Island's law enforcer to convey into the record two aerial photographs over Sevier's objection. Berman continued with Master Sergeant John E. Clement, who succeeded Major McLeod.

BERMAN: Tell me this: In all the years you have been on this base have you ever seen platoons marching in the swamps, marshes, and creeks, Sergeant Clement?

SEVIER: May it please the Court: We would like to object to that question. It's beyond the scope of direct examination. All this witness has testified to today is about the area—

BERMAN: He has been speaking about the area and that's what I want to ask him about.

KLEIN: I don't think he testified he ever saw anybody marching in the area.

SEVIER: Further, we think it's irrelevant and immaterial.

KLEIN: I will admit the question of the witness, who has expressed familiarity with the area. It hasn't been limited to the present time by either Prosecution or Defense.

SEVIER: May it please the Court: The only purpose we can see that Defense has got in asking this question and attempting to elicit his answer—and it also applied to witnesses whose names have been submitted to us to bring down here and testify—is to show some custom or usage in going into these—

BERMAN: Custom, usage, or practice.

This was an entirely different question on which Judge Klein was withholding decision until both sides could prepare briefs and deliver their arguments. So Berman held his ground and passed over the next witness, Sergeant Algin Nolan, Sevier's "tidal expert," who couldn't serve the Defense objective. Then

Corporal Richard J. King, McKeon's rommate April 8, was called to testify and Berman drummed out his rhythmic offensive:

"Now, in connection with Platoon 71 and in connection with your going to Drill Instructors' School—which Counsel for the Government has brought out here—was it your understanding that when you had the duty the matter of teaching discipline was an obligation and largely at the discretion of the Drill Instructor?"

SEVIER: I object. Outside the scope of direct examination—immaterial and irrelevant.

KLEIN: Do you claim teaching of discipline is not relevant?

SEVIER: My questioning was as to whether or not this witness knew the Accused; we wanted to know when he met the Accused. But what went on at Drill Instructors' School—something like that—has nothing to do with the charges alleged.

KLEIN: I will allow the question.

Judge Klein had in effect joined forces with Attorney Berman. Sevier's position had fallen. It was now just mopping up. Staff Sergeant Edward R. Huff, Senior DI of Platoon 71, was next and with him Berman consolidated the Defense position:

"What was it that you found out in your official duties regarding duties imposed upon Sergeant McKeon as Junior Drill Instructor?"

SEVIER: I am going to object. It's outside the scope of the direct examination, sir.

KLEIN: Would you amplify your objection, please, sir? Specifically, what has been covered in your direct examination? Refresh my recollection.

SEVIER: I will try. The Sergeant introduced the roster of the platoon; he introduced the platoon schedule for Sunday, April 8; he identified himself as Drill Instructor in A Company, Third Training Battalion; he identified, I believe, who his Junior Drill Instructors were.

KLEIN: Of whom Sergeant McKeon was one?

SEVIER: Yes, sir.

KLEIN: Objection overruled.

BERMAN: Now then, in the course of your duties as Senior Drill Instructor of Platoon 71 were you aware of the state of training with respect to that platoon on or about April 8, 1956, with regard to their response to discipline and to the morale of the platoon as a unit?

SEVIER: Objection. Outside the scope of direct examination.
KLEIN: Overruled.

In this territory Emile Berman's generalship had triumphed. His victory was timely. Before the parade of recruit witnesses began the following day, Defense had won the right to fight parallel with the Prosecution rather than in its trace. Klein's later rulings were consistent. On this issue Sevier folded.

When Provost Marshal McLeod, who had directed they be taken as routine procedure, resumed the stand on the fourth trial day, Prosecutor Sevier offered into evidence photographs of the dead. He began with the first pair.

BERMAN: I object to them on the grounds that they are inflammatory and of no purpose in this trial. I repeat what I said at the pretrial conference and state in open Court that this is no issue as far as Defense is concerned. It is conceded in the record that the persons named in the charges lost their lives as a result of drowning in Ribbon Creek while on a march on April 8. There is no need for proof of this kind except to encumber the record with inflammatory and gruesome material.

SEVIER: My colleague has legal authorities to present on this.

CAPTAIN OTTEN, ASSISTANT TRIAL COUNSEL: The Prosecution feels that we should not be restricted as to how we present our case. We feel that the best way to establish identification of the deceased persons is by the use of the photographs which we intend to enter into evidence. It has been held that a photograph may be admitted for the purpose of identifying a person even though it presents a shocking aspect—which in this case it may not necessarily do—which might conceivably incite the passion of the triers of the facts. (*Otten cited four authorities.*)

KLEIN: May I interrupt for a moment? I think Trial Counsel might permit the Law Officer to see what you are offering in evidence and then I may be in a position to judge the inflammatory aspects of it, if any.

Trial Counsel handed the photographs to the Law Officer.

OTTEN: It is also held that they are admissible, even though inflammatory, if for a legitimate purpose. The fact that they may possibly tend to have undesirable aspects is irrelevant and is no ground for reversal. Wigmore on Evidence, Third Edition, 1940, page 1167, in speaking of possible prejudice cites what Dean Wigmore—and I ask the Court to take judicial notice that Dean Wigmore is an authority on evidence—quotes as follows, if you'll bear with me a moment please—

BERMAN: What edition?

SEVIER: Just a second, sir. I think he can tell you. The Third Edition.

OTTEN: Now, this case was pertaining to—

KLEIN: At this point in regard to your argument, having looked at the photographs and having been offered for the purpose of identification, I cannot say there is anything of an inflammatory nature concerning these photographs and I accept them in evidence.

BERMAN: I would like to make one further objection. I don't think it is required to state that the photograph of a corpse recently recovered and removed from the drink requires a legal definition as to whether it is inflammatory or not. At least it is gruesome. Identification in this case has been made and established for Trial Counsel by persons who knew the deceased. I state that this evidence is only cumulative and should be excluded because of its gruesome character.

KLEIN: Regarding Mr. Berman's argument, do you accept his stipulation?

SEVIER: Sir, I always considered it improper to make such an argument as Mr. Berman has just made. I think that was taken up at the pretrial hearing. Since no agreement could be reached then, I would like to have Counsel refrain from making those statements in this record.

BERMAN: I'm conceding it on this record of trial—before this Court. There is no issue on this.

SEVIER: We informed Mr. Berman we did not desire to stipulate.

KLEIN: Even accepted in stipulation, you could nevertheless go ahead with such proof as you desire to offer.

SEVIER: Yes, sir. I understand that.

KLEIN: It's admitted into evidence.

SEVIER: I show you Prosecution Exhibits 6 and 7 for identification and ask you—

BERMAN: I thought they had been offered in evidence.

SEVIER: These are additional.

BERMAN: I'm sorry. [Before Sevier could get pictures of the

second victim in the record, Defense was off again.] I object to each of them on grounds previously stated. They are of no issue in the matter attempting to be proven. There is available other means for identification that would not tend to incite or inflame or involve emotional content.

KLEIN: It is offered for identification and subject to connection with additional identification.

BERMAN: That is not the basis of my objection.

KLEIN: I'll permit the introduction of the one you have marked 6. Make sure you have the right one. Show that to him.

BERMAN: If you would permit—I thank you for permitting me to see that which has been ruled upon as admissible. I stand upon my objection for the record.

KLEIN: I didn't let you see it in the hope that I could obtain a concession from you.

Photographs of the third victim were introduced. Berman repeated his previous objections and added: "I object further that these exhibits probably show *rigor mortis,* an unpalatable showing of *rigor mortis.*"

KLEIN: We'll admit 8 and not admit 9.

BERMAN: Can I see 8 again please? Do I have your permission to see it again for just a moment?

KLEIN: Yes, sir.

BERMAN: I observe there is a bit of writing on the back of these. I don't see how the exhibit can go into evidence without the writing going in, too. I have no idea that this writing has been identified with anyone—with regard to its significance or just what is meant. [The writing was merely an official Marine Corps stamp with serial number and date.]

KLEIN: We will accept them without the writing. The Court is instructed to disregard any writing on the face or back. They are Government documents and we are accepting them as a true representation.

BERMAN: In that case, since they are being exhibited to the Court, may I respectfully request the Law Officer to make some instruction to the Court?

KLEIN: I instruct the members of the Court to totally disregard anything which may be written on the reverse side of each of the Government's exhibits that have been introduced in this case without evidence showing the admissibility of any writing on them.

SEVIER: At this time I would also like to call the Court's attention to the fact that these are official photographs and not for publication. They can be accepted in that manner.

KLEIN: They will be accepted in that manner.

Sevier attempted only one photograph of the fourth victim. "I offer Prosecution Exhibit 10 into evidence and show it to the Defense for possible objection."

BERMAN: Mr. Law Officer, I respectfully invite your attention to the fact that, under the terms of the charges, the incident which formed the basis of charges of criminality occurred about 2030 hours on the evening of April 8, 1956. As I understand the testimony of this witness, this proffered exhibit had its origin forty-three hours thereafter. I ask you to take judicial notice of these forty-three hours' variation. With respect to this I urge it is prejudicial and is not a fair representation of the deceased—except the remains—and there is no admission of identity. The whole purpose of flooding this record with exhibits at this time is inflammatory.

SEVIER: I show this to the Court and state, as to the time element, one of the essential elements of proof which the Prosecution has the burden of proving is the identification of the deceased.

KLEIN: You're offering it for that?

SEVIER: Yes, sir.

KLEIN: I think it is clear, from the ruling of the Law Officer, that these exhibits are admitted to be used for the purpose of identification only. That is my ruling. That is what they are offered for.

BERMAN: I would like to make the suggestion now that should the Prosecution use them for anything else I'll make a motion for a mistrial. I don't want them used to confront the Accused with on cross-examination.

SEVIER: I have no answer. There is nothing that has come up to answer so far, sir.

KLEIN: To your remarks, I should say now they are offered for identification only. They are not and they will not be permitted used for the purpose of shaking the Accused or any other person. That is in answer to your observations.

Remembering that these pictures were, after all, photos of dead marines, they were not remarkably unesthetic. All the bodies were fully clothed. Minor wounds on some faces were not particularly noticeable. True, their limbs were all in grotesque positions of *rigor mortis,* yet members of the Court had seen much worse in still life during their experience in combat. Yet it was truly shameful these pictures were appended to the trial record. They served no useful purpose.

Later that same day Richard J. King, DI in Platoon 71 junior to McKeon and now a corporal, was on the stand. Sevier confronted King with the seven photographs admitted. King had been required to go to the morgue and view the bodies for identification; three months later he could name only *Thomas Hardeman* though he did recognize all as members of Platoon 71. Attorney Berman renewed his previous offers to stipulate.

KLEIN: Before the witness leaves it might be desirable for Mr. Berman to indicate the extent of his concession. At a pre-trial discussion that we had he indicated a willingness to make a specific concession on this subject. It might expedite considerably proof of death and other things if we had for the record that concession at this time —assuming Mr. Berman is of a mind to do precisely what he indicated he wanted to do a little while ago.

BERMAN: I am of that mind.

KLEIN: In other words, I don't want to appear to be eliciting from you something you don't want to do.

BERMAN: Not at all. At the pretrial conference I offered to concede that the persons named in the specifications were members of Platoon 71 who participated in a night exercise on April 9th [sic], 1956, and that they lost their lives by drowning in Ribbon Creek.

KLEIN: You say, "who participated in the exercise." You mean were led in it?

BERMAN: Were led by platoon into the area of Ribbon Creek and lost their lives by drowning.

KLEIN: And that they are dead, of course?

BERMAN: The legal presumption, Mr. Legal Officer, is that when one loses his life there is a certain degree of permanency about it.

SEVIER: I can't accept any stipulation that includes any exercise.

BERMAN: We concede that the members of Platoon 71 designated in the specification and now identified in and depicted by the exhibits lost their lives by drowning in Ribbon Creek while members of Platoon 71. I concede identification and death.

SEVIER: And the time?

BERMAN: Yes, of course; April 8, 1956.

KLEIN: All right. That will facilitate our hearing proof.

SEVIER: We accept the stipulation as most recently stated by Defense Counsel.

KLEIN: That does not bar you from going ahead with such additional proof as you consider necessary to prove the offense or any element of it.

BERMAN: Your Honor, I have just one other question of the witness. [That time Attorney Berman limited himself to one question!]

We recall Judge Klein's instructions that these photographs were not to be used "for the purpose of shaking the Accused or any other person." Monday of the second week when he had for cross-examination the most impressionable of all witnesses at the trial, the one who admitted he was scared—and vomited when he emerged from Ribbon Creek, the small Negro boy, Attorney Berman showed the picture of Private *Norman Wood,* Negro leader in Platoon 71, to him "for identification."

Classic military tactics generally involve "holding attacks" on all fronts except one selected for the "main effort," though several generations of German strategists did favor the "double envelopment" inherited from the Punic wars. And so Emile Berman's tactics may have been a surprise to the military: He kept hammering on all fronts. Besides his public relations drive, and his operation to keep both sides of the case moving in parallel, Attorney Berman embarrassed the Prosecution in summoning witnesses.

Article 115, *Manual for Courts-Martial,* provides a solution for this problem: Witnesses are subpoenaed by Trial Counsel, who may evaluate the weight of testimony expected from them. In case of dispute when the trial is under way, the Court rules. But to save money when introducing minor evidence the Manual emphasizes reliance on stipulations and depositions. Berman took the initiative in this by offering to stipulate even before Court met—and Sevier refused it. After that Berman asked for witnesses in profusion. Even before opening arguments, Defense Counsel was on his feet when Court met the third morning.

BERMAN: Mr. President, Mr. Law Officer: We had a list of names, furnished Trial Counsel, respectfully asking subpoenas be issued on the basis of our interview with them.

KLEIN: I think you can transact that kind of business directly with Trial Counsel and not consume the Court's time.

SEVIER: If it please the Court: I requested Mr. Berman to make that request since the procedure required it.

KLEIN: What is your authority for that? Would you cite my attention to it? I think we can expedite many of these things—despite what your Manual says—outside the courtroom.

BERMAN: I'm simply following the procedure given to me.

KLEIN: I appreciate that. I'm sorry.

In his drive for witnesses Berman was operating on two fronts: A public psychological offensive indicating refusal of Defense needs and simultaneously a concerted effort to get before the Court evidence of swamp marches being a custom. Resolution of this brought on an out-of-Court hearing, but Attorney Berman didn't boat his oars. The seventh trial day opened similarly.

BERMAN: Before you call your witness, Mr. President—with your permission, Mr. Law Officer—I have here a list of 108 former marines I desire the Government to issue subpoenas for.

KLEIN: I prefer that any discussion you have to make on the subject be made in the absence of the Court. I have, however, a preliminary request—or inquiry rather—to make of you. Have you complied with Paragraph 115 in the Manual?

BERMAN: I can't tell you until I look it up, sir. [Maybe Counselor didn't recall the paragraph number, but his tremendous capacity for absorbing detail makes that doubtful. These procedures were thoroughly reviewed the previous Wednesday when Sevier egged Berman into asking in open Court for seventeen witnesses. Now Berman would be polite, co-operative, ignorant of military red tape.]

KLEIN: Look it up. I would know without your telling me if you knew about 115—you would be prepared to speak. If you did not know about it you couldn't tell me without looking it up and—if you are requesting an opportunity to look it up—you may look it up.

BERMAN: Very well, sir. Thank you.

Klein offered a recess, which Berman declined, then went on to read the whole procedure, twice. Finally he directed members of the Court to withdraw and opened debate on admissibility of evidence about the practice of teaching discipline by marches into swamps. Getting back to the question of summoning witnesses, Sevier pled that he couldn't refuse any request he hadn't received. Judge Klein agreed. After long debate Captain Klein instructed both Counsel regarding the three avenues by which information might come before the Court: witnesses, depositions, stipulations. A long recess was agreed upon. Following that, Berman grabbed the floor as soon as it was available:

> Mr. President, Mr. Law Officer: This morning I stated in open Court that I was calling upon Trial Counsel to issue subpoenas for the production of a list of persons whose names are numbered 108. I have reconstituted that list and I have cut that number down to eighty-two. However, I would like for the record to show now that I am presently furnishing, together with that list, a list to Trial Counsel of just eighteen names, eighteen out of the list of eighty-two. If those eighteen persons are subpoenaed, I will not request any others until those have testified and then only upon reflection as to whether there is a necessity for additional proof. In the event that such reasons commend themselves to me—suggest that there is such a necessity—I would like the record to show that I feel free to then again press my request for the calling of witnesses by subpoena.

These remarks continued at length. Berman told the Court that all witnesses had served at Parris Island and would testify they were led on unscheduled night marches into swamps. He then explained he had only obtained their names after McKeon's trial began. He wanted Court to understand that written depositions would delay progress of the trial. More important, the Court would now be able to judge the credibility of witnesses by their demeanor, whether they were frank and aboveboard or suspicious and evasive. Berman concluded:

> This is respectfully submitted by me, Emile Zola Berman, requested civilian Counsel. I am now reading from handwritten material. I shall, without interrupting the trial, see to it that this request is prepared in the approved form and that the names of the eyewitnesses are typed out together with such addresses as

we have. Thank you, Mr. President. Thank you, Mr. Law Officer.

Again there was verbose three-cornered debate. Sevier agreed to accept the list "for consideration," wanted assurance this would not establish a precedent, and reported he already had fourteen military witnesses standing by for the Defense. Klein's remarks generally interpreted Berman's while assuaging Sevier, though he did instruct the latter to report his decision. Berman used his time to insist he was waiving none of the Accused's rights. Next morning there was an early recess to facilitate issuing subpoenas: Berman got his witnesses.

Now we leaf the calendar ahead nine days. Attorney Berman had just announced, "The Defense rests":

SEVIER: At this time, sir, at the insistence of the Defense, I have sixteen civilian witnesses who were subpoenaed and were not called, all of whom I am required to sign vouchers for—for their costs. I have seventeen United States Marines who were requested by the Defense and were ordered here at expense to the Government and were not called. I wish Defense would indicate for the record whether or not they intend to call them, or whether I can release them. I cannot release them.

BERMAN: I have indicated for the record we rested. But, in response to your direct inquiry, having rested, we propose to call no other witnesses.

KLEIN: I think Mr. Berman is indicating to you that you may release those witnesses and send them home.

SEVIER: I shall take that as an order of the Court.

KLEIN: Mr. Berman nods assent to that.

On the seventh trial day Prosecutor Sevier wanted to bring copies of the six death certificates into evidence. This move was uncalled for. Attorney Berman, with Accused McKeon's consent in open Court, had on the fourth day made stipulations of all facts necessary to prove identity, death, and cause. On the morrow he would again stipulate those facts.

The Navy pathologist had been ultra-scientific when he did his autopsy on the six bodies. Details are morbid:

Congestion and edema of the lungs.

White foam in the larynx, trachea, and bronchi.
Pleural effusion, right 400 cc, left 290 cc.
Congestion of the conjunctiva and of the mucous membrane of the larynx, trachea, bronchi, and urinary bladder.
Increased NaCl content of the blood in the left auricle.
Cutis aserina.
Avulsion of the edge of the left ear, of the skin above the left eye, of the right upper eyelid and of the tip of the nose.
Multiple lacerations of the right lower eyelid and of the upper lip.
Undigested food in the stomach.
Fibrous adhesions over the upper lobe of the right lung.
Emphysematous bulli at the apex of the upper lobes of both lungs.
Intramural mass in the mid ileum.
Lymphoid hyperplasis in the distal ileum and in the cecum.
PROBABLE CAUSE OF DEATH: Drowning.

Each certificate bore a post-mortem fingerprint. It is unnecessary that one be trained in anatomy and physiology—or even have access to an ordinary dictionary—to sense unpleasantness in reading this typical report.

Sevier handed the documents to Klein.

BERMAN: I could save a lot of time, Mr. Law Officer, by saying that I raise no question whatsoever of the authenticity of the papers being shown you and raise no objection to the papers going into evidence insofar as it is an autopsy report and shows the cause of death, as stated in each of those papers. I am satisfied for them to go into evidence. I repeat my stipulation that we do not put in issue that the deceased lost their lives by drowning in Ribbon Creek.

KLEIN: That is the cause of death as I read it.

BERMAN: That's what we conceded from the beginning.

KLEIN: That is the cause of death in this document—the stated cause.

BERMAN: My objection is to the anatomical detail of the autopsy report. That has no place in here. That this was a post-mortem examination intended to come to an ultimate conclusion of what is the cause of death—as to that I have no objection.

KLEIN: In connection with these individuals?

BERMAN: Yes, sir.

KLEIN: Specific individuals? Six of them, by name?

BERMAN: Certainly, sir. That's what we are talking about.

KLEIN: There's no objection to the offer in evidence?

BERMAN: All I am objecting to is the autopsy techniques and the autopsy itself. I do not object to the identification of the individual and the cause of death as stated in the paper shown you. I raise no objection to their authenticity.

KLEIN: That's the only reason you're offering it?

SEVIER: I'm offering to show proof of death.

KLEIN: By drowning?

SEVIER: By drowning. As to the death certificates, any mention of autopsy, of course, just goes to support the findings of the final opinion stated there.

BERMAN: I withdraw all objections. I have no objection to the whole thing.

SEVIER: I introduce this as Prosecution Exhibit 16.

Lawyer Berman scored an overwhelming psychological victory in this action. He kept the subject alive long enough to show that Defense Counsel favored decency, respect for the privacy of the deceased. Perhaps Defense had become victim of oppression.

Wednesday morning of the second week Counselor Berman with the bottle of vodka in his hand was cross-examining PFC Fred A. Magruder, the MP who took McKeon in custody the night of April 8.

BERMAN: In any event, this is in all respects similar to what was found there at that time. Is that correct?

MAGRUDER: Yes, sir.

BERMAN: I offer it in evidence.

SEVIER: No objection, sir. We request the Law Officer rule that Defense Exhibit E for identification be admitted as Defense Exhibit E and that a description be included in the record in lieu of the Exhibit.

KLEIN: That is, if it meets with the approval of Defense Counsel.

BERMAN: Very well. There is nothing mysterious about a fifth of vodka. I think if you say it is a fifth of vodka that pretty well describes it. All you have to describe is how much is in it.

KLEIN: You already have a description of the bottle?

SEVIER: Yes, sir.

BERMAN: Anything that adequately describes it is all right with us. The Court has seen it.

KLEIN: I mean for the reviewing authorities.

BERMAN: Well, I presume an exhibit of this kind might become the original to be handed up to the reviewing authorities as we do with all living exhibits in a trial when it is appealed. However, what you suggest, Mr. Law Officer, is certainly acceptable to me.

KLEIN: If we wait long enough we don't know what evaporation might do.

BERMAN: There are two ways of vodka being evaporated, sir.

KLEIN: At all court levels.

BERMAN: I don't presume to speak for anyone but myself.

18

Trial Begins

WEDNESDAY, JULY 18, third day of McKeon's trial, Defender Berman's opening salvo was veiled suggestion making his client victim of arbitrary martial tyranny. Berman inferred Prosecutor Sevier was unwilling to summon witnesses needed for Defense. Judge Klein pigeonholed this problem for the moment, but it would recur. Neither party wished to present legal authorities other than those briefs given Klein when members of the Court were excused. It was time for opening arguments.

Sevier outlined his case with 250 words of generality: By direct testimony he would present relevant, material facts which would enable the Court to make fair, just, impartial decision. The trial would be long because much detail need be reconstructed, but Trial Counsel was confident members of the Court would give their concentrated attention. It would be essential for the Court, in the presence of all parties, to view Ribbon Creek.

Major Sevier was playing his cards close to the chest; he advocated "military security." Unless one knew he had spent more than two months preparing his case, one might surmise he composed it as the trial progressed. Sevier never did reveal how his material was structured and organized, which was probably rather loosely. Then Berman succeeded in so disrupting Sevier's organization that little is apparent in the record of proceedings.

Unlike Berman, Sevier didn't subscribe to the old maxim: Tell them what you're going to tell them, tell them, tell them what you've told them. Contrast Berman's opening:

> If it please you, Mr. President, gentlemen of the Court, with your permission, Mr. Law Officer: Not knowing what particular experience any of you officers have had with courts-martial, it might be helpful if I suggested to you that when lawyers in a tribunal such as this rise to talk to you, before any evidence, if it has any useful purpose at all, it is because it can give you a synoptic view—a run-down—of the evidence that will follow. In so far as I am concerned, it is not for the purpose of persuading you—and certainly not for the purpose of inculcating in you any hostility toward anyone in this case—but with the general view if you have in mind what the main issues and circumstances are—and the evidence which supports them—it will make it more simple for you to follow the evidence in its proper context. Moreover, it will make it easier for you to exercise your combined intelligence on the evidence as it comes from the witness stand so that you may then analyze it in conjunction with what each lawyer says—and then accept it or reject it.
>
> There is much publicity in a case such as this, and so I propose to outline for you—briefly, I hope—the facts of this situation as we understand it. I think it has already been stated to you that I am not a witness to any of the events or evidence of this tragic day. What I tell you are things I have been told by others. Primarily, Mr. President and gentlemen, I would ask your indulgence for myself, for I have not learned all the idiomatics—technical expressions of the Marine Corps—although I have studied mightily so that I may speak to you in a language that is not more unfamiliar to you than Marine Corps language to me. So I hope you will excuse any technical terms I do not have and charge it only to unfamiliarity with this language.

Berman then ventured into his outline: Nowhere in the charges was there even a suggestion that McKeon was under the slightest influence of alcohol, though the mere presence of charges of wrongful possession and wrongful drinking would unjustifiably suggest that alcohol affected McKeon in the performance of his duties. "Oppression is tyrannical use of power for one's own advantage. I doubt if you will find anywhere in any branch of the maritime service—going back to that time where it was lifted bodily from the laws of the British Royal Navy—where there is such a term." McKeon's upbringing and character would contradict any inference of oppressive behavior; Berman outlined McKeon's career in the Navy and Marine Corps and told of his family. He described the lack of discipline—absence of team spirit—in Platoon 71 and his client's decision to teach his men those virtues. Berman mentioned McKeon's physical affliction. He emphasized McKeon's seriousness in giving instruction while in Ribbon Creek in the light of a faint moon. Counsel then noted the recruits in Platoon 71 considered themselves on a lark until panic broke out; he described the madness of panic. He suggested that had the recruits followed McKeon's leadership with disciplined observance there would have been no tragic accident. He concluded:

> What was this march for? What was its purpose and what was intended to be accomplished by it? This thing will go down as one of the more tragic accidents which our civilized community finds more and more multiplied. We shall prove to you, Mr. President and officers of the Court, that the mission of this command was to produce marines and to produce them within a period of time given to the Drill Instructor—which at that time was ten weeks—that that mission and the methods employed to accomplish it were indeed part and parcel, the very warp and woof by which this Corps has earned its wondrous traditions and its well-deserved history. We shall prove to you, in our view, that Sergeant McKeon was a dedicated member of that Corps, trying to accomplish its purpose, not for self-benefit, not for sadistic pleasure, not for a casual indifference to life and limb, but for the dedicated purpose of making marines of those entrusted to him. These methods require no apology either by the Corps or by Sergeant McKeon. But if there be others who think so, that apology should not have to be made by the Sergeant who is on trial before you. Thank you for your attention to what I have said. I like to think of myself as a responsible lawyer, Mr. President and officers of the Court. I believe that

when the time comes for evidence to come in, you'll say to yourself, "Mr. Berman told us several days ago that this will be his proof. We have a right to measure him by accepting that proof." I accept that responsibility. I have not spoken lightly or loosely to you and I welcome your attention to this case against the background we say the proof will be.

Though it took Attorney Berman 3,000 words to outline his side of the case, it was worth the effort: He induced in the jury that psychological set he desired without revealing too many details of the plot. He retained that flexibility which would permit a series of surprises disclosed through master showmanship; yet those surprises would dovetail in the structure he described.

The Prosecution began.

Major Sevier called Captain Charles Robert Weddel, Depot Adjutant, as first witness. His purpose was to read into the record orders pertaining to possession of alcoholic beverages and prohibiting swimming in the waters adjacent to Parris Island. Sevier could anticipate this would be straightforward procedure insuring him a quiet beginning. It was not so.

Had Berman wanted to be antagonistic, he could have made public ridicule of Post Regulations. These had been effective more than five years through the regimes of four Commanding Generals. They contained over forty changes. The paragraph concerning alcoholic beverages had been rewritten in Changes No. 16 and 24, a clue to the fact that restrictions were difficult to enforce. The current version was suggested in January 1954 by Colonel John Alexander White, then in command of Headquarters and Service Battalion, after one of his marines was acquitted of illegal possession. But it was the paragraph prohibiting swimming that gave Berman opportunity for logical reasoning. That paragraph states: "Because of the contamination of the water adjacent to Parris Island, all personnel of this Command are prohibited from bathing or swimming therein."

BERMAN: Does Trial Counsel suggest that 19-20 prohibiting that personnel bathe because of the pollution of the water is material in this case?

SEVIER: I think my action is very evident.

BERMAN: I certainly attack the relevancy of such order to this case. Nobody has suggested that anyone has gone out swimming or bathing.

KLEIN: I will admit it is a prohibition against swimming and bathing—it is at least a procedure of entering on the circumstances for the purpose of swimming and bathing.

BERMAN: It seems to me someone who offers evidence should show the relevancy and materiality. The language is specific: It prohibits the act of swimming and bathing. Does that prohibition apply to the facts of this case?

KLEIN: Certainly it is the prohibition against entering the water adjacent to Parris Island.

BERMAN: Oh, no, it is not. It is a prohibition against swimming and bathing because of pollution.

KLEIN: I believe it is self-evident.

BERMAN: I present my objection on the ground there has been no showing of materiality whatsoever.

KLEIN: I will admit it on the basis that the reason—because of pollution—implicitly carries with it the question of entering.

BERMAN: I must respectfully except. The language of the proffered offer is plain and clear, requires no interpretation.

KLEIN: It is admitted.

BERMAN: I trust that my exception will be noted.

KLEIN: Yes.

SEVIER: I believe it is my understanding in the procedure—in a court-martial proceeding—that all objections are saved and that exceptions need not be noted.

KLEIN: I have said that but Mr. Berman has the right to know that is so.

BERMAN: I am happy to know that this is so and I will not cumber the record with any further exceptions.

While Adjutant Weddel was on the stand Emile Berman won his first skirmish against limiting cross-examination and was introducing his first Exhibit:

"If it pleases the Court: I offer into evidence Defense Exhibit A for identification—" An aide whispered. "I have been advised that General Pate's secretary, Colonel Simpson, is on the telephone. It has been reported to me that this is an emergency call. Do I have your permission, Mr. President, to respond to that call?"

HUTCHINSON: Yes, you do.

Berman turned to Klein: "Do I have yours, sir?"

KLEIN: Yes.

BERMAN: I shall return once again to carry out the proceedings. With your permission, gentlemen?

KLEIN: May I see this piece of paper?

BERMAN: Yes, sir. (Berman handed the Exhibit to the Law Officer.) Thank you, Mr. President, and members, and, of course, the Law Officer. (He withdrew from the courtroom.)

That scene was enough to inspire news tipsters, generate speculation among the jurors, throw the Prosecution off balance, and keep Parris Island's network of rumor factories working overtime.

Master Sergeant Hans C. Manthey, McKeon's Chief Drill Instructor, was second witness. Manthey testified that orders concerning possession of alcohol and forbidding swimming in local waters were posted on a bulletin board where McKeon could read them. That ended Wednesday's morning session.

Since Mr. Berman sent Captain Weddel away to search his files and Judge Klein bumbled when instructing the Court about questioning Sergeant Manthey, both were recalled immediately after lunch. Then Lieutenant Colonel Robert Almond Thompson, McKeon's Battalion Commander was called as third witness. Sevier got Thompson to describe how he had warned McKeon about the pitfalls of financial dealings with recruits and maltreatment. On cross-examination Berman won the skirmish in which Sevier attempted to limit the scope to matters brought out in direct examination. Attorney Berman consolidated the advantageous position he gained.

BERMAN: I am asking you, quite apart from any other circumstance, Colonel Thompson, quite apart from the result, quite apart from any regulations—if such there were—would you equate the taking of men on a march across a rifle range where they were at that time—they were billeted at the Range, at Weapons Training Battalion—across the drill field and possibly one hundred yards beyond that into the marshes of a creek—quite apart—for the avowed purpose of teaching them discipline and improving their morale, would you consider that, in your view, a kind of maltreatment that your orientation lecture was intended to point out to a Drill Instructor?

THOMPSON: In the absence of—

SEVIER: If it please the Court: I feel constrained to object to that question. He is asking the witness a hypothetical question and I feel the Law officer will agree that a hypothetical question must be based on facts in evidence and those facts that he has related are not now in evidence. I think that the question is improper.

BERMAN: Well, we've gone all through that, sir. I'm offering this subject to connection. Subject to connection I am permitted—

KLEIN: I assume that you will offer testimony to establish the basis for the assumed facts.

BERMAN: I am now put to the necessity of asking you whether you have the question in mind, sir.

THOMPSON: I have the question in mind.

BERMAN: I would be delighted to hear your answer, sir.

THOMPSON: If this hypothetical march had taken place without adequate reconnaissance, without adequate means to safeguard the members of that platoon, without adequate medical personnel to accompany it, without adequate communications with its rear base and with full knowledge that certain members of that platoon could not swim and with the intention of taking them into the water, I would definitely consider it maltreatment.

BERMAN: I wonder if you would answer the question that I asked you, limited to the facts that I mentioned to you? We will strike out the answer as being not responsive.

KLEIN: I will permit the answer to stand.

BERMAN: What base are you referring to when you keep in mind that this entire march was less than 1,000 yards?

THOMPSON: From your headquarters of operations—your point of departure—with whom you would have arranged the march previously.

BERMAN: And now you are contemplating the tragic results, are you? I am asking you quite apart from the results.

THOMPSON: I am contemplating getting the troops there and back in the best condition, if that is what you mean.

BERMAN: But I am asking you quite apart from what you now know to be the results—

SEVIER: I object. It is argumentative—

BERMAN: Excuse me, sir. Are you in a position—

SEVIER: My objection goes in now.

KLEIN: Let's get the question. One moment. (Judge Klein turned to the side door of the courtroom). Will you clear that area? Back up, please! But don't stand beside the door.

BERMAN: May I restate the question I'm asking, sir?

KLEIN: Yes.

BERMAN: I would like to know, quite apart from introducing into your mind anything other than the bare facts as stated in the question—not end results, not the occasioning of an accident—I'm asking you whether it would be your view, even if a regulation was violated, that if a Drill Instructor, to improve—teach discipline and improve morale, took his troops on a night exercise in which he marched them into a swamp, would you take the position that that was maltreatment under the context of your orientation lecture, sir?

THOMPSON: I would.

BERMAN: In that case I have no further cross-examination.

Prosecutor Sevier countered with his own hypothetical question, "subject to connection," which added features Berman had omitted. The question was admitted over Defense objection and Thompson gave the answer Sevier expected. But Defender Berman had the last word.

BERMAN: Did you ever issue any instructions about whether the training or drills should be—or exercises should be conducted day or night in marshes or swamp land? You can answer that—if you can answer that "yes" or "no," please do that, sir.

SEVIER: The Manual states that no witness may be required to answer "yes" or "no."

KLEIN: Provided the answer isn't capable of "yes" or "no."

Judge Klein should have asked for a recess to review his book, which says:

> A witness should be required to limit his answers to the question asked. He cannot, however, be required to answer categorically by a simple "yes" or "no" unless it is clear that such an answer will be a complete response to the question. A witness may always be permitted at some time before completing his testimony to explain any of his testimony.

BERMAN: I simply want to know from the witness if he had ever given such an instruction. He can be confined to a "yes" or "no" if he is capable of answering "yes" or "no." You can have a man—

THOMPSON: My answer is "no."

Klein, Sevier, even Thompson were dupes. Klein made the wrong ruling; Sevier could have further questioned the witness; Thompson could have claimed privilege to explain his testimony. Berman scored on that hoary trick question: "Have you quit beating your wife?" Lawyer Berman was aware of what Thompson had said at the Inquiry and wished to keep it out of the Court-Martial record:

Q. In your orientation of the new Drill Instructors that come to you, do you ever personally tell them not to go into the swamps with troops?

A. No, sir. Nor have I told them not to jump their troops off the tops of buildings. That is just one thing common sense would tell you not to do.

Major Stanley Norman McLeod, Depot Provost Marshal, was fourth witness. He briefly described the terrain near Ribbon Creek and the search and rescue operations. Why Counsel Sevier called McLeod or what he contributed is not apparent. Berman, on the other hand, made McLeod his witness, raised doubts about observations of the moon and weather, and then used McLeod as the vehicle for introducing into evidence two aerial photographs of Ribbon Creek. Sevier's objections were to no avail. McLeod then escorted the Court out to Ribbon Creek and oriented them at the scene of the tragedy. With that the Court-Martial adjourned at the end of the third day. Four witnesses had been heard, two appeared twice, three would appear again. Lieutenant Colonel Thompson would not be recalled.

Major McLeod was back on the witness stand when Court opened Thursday, fourth day of the trial. Forty-five minutes were spent getting into the record—needlessly—photographs taken of the deceased as their bodies were removed from Ribbon Creek. That was McLeod's final appearance.

Master Sergeant John E. Clement was the next witness. His testimony would last two hours, consuming the rest of the morning. Clement might have been one of the few important witnesses in the whole trial, but neither party took full advantage of his superior knowledge of both the hydrography and customs of Parris Island. In fact, Major Sevier turned Clement over to one of his assistants, either Frederick Haden or William Otten, the record fails to indicate whom. Clement had eighteen years' service and had spent eight of the last eleven years at Parris Island. A good part of his experience was with the Water Transportation Unit and when he was with Weapons Battalion he spent all of his spare time on the water. Trial Counsel should have qualified John Clement as an "expert" and announced this openly to avoid misunderstanding. Instead, the Prosecution actually depreciated the ability of its own witness.

BERMAN: What do you consider that that area I have indicated —shown lighter in the photograph—is compared to the darker areas shown here?

PROSECUTOR: I object here. I believe it would be improper, the Sergeant having had no prior experience in the interpretation of aerial photographs.

BERMAN: I am talking about his knowledge of the terrain.

Judge Klein ignored Trial Counsel's objection, but either party by questioning Clement would have determined that he had sound reading knowledge of aerial photographs. In this age of ultraspecialization marine officers too often presume that an individual's military qualification is limited strictly to his occupational specialty. And naturally Counselor Berman wished to stress the opinion that Clement was no "expert."

BERMAN: Do you happen to know that at the highest possible tide at that point which you have indicated—the lowest point in the creek bed—the highest possible tide except monsoons or typhoons—the greatest possible depth of water at that particular moment of the highest possible tide is eight feet—or would you agree with that?

CLEMENT: I wouldn't go along with it, no.

BERMAN: Do you think it's greater or less?

CLEMENT: I think it's greater.

BERMAN: By how much do you think it's greater? I am speaking now of this highest tide and the six-foot rise.

CLEMENT: I would say about two and a half feet more than that.

BERMAN: But yours is based on observation. Is that correct?

CLEMENT: That's correct. It definitely isn't based on survey because I haven't surveyed the place.

BERMAN: No surveying; no plumbing of it; that's the way it appears to you?

CLEMENT: Yes, sir.

BERMAN: All right. Thank you.

John Clement already had testified he observed Sergeant Seybold the frogman, neck-deep in Ribbon Creek at low tide. Also Clement could have told that he sounded the "trout hole" with a boathook. Certainly this wasn't a precise survey, but it was a mighty valid observation. Just before Sergeant Clement left the courtroom, Berman dealt his prestige the final blow.

HUTCHINSON: Major Sevier, the witness may be excused. We have no further questions by the Court.

BERMAN: That is with the admonition, Mr. Law Officer, that you give the witnesses generally. And since I propose to recall him, I take it he will be available to me for interview.

KLEIN: The admonition provides that Counsel may talk to the witnesses.

HUTCHINSON: Did I understand, Mr. Berman, that you will produce more evidence later with reference to the hydrography of the creek—the details?

BERMAN: Yes, sir, we propose to produce the trained men who have prepared it, based on their own studies of that creek.

Defense Counsel would produce his own "expert." This is a reminder of the Naval War College unofficial definition of *expert:* any sonofabitch from out of town.

Prosecution apparently called Clement to establish the depth of water in Ribbon Creek. There were difficulties.

PROSECUTOR: At what time did you begin the dragging operations?

CLEMENT: The dragging operation began—

BERMAN: I can see no reason whatsoever for any of this testimony.

KLEIN: What are you trying to establish?

PROSECUTOR: We are trying to establish—we are going to show that Sergeant Clement was there and took part in the operation in which the boys were drowned [sic] and that Sergeant Clement is acquainted with and has a knowledge of the terrain and the actual river bottom. He is going to testify as to certain features of the river.

Klein spoke to Berman: "Will you concede if it will save time?"

BERMAN: I certainly will agree that he worked on that creek. There's nothing unusual about that. I concede that he worked on that creek in grappling operations.

KLEIN: With that I think you are in position to proceed concerning the terrain. Ask him whether he observed the terrain at such and such a time and so on.

PROSECUTOR: I also want to establish—if I could ask—

KLEIN: Well, you may ask any question. I'm merely suggesting in order to speed things.

Legal skirmishing continued until Trial Counsel finally achieved the essence of testimony desired.

Major Sevier wouldn't concede to Mr. Berman Thursday morning. The former was still attempting to have the two sides of his case presented in series; the latter had already established a fairly strong beachhead for presenting both sides in parallel. And while he was doing that, Berman did what he intended in any event: to shroud in doubt location of the point of drowning any time it did not agree with his own hypothesis. One way Berman did this was by asking long, somewhat confusing questions requiring short answers.

BERMAN: Just tell us what you mean—indigenous with that matter—as it is influenced by the tide—what is the influence of a high rise in tide on the area between the marsh grass and the bank you have described as the fill bank—how much water would you get in that area?

CLEMENT: I do not know how much water could get in that area.

BERMAN: Now I want to ask you—I think it is already implicit in your testimony that the observation that you were asked about in your direct examination of the deepest point that you saw a man in the water on the following day—or the tenth, two days following—is at the place where you put the letter *m,* which you estimate to be—which you approximated, in any event—to be about fifty feet actually from the side of the creek itself—behind Charlie Butts, toward the opposite bank. Is that correct?

CLEMENT: Let's have that again.

BERMAN: I will put it this way: When you put this letter *m* on this picture, Defendant's Exhibit B, that was supposed to point where a man had been in the creek bed—in the stream on his feet—and the deepest place where you had seen him or any other man at any time on that day?

CLEMENT: Approximately. Yes, sir.

Clement's "approximately" is an important cue which discloses another Berman tactic in casting doubt. Defense Exhibit B is an oblique aerial photograph of Ribbon Creek taken in June from an altitude of 1,500 feet. As with any aerial photograph, most particularly an oblique, the scale varies considerably over all parts of the picture. Estimation of distances on this photograph is virtually impossible, even directions are rather confusing. In comparison Berman introduced Defense Exhibit D, a precision survey made in June to the scale of one inch equals fifty feet. Berman folded that survey so that soundings of Ribbon Creek would not show. Then he required Clement to estimate the distance to the same spot!

Attorney Berman also used Clement to cast doubt on the existence of a drop-off into the "trout hole." He wanted to prove that the only drop-off was at the bank of Ribbon Creek where water was not more than waist-deep at high tide. This is how he went about it:

BERMAN: Have you ever estimated how much of a drop-off there is from the shallow area to the depth of the deepest area in the creek; that is, is it a sheer drop, is it a gradual drop, or what kind of drop-off is it?

CLEMENT: I don't know, personally. But talking to a man who was in there, he said that the bottom sloped off—didn't drop off.

We review all the testimony about this drop-off while considering tidal phenomena and the depth of water in Ribbon Creek. But it is interesting to point out here two aspects of Clement's observations: First, Sergeant Seybold never entered the "trout hole," he recovered *Thomas Hardeman*'s body from the very edge of it, he wasn't forced to use the oxygen-breather. Second, Seybold approached the hole from "downstream"—seaward; Platoon 71 approached the hole from upstream.

Berman used Clement to sustain another hypothesis: that the point from which the bodies were recovered was unrelated to the spot where the recruits drowned. (Major Sevier couldn't challenge this, of course, since he didn't learn from Sheriff McTeer that a drowned body doesn't shift position even in a strong current.)

PROSECUTOR: Sergeant Clement, I wonder if you could show us on the photograph where the bodies were found?

BERMAN: I object to this and ask for the right of preliminary inquiry, please. This being a tidal stream, it is influenced by the action of the tide in respect to some current, is it not?

CLEMENT: Right.

BERMAN: So on an outgoing tide there is a current that is going out toward sea; is that right?

CLEMENT: Correct.

BERMAN: And if there was an object such as a piece of wood or even a body that was doing nothing but floating or being carried under water, that would be carried downstream during the tide that is going in ebb; isn't that so?

CLEMENT: Correct.

Throughout the trial Defender Berman would harp on the custom of marching platoons through swamps to teach discipline. He started the campaign Wednesday with Lieutenant Colonel Thompson. Before he went much further there would be an out-of-Court argument, which we consider in that context. But while John Clement was on the stand, Emile Berman continued this drive.

BERMAN: Tell me this: In all the years you have been on this base, have you ever seen platoons marching in the swamps, marshes, and creeks in the area of the Weapons Training Battalion, or the Third Battalion, or any other area, Sergeant Clement?

John Clement never got a chance to answer this one, nor do I know what his answer would have been. But I do know that he would have contributed rather convincing circumstantial evidence. Berman was stymied for the moment and this is how the record shows it:

KLEIN: I take it you are withdrawing the question at this time?

BERMAN: I am, sir.

KLEIN: Is it your intention to present this question when the witness is recalled to the stand, or will you defer presentation of that question?

BERMAN: I propose to present it when the witness is recalled. It is my expectation to present that issue continuously in this trial. In my view, it is the major issue in the case.

John Clement was not recalled.

Sergeant Algin H. Nolan, "tidal expert," was lead-off man for the Prosecution Thursday afternoon. The only thing we learn from his testimony is that since the Inquiry he had been transferred from administrative clerk in the Depot Sergeant Major's Office to on-the-job training in the Area Auditor's Office. In the last three months Nolan had learned nothing more about tides. Major Sevier might just as well have had the Court take judicial notice of *Tide Tables of the East Coast,* U. S. Department of Commerce.

Next witness was Richard J. King, once colleague of Matthew McKeon, now a corporal in Headquarters and Service Battalion. King related his version of drinking in Barracks 761, told of his activities April 8, and was on the stand when Prosecutor Sevier finally decided to accept Defender Berman's first stipulation admitting identity of the six named recruits and that they died from drowning in Ribbon Creek April 8. Fireworks during King's appearance in court were few. One exchange shows Judge Klein's disposition that hot afternoon:

BERMAN: Are you aware of any orders given by Sergeant Huff regarding seconds of desserts at chow?

KING: He didn't say it in front of me.

BERMAN: Had you heard of it? Are you aware of it?

SEVIER: I object. The question has been asked and answered twice.

KLEIN: I think he can continue.

BERMAN: Were you aware?

KING: Yes, sir.

SEVIER: Objection, answer, hearsay. Ask it be stricken.

BERMAN: I haven't even finished my question. I'm on the question. When you say you were aware of it, were you aware that Sergeant Huff had given orders to someone that the platoon was not to have seconds at chow?

KING: No, sir; I wasn't.

SEVIER: I object. The answer is hearsay—the question before this.

KLEIN: He has answered the question.

SEVIER: Does the Law Officer overrule my question?

KLEIN: You are objecting to questions and answers somewhere back?

SEVIER: I want a ruling.

KLEIN: We will have the question read.

REPORTER: Q. Were you aware? A. Yes, sir.

KLEIN: Overruled.

The only bright spot in Corporal King's testimony was provided by Lawyer Berman's antics while exhibiting the vodka bottle for the first time:

BERMAN: Do you have the bottle here?

Trial Counsel handed Defense Counsel a bottle.

BERMAN: Would you take off this tag just for a moment?

SEVIER: Just for the moment, but I will put it back on.

BERMAN: I'm inclined to take out this cork and smell it. I would like for you to tell me whether the contents are the same as the contents when it came into your possession.

SEVIER: Yes, sir.

BERMAN: I show you this bottle and without trying to identify it specifically, was it a bottle such as you are shown now—that I am holding?

KING: Yes, sir. It was the same category, same size and description.

BERMAN: Yes, sir; very good. I ask that this bottle be marked for identification.

SEVIER: I have no objection to its introduction.

REPORTER: It is marked "Defense Exhibit E for identification."

BERMAN: In connection with your drink—such as it was—did you have a drink out of a cup or a glass, or how?

KING: Out of the bottle.

BERMAN: What is known in some circles as a *swig?*

KING: Yes, sir.

When Corporal King was excused there remained twenty minutes of Working Hours.

SEVIER: Sir, I have more witnesses I can call, but I have no witness that I can finish with during the time we have set for today.

KLEIN: What are your wishes, Mr. Berman?

BERMAN: I am ready to proceed or—

KLEIN: *(to the Court):* What are your wishes?

HUTCHINSON: We would like to make it a policy that we utilize to the maximum all the Working Hours we have established and have agreed upon.

KLEIN: Call your witness. I shouldn't say, "Call your witness." Proceed.

SEVIER: I will call Sergeant Huff.

Staff Sergeant Edward A. Huff, once Senior DI of Platoon 71, was custodian of a neat, clean roster of the platoon, obviously not the one he used April 8 but a copy worthy of the National Archives. Defender Berman came to his feet to emphasize some material he would use later.

SEVIER: I offer this into evidence as Prosecution Exhibit 14.

BERMAN: May I just ask two questions about it preliminarily?

KLEIN: Yes, sir.

BERMAN: I notice there is a column on the roster called "GCT." Am I correct that this is the General Classification Test?

HUFF: Yes.

BERMAN: Are the entries contained in the column under GCT your own markings and evaluations or merely translating somebody else's test?

HUFF: They are somebody else's test.

BERMAN: Alongside that is a column headed "15-day." Does that also refer to the GCT test retaken fifteen days after the recruits have been with the platoon?

HUFF: That is a test they take on general knowledge of what they have accumulated.

BERMAN: Is it you who go there and mark that test?

HUFF: No, sir.

BERMAN: You simply again enter marks or grades that are given to you by someone else, so that you neither give the test nor evaluate it or know what the marking system is?

HUFF: That's right, sir.

BERMAN: With that understanding, I have no objection to this going into the record.

KLEIN: Admitted.

The next document Sevier wanted Huff to identify was the Weapons Training Battalion schedule for April 8. Weapons' schedules caused headaches among legal beagles at times because they were not authenticated. Multiple copies were mimeographed daily and distributed throughout the area. Having someone sign each stencil served no useful purpose, a copy could be received as "real evidence." But some law specialists have refused to accept them, thus occasionally forcing acquittal of a malefactor through their own stubbornness. At the Inquiry, Major Holben introduced a copy as part of the Platoon Log. Major Sevier followed suit. He was then finished with direct examination.

Both Counsel and Judge Klein agreed the hour appropriate for a break. Klein warned Huff he would be recalled in the morning. President Hutchinson announced the adjournment.

Friday, July 20, McKeon's Court-Martial came to order one hour late. Trial Counsel just had time to swear in a new Reporter, Margaret Heustess, before Counselor Berman was on his feet:

> Before the witness is called, Mr. President and members of the Court—and Mr. Law Officer, I would like to make an application to the Court.

A matter has come up very, very recently which requires my personal attention at some distance from Parris Island. It is a matter of serious purport and I have no way of delegating this to anyone else. It will require my leaving Charleston by the first available plane on Saturday—which is one o'clock—and my experience with transportation across from this place and vice versa is that if I allow two and a half hours, especially on Saturday, I would be operating on a very, very thin line indeed.

I respectfully request that, since at best—if you honor my request to attend this important business—at best the session of our Court would be limited to an hour, or possibly an hour and fifteen minutes on Saturday morning—and no great useful purpose will be served by such a brief session—therefore, I am making the request now to you, as President of the Court, and you, sir, the Law Officer, for an adjournment at the conclusion of today's business until Monday morning at our usual convening hour. I can only assure you that my purpose is not trivial; that it has, in my view, serious connotations, and I ask that you give me the tolerance of ability to perform this business.

KLEIN: Has Trial Counsel any views in connection with that request?

SEVIER: Trial Counsel has no objection, sir.

KLEIN: The Law Officer has no objection. The President, I think, will, under those circumstances, make a determination.

HUTCHINSON: In view of the request of Counsel for the Defense, this Court will adjourn at the close of hearings today until nine o'clock Monday.

Berman's secret mission, ostensibly connected with Matthew McKeon's defense, bathed the working press in an aura of mystery. There was much speculation in next morning's newspapers. Parris Island was clouded with rumors. The most credible hearsay is that Emile Berman flew to Washington for a visit with Randolph Pate—and cooled his heels several hours while Pate attended his duties at a cocktail party.

Edward Huff then came back for cross-examination. Before Defense could establish rapport with the witness the Prosecution fired a barrage of objections. We tune in near the climax of this issue:

BERMAN: Have you, in your acquaintanceship with a large number of Drill Instructors over a period of almost two years, acquired any knowledge as to whether or not there was a practice amongst Drill Instructors in dealing with a laggard platoon—for the purposes of teaching discipline and boosting morale of a platoon as an organization—become aware of a practice of marching men into boondocks or swamps—marshes and creek waters?

SEVIER: We object to that question, may it please the Court.

KLEIN: Objection sustained.

HUFF: I think it was common knowledge—

KLEIN: Don't answer that question.

BERMAN: I didn't hear the grounds of the objection and I am certainly unaware of the grounds for the ruling. If it is the form of the question that was objected to—no grounds were stated—is it as to form?

KLEIN: As to form without going back to have the Law Officer say more than he is inclined to say.

BERMAN: All right, sir. (*Then to Huff*) Sergeant Huff, do you know of a practice on Parris Island in the training of recruits with respect to discipline and the inculcating or boosting of morale in the unit—as well as for the training of interdependence amongst the men of that unit—of marching men at night into the boondocks, marshes, swamp water, or creek water, in the waters abutting or within Parris Island?

SEVIER: May it please the Court: We object to that question. One, on the basis that it is a leading question and this is in the nature of direct examination which has exceeded the scope of the previous examination of the Prosecution; and secondly, that this is an attempt to inject a custom, practice, or usage—whatever you call it—which was objected to yesterday. If the Court is ready to hear our argument, we have a strong argument on that point.

BERMAN: As far as the form of the question, I have not led—have not suggested an answer. I have simply directed attention to the field in which the testimony is cast. As far as the ruling of the Law Officer on the admissibility of a common practice, it is true there hasn't been any such ruling. As far as making the witness my own witness at this point, I agree that, for this inquiry, I am making this witness my witness.

KLEIN: Are you both prepared to present argument on the question of the custom or practice—Trial Counsel and Defense Counsel—and the admissibility of evidence of practice or custom as it may affect the issues in this case?

SEVIER: Yes, sir.

BERMAN: I am prepared to argue the question briefly and—I hope—concisely.

The witness was warned and excused.

KLEIN: The Court will please retire until such time as they are advised that the Court will again reconvene.

The argument lasted forty minutes. Judge Klein made up his mind before the debate got under way. He listened—in his fashion—making frequent interruptions. Attorney Berman won. Klein would admit evidence of customs or practice, though he restricted it to the same or similar circumstances. That left Sevier's foot in the door.

BERMAN: Sergeant Huff, in connection with your having been a Drill Instructor of five platoons and having been on Parris Island for approximately two years—and in connection with your knowing a great many of the Drill Instructors, were you or were you not aware of a practice of marching platoons at night into the swamps, marshes, boondocks and waters in the vicinity of Parris Island for the purpose of teaching discipline—not disciplining troops, but teaching discipline and boosting their morale?

SEVIER: Objection. First of all, it calls for hearsay; second, it is irrelevant and immaterial; third, it presumes facts not in evidence.

KLEIN: Objection sustained.

BERMAN: I don't see that there is anything, sir—if I may respectfully refresh your recollection—I don't see anything in the question that calls for hearsay. It is a matter of cross-examination and I asked him whether he knows of a practice.

SEVIER: If he would say "do you know of your own knowledge" rather than call for hearsay information—but it still assumes facts not in evidence.

BERMAN: As to facts not in evidence, no one has as yet testified to the events which form the subject matter of the charge and the specification thereunder—Charge II—or the specification thereunder, 1 and 2 of Charge III. It's a charge that's laid—and we presume there will be proof on that issue.

KLEIN: Without arguing the point, the question also says "for training purposes."

BERMAN: That's all right. I am offering the question as stated subject to connection. We will offer proof. I said, "for training purposes."

KLEIN: Since the question does not pinpoint his knowledge of a general awareness, I will sustain the objection. Had it been brought to your attention—did you ever observe—do you know?

BERMAN: That is what I am asking him. I am stating the question: "Do you know of a practice among Drill Instructors?" Do I have to restate the entire question?

KLEIN: Yes, sir.

BERMAN: Sergeant Huff, I am asking you whether as a result of having been on Parris Island for almost two years prior to April 8, 1956, and with your knowledge and acquaintanceship of a great many Drill Instructors and other noncommissioned personnel at Parris Island, did you know of a practice—for the purpose of training discipline and boosting morale—of taking platoons on night marches into boondocks, swamps, marshes and waters in the area of Parris Island?

SEVIER: Objection. It still calls for hearsay. In addition, this is now direct evidence produced by the Defense, and it is leading and suggestive.

KLEIN: Objection overruled, subject to connection.

BERMAN: You may answer, Sergeant.

HUFF: Yes, sir.

BERMAN: And was it the practice?

HUFF: As far as I know; yes, sir.

Counselor Berman knew that at the Inquiry Sergeant Huff made a startling revelation not yet known to the press. He made reference to Huff's previous testimony, but Prosecutor Sevier charged Berman with impeaching his own witness.

BERMAN: In the first place, he is a Defense witness only for the question last asked him—

KLEIN: Correct.

BERMAN: Also, he was called for general examination. I can ask him if he made certain answers under oath and he can say "yes" or "no."

KLEIN: We will hear the question and then determine whether it goes to his credibility.

BERMAN: I withdraw the question. *(Then to the witness)* Did you, yourself, ever tell your platoon—in connection with their lack of discipline and to train them in discipline—that if they didn't snap out of their hockey "I will take you down to the swamps?"

HUFF: I did, sir.

KLEIN: What is that, sir; snap out of what?

BERMAN: That is one of the terms I apologize to the Court for unfamiliarity with. May I adduce from the witness what *hockey* is? *(Then to the witness)* When you used the phrase, "if you don't snap out of your hockey," will you tell the Law Officer and the members of the Court just what you meant by that expression? May I suggest that you remember there are certain terms which cannot be translated into parlor language—I have reason to think that it is a term which would be understood by all marines—

KLEIN: But the record will be reviewed by some who may not be United States Marines.

BERMAN: Please give it some thought and answer the question.

HUFF: Well, sir; in training marines down here, it's a job that's very tedious and tiring, and *hockey,* the way I meant it, was that if they didn't start doing a little better—putting a little more effort into it—I would have to do something about it, sir.

BERMAN: And that something you told them you would have to do would be to take them down to the swamps?

HUFF: I made that statement; yes, sir.

It is useless to speculate on the word Sergeant Huff actually used when he threatened the platoon; needless to say, it was one of venerable Anglo-Saxon origin traditionally scorned by lexicographers. But it is important to note that Berman created headlines for the next day: "McKEON'S SUPERIOR THREATENED SWAMP MARCH." Sevier tried to shake Huff, only to learn—as was apparent at the Inquiry—that Huff was too shrewd to admit his own guilt and too loyal to the DIPA (Drill Instructors' Protective Association) to squeal on fellow sufferers:

SEVIER: Sergeant Huff, did you ever see any platoons marched in the swamp?

HUFF: I have never seen a platoon marched into the swamps.

SEVIER: Then can you say of your own knowledge that you, yourself, actually know of a platoon being marched in the swamp?

HUFF: Well, sir; I think among the Drill Instructors at Parris Island the word gets from one to the other.

SEVIER: But do you know of your own knowledge—from what you saw and what you, yourself, know—without some third party telling you?

HUFF: Like I say, sir; I have not seen them in the swamps, but I have heard it, sir.

SEVIER: Then what you are saying is that you, of your own knowledge, don't know about it?

KLEIN: In other words, you never saw anyone marched into the swamps; you did or did not see anybody marched into the swamps?

HUFF: I did not see, sir.

SEVIER: To get this down specifically: Did you, yourself, ever see any platoon marched into Ribbon Creek?

HUFF: No, sir.

SEVIER: Do you, yourself, know of any platoon numbers—the number or designation of any platoon that was taken into the swamps?

HUFF: None that I can recall, sir.

SEVIER: You don't know of any then?

HUFF: I do not know, sir.

SEVIER: You stated that you informed the members of Platoon 71 that if they didn't snap out of their hockey you would take them into the swamp. Did you take them into the swamp?

HUFF: I did not, sir.

SEVIER: Did you intend to take them into the swamp?

HUFF: Yes, sir.

SEVIER: But you did not?

HUFF: That's right, sir.

SEVIER: Why didn't you take them in?

BERMAN: I object to that. Why an act was or was not committed, why one didn't do something or one does something is a conclusion that does not come within the ambit of a witness' testimony—except for an expert, who may express reasons for an opinion where opinion evidence is required.

KLEIN: I will allow the question. Objection overruled.

HUFF: Would you please repeat the question, sir?

SEVIER: You said you didn't take them into the swamp but at the time when you said it you intended to, and I wanted to know why you didn't take them in.

HUFF: Because I had a training schedule to meet and I didn't have the time, sir.

Sevier continued this line of questioning with little success. Then he shifted to what Huff might have told McKeon:

SEVIER: Directing your attention to pretrial interview in the conference room of the Administration Building, you were asked whether or not you had told the Accused not to take the platoon into the swamp and you answered, "Neither told him to nor told him not to." Do you recall that answer?

BERMAN: I object to that. If that is referring to a question and answer, the custom is to ask were you asked this question and did you make this answer. Does this purport to be a series of questions and answers, reduced to writing, and signed by the witness?

SEVIER: This was a pretrial interview between the witness and Counsel.

BERMAN: I am just asking you whether you are referring to written statements or questions and answers reduced to writing and submitted to the witness for signature.

SEVIER: I am not; and I am not required to do so.

KLEIN: The question has been asked. You have no objection?

BERMAN: No, sir.

HUFF: Will you re-ask that statement, sir?

SEVIER: Do you want me to name the place again?

HUFF: No, sir. I have forgotten now what the question was about.

SEVIER: You were asked the question whether you had authorized Sergeant McKeon to take the platoon into the swamp and your answer was that you neither authorized him to nor did you forbid him to.

HUFF: I think I did, sir.

SEVIER: You recall that question and answer?

HUFF: I think so, sir.

SEVIER: Further, and following that question and answer, you were asked, in your opinion as Senior DI, did you consider Sergeant McKeon authorized to take the platoon into the swamp, and your answer was that you did not consider him authorized to. Do you recall that?

HUFF: I don't remember it, sir.

SEVIER: Do you recall being at that place at that time for that interview?

HUFF: I remember when you were speaking to me; yes, sir.

SEVIER: You recall the first question but not the second?

HUFF: I have forgotten many of those questions you have asked me. I have been asked questions day and night and I don't actually know now what you asked me, sir.

BERMAN: May I ask the Law Officer at this point, because it seems to me a good time to do so, to instruct the members of the Court that a question, itself, has no testimonial value?

SEVIER: I agree. I have no objection.

KLEIN: They are so instructed.

Staff Sergeant Edward A. Huff had finished his day in court. While he was called by the Prosecution, he was a material asset to the Defense. President Hutchinson announced a recess; it was time for lunch.

Friday afternoon Captain Charles E. Patrick, Weapons Battalion Officer of the Day at the time of the Ribbon Creek tragedy, was first witness. He was on the stand only six minutes. Sevier might have used Patrick to develop *res gestae,* but he only brought out that McKeon "thought there was three or four left back down in the water." Sevier didn't even ask Patrick about his placing McKeon under arrest, or why. Naturally Berman was delighted to get Patrick off the stand; the Defense asked but one question in cross-examination.

Technical Sergeant Johnny B. Taylor, Patrick's deputy at the time, was next to testify. It took him twenty minutes, but the only *res gestae* adduced was McKeon's saying, "Sergeant, I'm responsible for this." Berman's cross-examination of Taylor was with aid of aerial photographs and related to the location of sentry posts. No one seemed interested when Taylor stated that the first alarm was sounded by Post No. 4, rather than Post No. 3, as developed at the Inquiry.

Private Thomas Grabowski followed Taylor and headed the parade of recruit witnesses. The Prosecution used Grabowski as principal narrator of the events of April 8 while the Defense artfully fell in step and used him to establish its hypothesis pinpointing the location of Platoon 71 in Ribbon Creek at the time of panic. This is what happened when Sevier first released Grabowski to Berman for cross-examination:

BERMAN: In other words, to follow this out, if he was coming along following the bank on his right, he then made a turn or changed his course and walked out toward his left about from where you sit to the table?

GRABOWSKI: Yes, sir.

BERMAN: Where he then changed his course and resumed a line back parallel to the line along which you had come; correct?

GRABOWSKI: Yes, sir.

BERMAN: May we have that measured, Mr. Law Officer, from the witness stand to the table?

KLEIN: Have you any rule or measure to measure it?

SEVIER: I will accept an estimate from the witness.

BERMAN: I would estimate it, but I might be wrong on it.

KLEIN: Do you want the exact measurement?

BERMAN: Yes, sir. I prefer that exact measurement.

KLEIN: Then let's get a rule and measure it.

SEVIER: I take it the Law Officer desires to recess the Court until I get the means to measure it?

KLEIN: Exactly.

There followed a 17-minute recess.

BERMAN: Let the record show that, by measurement and by agreement, the distance is measured as approximately thirteen and a half feet.

Thomas Grabowski's testimony is divided into six parts; he was volleyed between Prosecution and Defense like a tennis ball. Even President Hutchinson made two unusual interruptions. This was the first: "Major, just a minute—Sergeant, tell the man in charge of the sound equipment to come in here." There was a pause while an anonymous technician adjusted the witness' microphone. A few minutes later the President interposed with a mild blunder.

HUTCHINSON: In order to avoid any possible confusion in the minds of members of the Court, it would be helpful if the Accused would point out—trace on the map or chart, whichever you choose—the general course that he followed from the time he left the rear of the butts until they returned to the river bank and where they made these turns. Any reason why that can't be done?

BERMAN: Do you suggest the *Accused* draw that line?
HUTCHINSON: The witness.
BERMAN: I believe you said "the Accused."

President, Trial Counsel, Defense Counsel, and Law Officer collaborated in assisting Private Grabowski to sketch on the oblique aerial photograph where he and McKeon were at the time of panic. The misfortune is that Grabowski hadn't seen the area in daylight prior to the tragedy except from D-Butts, 300 yards away; Grabowski had no training in reading aerial photographs; and the photograph itself was greatly distorted. Yet Grabowski's testimony was later the basis for Defense "scientific" reasoning to fix the depth of Ribbon Creek.

Last up that humid Friday afternoon was Private Melvin Barber, the nonswimmer who held back when the column turned downstream and then yelled "form a chain" when panic erupted. Even in discomfort all parties kept alert. Barber was telling of a conversation that Matthew McKeon had with Private *Wood* and him.

SEVIER: Were there any other nonswimmers in your platoon?
BARBER: Yes, sir. There was.
SEVIER: Where were these people located at this time?
BARBER: They were in the same vicinity, but they wasn't close enough to hear anything.
SEVIER: Were they within seeing distance of yourself?
BARBER: Yes, sir.
BERMAN: Have you got that time fixed in relationship to their instruction?
SEVIER: Private Barber, calling your attention to Sunday, April 8, 1956—
BERMAN: I respectfully request that the time—
KLEIN: He wants the time that that conversation—
SEVIER: If the Court please: If that's in the form of an objection, that's fine. If not, I feel Counsel can cover it on cross-examination.
BERMAN: Very well, sir.
SEVIER: We are interrogating the witness at this time, sir.
KLEIN: You have indicated that it was during the period of

swimming instruction which there is testimony—concerning which there is testimony covering a period of a week. Is that correct?

SEVIER: That's correct.

BERMAN: I understood the rule of evidence to be that any conversation must have as a foundation the time and place at which it took place.

KLEIN: It should, but after—

BERMAN: But, however, since the Captain doesn't desire to go forward with that I shall sit down.

SEVIER: If the Court please: Since Mr. Berman has made a statement, it's not a question of going forward and I would like to call to the Court's attention right here that there was no objection raised when—

KLEIN: Proceed.

SEVIER: Now, Private Barber, we will go on here uninterruptedly, I hope. Calling your attention to Sunday, April 8—

KLEIN: I can tell you about that, if you want, because there will be objections.

SEVIER: What, sir?

KLEIN: About going on uninterruptedly. You may expect that from time to time you will be interrupted by an objection if any question occurs to Counsel to be objectionable.

SEVIER: Of course. That's expected, sir.

KLEIN: I want you to expect it.

SEVIER: I expect it, sir, if it is objectionable. *(He turned back.)* Now, Private Barber, calling your attention to April 8, 1956, where were you located at that time?

BARBER: On the Rifle Range, sir.

Fifteen questions and answers followed.

SEVIER: Did you consider these field days in the form of punishment?

BERMAN: I object to that.

BARBER: Yes, sir.

BERMAN: Wait a minute! When I rise to object, would you please permit the Law Officer to rule on it, Private? I object to that as to what he considered the field days have been motivated by or what his description of them was, whether as discipline or anything else.

KLEIN: I will allow the question. Objection overruled.

This time there were twenty questions and answers.

SEVIER: Did you go as far as the rest of the people went?

BARBER: No, sir. I didn't.

SEVIER: Why didn't you, Private Barber?

BERMAN: I object to that. It's a question which calls for the operation of a witness' mind. I have objected to it previously.

KLEIN: The question is, "Did he go as far as the other people."

BERMAN: The question is why he didn't do something.

KLEIN: The question is why he didn't?

SEVIER: I think he's entitled to tell why he didn't go further—in answer to Mr. Berman's objection.

BERMAN: I withdraw my objection.

KLEIN: I think it's a question of senses, what he sensed at that time.

BARBER: Repeat the question.

Again there were twenty questions and answers.

SEVIER: Your witness.

BERMAN: I presume that we are going to conclude at the end of the direct. May I make a request of you, Major Sevier, for both our conveniences? We are going to recess now for approximately forty-eight hours. At least to refresh my recollection of this witness' testimony, could the Reporter get the brief testimony of this witness out so that we could have it by tomorrow afternoon? That doesn't seem like a major job.

SEVIER: We hope to be able to catch up with the rough on the entire record.

KLEIN: Since the first order of business will be cross-examination, this is brief testimony—

SEVIER: I was about to agree with him that I would.

BERMAN: Thank you, sir. In that case I'll abstain from examining at this time, if that's agreeable to you, Mr. President?

HUTCHINSON: Very well.

McKeon's trial ended its first week Friday, July 20, at 4:10 P.M. Showman Berman was in command.

19

Customs

THE CUSTOM OF NIGHT marches into Parris Island swamps was a hot issue from the beginning of the Inquiry into the Ribbon Creek tragedy until the end of Matthew McKeon's Court-Martial. This issue may be debated ad infinitum by partisans choosing either side because never in the history of this case was there agreement on definitions. Counsel for Inquiry and Prosecution lent added meaning to existing orders; Counsel for Party and Defense relied on evidence of custom as a criterion of sound judgment, which in turn was minor premise of the syllogism determining McKeon's guilt under the manslaughter charge. Let's see if we can examine the argument in its logical structure.

Custom in its generally accepted sense means habitual or usual practice, the usual way of acting in given circumstances. Sociologists say *custom* is a pattern of habitual activity transmitted from one generation to another. It has been established that generations of DIs made a practice of marching wayward platoons into Parris Island swamps at night. It is not necessary to question the motivation of these DIs or bases of their opinions. They did it; the custom in fact existed.

But we can't stop here. *Custom* means something more specific in the eyes of the law: a long-established usage which by continuance has acquired the force of unwritten law or a right. The criteria of a *valid custom* have been spelled out by authorities in military law: certain and uniform; long continued; compulsory; consistent; known; not contrary to any law or regulation. Night marches at Parris Island were not certain and uniform, not compulsory, not consistent; hence, they were not a *valid legal custom,* though they might still be considered *usage* or *practice.* The important point here is that we can try a marine for failure to conform with a valid legal custom, which is demonstrated in the oath taken by court-martial members to: "faithfully and impartially try, according to the evidence, your conscience, and the laws and regulations provided for trials by courts-martial; and if any doubt should arise not explained by the laws and regulations, then according to the best of your understanding and the custom of war in like cases." Yet this is only one side of the coin.

Before we look at the other side let's dispose of that sixth criterion of a valid legal custom: "not contrary to any law or regulation." Major Holben, General Burger, and Major Sevier all attempted to prove that night marches into swamps were prohibited, therefore contrary to regulations. Their argument was tenuous. First, Post Regulations said: "Because of the contamination of the water adjacent to Parris Island, all personnel of this Command are prohibited from bathing or swimming therein." Certainly this didn't restrict wading in the water, for instance, by surf fishermen. Next, these advocates cited a series of Depot Training Orders which said about the Elliott's Beach area: "The picnic ground, Whale Creek, beaches and all marshes are out of bounds," and in its context this applied only to recruits. By analogy they claimed other waters, beaches, and marshes were out of bounds to recruits. Sergeant Leland Blanding pointed out during the Court-Martial that DIs had read this order closely, that the Dredge Cut wasn't out of bounds, and that when the training order required exercises in scouting and patrolling on the Elliott's Beach hike it could rightfully be considered necessary to enter the Dredge Cut.

But the campaign of Holben, Burger, and Sevier—continually abetted by Trainer Silvey—argued the same point from another aspect. There was a standard paragraph in Recruit

Training Battalion schedules: "No deviation will be made from these schedules without specific authorization by this Headquarters (S-3)." These weekly schedules had an open-ended period in the evening denoted "review." Silvey pinpointed this argument by quoting from another order: "No extra instruction will take place on Sundays except during the evening periods in preparation for the following day." Silvey realized his "no deviation from schedule" rule wouldn't hold water—except, he hoped, by analogy—because that prohibition wasn't part of Weapons Battalion schedules which governed Platoon 71 at the time. He gave weight to "preparation for the following day," however, because night marches are certainly not preparation for marksmanship.

Then our apologists had a third aspect even less tenable: They maintained that any act by a DI not specifically authorized was prohibited; if it wasn't on the Schedule or in the Lesson Plan, the DI couldn't do it. This viewpoint was untenable because in other parts of Silvey's own Standard Operating Procedure it said:

> Drill Instructors will use waiting periods to instruct recruits or to have recruits study the Guidebook or classroom notes. Drill Instructors are encouraged to conduct extra instruction of a constructive nature which will assist the recruit in becoming a good basic marine. The value of extra instruction is lost if it is approached from a disciplinary or harassing point of view.

This repudiates Silvey's contention that the DI had no initiative, that his every move was spelled out. Moreover, as a "training expert," he should have known about the phenomenon of individual differences: No two recruits, no two platoons are the same; they learn different things at different rates; time must be adjusted by the Drill Instructor, cut short when his troops learn quickly, lengthened when they learn slowly. (Silvey is an advocate of uniform weekly schedules which make no allowance for uncertainties, like weather.)

And so now we must look at extra instruction as "diciplinary or harassing" in connection with another item in the SOP:

> Drill Instructors are required to include adequate physical drill as a part of recruit training. Physical drill will not be

employed for individual or mass punishment. Drill Instructors are, however, encouraged to utilize such free time as may be available for physical conditioning beyond the specific requirements of the training schedule. A Drill Instructor will execute the movement with his platoon.

This leads us into semantics because *discipline* has more different meanings than the old Gatling gun had barrels. In our situation we select just three: (1) *discipline* as the process of training, (2) *discipline* as maintenance of a state of order and control, (3) *discipline* as correction, chastisement, or the infliction of punishment. Silvey's SOP says:

> The recruit will immediately be taught that all persons in the naval service are required to obey readily and strictly, and to execute promptly the lawful orders of their superiors.

This injunction involves all three meanings: training, control, punishment.

These three meanings of *discipline* have been part of our language 300 years, but during Inquiry, Court-Martial, and letter-writing in between Silvey maintained that *discipline* is a state of order while *punishment* is something different, and is only inflicted by the Commanding Officer. Silvey's position was upheld by the triumvirate: Holben, Burger, Sevier. All quote their authority from *Manual for Courts-Martial,* which does in fact limit to the Commanding Officer administration of both judicial and nonjudicial punishment. But here we again venture into semantics. To begin with, judicial and nonjudicial punishment are formal, defined in the *Manual,* and required to be a matter of record. Yet the Manual says:

> The provisions do not apply to, include, or limit the use of nonpunitive measures that a Commanding Officer is authorized and expected to use to further the efficiency of his command, such as admonitions, reprimands, exhortations, disapprovals, criticisms, censures, reproofs, and rebukes, written or oral, not as a penalty but as a purely corrective measure, more analogous to instruction than to punishment, in the strict line of his duty to create and maintain efficiency.

Our manual also prohibits:

> Punishment by flogging, branding, marking, tattooing on the body, or any other cruel or unusual punishment; the use of irons, single or double, except for the purpose of safe custody; punishment not sanctioned by custom of the service, such as carrying a loaded knapsack, shaving the head, placarding, pillorying, placing in stocks, or tying up by the thumbs; imposing as punishment formal military duties, such as assignment to a guard of honor, and duties requiring the exercise of a high sense of responsibility, such as guard or watch duties.

And so we have a continuum labeled "discipline" with punishment at one extreme, training at the other, a hazy band in between. It would seem lawful to revive that old tradition of publicly stripping the buttons from a convicted deserter (or coward) and having the field music follow him out to the gate playing the "Rogue's March," which is still in the book. If at the end of Working Hours there is necessary police work left to be done, it seems lawful to select "volunteers" from among those sloughing off at drill. There was no positive rule preventing a recruit platoon doing physical drill all day long—provided one of its three DIs participated; nothing prevented this but the sound judgment and moral values of the Drill Instructor. Hence, if we're disciplining (training) an outfit to instill discipline (control and order) it may or may not be discipline (punishment) depending on our own personal motivation, which can neither be seen nor measured, which in a court of law must be inferred —beyond reasonable doubt.

Joseph Burger's permitting a press release stating Platoon 71 had been on a night *training* march and then on the record of Inquiry trying to prove that no practice of night marches into swamps existed, led to threefold results: publicly discrediting the integrity of Marine Corps commanders; providing a firm base for Matthew McKeon's defense strategy; comprising logical analysis of the Ribbon Creek *affaire*.

Had the whole truth been revealed at the outset, custom law would have been on the side of Government. Discrediting Inquiry testimony as hearsay was poor tactics: Hearsay may be admitted freely during investigations—though it is rigidly excluded from trials—because hearsay yields clues which may lead to truth, General Burger could have given blanket immunity to witnesses so that he might develop further truths. Our whole system at Parris Island was under the guns, under attack by the American public we serve and who ultimately render final judgment. Let's speculate on what might have happened if Burger's tactics (and that includes Staff, organs in the body of his command) had been different.

Admit that maltreatment and extortion are the two outstanding vices of Boot Camp—this is eloquently demonstrated by Depot Orders. Admit that we maintain constant vigilance to suppress maltreatment, that we're continually bringing DIs to trial for cruelty to recruits, that we try to keep maltreatment under control—then confess we don't believe we can ever eliminate it completely. Admit that our philosophy of training vests powerful authority (and initiative) in the DI and that while we try to restrain him, ultimate control rests in his good judgment. Then let's get specific. Document cases of maltreatment—in its hundreds of different manifestations—through the years; this could be kept private in official records and not released to the press. Give them immunity and call every witness we can find, learn everything possible about night swamp marches, particularly what motivated them. Now ask each witness, "What would have happened had you been caught?" There is just one logical answer, "I'd have been punished for maltreatment." Now we have the custom established, but from a completely different viewpoint: In the culture of Parris Island it is known to be illegal.

Considering the Ribbon Creek incident specifically, that night march wasn't prohibited (1) because the area was out of bounds, (2) because the DI lacked authority, (3) because it didn't appear in the training schedule, or (4) because it was in fact punishment rather than training. That march violated no positive law directly, but through the mediation of Parris Island custom-law and as judged by Parris Island values, it was unquestionably maltreatment—unless Matthew Charles McKeon led that march with sincere good purpose; in other words, we need to know his motivation. Viewed in a different way, our question is this: "Having been on Parris Island three months, was McKeon part of its culture, party to its customs?"

Throughout this analysis we're completely disregarding the two Court-Martial charges involving use of alcohol while we concentrate on the two involving oppression and manslaughter. We substitute *maltreatment* for *oppression* because the former was Parris Island usage and the two are equivalent under the law. Now we are forced to look at *custom* from a different angle. If McKeon was guilty of maltreatment, he was automatically guilty of involuntary manslaughter while perpetrating maltreatment; conviction on both counts might lead to four years' imprisonment. But if McKeon were acquitted of maltreatment, then the custom of night swamp marches would determine whether he was guilty of manslaughter by culpable negligence or homicide by simple negligence; conviction on the former count might lead to three years' imprisonment, while conviction on the latter carries a maximum of one year. It is most interesting to see what bearing *custom* has on this determination. Here we turn to out-of-Court hearings of July 20:

KLEIN: I want to say at the outset that I am inclined to rule—on my own research thus far—that evidence of custom or common practice is not admissible with respect to any of the other charges. I would first like to have Defense Counsel then Trial Counsel state his position. After that we will hear arguments.

BERMAN: We are in complete accord with your view that this evidence is admissible on the charge of culpable negligence, since the evidence has to do with reasonableness of the conduct of the Accused, whether it was either culpable or simple negligence—the test always being: "Was it the act of a reasonable and prudent person?"

KLEIN: Under the same circumstances.

BERMAN: Or circumstances similar or analogous, I believe. The practice must fall into the pattern of the charge and be reasonably similar to it; we agree to that. Now if we are correct in that premise, I will address myself to the specifications alleging oppression. Indefatigable research—and I am trying to say this modestly—has produced no definition of *oppression* as a legal concept in the military or civilian field. It may well have been that we should have searched for this in the field of international law, but we feel that we have enough to do in this case without going so far afield. However, there can be no doubt that by common understanding as well as by various and sundry standard dictionary definitions as well as by the implication of reading the specification—the oppression spoken of must have the meaning that the Accused abused his office to exercise a tyrannical power over those who were responsive to his command, for his own satisfaction and purposes. When I use the term, I have in mind personal satisfaction as distinguished from the satisfaction one generally receives from a job well done. Now if that be so, then the test of the reasonableness of the conduct of the Accused becomes far more persuasive and far more at issue in considering oppression than it does in culpable negligence, where the cases are legion, both as to culpable and simple negligence. We have found no decision in the military courts, and since this is not an offense or crime found ordinarily in civilian life, we have found no decision, no case law to which we can refer you under any doctrine of *stare decisis*. But if it is true that reasonableness of one's conduct is the very antithesis of the tyrannical exercise of power for the purpose of oppression—for the satisfaction of personal desires—then there can be no logical doubt that if the evidence has some value on the question of reasonableness of the Accused's behavior, it *ipso facto* stands as a defense to the charges of oppression. What may be deemed reasonable conduct because of long-established practices is the very antithesis of oppression under any kind of definition. Being the issue created by the Government, it warrants the reception of evidence tending to prove reasonableness on both counts.

OTTEN: If it please the Court: The theory of the Prosecution is best set forth in Winthrop's *Military Law and Precedents* where he states: "An alleged military usage cannot avail an officer or soldier charged with a military offense to vindicate this act, except where its existence and its lawfulness are susceptible of exact proof. Custom of the service is a treacherous tribunal. The existence in a command of an unauthorized practice, sanctioned by a commanding or superior officer, may sometimes extenuate the act of a subordinate who adopts it, but unlike a legal custom it cannot serve as a defense—

KLEIN: Unlike a what?

OTTEN: A legal custom. There appear to be actually two rules which may be in issue. One is the normally adopted, legal rule of custom and usage, which the Prosecution will concede can be evidence in negligence cases. The other is the purported term which Mr. Berman is using as a practice. We contend that a practice is akin to an illegal custom and cannot be a defense. The law is well settled that custom and usage is no defense to a crime. I would like to cite the case of Burnett vs. the United States, 222 Federal 2d 426—

KLEIN: What is that citation?

OTTEN: I have most of these citations written on a piece of paper if you would like to have a copy. *(He handed the document to Judge Klein. Assistant Prosecutor Otten continued:)* It is likewise a well established principle of law that negligence cannot be excused by custom and usage. *(Otten gave six citations.)* We concede there is a well-recognized exception to this ruling first stated by Justice Holmes in Texas and Pacific Railway Company vs. Behyner; he stated what is usually done may be evidence if what ought to be done, but what ought to be done is fixed by a standard of reasonable prudence whether it's usually complied with or not. So the rule is that evidence of custom may be admitted as what the standard of care is and not what is reasonable. I have been unable to find any rule that evidence of custom is to show reasonableness, rather it is to show what is the standard of care. There are, however, several exceptions to this rule. The first exception in 38 American Jurisprudence 319 is: where an act is clearly negligent evidence of custom is inadmissible. Now on the very facts of this case, we contend that he took nonswimmers into ten feet of water and that, sir, is clearly negligent. Another exception is where the manner of performing the act is of common knowledge and I think it is common knowledge you do not take nonswimmers into water ten feet deep. The third exception is that evidence of custom is not admissible where the circumstances are dissimilar, and we feel there is one great dissimilarity between the facts of this case and any other custom which the Defense might be able to offer. Now I would like to cite one case which I think amply illustrates the exception, Klaus vs. Yellow Cab Company, 106 Federal 2d 935. This involved an automobile accident in which a left turn was made. There was a sign at the intersection, "No Left Turn," and it was held in that case that evidence of a custom of making a left turn in violation of that sign was inadmissible. That brings up the rule, then, that evidence of a custom contrary to an established law or ordinance—or in our case an established order—is inadmissible. We have already introduced one order—

KLEIN: I don't think anyone will say that evidence of a custom or practice in violation of a lawful order is admissible for the purpose of defense. It may be admissible in extenuation or mitigation. That isn't the question here.

OTTEN: That is exactly our point. Any evidence that would show a custom of taking people into water around this base would be in violation of the order already introduced and other orders we are prepared to introduce if we have to.

KLEIN: That's to be litigated.

OTTEN: We feel, anyway, that evidence of any custom for any of the three specifications about which this argument is concerned would be inadmissible. We contend that if any evidence is produced of a custom the facts of which are the same as what the Accused did, that would be an inherently dangerous custom. Thank you.

BERMAN: So far as Mr. Winthrop's observations written in 19—

KLEIN: Have you a brief?

BERMAN: It's not in submissible form. We have a paper. We will try to put it together for you. [No such brief is included with Appellate Exhibits.]

KLEIN: When do you expect you will have it?

BERMAN: We will work on it all this afternoon. We've been working ever since the question has been raised. So far as Mr. Winthrop's 1920 observations are concerned, I will ask Mr. Lester of my office to make some comment. I think the real problem with the argument advanced by Trial Counsel lies in the distinction of what is evidence of reasonable care against his view that admission of this evidence forecloses the jurors from considering what is reasonable care. We are not bold enough to say the jurors are foreclosed from making findings on what is or is not reasonable; we simply say that this is some evidence along with the rest of the case which they may consider. Viewed in that light, I think in large measure it disposes of what has been said here by Trial Counsel, except his statement that the act is clearly negligent. This is another way of saying that on the specifications alone they are entitled to a direction of a verdict in their favor. The act is not clearly negligent because the facts have not been fully elicited. Supposing I would pose to him the question that this man led his platoon, nonswimmers, if you please—even that's debatable—into water which at no time extended over their chests. Would you then say that we, sir, are entitled to a directed verdict since the issue is not the problem of night marches and is not the problem of going into water, but only that you take people into a depth of ten feet of water? This notion of what's clearly negligent depends in large measure adversely on the facts, and surely the facts are not at all conceded. That this platoon was led into ten feet of water, I could state for the record, will not be the evidence adduced in this case. So we are left with the proposition that ultimately, on the question of culpable negligence, possibly on some lesser degree of negligence, this case most likely will have to be decided by members of this Court. I'm not sure that the issue of oppression will ever reach the members of this Court and I am not sure that the issue of culpable negligence—since the term has been considerably defined both in United States Courts and the Court of Military Appeals—as well as a very recent development, a recodification for the benefit of the Law Officer's instruction on that subject, which we will call to your attention at the appropriate time—may take away from the triers of the fact—but even if they all eventually go to the jury, the over-all question—no matter how this case is charged, and I am not presumptuous enough to indicate now what I believe an appropriate charge is—

KLEIN: May I interrupt? I will welcome matter concerning instructions to the members and request it at the earliest.

BERMAN: We understand the procedure in Federal Courts where we are required to submit written requested charges to the Court—and we presume that the same procedure follows here—but as I was suggesting, on both the issue of oppression and culpable negligence the Law Officer will be obligated to charge the members of the Court that the standard imposed on the Sergeant accused here was a standard of reasonable care—that of a reasonable Drill Instructor attempting reasonably to fulfill his functions by the exercise of the care that a prudent Drill Instructor would have employed under all circumstances. That's how substantially close the case will narrow itself on legal terminology. If that crystallizes as a major legal issue in the case, then the evidence we propose to submit—practice regarding night marches into boondocks, swamps, creeks—is relevant and is evidence from which the triers of the fact may decide a reasonableness of the conduct of the Accused. Would you, Mr. Lester, please add briefly to what Mr. Winthrop was referring in the cited portion of the Captain's argument to the Court?

LESTER: May it please the Law Officer: The authority relied upon by Trial Counsel, Mr. Winthrop's treatise on military law, published in 1921, is rather distinguishable and inapplicable to the facts in this case. The chapter from which he quoted is entitled, "The Unwritten Military Law," and makes reference to the old Articles of War. The matter referred to, with adoption of the Uniform Military Code, is now Article 134. It referred to a standard created by practice in the military and makes references to standards adopted by the British Military and is an adoption into the American Military System. Mr. Winthrop makes reference to matters to the prejudice of good order. The standards can only be admissible as a violation of an order, in mitigation, or an explanation of the offense, but is not a defense in itself because it's a violation of the standards. In other words, Mr. Winthrop's entire proposition is that there is a body of law under the unwritten military code which creates a valid standard in violation of the law.

KLEIN: You mean by that they cannot be offered to set up a standard but may be offered on the evidence of negligence?

LESTER: That's right, sir.

KLEIN: The reasonableness as to whether or not the ordinary man would or would not have done this?

LESTER: That's correct, sir.

KLEIN: Only that some evidence would come to a determination of whether he would or would not?

BERMAN: May I say one other word since the Prosecution is apparently aware of the fact that exceptions they are trying to hew out from under depend on the existence of a valid order? It is now urged upon you to pass, as a matter of law, upon a proposition which prohibits the use of water for swimming and bathing because of the pollution of the water—is such an order in the circumstances of this case, the violation of which was intended to preclude the activities that are here at issue? I should say that the language of that cited portion of the order speaks very clearly for itself. I have very, very grave doubts indeed that you, sir, will undertake to say that's an order that has direct application to the facts in this case.

OTTEN: If it please the Court: Professor Wigmore makes the statement that evidence of custom or usage to be admissible must be relevant. I have made as thorough a search as possible in this area to try to find one manslaughter case in which evidence of custom and usage was admissible—and I was unable to find one. So the question is, "Why?" Because we are dealing here with culpable negligence and any custom which would tend to show that culpable, criminal, reckless disregard of the lives of other people was a customary practice would be illegal, therefore inadmissible. If the custom did not pertain to reckless and culpable negligence, it would be dissimilar and would not be relevant.

KLEIN: Isn't culpable negligence the ultimate issue—and has a lesser included offense? Isn't that a defense of simple negligence? Doesn't that then become one of the possible ultimate issues?

OTTEN: Once again, any evidence of a custom of doing a similar act would be a custom clearly negligent and would be inadmissible for that reason; but for another reason the act is also illegal and in violation of an order. I have a reason to believe—though we have no offer of proof from the Defense—that many of the instances which they might introduce would be concerned with a march to Elliott's Beach; there's been an order which forbids any marching through the swamps on the way to Ellott's Beach; and we are prepared to introduce that order. Winthrop says a prevailing usage is superseded when an enactment is made covering the subject. A usage can grow up or continue only when the written law is silent or quite obscure. We feel any custom or usage which is contrary to the written laws is inadmissible.

KLEIN: I said if it violates an order or a law, as a matter of defense. I think we concurred in that. But on the question of negligence—where negligence becomes a part of the case—apart from any order.

OTTEN: The point is where you are considering negligence, if the custom is an illegal custom, just as the custom of turning left where a sign says, "No Left Turn—"

KLEIN: You're getting into an order. I want to make this distinction and then you will be permitted to argue it. If a matter is prohibited, you may have a question of what is reasonable under the circumstances. You referred to distinct prohibitions. But where the offense is one such as involuntary manslaughter, where the question to be determined is, "Was or was not this man culpably negligent?" then it is a question of reasonableness or unreasonableness that comes into play for that purpose and for aiding the members of the Court in a determination. With that concept, I would like to hear your views.

OTTEN: If the Law Officer please: With regard to what is reasonable, it is stated in 26 American Jurisprudence 206 that a person of average intelligence is presumed to know what the average man knows. Our theory is that the average man has enough sense not to take nonswimmers into water over their heads and therefore any attempt to show a custom of something less than that is irrelevant.

KLEIN: But over their heads is one of the issues again.

OTTEN: That is the issue of fact for the Court—and any custom that shows that people were taken into ankle-deep water is irrelevant to this case.

KLEIN: That goes to the question of weight—to the question of similarities—that's one thing to be ruled upon when presented.

OTTEN: The Law Officer also brought up this question of the statute and I did find one case that is in the reverse—concerning the purpose of the statute—that is the case of Commonwealth vs. Wilansky, 316 Massachusetts 383, in which the problem was whether the owner of a night club had committed manslaughter by not complying with the building code.

BERMAN: Building code?

OTTEN: It's in the nature of a statute or ordinance, I believe.

BERMAN: I'm sorry to interrupt.

OTTEN: In any event, let us say it's a rule. Evidence of the building code was admitted in that case even though the purpose was not to prevent manslaughter.

KLEIN: That case doesn't go to the introduction of practices or customs. You are telling me that the evidence of a building code is admissible in a question of manslaughter?

OTTEN: The statute is admissible because it was an illegal act and manslaughter is based on the fact that if you do an illegal act and homicide results, it's manslaughter.

KLEIN: But still a reasonableness of the act involved in determining whether it is or is not unlawful. The point I make is that culpable negligence is not a matter of prohibition.

OTTEN: Once again, the act in question is one which is unreasonable, culpably negligent, a gross indifference, a reckless disregard for the rights and lives of other people, and no custom can be relevant to such an act.

KLEIN: Not custom, but practice, for the purpose of determining whether it is all those things you say it is. It's offered only to aid in arriving at a determination. I am of the opinion that it is admissible. I will grant the motion but I would rather rule on it. I will rule that evidence of other similar practices under the same or similar circumstances will be held to be admissible. With regard to oppression, questions of involuntary manslaughter as a result of an unlawful act, my ultimate instruction to the Court, upon the evidence, will cover and protect—

OTTEN: May it please the Court: I have one clarification. In any event where the Prosecution may be able to produce an order which any of this so-called custom will be in violation of, will the custom be admissible?

KLEIN: I will rule at the appropriate time on what is before me.

OTTEN: We have the right to make objection.

KLEIN: You may make every objection as we go along and you have an exception.

BERMAN: Since we have been here consecutively for quite some time—and as long as the Court is recessed now—may we have a ten-minute recess?

That's how Emile Berman got his favorable ruling—apparently without submitting a brief—permitting introduction in evidence of the custom of night marches into Parris Island swamps so that the Court might judge the reasonableness of Matthew McKeon's behavior. This will lead us to weighing ethical considerations, but first we have another question: "Was the custom of night marches into swamps condoned by McKeon's superiors?"

This question must be analyzed with respect to knowledge of the practice and at different levels of command. Unquestionably there was specific knowledge among DIs and agreement at their level that the practice helped to instill obedience and control in their platoons. While they valued the practice as an effective training measure, they seemed to know it could only be done surreptitiously: The custom was regarded as maltreatment and disapproved at higher levels in the command. But in the intermediate zone were company officers—captains and lieutenants—who defined *maltreatment* rather generously and either overlooked or failed to make an issue of minor acts of maltreatment.

At this level there was obviously general knowledge, and unquestionably knowledge of specific instances which company officers condoned by handling informally and not bringing to trial. In the upper zone of command, beginning with Battalion Commanders, there was general knowledge with readiness to punish in any specific instance discovered.

Our dictionary calls *ethics* "rules of conduct recognized in respect to a particular class of human actions." Fortunately Defense strategy in the case of the United States vs. McKeon was analyzed by Fr. Jerome A. Petz, SJ, in the August 18, 1956 issue of *America*. Fr. Petz teaches at the University of Detroit Law School and like other members of the Jesuit order is skilled in moral philosophy. While he had a different purpose in his analysis, which we point out later, we shall be guided by Fr. Petz' study.

The first question is: "Did Matthew McKeon have good purpose in his action?" The Defense insisted that Platoon 71 was led on the Ribbon Creek march for the purpose of instilling obedience and control. If that be true, there is no criticism of McKeon's goal. But the morality of our culture cannot tolerate the principle, "the end justifies the means." Certainly McKeon couldn't foresee that the march would end in tragedy. But did he know his act was, in violation of Parris Island custom-law, maltreatment? That is an issue which remains hidden in his own conscience.

The second question is: "Did Matthew McKeon believe that he was obeying orders, that his superiors condoned his action?" The Defense insisted that night marches were common practice while the Prosecution failed to show that these were frowned upon by custom-law. But mere obedience is no moral defense; obedience does not in itself justify wrongful actions. For our answer to this question we again refer to McKeon's conscience.

The third question is: "Did Matthew McKeon believe he was in the right because other Drill Instructors commonly followed the same practice?" On this issue the Defense used evidence of custom to gauge McKeon's reasonableness. The basic question we can resolve. Matthew McKeon's moral training was such that he knew, beyond any doubt, that common practice doesn't justify an immoral act. Even though drunkenness, fornication, and sloth continue to be well-established practices, we don't plead custom-law in self-defense. Yet on this issue McKeon's conscience might be clear: He knew others did it; he didn't believe it was wrong.

Fr. Petz was alarmed by public reaction to these three points in McKeon's defense. He felt that the American public sitting in judgment on this case manifested reasoning far removed from traditional Western thinking on moral questions. This he considered a sign of weakening in the moral fiber of the whole nation. There is cause for alarm if we rationalize: "The end justifies the means"; "Carrying out orders is in itself good"; "What everyone does can't be wrong."

Peculiarly, custom may prevail over both law and ethics. George D. Birkhoff, mathematician who studied at Chicago and Harvard, taught at Wisconsin and Princeton, has this to say: "Religious leaders, statesmen, judges, and the socially elect are regarded as the best judges in their several ethical fields. But the general intuitive opinion of mankind often has decisive weight."

The public decided: Matthew McKeon's intentions were good; he made a grievous error.

20

Prosecution Rests

MONDAY, JULY 23, was sixth trial day and beginning of the second week. Morton Janklow withdrew from the Defense team after completing his share of legwork Emile Berman needed. Seven recruit survivors of Platoon 71 paraded through the courtroom: Melvin Barber, John Maloof, Louis Leake, Lester Hendrix, Eugene Ervin, Gerald Langone, and Robert Veney. Prosecutor Sevier wanted to show that McKeon knew of nonswimmers in the platoon and that his recruits viewed the two Sunday field days and the night march as punishment. Defender Berman emphasized joking and horseplay during the march; lack of discipline in the platoon; that the recruits held Matthew McKeon in high regard. Through his suggestive questions Berman reinforced the idea that McKeon used the traditional Infantry slogan "Follow me!" as he entered Ribbon Creek. (My study of the case would cast doubt on the validity of that assumption.)

Berman was also strengthening his hypothesis that with adequate discipline there would have been no drownings, that the cause of the tragedy was the recruits' straying from their ordered column. It was necessary for him to emphasize measures which fitted this hypothesis and to disregard others. Such flexibility was revealed when he cross-examined Private Melvin Barber, first on the stand that morning. This concerned the distance marched up Ribbon Creek after Barber agreed he had gone only a few steps into the water:

BERMAN: Come right down and show us what you mean by a few feet.

Barber left the stand and demonstrated: "He walked over here, a little further than this."

BERMAN: A little further than that?
BARBER: Yes, sir. It was.
BERMAN: How much further?
BARBER: I couldn't tell—
BERMAN: To what point? To the middle aisle, the middle rail in the jury box?
BARBER: It might be just about to the wall, but I'm not sure. I couldn't say for sure.
BERMAN: All right. Thank you very much. *(He turned to Major Sevier:)* Could we have an agreement that what the witness indicates is somewhere between thirty-five and forty feet? This is only my judgment. If the Major would agree with that, I see no reason to waste the time to have it taped off.
SEVIER: I will agree.

Defense Counsel "signed off," asking each recruit witness to appraise Platoon 71 and Matthew McKeon. This was typical:

BERMAN: I say, as you think about it now, considering what the attitude or what the problems were with the platoon then—in the character of the man that you told us about—as you reflect on it now—don't you think it was intended to teach this platoon how to be a disciplined platoon, how to sharpen up, how to improve in the seriousness of their purpose?
BARBER: Yes, sir.
BERMAN: That's all.

Defender Berman did have one misfortune launching a trial balloon that burst:

BERMAN: There is a pier way up there somewhere behind one of the butts. Are you familiar with that?
MALOOF: No, sir.
BERMAN: Weren't you and some other men of this platoon just a few weeks ago taken by some member of the Trial Counsel's office down to Ribbon Creek?
MALOOF: No, sir.

BERMAN: You haven't been there from the date of this tragedy until now; correct?

MALOOF: No, sir. Correct.

While opposing counsel prodded recruit witnesses Judge Klein helped keep the record straight:

BERMAN: But the platoon still—to use the expression—still was goofing off?

ERVIN: That's right, sir.

KLEIN: I don't suppose the term *goofing off* needs any definition?

BERMAN: I think it has its equivalent even in civilian life, Mr. Law Officer.

Judge Klein also tried to get the parties to agree:

SEVIER: How far out did you go? What was the depth that you stopped at?

VENEY: It was up to about my shoulders, right along here.

BERMAN: I think the record ought to show that while he called it his shoulders, he is indicating a point below his armpits.

SEVIER: Would you indicate where you think it came the highest?

VENEY: About right along in here, I guess.

SEVIER: About even with the pockets of your shirt?

VENEY: Yes, sir; something like that.

SEVIER: Was the water getting deeper as you went out?

KLEIN: Won't you accept the armpits instead of the top of the pocket of the shirt?

SEVIER: Sir, I am not arguing about anything. If the Law Officer wants armpits, armpits it will be, sir.

Private Earl Hendrix, fifth member of Platoon 71 on the stand, was a difficult witness, though Major Sevier obviously expected to get important testimony from him:

SEVIER: Why did you stop?

HENDRIX: Everybody else stopped.

SEVIER: Was the water getting deeper?

BERMAN: Object to leading.

Now Emile Zola Berman, one of the nation's foremost trial lawyers, knew the exceptions to that rule: When, from the nature of the case, the mind of the witness cannot be directed to the subject without particular specification of it; or, when a witness is obviously embarrassed and timid through fear of strange surrounding or for other reasons. Both exceptions applied to Private Hendrix, but Attorney Berman showed his compulsion to remain in the driver's seat.

SEVIER: I believe it is fairly obvious he is scared and that he is nervous. I think this is an exception.

BERMAN: Reassure him.

KLEIN: You shouldn't say anything about the water getting deeper because now he knows the subject.

BERMAN: Let's try to make him feel a little more at home.

KLEIN: Try not to lead. Counsel is correct.

Judge Klein let eight questions get by before he again cautioned Sevier.

SEVIER: Were you cold?

HENDRIX: Yes, sir.

KLEIN: Without leading you can ask him a disjunctive question: "Were you wet or dry? Were you cold or warm?" Make him make the choice instead of using the one—and we will get on.

This coaching of Trial Counsel lasted all three weeks. It served only to make Major Sevier obstinate and belittle his ability in the eyes of spectators.

Monday there were few objections; Counsel usually withdrew challenged questions. During a seven-hour day Court was in session four hours and fifty minutes while 111 pages were added to the record. But this voluminous testimony was not particularly fruitful. There was considerable variation in estimates of the distance marched in Ribbon Creek, the distance of the column from the bank, directions, and the depth of water. Much of this variation can be attributed to the different location of each individual in the column, but the Court surely noted confusion in orientation and outright refusal of some witnesses to estimate. In spite of this Attorney Berman succeeded in getting Gerald Langone to mark on the oblique aerial photograph where Platoon 71 entered Ribbon Creek and this neatly substantiated the opinion of Earl Grabowski. It was a triumph for the Defense which went virtually unnoticed. (My reconstruction of the incident would place the entry point much further downstream.)

Tuesday of the second week was much like Monday except for Emile Berman's opening salvo requiring 108 ex-marine witnesses, later reduced to eighteen, which led to an out-of-Court hearing. After that six Platoon 71 recruits testified but added little to information previously obtained. It was consensus that the platoon lacked discipline and that McKeon was a sympathetic DI. Variation in estimating critical distances in Ribbon Creek continued. But the Court was in open session just three hours while a mere seventy-eight pages were added to the record. Except for conflict over subpoenaing witnesses, relations between opposite Counsel appeared friendly. Still there were interesting points.

Private McPherson was the first witness that day and the only witness with knowledge of McKeon's alleged drinking in the presence of a recruit. We need examine this point thoroughly.

At the Inquiry on the morning of April 11, only sixty-three hours after the fact, McPherson testified that he saw McKeon take one drink from the vodka bottle. There were eight questions about this on direct examination. Obviously McPherson had no doubt in his mind. Lieutenant Collins, McKeon's Appointed Counsel, waived cross-examination. Attorney Costello had not yet been summoned to Parris Island.

Charge IV at the Court-Martial alleged McKeon unlawfully drank intoxicating liquor in McPherson's presence. When McPherson took the stand July 24, fifteen weeks had passed. He had finished combat training at Camp LeJeune. He had been to his home in Chatham, New Jersey, on leave. Both Trial Counsel and Defense Counsel had questioned him repeatedly. He had been warned of his oath—the penalties of perjury. He must be absolutely certain! McPherson labored under a terrific burden. His word alone could send a man to prison. He respected McKeon. At the Court-Martial he testified: "I thought he was an excellent DI—a man with great patience." Legal pyrotechnics at the trial are a classic in psychology:

McPHERSON: A little while later he went across the room and picked up a bottle sitting under the desk or next to the desk on the floor, brought the bottle over, and I saw him raise the bottle to his mouth and bring it down.

SEVIER: A bottle. Can you describe that bottle?

McPHERSON: It was a clear bottle with a label marked "vodka."

SEVIER: Did you see that label?

McPHERSON: Yes, sir.

SEVIER: What did he do with it?

McPHERSON: I saw him raise it to his mouth and presume take a drink and take it down.

SEVIER: Go ahead.

Berman sprang forward, catlike: "I move to strike out the presumption of the witness—or that part of the answer, sir, which says in substance 'I presume take a drink'—on the ground that that part of the answer is speculation."

In elementary Rules of Evidence, Berman's objection was based on "incompetency" since the answer was an opinion of the witness. But an exception to that rule permits opinions concerning matters of everyday experience and knowledge. One would need be a hermit not to see people drinking every day.

Sevier was mute. Klein stepped in: "I think the word *presume* in that context is a colloquialism, but I will grant your motion. Strike it out."

SEVIER: What did you actually see there, McPherson?

McPHERSON: Actually, I saw him raise the bottle to his mouth and bring it back down.

SEVIER: Was the cork on or off?

McPHERSON: I don't know, sir. I don't know if there was a cork.

SEVIER: You don't even know if there was a cork?

McPHERSON: No, sir.

SEVIER: In your opinion from what you observed at that time and that place, what do you think—of what, in your opinion, did he do?

The answer was legally admissible, yet Berman squelched it. Now he was ready to demonstrate the artistry of a big-league trial lawyer. He was confident of his witness. He would show the Court that he had nothing to hide—was always co-operative —never stooped to the suppression of evidence by invoking rules. He would flaunt this point before the Prosecution in cross-examining the Government's own witness. A few personal questions served to enhance McPherson's prestige. Berman called him "sir."

"And in addition to being one of the larger men—physically —in the platoon, you enjoyed the confidence and good feeling of a good many of the men in that platoon. Did you not?"

"Yes, sir."

"And it was in that connection—you were one of the popular lads in the platoon—that Sergeant McKeon called you into his room to talk to you. Isn't that so?"

"Yes, sir. I guess so."

"Did you agree with what he said about the status of the platoon with regard to their lack of earnestness and lack of discipline and lack of sharpness?"

"Yes, sir."

"And as you look back at it now, tell us what your view is about the status of discipline and morale in that platoon on April 8, and before that day."

"I definitely felt the platoon was very poorly disciplined and had no spirit at all. They worked individually and never worked together."

"Now you say that when this subject came up that evening and Sergeant McKeon was asking you why you—one of the big popular men in the platoon—didn't do something about squaring them away, it was you who said you felt they had it too easy?"

"Yes, sir."

"Just one thing now about this bottle: Of course, I didn't know you knew anything about drinking vodka; but as long as you do, I want to ask you about that phase of it. Ordinarily when a man takes a drink from a bottle the least you could see is his gullet swallowing. Sometimes you could hear the swish of the drink. Frequently a man drinking from a bottle would wipe his lips or chin. Did you observe any one of these things when Sergeant McKeon lifted that bottle up to his lips?"

"I don't remember, sir."

"In other words, you can't tell us that you saw any one of those things?"

"No, sir."

"Can you tell us whether or not he lifted this bottle to his lips as a gesture to you—merely that he was making the gesture? You don't know, do you?"

"I don't know, sir."

"So the truth is, that except for the fact this bottle was lifted to his lips and put down, you have no other single fact to which you can testify concerning whether or not a drink was taken on that occasion?"

"No, sir."

"You are not even in a position to say whether the bottle was open or closed at the time. Is that correct?"

"I don't remember. No, sir."

That satisfied Counselor Berman but not Judge Klein. He called for the vodka bottle and put some questions of his own.

"Do you recall whether the cork was or was not on this bottle when the Accused raised it to his lips?"

"Yes, sir. I hadn't seen the cork."

"You had never seen the cork?"

"I don't remember seeing the cork on it."

"Will you take this bottle and hold it in the position you say the Accused held it at that time when he had it to his lips?"

McPherson demonstrated.

"Was the fluid at the neck of the bottle at that time, as you observed it?"

"I don't remember noticing the fluid, sir, but the bottle was tilted this way [demonstrating]."

"Will you hold it up so we can see how it was."

The record notes that on this third demonstration the fluid flowed into the neck of the bottle.

At this point one salient in the Government position was overrun. Berman scored a decisive victory on Charge IV.

Walter Nehrenz followed David McPherson to the stand. The beginning of his cross-examination is typical of the manner in which Attorney Berman established rapport with a favorable witness:

BERMAN: Private Nehrenz, relax a little bit; will you? Just take it easy. If you don't understand any question that is being asked of you by me—or anyone else—just say so.

NEHRENZ: Yes, sir.

BERMAN: Don't try to guess about things. If you know the answer, state it, if you don't know the answer, just say you don't know about it. Is that all right?

NEHRENZ: Yes, sir.

BERMAN: Don't tighten up. Just take it easy.

NEHRENZ: Yes, sir.

BERMAN: One of the things I really want you to draw on your memory for—and if your memory doesn't serve you, just say so—I want you to tell us as a fact whether you started swimming after you heard the cry and confusion, or before. Just try and think about it and do the best you can in trying to give us the answer.

NEHRENZ: I imagine, sir, it was about the same time. It was about the same time I started swimming.

Dewin Leonard followed Walter Nehrenz. Major Sevier had delegated direct examination to Captain William Otten. With several previous witnesses when Emile Berman would cut their answers short Sevier lodged formal objection. Berman demonstrated how the same result may be accomplished tactfully:

OTTEN: Now what did you do after that?

LEONARD: After I went up front, sir, he started talking to us and telling what we would do in combat—

OTTEN: At that point, how deep was the water?

BERMAN: I know that this is not intentional on the part of Captain Otten, but I think the witness should be permitted to finish his answer. Several times Counsel has cut off the witness.

OTTEN: Would you finish your previous answer?

LEONARD: Sergeant McKeon was telling us when we were in combat or anything like that we should stick close to the shore and shadows and not go out in the middle where the enemy could pick us off easy and things like that.

Richard Drown followed. Sevier wanted him to compare the Ribbon Creek current with those of the Ohio River. Klein sustained Berman's objection to that. Then Drown told the Court that McKeon's shirt-tail was hanging out when he formed Platoon 71 for the night march.

Carmac Brennan was next. Brennan was a confused and confusing witness. Apparently he told three stories: one in his statement written April 9, one during the Prosecution interview, one during the Defense interview. Emile Berman solved this problem by having Brennan identify his earlier written statement, marking it for identification only, and then appending it to the record where it could have no testimonial value. It was a dramatic way to show the confusion.

Joseph Moran was the last witness Tuesday of this second week. He was the youngster who insisted that Platoon 71 made three column movements, whereas all other witnesses described only two. This excerpt is in contrast with Emile Berman's coaching William Otten:

BERMAN: I thought before, you said that the column had turned in order to get back to the place they started from. Is that right?

MORAN: Yes, sir.

BERMAN: That would be to the left, wouldn't it?

MORAN: Yes, sir; only it went past—

BERMAN: Then would it—

SEVIER: Just a moment—

BERMAN: —would it be a right turn if they were closing the circle and getting back to where they had started from?

SEVIER: May the witness complete the answer he is making?

BERMAN: I withdraw the question. Let's put it concretely. Whatever question is before the witness is withdrawn.

KLEIN: I will let the witness answer the question. He had a question before him and you interrupted him when he was answering the question. I will permit him to complete his answer.

BERMAN: I apologize, sir.

MORAN: Tell me what the question is, sir.

KLEIN: Will you read the question and let the witness continue with his answer, if he desires to continue with it?

REPORTER: "Q. That would be to his left, wouldn't it? A. Yes, sir; only it went past—"

KLEIN: Continue. Went past what? What were you trying to say?

MORAN: Went to the right first after we went in the water, went back to the left, and then we passed the point where we went in and came back and went to the right again. That's what I did.

Joseph Moran was warned and excused. Judge Klein looked at his watch: "Does the President have any desires as to continuing?"

HUTCHINSON: What are your desires, Major?
SEVIER: I can either proceed, or we can stop and I can start preparing for tomorrow.
KLEIN: What are your wishes, Mr. Berman?
BERMAN: It is now ten minutes of four and I doubt that anything much would be accomplished in ten minutes. I defer to the wishes of the Court.
HUTCHINSON: I suggest a recess until nine o'clock in the morning.

Eighth trial day was Wednesday, July 25. First up was Private Hector Osvaldo Serantes, native of Buenos Aires, who joined the Marine Corps after living in New York a year, and who offered nothing important for the Prosecution. As might have been expected, Serantes talked rapidly and constructed his sentences peculiarly, for example: "Well, sir, the first time everybody thought they were kidding—making funny things. Suddenly, sir, I didn't see any recruit in trouble because I was one of the last squads."

Berman asked Serantes if he understood *embankment* and *abuse,* then turned to Klein: "I am going to ask for a little leeway in expressions here. They may be very leading, but because of the language barrier I ask that a certain amount of tolerance be given."

KLEIN: Yes, sir. We will see what develops.
BERMAN: Did you think he was a good Drill Instructor?
SERANTES: Well, sir, he was not only one of the finest of instructors, but he was also one of the most human sergeants that I have ever served under, sir.
KLEIN: I don't think you have to worry any more about the language barrier.

The sixteenth recruit witness was Private Carl Whitmore, Jr., who did mention Sygman, Leake, *Thomas,* and *Hardeman,* but whose important observation was that when Mathew McKeon formed the platoon for the march his right trouser leg was "unbloused." Then Ronald William Geckle appeared for ten minutes; though questioned by Sevier, Berman, and Hutchinson, he had little to offer. Judge Klein took him on to find out Ribbon Creek had a slippery bottom.

At the end of the first hour of Wednesday's session the parade of recruit witnesses ended. The last two of nineteen were Jerome Daszo and Thomas Oshal Truitt. We hear the experience of the first in different context; Truitt had little more to offer than the claim he was swimming before the column reversed its route of march in Ribbon Creek. Major Sevier added nothing to his case by calling these witnesses. Attorney Berman, on the other hand, fired a barrage of questions about the depth of water, keeping in line, joking while in the creek, and the esteem felt for Matthew McKeon. Moreover, Berman was able to emphasize the idea that McKeon was continually in the lead, despite the fact that the witnesses couldn't see him in the darkness and their answers to questions were that they *thought* he was at the head of the column.

A half-hour recess was granted Prosecutor Sevier to perform a task more appropriately done after Working Hours: issuing subpoenas for witnesses desired by Defender Berman. Then PFC Fred A. Magruder, the MP guardian of McKeon, took the stand. Apparently Sevier was going to trace custody of the vodka bottle from hand to hand as Holben had done at the Inquiry, even though Berman would expedite this evidence with a stipulation Thursday. Magruder's story is interesting, nonetheless, because he tells how Staff Sergeant Edward A. Huff, Senior DI of Platoon 71, was erroneously arrested, but omits telling that he drew a pistol on McKeon:

> Sir, I had just completed security at the Lyceum, and the Road Patrol had picked me up and was bringing me back to the PMO. The Sergeant of the Guard came out and got in the truck and we proceeded to Weapons Battalion. Upon arriving at Weapons Battalion, the Officer of the Day told the Sergeant of

the Guard to place Staff Sergeant McKeon under arrest. I was left in charge holding Sergeant Matthew McKeon under arrest. Whilst I was guarding Sergeant Matthew McKeon, I observed that he was very nervous, sir. There was a call by one of the men to the Officer of the Day at the Infirmary at the Rifle Range to place the Senior Drill Instructor under arrest. Well, sir, during the time I was guarding Sergeant McKeon he was standing in the door of his room and I was trying to get him to relax—let him smoke and move about freely, sir. The Senior Drill Instructor was trying to get the men to go to bed and everything like that and one of the men called the Officer of the Day and got permission to have him put under arrest.

He wouldn't listen to the sentry, so I had to tell him myself that he was under arrest. He was standing in the hallway and I asked him to step in the room with Sergeant McKeon. Whilst I was in the process of arresting this man I noticed Sergeant McKeon had picked up something and was started into the head—it was attached to his quarters there, sir. I followed him into the room and noticed that he was placing something behind the toilet in the head, sir. I told him to return into the room and then I took up my position at the door and asked Corporal Lyons to go into the head and retrieve the object he had placed behind the stool there, sir. Upon doing that Corporal Lyons brought me a fifth of vodka—I believe, sir—that was almost empty. It had about a fourth or less in the bottle, sir.

During Sevier's direct examination of Magruder, Berman made one of his many interruptions. This time is was for clarifying a point in his own mind rather than guiding testimony in another direction:

SEVIER: And did the label say anything? Did you see the label as to any kind of fluid in there?

MAGRUDER: Yes, sir. I do not remember the name of the fluid, sir.

SEVIER: All right. Was it a clear bottle or cloudy bottle?

MAGRUDER: It was a clear bottle and the fluid in the bottle was clear, sir.

BERMAN: May I ask one question at this point to clarify something in my mind? It is a little irregular, but do I have your permission?

SEVIER: Certainly, sir.

BERMAN: Didn't you say that it said "vodka"?

MAGRUDER: Yes, sir. I do remember that.

BERMAN: I heard you say you didn't remember the name of the fluid.

MAGRUDER: I meant I didn't know the name of the brand, sir.

BERMAN: Oh. But you did know it said "vodka"?

MAGRUDER: Yes, sir; I did.

BERMAN: All right. That is all I wanted to know.

During cross-examination Berman finally placed the bottle in evidence. Then Corporal Ronald J. Lyons, member of the Weapons Training Battalion Guard, was called to testify. Magruder, being a professional MP, had superordinated himself over Lyons without the requisite jurisdiction. But since Lyons had learned to respect MPs, there was no conflict. Actually Lyons had been placed in charge of Matthew McKeon by the Weapons Commander of the Guard. Lyons didn't appear at the Inquiry and so his testimony at the Court-Martial, though he was rather nervous, adds a few bits which clarify the scene in Barracks 761:

Q. Where did you see Sergeant McKeon?

A. The first time was behind Charlie Butts and the second time in the barracks.

Q. Did Sergeant McKeon say anything while you were there in the room?

A. Yes, sir. One statement was directed to Sergeant Huff. He said, "What can you say? Two of them were eaten up." And he asked the MP if he could wear dress shoes.

Q. What was your impression of his condition?

A. Behind the butts he looked tired—real tired—and in the barracks he was shivering.

Q. Sad? Dejected?

A. He was quiet.

Q. In the twenty-one years of your life I suppose you have seen people who have been sad, who have taken some calamity hard; haven't you seen them in your life?

A. Yes, sir.

Q. Well; how did he look?

A. I don't remember, sir.

Next on the docket Wednesday morning was Hospitalman Third Class Robert G. Gentry, who had been on duty at the

Rifle Range Dispensary. Prosecutor Sevier summoned Gentry without warning the Defense, but Defender Berman politely waived making that an issue. Gentry didn't contribute much to our knowledge of the Ribbon Creek affair though he gives us some insight concerning the operation of Parris Island's Food Service and its Medical Department:

Q. Did anything unusual occur during your duty tour that evening?

A. Well, about 2145—approximately—four or five people came in that had been swimming.

BERMAN: I move to strike the characterization as to what their activities had been. That is clearly hearsay and it is a description which comes from him alone.

SEVIER: May I ask a few questions? I will clarify it. If it's hearsay, I will agree.

KLEIN: I will sustain that objection. I will grant the motion to strike that part of the answer which refers to swimming.

Q. What was their condition when you saw them?

A. Well, they were pretty well in chills. I wrapped them up in blankets to get them warm and we tried to get some coffee but we couldn't get any. We put them to bed and wrapped them up in heat pads.

Q. Did you have any occasion or would you be required at that time to determine their temperatures?

A. Yes, sir. I took all of them.

Q. And what was the temperature, as you recall?

A. Well—on Private Leake—his temperature was ninety-three. I think the other guys were around ninety-five, if I'm not mistaken. They were subnormal.

Q. Whatever their condition seemed to be to you, you felt that wrapping them in a warm blanket and—if possible—getting them some coffee ought to do the trick; is that right?

A. I took the advice from the Medical Officer and did what he said.

Q. In other words, these men were examined medically?

A. No, sir. The Medical Officer did not see them until next morning.

Q. Did you inquire about what to do and he said to get them warm and get them some coffee?

A. Yes, sir.

Q. Nobody suggested any medication, nobody suggested any kind of medical treatment?

A. They didn't have any medicine at all.

Major Sevier's next step Wednesday morning of the second week was offering into evidence six death certificates. We note Counselor Berman's reaction in another chapter. Then just before lunch Sevier asked the Court to take judicial notice of Article 15, Uniform Code of Military Justice, which governs non-judicial, Commanding Officer's punishment. This procedure was superfluous: Each member of the Court had spent five years exercising his authority under that article and by virtue of his office was obligated to know it verbatim.

The midday recess lasted nearly two hours because Court closed early and opened late. Back on the stand for his third appearance was Captain Charles R. Weddel, who would have done better to send his capable assistant, Captain "J." "D." Green. This time Weddel brought a series of five orders, extending from 1953 until 1956, each rescinding the former one in the series, which placed the picnic ground, Whale Creek, and beaches and marshes in the Elliott's Beach area out of bounds to recruits making their scheduled march out there. Berman discovered the most recent order had been canceled by the Recruit Training Command, Commandant Pate's task force organized May 4. The order, however, was ostensibly issued March 8 and in effect on April 8. Since the witness didn't know the date of cancellation, Berman objected to an ineffective order. Judge Klein called a recess to examine the documents and got himself into another out-of-Court hearing. After the recess Sevier withdrew the proffered exhibits. Then Berman turned right around and sent Weddel back to his office to obtain a different order effective April 8 which had unquestionably since been canceled because it was the Standing Operating Procedure for Recruit Training Battalions (Male), now divorced from Parris Island's operational control.

Next on the stand, again without warning to the Defense, who again waived objection, was Hospitalman First Class Billy Redmond, who performed the Bogens test on blood drawn from

Mathew McKeon. Berman effectively, though unjustifiably, discredited Redmond's expertness in blood chemistry and qualification to perform the Bogens. Judge Klein admitted the Bogens Log and got himself in his fourth out-of-Court hearing, second for the day.

Technical Sergeant Samuel L. Cummings, Chief Investigator for the Recruit Depot, was then called. Cummings had been thoroughly trained in Army MP schools and had been in the same assignment at Parris Island thirty-five months. A skillful witness, he introduced Mathew McKeon's 20-page confession of April 9 along with the map on which McKeon had sketched the route of march. Berman exercised his "right of preliminary inquiry" and then offered no objection; he reserved cross-examination for Thursday morning. The afternoon had been so hot that Attorney Berman apologized for loosening his necktie. Court adjourned Wednesday after being in effective open session three hours and twenty-three minutes.

Thursday, July 26, was ninth trial day. Samuel Cummings was the first witness, recalled for cross-examination. Counselor Berman might have used Cummings Wednesday afternoon to show a valid objection to the admission into evidence of McKeon's confession, but that would have been incongruous with Berman's psychological strategy. Instead, he used Cummings to describe McKeon's remorse and to suggest that his client was the victim of injustice:

Q. Did he seem to be nervous and anxious and tense?

A. He was concerned over the event.

Q. Did he seem to be nervous and anxious and tense, Sergeant?

A. He was quite nervous; yes, sir.

Q. And in what way—in his talk with you or in the statements that he made—did his nervousness and concern show itself?

A. Well, at that time of morning neither he nor I knew what the condition of the men were. He was concerned over the—his main concern was about those boys, the men who had been out there. He didn't know what had occurred to them.

Q. In what way did he manifest that concern? What did he say?

A. I recall him making statements to the effect: "poor devils" and "those poor boys" and that sort of thing.

Q. Did you gather the impression that he was despondent?

A. In their regard; yes, sir.

Q. You gained the impression that he was co-operative and not attempting to hide or conceal anything from you?

A. No, sir; nothing whatever. It wasn't actually an interrogation, it was an interview.

Q. You didn't understand my question. The way it appears on the record, when you said "No, sir" it might seem that you meant he wasn't co-operative. I asked you if you received the impression he was co-operative and trying to tell you everything he knew and recalled.

A. Yes, sir. He was extremely co-operative.

Q. Well, hadn't you told him and wasn't it a fact that you had been asked to procure a statement for the General as quickly as possible?

A. Yes, sir.

Q. And you advised him of that, or mentioned it, in any event?

A. Yes, sir.

In a military environment, telling an Accused that his Commanding General wanted a statement right away is unquestionably coercion and would be so held in the Court of Military Appeals. Yet as soon as Lawyer Berman revealed this fact he left it dangling. Changing the subject Berman questioned Cummings about other drownings in Parris Island waters: The body of an AWOL recruit had been recovered near Horse Island in November 1952. Berman considered it irrelevant that other Parris Island people had drowned further away but more recently.

Technical Sergeant Cummings was on the witness stand just fifteen minutes while it took eighty for Dr. Robert J. Atcheson, whose duty it was to examine Matthew McKeon for sobriety. Unlike Counselor Holben at the Inquiry, Prosecutor Sevier did acquire some familiarity with the Bogens. But neither Sevier nor Atcheson possessed the intimate knowledge of Emile Zola Berman, which led to their embarrassment. We examine this facet of evidence in its medical context.

Following a mid-morning recess, Defender Berman took the floor:

Before you call a witness, Trial Counsel, I would like to make an application to the Court. Mr. President, Mr. Law Officer and members: It is with greatest reluctance that I am compelled to address myself to you regarding an adjournment at the conclusion of today's session until Monday morning. I am under an obligation to undertake a mission, which I regard as of the highest importance, connected with this case—and it cannot be done in any other way. By that I mean that I could not possibly do it at a time when the Court would ordinarily not be in session. This is the only opportunity in which I could perform this particular mission. You have my assurance that I regard it as a matter of importance in connection with this trial, regretful as I am. I respectfully request, Mr. President, that when Court adjourns today it adjourn until Monday morning at nine A.M.

COLONEL HUTCHINSON: You have approval of your request, Mr. Berman. We will adjourn this evening until nine o'clock Monday morning.

BERMAN: Thank you very kindly, sir.

KLEIN: Do you have any objection? (Klein addressed this to Trial Counsel, thinking, perhaps, he might make it an "interlocutory question.")

SEVIER: I do not wish to enter any objection, sir.

Then Prosecutor Sevier recalled PFC Fred Magruder, the MP who stood guard over McKeon. It is not apparent what Sevier intended to accomplish, but Magruder testified he took Mathew McKeon into custody about 9:30 P.M. April 8, and escorted him to the Depot Brig about 10:30. During that interval he was certain the Accused did not drink any kind of intoxicant.

Shortly before noon Captain Weddel made his fourth appearance to read from Depot Orders about extra instruction, maltreatment, mass punishment, and conditioning marches. After lunch Berman brought Weddel back to read about discipline and the objectives of recruit training. Here we should contrast the Court's reaction to both Adjutant Weddel and Trainer Silvey, who would be on the stand that afternoon. We reverse their order of appearance and begin with Silvey:

SEVIER: As the officer under whose supervision this section was prepared, what did you consider the scope of acceptable activity there on a Sunday or a holiday?

BERMAN: I object to that. The section and the language speaks for itself. If the witness is asked to define his language, I presume that this is permissible, but for him to give a dissertation as to what he considers to be acceptable—which is not contained within the language—I submit it is inappropriate, and has no probative value.

KLEIN: Sustained. Proceed in the fashion by Mr. Berman.

SEVIER: Aye, aye, sir.

Yet Berman failed to state ground for his objection. The witness had composed this training order and was responsible for "Staff supervision" to exact compliance. His answer was relevant, material, and competent as "expert opinion." Now we return to Weddel, not a policy maker but a sort of superior clerk or office manager:

BERMAN: And I call your attention to the following language: "The value of extra instruction is lost if it is approached from a disciplinary point of view." I ask you whether or not the term *disciplinary,* as intended in that paragraph, is punitive rather than the teaching of discipline?

SEVIER: I object. The officer is merely the custodian of documents. He does not prepare them or interpret them.

KLEIN: He didn't write that. Do you want to ask him what his understanding is?

BERMAN: This is a United States Marine, sir!

KLEIN: You want to ask him what his understanding is?

BERMAN: Yes. I'll reframe the question in the light of your objection. *(Then to the witness)* I quote, "The value of extra instruction is lost if it is approached from a disciplinary or harassing point of view." Is it your understanding that that term *disciplinary* in connection with the word *harassing* applies to punitive action rather than to the teaching of discipline?

WEDDEL: I don't know, sir. I don't know what my opinion would be on that and it would strictly be an opinion.

BERMAN: Do you have any doubt at all that it does not prohibit the teaching of discipline?

WEDDEL: No, sir.

Then Hans Manthey, McKeon's Chief Drill Instructor, returned to introduce a document showing the Accused signed a certificate acknowledging that he had read pertinent orders. None of this testimony contributed materially to structure of the Government's case.

The last Prosecution witness was Colonel David Wray Silvey, Assistant Chief of Staff G-3 (Training). Silvey had completed his tour at Parris Island and had been posted to North Africa but was held over for the trial. Major Sevier apparently hoped with this witness to integrate and to structure his whole case.

Dave Silvey was born April 21, 1914, and commissioned in July 1937. He went to Basic School and Basc Defense Weapons Class while a second lieutenant. During World War II Dave was stuck in the mire of Defense Battalions; one was a "Composite" Defense Battalion—a designation indicating enlisted marines were all Negro. Some Defense Battalions, later reorganized as Antiaircraft Artillery Battalions, got a bellyful of action. Dave Silvey's outfits didn't. After the war he was shuffled through various units at Camp LeJeune while the Marine Corps recovered from the trauma of too hasty demobilization. Then Dave went to Command and General Staff College at Fort Leavenworth, Kansas, for a year as a student and stayed on two more years as an instructor. This was abstract, high-level training—not the nuts and bolts variety where we teach a marine to take care of his feet, wear his uniform, and fire the rifle. After Leavenworth, Dave went overseas to Matthew McKeon's old outfit, the staff of Commander Naval Forces Eastern Atlantic and Mediterranean, with headquarters in London. Dave was able to have his family there and become moderately Anglicized. He arrived with his wife and four children from England on September 21, 1953. Parris Island was a strange world.

Dave delivered lengthy testimony at both Inquiry and Court-Martial. During the former Attorney Costello gave him a healthy workout, while in direct examination at the latter there was verbose argument between Emile Berman and Irving Klein, who overruled a Defense suggestion that the Law Officer was misinterpreting the evidence. But we can pass over those details, interesting as they were, because Berman's cross-examination neatly summarizes the whole story.

BERMAN: Do you agree that the Drill Instructor has latitude and discretion in teaching and maintaining discipline?

SILVEY: Within certain limitations.

BERMAN: In other words you do not take the position that the only things that could be done in connection with instruction and training for the purpose of turning out an excellent basic marine are contained in the lesson plans which form a part of the exhibit shown to you?

SILVEY: I believe—if I understand your question correctly, Counselor—you are saying that everything is in the lesson plan.

BERMAN: I am saying that you don't think that everything to be done in the training of discipline and the maintenance of it are contained in the lesson plans. Do you?

SILVEY: I don't think that everything is in the lesson plans; no, sir.

BERMAN: Now then, when you referred to the fact that there was no authority for Drill Instructors to take their platoons or recruits into the marshes or swamps or waters bounding Parris Island—and quite apart from the march to Elliott's Beach—you meant to say, did you not—that there was no lesson plan and no order or regulation on the Depot which instructed them to do so?

SILVEY: There is no order on the Depot—that I know of—that instructs the Drill Instructor to take his platoon into the swamps or marshes.

BERMAN: That's right. That's what you meant to say?

SILVEY: No; I don't think so. No; I disagree with you.

BERMAN: I am asking you, when you said there was no authorization to take men into swamps and creeks—I guess that's the word you used, or similar to it—that they were not authorized to take men into the swamps and creeks and boondocks of the Parris Island area—quite apart from Elliott's Beach—you meant by that, did you not, that there was no lesson plan that scheduled it and no Depot Order or regulation which required it?

SILVEY: No. I didn't say they were required to go into the swamps or marshes or into the creeks.

BERMAN: Perhaps I didn't make myself clear to you, Colonel. The fault, perhaps, is mine. Do you remember testifying in answer to Major Sevier's—Trial Counsel's question, that Drill Instructors and personnel were not authorized to take recruits into the swamps, marshes, boondocks and waters of Parris Island—exclusive now, and quite apart from Elliott's Beach—do you recall testifying to that?

SILVEY: I recall saying that no such night march was authorized.

BERMAN: No such night march was authorized; all right. When you used the word *authorized* you meant, did you not, that there was no such scheduled march and that there was no order or regulation which required it? Is there something about that question that you don't understand, Colonel?

SILVEY: Well, there's two parts there. I said, I believe, that marches into the swamps—to Elliott's Beach, or other marshes, or Wales Creek—were prohibited. I also said there was no authorization for a march—or a night march—to any other swamps or marshes, under the regulations.

BERMAN *(To Klein):* Instead of moving to strike the answer, I can dig it out from here. *(Then to the witness)* Did you say and do you say now that those marches, walks—or whatever else you may call it—into marshes, creeks, boondocks and swamps—is not authorized?

SILVEY: There are only four authorized marches in the training program—

BERMAN: Please, Colonel Silvey, will you kindly answer my question? I asked you—

SEVIER: I object. The witness should have the opportunity of answering the question in his own manner.

BERMAN: That is true, but it has to be my question that he is answering.

KLEIN: Read the question, Mr. Reporter.

The Reporter read the question.

KLEIN: You started to say there were four marches authorized.

SILVEY: I started to say there were four authorized marches.

BERMAN: Will you please answer my question, Colonel?

SILVEY: I did answer your question saying there are four authorized marches.

BERMAN: That doesn't seem to me to be an answer. I will ask you the question again, sir: Do you say that marches into the boondocks, swamps and marshes and creeks bounding Parris Island—not including the march to and from Elliott's Beach, and not including scheduled, authorized marches—that all others are unauthorized?

SILVEY: I would say that, yes.

BERMAN: When you say that they are unauthorized, do you say that because they are both unscheduled as well as the fact that there is no order or regulation permitting them—is that the reason you say they are unauthorized?

SILVEY: No. I say it because the Commanding General is the only one that could authorize a march—a troop movement.

BERMAN: A troop movement?

SILVEY: Right.

BERMAN: You consider a march of about—a little less—a march formation moving less than 850 yards from a barracks behind a rifle range with which they are completely familiar and back—is a troop movement in the sense in which you use the term?

SILVEY: I believe I would, yes.

BERMAN: All right. Well now, you have been here since 1953?

SILVEY: Yes.

BERMAN: And all of that time in the Operations of the Base Command here?

SILVEY: Yes.

BERMAN: So you were considerably concerned directly with the training methods and practices, were you?

SILVEY: I'm the supervisor of the recruit training, yes.

BERMAN: Yes, sir.

SILVEY: For the Commanding General.

BERMAN: Let me ask you: Have you since 1953 up until April 8, 1956, ever had it come to your knowledge that for purposes of teaching—teaching discipline, boosting morale, cultivating pride of organization—men were taken in—recruits were taken into the marshes and swamps and boondocks and waters around Parris Island—without regard to what happened on the marches to and from Elliott's Beach?

SILVEY: I know of only one report.

BERMAN: In other words, in three years—approximately three years, you've only heard of one such instance?

SILVEY: Yes, sir. That's true.

BERMAN: Did you make specific inquiries or inspections to determine whether there was such a practice?

SILVEY: I think. I have been around the Depot day and night. What do you mean by *sufficient?*

BERMAN: I didn't say *sufficient,* I said *specific.*

SILVEY: Specific? Well, yes. I made specific trips out around the Depot during the day and night.

BERMAN: How often?

SILVEY: Well it was my policy to leave my office at least once a day.

BERMAN: Well, did you go to any area behind the Rifle Range?

SILVEY: Only during the daytime.

BERMAN: Well I'm speaking now of night. Did you go in the area behind the Third Battalion?

SILVEY: Not during the night.

BERMAN: Well did you go in any—

SILVEY: I have been in the area during the daytime, though.

BERMAN: I'm speaking about the night, Colonel. You made no such inspections yourself at night?

SILVEY: Not in that area, no.

BERMAN: Well take the area the other side of the barracks in the Weapons Training Battalion area; did you go there and inspect the marshes and swamps on the other side of the area in that place?

SILVEY: During the night?

BERMAN: Yes, sir.

SILVEY: Negative. Not to inspect the marshes and swamps.

BERMAN: Now you say you know of no night marches at all?

SILVEY: No. I said I have known of one instance.

BERMAN: One instance?

KLEIN: Was that night or day?

SILVEY: That was at night.

BERMAN: Now let me ask you this: Isn't the Elliott's Beach situation—that's an overnight bivouac march, isn't it—a march to an overnight bivouac area?

SILVEY: It's a march to Elliott's Beach in the morning—they pitch their shelter tents and bivouac overnight and go back the next morning.

BERMAN: That's what I asked you. A march to and from an overnight bivouac area?

SILVEY: Yes, sir.

BERMAN: Do you know that when they start out from both ends they start out between 0500 and 0600 hours?

SILVEY: I can't say the exact time. It's in the lesson plan which requires them to get on the road by about 0615 in order to clear the traffic. They are scheduled by the Battalions.

BERMAN: You know in the wintertime—it's standard time—it's

pretty dark at that time, isn't it? Wouldn't you call that nightfall—or night—or dark?

SILVEY: I don't think so, sir.

BERMAN: Well if they started out at 0500 would you call that dark in the winter months?

SILVEY: I would have to check it. It might be dark at 0500, yes, sir. I would have to check the sunrise and sunset tables on that specific point.

BERMAN: Now apart from the one order that you say makes reference to Elliott's Beach, is there a single order or regulation to your knowledge—order or regulation, in writing, to your knowledge—that puts the area behind the rifle butts—Rifle Range butts—out of bounds?

SILVEY: There's one Depot Regulation to put all water out of bounds around the area. I don't know the specific regulation that puts that area—

BERMAN: About the water out of bounds, that's to prohibit people from being infected by swimming in polluted water, isn't that so?

SILVEY: That's so stated.

BERMAN: That's the sole purpose. Isn't that so?

SILVEY: It's so stated.

KLEIN: I didn't hear the answer.

SILVEY: Yes, sir. It's so stated.

BERMAN: That is the whole purpose of that regulation—that if you swim in that water there's a chance of being infected because the water is polluted—so don't swim in there?

SEVIER: I object. I stand on Mr. Berman's objection a while ago and let the language of the order speak for itself.

BERMAN: You say that the order you are referring to—

SEVIER: I have an objection.

BERMAN: I withdraw my question. Are you referring to one order—

SEVIER: Sir, pardon—

KLEIN: Let him ask the question.

BERMAN: When you made reference to the fact that you know of one regulation—I believe you said, one regulation, or order—what word did you use in connection with this polluted water?

SILVEY: I said there was one Depot Regulation.

BERMAN: Oh. When you referred to one Depot Regulation you were referring, were you not, to that regulation which prohibits men from swimming or bathing in the waters—all of the waters around

Parris Island—because they are polluted and thereby might become infected?

SILVEY: Yes. That's correct.

BERMAN: I see. So you don't know of a single order that puts the area—any of the swamp or marsh areas—except the one to and from Elliott's Beach, out of bounds, do you?

SILVEY: No. There is no other.

BERMAN: That's to this day—by the way—isn't that so? Up to the very moment we are standing here speaking to each other?

SILVEY: If I knew of one I would say so.

BERMAN: I didn't get the answer.

SILVEY: If I knew of one I would say so.

BERMAN: Yes, sir; and the only report you ever heard of anyone marching into the swamp was one solitary instance on a night march into a swamp?

SILVEY: It wasn't a night march into a swamp. I didn't say that.

BERMAN: Well, tell me what it was.

SILVEY: It was the report I received, Counselor—after I first arrived here—that troops may have gotten in the swamps or marshes in the Elliott's Beach maneuver area.

BERMAN: So that refers to Elliott's Beach—the report you had?

SILVEY: It did.

BERMAN: I see. Did you yourself know anything about the waters of Ribbon Creek?

SILVEY: Not prior to April 8.

BERMAN: Colonel Silvey, would you agree that a Drill Instructor has an overwhelming responsibility in the proper performance of his duties to make a recruit a basic marine to teach and maintain discipline?

SILVEY: You say "overwhelming"—I think a Drill Instructor has a very important assignment.

BERMAN: Well, Colonel, if it's the word *overwhelming* that you disagree with I will reframe the question. Do you agree that the Drill Instructor's obligation—in the performance of his duties, for the over-all purpose of turning out or training a marine—a basic marine—is to teach and maintain discipline?

SILVEY: Yes, it is so stated in the SOP.

BERMAN: I am asking whether you agree with it.

SILVEY: Yes, I do.

BERMAN: I presume you agree with this statement: "The objective of recruit training is to indoctrinate the recruit in the fundamentals of service life and develop pride, loyalty, self-confidence, discipline, physical fitness, initiative, adaptability, teamwork, and proficiency in small arms marksmanship, with priority given to discipline." Do you agree with that?

SILVEY: Yes, sir.

BERMAN: As being a primary objective—priority given to discipline?

SILVEY: That's one of the primary objectives, sir.

BERMAN: Now do all platoons in training respond identically to the period of learning—a period of time as it progresses?

SILVEY: I'm afraid not.

BERMAN: There are some platoons that may be laggard. Isn't that so?

SILVEY: There are some that progress faster than others; that's true.

BERMAN: And there are some platoons—I presume you know—have greater spirit than others?

SILVEY: Yes, sir.

BERMAN: And there are some platoons who have less discipline than others?

SILVEY: Yes.

BERMAN: It's the job of the Drill Instructor—is it not—to correct these things and teach them in accordance with the objectives stated in this exhibit that you are now referring to?

SILVEY: It's not the job of the Drill Instructor. It is the job of the rifle coaches—and all other instructors—and officers over them.

BERMAN: The man that is closest to the platoon—the man that has the responsibility for that platoon—recruits—fundamental overall training as an excellent basic marine—is the Drill Instructor. Is that so?

SILVEY: I would say the Drill Instructor has a most important responsibility in that respect, sir.

BERMAN: And so confronted with a platoon that's undisciplined—that lacks eagerness, lacks spirit—it is his job—within the bounds of his understanding—to correct the situation and instill discipline—instill pride, give some *esprit de corps,* some feeling of independence among those men who are to be prepared for fighting marines. Isn't that so?

SILVEY: You say, "within his bounds of understanding"?

BERMAN: Yes. Bounds of understanding.

SILVEY: Now—the understanding encompasses quite a bit.

BERMAN: I want to ask you one thing. Perhaps I misunderstood you. In any event I am asking this for clarification and because there are some things I don't understand and am trying to learn. Recall generally comes at 1600 hours, does it not?

SILVEY: No. For recruits it's normally 1700 on weekdays and 1130 on Saturdays.

BERMAN: How about—

SILVEY: That will vary with the procedure.

BERMAN: Well, 1700 hours—I will accept that. Am I to understand that you say that after 1700 hours—or the chow that follows 1700 hours—the recruits have nothing to do? Is that what you say?

SILVEY: No. I didn't say that.

BERMAN: Then—in that case—I did misunderstand you. Nothing further.

Colonel Silvey's testimony consumed the bulk of Thursday afternoon; he was on the stand one hour forty minutes, not counting the recess taken after his first hour. Then Major Sevier announced three stipulations: that Defense Exhibit E contained 80-proof vodka; that it was the same bottle found by Corporal Lyons in Barracks 761; and that *Thomas Hardeman, Donald O'Shea, Charles Reilly, Jerry Thomas, Leroy Thompson,* and *Norman Wood* died from drowning while on a march with Platoon 71 in Ribbon Creek. Matthew McKeon acquiesced to that concession in open Court.

As the second week ended Emile Berman remained in the saddle. Trial Counsel had rested his case. It was obvious to everyone that Berman would move for a directed acquittal.

KLEIN: Do you desire to make your motions at this time, Mr. Berman?

BERMAN: I prefer not to. I do not expect to make motions purely *pro forma,* so I would appreciate it if I could preserve my position until we reconvene.

KLEIN: The reason I asked you was—because of your earlier comment—I thought we might be able to dispose of the motions today. I do not intend, however, to urge that you do that *pro forma* or that you do that without full opportunity to present them fully.

BERMAN: Perhaps I owe an apology to the Court, but it is five minutes to our quitting time and it has been a fairly arduous day. I trust that at least five minutes can be dispensed with.

KLEIN: I would suggest at this time, then, that we adjourn until Monday morning, as you had indicated.

HUTCHINSON: Very well, if the Court has no objection, we will adjourn until Monday at nine.

21

Tides

THE MARINE CORPS had been studying amphibious operations assiduously more than thirty years when Matthew McKeon came to trial. Quantico Schools were devoted to the analysis of ship-to-shore operations described in historical combat records and observed on continuing maneuvers. Those schools generated doctrine which was tested by experience in the Pacific War from Guadalcanal to Okinawa. But professional soldiers lean toward conservatism. Mistakes too frequently are repeated before their obvious lessons are grasped. There continues to be a Marine Corps weakness in completely ignoring tidal phenomena.

Even though tides can be of crucial importance in a landing operation, marines relegate them to Navy "cognizance." As a result, the Navy frequently lets the Marine Corps down. This was true at Tarawa, where historical analysts mention the hazards encountered in low water and the barrier reef. These should have been anticipated and surmounted. Even the Quartermaster General of the Marine Corps, William Pendleton Thompson Hill, astute geologist and recognized world authority on coral, emphatically denounced that improvidence. But marines still ignore the tide.

Tidal phenomena are easy to understand. They have been known to oceanographers, or their predecessors in science, for centuries. They can be learned through a few hours' study. Yet at the Inquiry Major Holben summoned Sergeant Algin H. Nolan as an "expert witness." Called to introduce tidal evidence, Nolan was a clerk-typist. His "expertness" was gained through a clerical task: transposing information from Department of Commerce tide tables. He learned this job from another sergeant whom he relieved when the former was about to be discharged.

Parris Island has traditionally published local tidal data in a monthly Depot Bulletin and in the *Boot,* its weekly newspaper. These data are valued by fishermen, marine and civilian. Also, Beaufort liquor stores rely on Parris Island to determine sunset, their legal closing time.

Back in October 1953 when Captain Homer King was adjutant, compiling tide tables was a lost art. But King's office had cognizance over local tides. Anticipating the next calendar year, Homer wrote to Sixth Naval District, Charleston, requesting 1954 data for Parris Island. In reply he received the standard Commerce Department pamphlet. Considering tides a Navy matter, King judged the Navy rather stupid for not answering his request directly. He repeated that request—and received another copy of the pamphlet. Homer brought his problem to me, filling in as Chief of Staff: What could we do to get the Navy to fulfill its obligation? I showed him how to use the tables and this information went through channels from the Depot Sergeant Major to his clerk-typist. But one can't learn about tides while mechanically transposing tables. One must understand how to apply the factors of time and motion.

Reference data are based on the Savannah River entrance. Adding twenty-five minutes to these gives the information for Parris Point, as seagulls fly about 3½ miles south of Ribbon Creek. But there is a time lag between Parris Point and the scene of drownings in Ribbon Creek, a much greater distance by boat. An incoming tide, for instance, must move up Broad River and then into the creek. Hence both high and low tides occur later in the creek. During the recovery operation we observed this lag to be forty minutes.

Nor was the Inquiry concerned with the form of tidal movement. Straight-line interpolation is erroneous. Mathematicians would call tidal movement "harmonic motion." Waters rise from low tide slowly, flow greatest at mid-tide, reach flood tide slowly. They ebb in the same manner. To determine depth between stages, we measure the time interval on the arc of a circle. Disregarding these scientific facts, simple interpolation would indicate a 4½-foot tide at the time of the drownings. In truth the tide exceeded six feet.

When Major Sevier took the helm at the Court-Martial, he called Sergeant Nolan again. By July, Nolan had been transferred to the Area Auditor's Office, but he was still the man who prepared the April tide table. Sevier had the local table admitted into evidence as an exhibit. Berman in cross-examination developed the fact there is a time lag, which Nolan erroneously estimated at ten minutes. Sevier would regret this when opposing Counsel re-opened the issue in defense.

Now it is a fact which no one bothered to mention at the trial that ordinary human beings are notoriously poor in estimating distance. Trained riflemen in range-estimation contests vary widely. Skilled topographers and experienced gunfire observers check their estimates against measured distance at every opportunity. Those Boot witnesses from Platoon 71 had no training in making such judgments. Their march was in darkness, where there was no opportunity for visual comparison of distances. Finally, they had three months in which to forget their hazy perceptions. But Attorney Berman asked for estimates from these witnesses both as to distance from that nebulous bank of Ribbon Creek and as to the depth of water. In one instance the Court recessed while Berman sent for a tape measure. He was trying to prove, "scientifically," that had Platoon 71 stayed in column behind their leader no one would have been in water higher than his chest.

Then Defense Counsel called Warrant Officer Leslie E. Volle, Platoon Leader, Survey Platoon, 2d Topographic Company, Camp LeJeune, North Carolina. With five years' experience in hydrographic work, Volle quickly qualified as an "expert." To add to Volle's prestige, Berman continued to question him:

"Have you performed any hydrographic surveys in recent years?"

"Yes, sir. I performed two years of hydrographic work overseas and about six months training personnel in hydrographic work at Camp LeJeune."

"What were your duties overseas?"

"I worked as a hydrographer."

"With whom?"

"I don't believe I am at liberty to say with whom or where it was. That information is classified." Mr. Volle didn't bother to add that practically all surveys done by the Marine Corps are "classified." Berman scored his point and didn't continue in that line.

Volle testified that he headed a five-man team which made precise measurements of Ribbon Creek during a ten-day period beginning June 19. Volle particularly stressed the fact he had been unable to locate any holes in that area in question. He searched for these with a "Philadelphia rod" as well as with a fishing seine. In later testimony, though, Volle disclosed that he found holes on the bottom of the Dredge Cut. This matter of a "trout hole" or "Spanish well" was vitally important. McKeon's defense created the impression that there was no hole in Ribbon Creek.

Three witnesses at the Inquiry, who testified when impressions were fresh, experienced a sudden change in depth of the water. Private Porter claimed that he was in water over his head before he knew it. Private Daniel stated that he stepped in a hole and had to tread water. Private Mulligan said, "The bottom dropped out at spots." These recruits were not called at the trial. But during the Court-Martial, Private Maloof indicated that he "dropped off a cliff."

In addition to the word of those four recruits who experienced a sudden drop, we have the observations of those marines who became intimately acquainted with Ribbon Creek through their efforts to recover the bodies. Sergeants Clement, Sparks, Whitlow, Edwards, and Hughes sounded the trout hole with boat hooks time after time, particularly at low water slack. They had its location so well fixed in their minds that they could approach it from any direction and indicate its outline. Moreover, Sergeant Seybold, the frogman, told me that he located *Thomas Hardeman's* body at the edge of the trout hole.

Unfortunately surveyor Volle didn't elaborate on the shifting of muddy bottoms. Ribbon Creek unquestionably changes with the run-off from heavy rains, with severe storms, and with spring tides. Volle implied this when he complained about the accuracy of our Public Works map. The whole channel of Ribbon Creek had shifted decidely between the time of their survey and his—if he surveyed enough of it.

Sheriff McTeer of Beaufort County could have added some expert advice. His experience, repeated many times, is that even in strong tideways bodies are recovered at the approximate spot where they go down. There is no doubt in my mind that on April 8 there was a trout hole in Ribbon Creek. I saw it sounded and know six bodies were pulled out of it.

Once the trout hole had been dismissed Defense Counsel used Volle's survey in conjunction with estimated distances from the bank to show how the depth of water varied in Ribbon Creek. In the area where Platoon 71 must have entered, regardless of the fact that we shall never be able to pinpoint the spot, the bank drops off abruptly three to four feet. Then there is a mud flat, studded with Savannah grass and quite level, which varies in width from fifty to seventy-five feet. That mud flat, in turn, slopes rapidly to the low-water mark, dropping six feet over a horizontal distance varying from fifteen to fifty.

We shall omit Mr. Volle's numerous hypotheses regarding the depth of water at specific points at the estimated time. Errors in witnesses' judging horizontal distance casts doubt on the validity of any of Volle's conclusions. His testimony July 30 consumed the better part of both the morning and afternoon courtroom sessions. Such detail must have been confusing to the Court.

But we can't dismiss Volle without a critique of his tidal information. He started out by saying that barometric pressure would have raised the water about seven-tenths of an inch above the norm. He claimed that the wind, on the other hand, would have lowered that level eight inches. Such a conclusion is farfetched. Volle based his estimate on a recorded *average* wind of thirteen miles per hour for April 8. Weather stations are at Charleston and Savannah, both quite distant from local Parris

Island weather. There's no dispute, of course, that when we speak in terms of continental land masses, winds lower tides on the lee shore. But winds on Saturday came in gusts exceeding fifty miles an hour and forced the Weapons Battalion picnic to move to shelter from its A-Range grove. Steady winds that day continued until late Sunday and were seldom less than thirty-five miles.

Marsh flats drained by Edding and Ribbon creeks, between Horse Island and Parris Island proper, blocked at one end by the causeway and bordered by Broad River on the other, cover an area about one mile wide and over two miles long. At high tide, according to Mr. Volle's survey, those flats with their heavy growth of Savannah grass were under 1.3 feet of water. This is confirmed by the fact that during the morning tide on April 9 Weapons Battalion boats were poled over a good portion of that area. Knowledge of meteorology confirms our observation that local winds served to increase the depth of water appreciably by pushing it onto the marshy flats where it took a relatively long time to drain off. This may explain why we observed a forty minute lag from the Parris Point forecast and why our observations differed from the reckoning of others.

Now we've reached the point where we can raise the crucial question: How deep was the water when Platoon 71 marched in? While the absolute answer will remain a mystery hidden in Ribbon Creek, we can fix some lower limits.

Mr. Volle testified that the tide was 5.3 feet above low water at the estimated time of the drownings. Had he made a straight-line interpolation, it would have been 5.0 feet; had he computed by the harmonic cycle, it would have been 5.5 feet. Based on timely observations at Weapons Battalion, we say it was 6.1 feet above low water.

The channel of Ribbon Creek when the tide is out varies in width between 75 and 125 feet. Minimum depth at that time, according to Mr. Volle's survey, is 2½ feet. This minimum is at the point where a steep-sided drainage ditch empties into Ribbon Creek. Downstream from that point the channel depth increases gradually. Upstream in a matter of 400 feet horizontally the depth increases to 7½ feet.

Disregarding the trout hole and accepting Mr. Volle's conservative estimate, the minimum depth in the channel at the time of the tragedy was 7.8 feet. In fact, on cross-examination Volle pointed out some hypothetical points where depths varied from 8.0 to 8.8 feet. Under the same assumptions, our computations show that the channel depth varied between 8.6 and 13.6 feet.

When you're wearing sweat shirts under utility jackets—and field boots, that's deep water! *Norman Wood,* tallest of the victims, measured 73¼ inches. *Jerry Thomas,* shortest, was 66½ inches in stocking feet. With no allowance for sinking in the bottom muck and assuming upright posture—impossible in the situation—those waters were at least 28 inches over *Norman Wood's* head under the most conservative hypothesis.

Thirty-one different recruits testified either at the Inquiry or the Court-Martial. We have mentioned four who experienced a sudden drop-off. Six others, Moran, Martinez, Grabowski, Leonard, Brennan, and Daszo, swore they were in water over their heads. Seven more, Rambo, McGuire, Bruner, Hendrix, Langone, Nehrenz, and Truitt, claimed they had to swim. Brewer struggled with *Wood,* Geckle with *Thomas,* and Acker with *Reilly*. They sensed, obviously, that they were in water over their depth. The other eleven, either poor swimmers or unqualified, held back and were never deeper than their shoulders. Some witnesses said McKeon was swimming before panic started.

Berman's theory was rather tenuous.

22

Medicine

Law and Medicine met on passionately contested ground at both Inquiry and Court-Martial. Testimony in the two records by sheer volume completely overbalances its practical significance in deciding the issues, even though interpretation of that testimony led to violent reaction in the court of public opinion. When anyone is particularly intrigued with the ramifications of legal medicine, or wishes to learn more about the art of cross-examination, or merely enjoys verbal duels which lay raw human frailty, reading those records is utterly fascinating. Unfortunately we but scan the picture here because it is not altogether pertinent to the Ribbon Creek story.

Navy medical practitioners got well involved in the incident and its sequel, certainly more involved than they would have desired. These medicos like to quarantine themselves from the courtroom. Theirs is more art than science and they know full well there are few clear-cut, straightforward answers the trial lawyer demands. Still ten of the profession were dragged into the affair.

Dr. Robert F. Sullivan, who ministered to Weapons Battalion, examined the first five bodies recovered and in consequence was elected to sign their death certificates even though the most important information those contained was the findings in autopsies performed at Beaufort Naval Hospital without Dr. Sullivan being present. When we finally got the body of *Thomas Hardeman* and I took the responsibility for declaring him dead, medical administrators were out on a limb, but they solved this problem by having Dr. William F. Bahnson sign this certificate because he was Medical Officer of the Day at Parris Island—yet Dr. Bahnson didn't see the body if the ambulance driver carried out my orders.

Dr. Charles E. Herlihy, Depot Psychiatrist, examined Matthew McKeon April 9 and gave his opinions at the Inquiry. Dr. Lowell J. Smythe, pathologist at the hospital, performed the autopsies and testified at the Inquiry. Dr. William D. Owen, Senior Dental Officer at Parris Island, examined the bodies at the Naval Hospital and was called to the Inquiry. Dr. Benjamin M. Kraynick, orthopedist at the hospital, examined McKeon June 18 and told his story at the Court-Martial. Dr. John P. J. Cummins, Jr., treated McKeon March 14, had his diagnosis questioned at the Court-Martial, but got no opportunity to defend himself at either tribunal, each of which had a medical-officer member.

But the star medical witness at both Courts—certainly for human interest—was Dr. Robert J. Atcheson, who examined Matthew McKeon the night of April 8 for sobriety. Atcheson attended Southwestern College at Memphis, then the University of Tennessee at Knoxville, then interned at Jacksonville, Florida, and later had a three-month course in radiology at Naval Medical Center, Bethesda, Maryland. At the time of the Ribbon Creek incident he had been fourteen months in the Navy and six on Parris Island, where he was the next to most junior of thirteen physicians at the Depot. Atcheson suffered through sieges of cross-examination both in April and July when McKeon's counsel, each erudite in the Bogens test, pressed him for details. He also suffered because he had been trained to shun yes-or-no questions.

Two years before Platoon 71 marched into Ribbon Creek I was forced by the Goulet incident to study that section of the Medical Department's book dealing with the Bogens test. The basic assumption for interpreting this test is that central nervous systems of all human beings are equally susceptible to alcohol carried there in the blood stream—or in other words, there are no individual differences. That assumption is biologically untenable. Moreover, slight contamination of laboratory equipment with something like glycerol or phenol is known to yield a high positive Bogens. Ketosis, an excess of acetone or other sugars in the organism, which occurs in diseases like diabetes and acidosis, will yield a false positive. The Bogens test is made by color comparison: Deteriorated reagents, old test-tube stoppers, or aging test material affects reliability of the standard, while poor lighting in the laboratory does the same thing. Before taking an ordinary blood sample, corpsmen are trained to swab the patient with ether or alcohol; this action by the unwary yields a false positive. Then the book warns that people having a Bogens score between 2.5 and 3.0 show observable evidence of intoxication in only eighty-five per cent of the cases, hence clinical judgment is the last resort.

Even more important is the fact that Bogens data were obtained from otherwise normal subjects; we have no data for people in shock, which is rather easily mistaken for drunkenness. Then we have Cannon's theory about emergency mobilization of bodily resources: When a person experiences emotional tension, such as fear or anger, the adrenal glands cause the liver to increase the sugar content of the blood. A close relative of alcohol, it is sugar which the Bogens Manual warns may yield a false positive. Matt McKeon's leg bothered him all day Sunday, which made him irritable. He considered Platoon 71 his children, and like an irritable parent, he became angry at behavior which normally would not bother him. Then in Ribbon Creek he had a magnificent opportunity to experience fear. His Bogens index was 1.5; my only wonder is that it wasn't higher.

Attorney Costello at the Inquiry and Lawyer Berman at the Court-Martial each did a magnificent job cross-examining Dr. Atcheson, who in turn was usually reluctant, frequently embarrassed, and occasionally antagonistic.

During both of Dr. Atcheson's appearances in the courtroom he described the Parris Island sobriety test and how he conducted it when he examined Matthew McKeon. His clinical findings were that McKeon appeared normal in post-pointing, self-balancing, gait, reflexes, speech, and visual accommodation. Opposite one item, "odor of breath," Atcheson wrote on the form: "suggestive of alcohol." He explained this by saying, "During my examination I had occasion to get rather close—particularly in the pupil reflexes—and it was my impression that there was a suggestive odor of alcohol on the patient's breath."

In friendly cross-examination Attorney Costello pointed out that the odor sensation might have been autosuggestion:

Q. During your questioning of Staff Sergeant McKeon did you ask him about what time he had these drinks of vodka that you refer to?

A. No specific time. I didn't ask him any time. I just said, "Have you had anything to drink lately?" and he said, "I have had a few shots of vodka this afternoon," and since that wasn't one of the questions—since that was only one of my personal questions—I did not pursue the subject further.

Dr. Atcheson was given the usual opportunity to make a statement after interrogation and had this to say:

> Only thing I had written down was things I had discussed —my own personal questions which I think I have brought out. The one where I referred to the few shots of vodka—I asked the Sergeant—it's not part of the test at all—it may shed some light on the question. I don't know—I asked the Sergeant why he marched the men into the swamp and asked him if he was mad at them and he said, "Yes," and I did not pursue that any further.

But Costello's development of Dr. Atcheson's attitude toward the Bogens might have flashed a warning light at the Inquiry:

Q. You mentioned, Doctor—correct me if I am wrong—you are not an expert as far as this Bogens test is concerned. Is that correct?

A. That is correct.

Q. And Doctor, as I understand your testimony you seem to have some question as to whether or not you are really qualified on the date here in question to administer this Bogens test?

A. Well, I don't know what you mean by *qualified*. I can render the test and that is all that is actually required of me. It is not up to me to interpret it, nor to have a theory of how it works—how it works or how good it is. I am—I will say—an expert in drawing blood and initiating the test, but I am not an expert in that I do not know all the ramifications of the Bogens and do not intend ever to know.

Q. Who is it up to to interpret this Bogens test?

A. Whoever—I suppose—whoever ordered the Bogens test to be run. I did not order it to be run.

Q. Who ordered it to be run?

A. I don't recall exactly. I received a written request. It was either from the Officer of the Day—or either from the Rifle Range—or over at the Provost Marshal's Office.

Q. This Officer of the Day—he is not a doctor, is he?

A. No, he isn't.

Q. So you say that you just expressed the opinion that the individual who made the request for this Bogens test would be the one who would interpret it. Is that right?

A. Well, I don't know who is going to interpret. It has never fallen my lot to interpret it and I don't see that it alters my findings or sobriety test one bit.

Speaking of the Bogens in a different part of his testimony Dr. Atcheson said, "I ignored it completely." This made Costello's summary of Atcheson's clinical examination the most important point in the hearing:

Q. So, Doctor, based on the clinical examination which you made of this patient, would you as a medical expert conclude that Staff Sergeant McKeon had full control of his physical and mental facilities?

A. I have already so stated. Yes, sir.

From the viewpoint of military law *drunkenness* is "any impairment of the physical or mental faculties, however slight." Yet when Costello acquitted his brother-in-law, the Court of Inquiry was not impressed. It found as a fact "that Staff Sergeant McKeon drank an unknown quantity of vodka during the morning, afternoon, and early evening of April 8 while on duty as the Drill Instructor of Platoon 71." That evening drink was not proved at the Court-Martial; Navy and Marine Corps custom permits a man to go on watch four hours after liberty (which tacitly assumes he can sober up in that interval); yet the Inquiry's opinion was "that Staff Sergeant McKeon at the time he marched his platoon into Ribbon Creek was under the influence of alcohol to an unknown degree." This opinion was obviously based on superficial knowledge of the Bogens and Dr. Atcheson's written remarks, which we come to understand later. But publishing the Inquiry findings did the Marine Corps irreparable damage by leading to headlines such as "DRUNK LEADS DEATH MARCH" and to editorials concluding "drinking is universal in the Marine Corps" while insinuating that duty status is irrelevant.

Dr. Atcheson noted on his report, appended as an Exhibit to each record: "Clinical evidence of intoxication: Yes. Possibly under the influence of alcohol but still is in control of himself." It took Emile Berman to explain this. Toward the end of Dr. Atcheson's direct examination at the Court-Martial, Trial Counsel Sevier raised the issue of interpreting the Bogens, and this gave the proceedings an unusual turn:

SEVIER: And when you made that comparison, do you recall what the results were?

ATCHESON: The nearest comparison was 1.5 milligrams per cc.

SEVIER: Do you consider yourself qualified to give an evaluation as to what amount of alcohol that would indicate in the blood system?

ATCHESON: In view of the fact that I have had no real authoritative training in the field and my contact with the test has only been since on active duty in military service here at Parris Island, I do not think I'm qualified to answer.

SEVIER: But on your general knowledge does the reading which you obtained indicate anything to you?

BERMAN: I object to that—if it please the Law Officer—upon the ground that the Doctor stated that he doesn't feel qualified to make any evaluation of it at all.

SEVIER: May it please the Court: I intend to see if he could give any evaluation of the exact amount of alcohol.

KLEIN: I will allow the question.

SEVIER: Does that have an indication to you upon which you could base an opinion?

BERMAN: Base an opinion as to what?

SEVIER: Blood alcohol content, sir.

ATCHESON: Well, in my own personal opinion—with limited experience as a preface—it does mean that there has been some contact with alcohol. The amount, or when, or anything like that I wouldn't say.

KLEIN: By *contact* you mean ingestion of alcohol?

ATCHESON: Yes; ingestion.

SEVIER: Did you ask Sergeant McKeon anything about his activities that night in order to help you carry out the test of that?

ATCHESON: To my recollection the Sergeant answered my questions directly and rather hesitantly and without elaboration. I didn't find it easy to discuss anything with him. I don't recall anything right now that I said to him.

SEVIER: Did you make any inquiries as to what he might have done or might not have done that evening?

ATCHESON: I made—I asked him some question with reference to why he was brought in—something like that—I don't recall exactly—I'm sorry.

SEVIER: Thank you. That's all. Then to Berman, Your witness, sir.

Major Sevier wanted the Bogens finding to substantiate Sergeant McKeon's having one or more drinks April 8—a fact Defense Counsel was ready to admit. Sevier's fallacy was in relying on the Bogens test as conclusive, which the Manual warns it is not. Yet we shouldn't criticize Sevier for this fallacy when the Depot Provost Marshal, the Court of Inquiry, the Depot Legal Officer, Parris Island's Commanding General, the Commandant of the Marine Corps, the Judge Advocate General of the Navy, and the Secretary of the Navy were apparently willing to rely on the same fallacious assumption.

But now Attorney Berman was burdened with an unjustified procedure: Though Matthew McKeon was not so charged, the evidence warranted damaging suspicion that during the march into Ribbon Creek he "was under the influence of alcohol to an unknown degree," as the Inquiry found. Contrary to recognized court-martial rules, erroneous but popular opinion shifted burden of proof to the Accused: Trial psychology made this unwarranted suspicion intolerable to the Defense. Emile Berman was forced to discredit the Bogens as much as he could against a preponderance of bias, and particularly to prove that during the time in question Matthew McKeon was sober.

And so it was cross-examination by Attorney Berman, expert in legal medicine, that kept Dr. Atcheson on the stand more than an hour. Defense Counsel questioned the clinical sobriety test item by item displaying consummate learning in the physiology of drunkenness. Then he went through the Bogens routine step by step, continually prompting the witness in details of that procedure. Berman cast doubt on sterility of apparatus, condition of reagents, accuracy of color matching without a spectrophotometer, reliability of standards; Atcheson couldn't reassure him. More important, Berman disclosed that Atcheson was unable to say whether or not an alcohol-soaked sponge was used in handing him the syringe and needle with which to draw Matthew McKeon's blood. (No one bothered to ask Corpsman Fox, who did the handing.)

Then Berman gave Atcheson, "to refresh his memory," Atcheson's own sobriety report, which remains in conflict with all other evidence. Let's ask the principals at the trial to speak for themselves:

BERMAN: What was your finding or opinion placed upon this sheet of paper as a result of the series of objective tests?

SEVIER: I object—

KLEIN: Don't answer the question.

SEVIER: He's not asking for an opinion, he's asking for the contents of the writing.

KLEIN: Ask for his opinion.

BERMAN: What is your opinion?

ATCHESON: Then my opinion does not have to be expressed as the words are placed on that paper. Is that correct?

Q. You are asked to express your opinion.

A. My opinion was that Sergeant McKeon was not clinically intoxicated—drunk, or under the influence of alcohol. However, in view of the fact that his breath was suggestive of alcohol to me, and a point there which maybe I shouldn't bring out—there's another question there which hasn't been brought out which I think probably has a significant answer.

Q. What is that?

A. As I recall—to the best of my recollection—he answered, "I had a few drinks—or a few shots—of vodka this afternoon." In view of the fact—in view of the finding that I had, namely, odor of alcohol—suggestive of alcohol on the Sergeant's breath—and the fact that he admitted having had something to drink, I concluded—which is a moot question—he may have possibly been under the influence of alcohol to a subclinical degree which no one, of course, can determine. Clinically he was not intoxicated.

Q. Doctor, as I understand it, among the other things that you are required to do is to ask someone whether he's had a drink or a few drinks and should you, in your view, get some suggestion of the odor of alcohol you put it down. Is that correct?

A. Yes.

Q. Well now, what I'm getting at—in this case or any other case—if a man is brought to you under military—that is, police custody—and you are asked to run a sobriety test and every test that you run is negative and normal, and your own observations of the man indicate to you that he is normal—let's take me, for instance, I'm a better specimen in this regard than some others—every test you run is normal and every observation that you would make concerning speech or articulateness, co-ordination, general rapport, orientation of time and place—all normal, within normal limits—but if I had told you, "Look, I've had a couple of drinks," and you gathered some suggestion of an odor from my breath, you would have to put down on the form I'm possibly intoxicated?

A. No.

Q. That's what you did here, isn't it?

A. No—not to my knowledge—it certainly isn't the idea I wanted to convey. I just stated my conclusion regarding it. If the same thing occurred, I would not attempt to be brief in that. I apparently have lost the idea that I wish to convey. I would be more verbose and more specific.

Q. Tell us again. What is the idea you wish to convey?

A. The idea I wish to convey is clinically Sergeant McKeon was not under the influence of alcohol. He was not drunk—not intoxicated—to any test. Anyway, I could gainfully—

Q. That's by examination—observation?

KLEIN: Let him answer.

A. —but in view of the fact he admitted to me having had a few drinks of vodka that afternoon and in view of the fact his breath was suggestive of alcohol to me, I could not say that he wasn't under the influence of alcohol to a subclinical degree. If you have one drink of alcohol you are under the influence of alcohol. It may not be clinical or sub—you can't say whether it's subclinical or not, but that's the point I wanted to make.

Q. So the point I'm making to you then, is that since you could not—having a history of a few drinks and a suggestive odor of alcohol, you felt that you were obligated to say—knowing that he had a few drinks—that you could not rule out every possibility. Is that correct?

A. Yes—to the best of my testing.

Q. So that means you would do the same for me under similar circumstances?

A. But I would say what I just said—on the back of the page—

Q. You mean you didn't make your—

A. I sacrificed details in order to be brief because that space was limited there.

Q. You are certainly pursuing an illusive quest for certainty since you think if a man has a drink or two there is that broad, vague possibility that to some extent he may be under the influence of alcohol. Is that correct?

A. It's a moot question.

SEVIER: I object. The question is argumentative. The question has been asked and answered three or four times.

BERMAN: I'm putting it now on a philosophical note. Wouldn't you consider that a pretty—

SEVIER: I object to the philosophical note.

BERMAN: I have nothing else for the Doctor.

Dr. Atcheson insisted the clinical examination was at nine o'clock while the record showed the blood for the Bogens wasn't drawn until eleven-thirty. (From reconstruction of the incident it seems rather improbable that McKeon reached the Main Dispensary before eleven.) Major Sevier tried to account for this delay and Atcheson said: "As I recall, there were other patients who came in; one specifically who had been in a fight and had several lacerations which needed immediate attention before I went and drew the blood."

SEVIER: Does the Court have any questions?

HUTCHINSON: We should assume then, Doctor, that in view of your answers to the questions that you have been asked that the question here [indicating Atcheson's report] which says "clinical evidence of intoxication," where you circled the word "yes" you should have circled the word "no." Is that correct?

ATCHESON: Yes; I would say, "no."

Of eleven Defense witnesses only five seemed to offer material testimony. Perhaps the least relevant came from Lieutenant Benjamin Michael Kraynick, Medical Corps, U. S. Naval Reserve, orthopedist at Beaufort Naval Hospital. Yet his appearance in Court is loaded with interest because it reflects Emile Berman's skill in dealing with a medical expert. We sample a few items:

Q. Did you obtain a history from the patient?

A. Yes, sir. He got out of bed approximately five o'clock the morning of March 12 and reached for his trousers. At this time he experienced a sharp, stabbing pain in the left cheek, and he fell down on his left knee.

Q. Let's clear that up. What cheek are you referring to?

A. The gluteal region; I have that in quotes.

Q. I presume you are referring to a buttock?

A. That is right.

Q. You referred to the term *spasm;* medically speaking, what does that mean?

A. It means tightening of the muscles.

Q. And that is Nature's way of splinting because of pain?

A. Yes, sir; it is.

Q. If you feel your spine, those muscles you feel alongside of it, running up and down, are the pericerebral muscles that you are referring to?

A. Yes, sir.

Q. And those were in spasm?

A. That's right; on the left.

Q. Go ahead.

A. Neurological examination revealed diminution of sensation to pinprick in the left great toe.

Q. That left great toe, both centrally and muscularly, is elevated by the distribution of one of the nerve roots that emanates from the spine. Isn't that so?
A. Yes, sir; one or more.
Q. Go right ahead.
A. There was a total loss of ankle jerk on the left.
Q. I believe you have already told us that that is a neurological deficit of great clinical importance. Is that right?
A. Yes, it is.

Doing more talking than his witness, Berman went from nerve function to spinal anatomy:

Q. In order to get a description in lay terms could this be compared, except for size and dimensions, just as a concept, to perhaps a jelly doughnut with the doughnut itself being the annulus fibrosis and the jelly within it being the equivalent of the nucleus pulposis?
A. That's as good as any.
Q. To reduce this to terms everyone can understand, it serves as a shock absorber for the ordinary shocks produced by activities such as walking and jumping?
A. That's right.
Q. And with respect to muscles that are elevated by distributions of the fifth lumbar nerve root, does that include in part the handspring muscles?
A. That's exactly what it includes.

Counselor Berman kept Dr. Kraynick on the stand perhaps an hour and forced the Court to work overtime. Prosecutor Sevier made the last play:

"I move to strike the testimony of the Doctor as immaterial and irrelevant. It's not been connected with anything in the charges—very interesting—but not connected with anything in the charges."
KLEIN: Your motion is denied.

Berman convinced the Court that on April 8 Matthew McKeon suffered from a herniated intervertebral disc near the fifth lumbar nerve. "Conservative therapy"—rest and a hard bunk in the Depot Brig—had alleviated the condition. Neither surgery nor even hospitalization were now indicated, but McKeon should be kept under observation and have a further diagnostic work-up.

Considering the psychology of testimony, Kraynick's description of McKeon's pain would unquestionably win a degree of sympathy from a civilian jury and might receive weight in the closing argument. Perhaps it did have some influence on members of the Court, but to echo Dr. Atcheson, "It's a moot question." Rather than feeling sympathetic toward a man suffering, the typical marine officer would react by saying, "That knucklehead should have gone to Sick Bay. Failing to get relief, he should have asked for transfer to the hospital."

In weighing the all-important medical question, being under the influence of alcohol, the issue is clear. It was never proved Matt McKeon had a drink in seven hours preceding the Ribbon Creek march; it was proved he had a long nap and supper during that time. On the stand McKeon admitted to such offenses as: unauthorized absence from his post of duty; unlawfully striking recruits; and while in a duty status taking a few sips of whiskey and drinking most of a beer—these latter facts he might prudently have omitted because they were revealed by no other witness. The question of "subliminal intoxication"—which Dr. Atcheson insisted might exist—had best be referred to psychoanalysts. But if ardent Prohibitionists lend credence to that phenomenon, they may well take another reading on their cough medicines and health tonics.

23

Accused Testifies

MONDAY, JULY 30, began the third week and was tenth day of McKeon's trial. Once the Court came to order Emile Berman arose to argue his motion for directed acquittal. His statement and Charles Sevier's reply took an hour and a quarter, yet all their words were futile: Judge Klein had previously made up his mind, "All motions presented by Defense Counsel this morning have been denied."

Affecting mild surprise Berman started his defense, which was little more than consolidation of the position he had already won. His first witness was Elwyn B. Scarborough, owner of the vodka bottle and now a staff sergeant. For his part in the incident Scarborough had been given a summary court-martial and reduced one rank with sentence suspended during exemplary behavior. The ink was hardly dry on Scarborough's trial record before he became involved with Beaufort police and the suspension was vacated. The interesting thing in Scarborough's appearance is Major Sevier's impeaching his testimony.

BERMAN: Do you know the difference between 80-proof and 100-proof vodka?

SCARBOROUGH: Yes, sir. I can read on the bottle, sir.

BERMAN: Will you give this Court and the Law Officer your best recollection of how much was left in the bottle, if anything, at that time?

SCARBOROUGH: I don't know exactly how much was in it, but I would say an inch or two or three. I don't remember because I didn't see it.

BERMAN: There was enough in it so that you were going to come back and get it?

SCARBOROUGH: Yes, sir.

BERMAN: Now, was the bottle similar in all respects so far as you can remember to what I am holding in my hand?

SCARBOROUGH: Yes, sir.

BERMAN: And so far as your recollection is concerned was there approximately left in that bottle what appears in this bottle now?

SCARBOROUGH: I think so, sir.

SEVIER: Now you testified at the Court of Inquiry, did you not?

SCARBOROUGH: Yes, sir.

SEVIER: And that was right shortly after this incident?

SCARBOROUGH: I don't remember just exactly how many days it was afterward, sir. [It was four days.]

SEVIER: It was pretty shortly thereafter, wasn't it?

SCARBOROUGH: Not too long.

SEVIER: Do you recall this question being asked you: Question 43, Page 144, "Q. Do you recall how much liquid was left in the bottle?" Your answer: "No, sir. I don't." Do you recall that question?

SCARBOROUGH: Well, to tell you the truth, Major, it's been a long time.

SEVIER: Do you recall them questioning you about the bottle?

SCARBOROUGH: Yes, sir.

SEVIER: And you remember the answer then, "No, sir. I don't."?

SCARBOROUGH: Yes, sir.

Defense Counsel was able to reconcile Scarborough's conflict, which was only a minor issue. Scarborough hadn't seen the bottle at the Inquiry. It was undoubtedly a relief for him to learn that McKeon hadn't been nipping after their visit to the Staff NCO Club.

Second Defense witness was Warrant Officer Leslie Edward Volle, the topographer who conducted a survey of Ribbon Creek. Volle enlisted in the Marine Corps in 1946, was commissioned a reserve lieutenant in 1954, and had recently been demoted to warrant grade. He had five years' experience in surveying and was a graduate of both the Photo-Topographic and Map-Compiling Schools conducted by Army Engineers. Either Lieutenant

Colonel Alaric Valentin or Major John DeBarr conducted the first questioning of Volle because the record shows that Mr. Berman left the courtroom while it was going on. When it came to being Volle's watchdog during cross-examination, however, Ex-Intelligence Officer Berman was at his post. Major Sevier had no previous opportunity to interview Volle; he had to obtain a special recess Monday afternoon to do that. Mr. Volle spent two and one half hours testifying, starting near the end of the morning session and extending well into the afternoon. He was recalled twice Wednesday.

In courtroom terminology Volle was unquestionably an "expert." Nor is there any doubt he was thoroughly familiar with the Ribbon Creek hydrography as it existed in late June. But Defense was using estimates made in darkness by untrained recruits as basic reference data—"bench marks"—and superimposing on those precise measurements with which to test "scientific" hypotheses. Even more disturbing was the fact Leslie Volle openly showed bias toward the party calling him while Judge Klein demonstrated ignorance of aerial photographs, maps, and tides.

Unless the reader were trained in mapping, he could make little sense from Witness Volle's testimony. Even with training and interest in the subject he would be quite bored. Defense had Volle trace three hypothetical lines entering Ribbon Creek approximately perpendicular to the bank. Along those lines Volle estimated the depth of water at the assumed stage of the tide. One could march between twenty and forty-eight feet, according to Volle's data, before reaching a depth of five feet. Moreover, there were no holes in the area he surveyed nor was there a steep gradient. Dovetailing this testimony with that of Privates Grabowski and Langone would indicate the six victims drowned in water no higher than their shoulders and—more important—that the recruits of Platoon 71 were never in water over their heads as alleged in Charge II and the second specification of Charge III. Volle's estimate of the stage of the tide compared with our observations at Ribbon Creek was thirty minutes in error, but that was unimportant.

On cross-examination Major Sevier induced Mr. Volle to

estimate that the maximum depth of water on the lines charted by the Defense varied between eight feet and eight feet nine inches, all other assumptions remaining unchanged. Sevier might well have stopped right there. Instead, he brought back Defense Exhibit B, an oblique aerial photograph, and Prosecution Exhibit 27, the Public Works map of Parris Island. From these he asked Volle to transfer data obtained from Langone and McKeon. The result was vigorous protest from Berman, vacillation by Klein, hostility in Volle. Their verbal tangle is interesting, though not enlightening.

Let's try with brevity to bring the problem into focus and to omit many pages of testimony. Matthew McKeon's sketch of the march was on the Public Works map; the estimates of Earl Grabowski and Gerald Langone were on the oblique photograph; Leslie Volle's hypothetical lines of march were on his precise survey. Counselor Sevier wanted Expert Volle to transfer the first two sets of data to the survey. Volle made a rough translation from photograph to survey but rightfully complained he could do no better than a "close guess." Then Berman pointed out that the scale ratio between survey and map was ten to one, errors would be greatly exaggerated. Overruled on that count, Berman insisted the map had been admitted into evidence by the Law Officer "not to show distance but only the route of march"—actually it was Berman himself who said, "With that understanding, I have no objection," and who reached that understanding questioning the witness. At this point Klein directed that Volle "translate the line of march without reference to scale," an impossibility.

Unfortunately the identical map had been posted in the Inquiry courtroom. On it Guard Commander Johnny Taylor marked where he saw men emerging from Ribbon Creek; later Provost Marshal McLeod marked the location of the bodies. These additional marks, which couldn't be identified by Witness Cummings, who introduced the map, led to ambiguity.

Prosecutor Sevier continued questioning Witness Volle but didn't succeed in getting him to draw another line on his prized survey. Volle was hedging to favor his party. He insisted that he couldn't disregard scale, which was true, but he went overboard in describing the error that would result. He insisted that Ribbon Creek wasn't as accurately depicted on the Public Works map as on his own survey. This was true, also, but not vitally important since the only data he would apply were from rough estimates. The really important measure was not scale, but *direction.* Defender Berman's smoke screen adequately shielded his maneuver.

Mr. Volle pointed out a discrepancy between the two maps in the width of Ribbon Creek. At low water behind C-Butts, the stream narrows to 60 feet; at high water, it exceeds 350 feet, disregarding many acres of inundated tidal flats on the far side. Mr. Berman didn't want data transferred from either the aerial photograph or the Public Works map—with good reason. Had he wished that he would have selected a plain vertical rather than an oblique photo. On the former directions are accurate and scales can be corrected; on the latter one can only estimate. Berman would have been foolhardy to have attempted through witnesses to fix the *direction* of march.

Matthew McKeon was a thoroughly trained combat soldier. He had experience in night operations. He was the only well-oriented marine who entered Ribbon Creek. He had two landmarks on the night of April 8: the first target shed in C-Butts and the drainage ditch which runs northward into Ribbon Creek from between B- and C-Ranges. On April 9, after twice viewing Ribbon Creek flooded with searchlights during the recovery operation, McKeon indicated his direction of approach on the Public Works map: It was fifty degrees to the left of those lines postulated by the Defense. The location agreed closely with the area indicated by Johnny Taylor, another combat-experienced marine, and with the spot from which six bodies were recovered—that of *Thomas Hardeman* trampled into the mud.

An air intelligence officer can't function without intimate knowledge of maps and photographs. A seagoing naval officer must be acquainted with charts, hydrography, and tides. Every marine officer has to use maps, charts, photographs—often his very life depends on them. Lieutenant Colonel Berman gained the major advantage on Ribbon Creek terrain.

The last hour Monday of this third week was spent with Attorney Berman displaying thorough knowledge of anatomy and physiology. He called as next Defense witness Benjamin Michael Kraynick, Lieutenant, Medical Corps, U. S. Naval Reserve. Dr. Kraynick was a graduate of Hahnemann Medical College, Philadelphia, and an intern in orthopedic surgery at Allentown, Pennsylvania. He examined Matthew McKeon on June 18 and recorded the history of a back injury dating back to March 12. Finding: A herniated intervertebral disc caused McKeon's limp. Much of Kraynick's testimony was hearsay; all was irrelevant. Judge Klein admitted it over Prosecutor Sevier's objection "subject to connection." It fitted Counselor Berman's strategy neatly in building up sympathy for his client: Though racked with pain, Sergeant McKeon carried on—devoted to duty.

Dr. Kraynick's testimony also cast a shadow over Parris Island's Medical Service. The day of his injury McKeon went to a Beaufort drugstore and purchased a bottle of patent medicine. Next day he went to the Main Dispensary and after a cursory examination received aspirin. Back at the Main Dispensary two days later he was administered mephenesin, a muscle relaxer. Subsequently McKeon treated himself. It was three months before thorough examination changed the diagnosis from sciatica, or neuralgia.

Attorney Berman kept the Court working a half-hour overtime Monday, thus enhancing the prestige of his expert witness: "I have been very anxious, at the Doctor's request, not to bring him back here. He's got work to do of a medical nature. Not as a privilege to me, but out of consideration to a medical man, I request that we sit a little longer."

Sevier acquiesced.

Tuesday, July 31, third week in the case of the United States vs. McKeon, was a banner day for newsmen: The Accused took the stand.

Masters of courtroom strategy invariably debate the problem of exposing an accused to rigorous cross-examination. The more conservative prefer to let him remain silent. In this case Counsel Berman in parallel with Prosecutor Sevier's structure of the evidence had most effectively shrouded in doubt Sevier's finished picture. Now that the burden of proceeding was on Berman he launched a two-pronged counterattack: showing Matthew McKeon as a professional marine of the highest character, and convincing the Court that night marches in swamps were the traditional method of molding disciplined soldiers. In loosing McKeon to the wolves Berman took a calculated risk, but he was sure of his client. Permitting members of the Court to judge McKeon's character from their own observations (and what military leader doesn't consider himself an expert judge of character?) would be a capstone to the psychological structure Berman built.

As in the rest of his campaign Attorney Berman had a nice sense of timing. He started Tuesday morning warming up enthusiasm with Staff Sergeant Earl A. Myers, administrative clerk at DI School. Myers was custodian of facts and figures. Records over twenty-seven months showed that 1,362 marines attended DI School while only 787 graduated. Their average grade was 80.77 per cent. Sergeant McKeon's average grade was 84.90 per cent. Of ninety in his original class, fifty-five completed the course and McKeon's standing was fourteen. Myers noted that all DI candidates receive psychiatric screening.

When Myers left the stand Berman personally introduced McKeon's record from the Psychiatric Observation Unit without protest from Trial Counsel. Yet this was not in accord with the "best evidence" rule: Paul Thomas Sayers, civilian psychologist who did the original screening, was on the Depot. Dr. Charles E. Herlihy, Depot Psychiatrist who examined McKeon after the Ribbon Creek incident, was also available. Major Sevier's legal position, on the other hand, can readily be defended: He considered his own action in the nature of stipulating minor evidence. But from that viewpoint he failed to perceive Defense strategy.

Psychologist Sayers' check list had this to say of McKeon: "Strong drive and desire for DI duty. Motivation appears sound and healthy. Unusually stable, well integrated, efficient defenses. Average amount of hostility, appropriately displayed and controlled. Better than average achievement." To these Sayers added in his own handwriting: "Mature, stable-appearing, career marine. Handles self well, denies hostility problems. Accept."

Then Emile Berman called in a stagehand to arrange the scenery. Staff Sergeant William E. Ferris, training aids artist, had spent three weeks constructing a mock-up of that part of Weapons Training Battalion area showing barracks, rifle ranges, and an adequate extent of Ribbon Creek. Photographs were available for the record. Berman emphasized that this model was not to exact scale and guided Ferris in pointing out all important features. The stage was set.

BERMAN: If it please you all, the Defense desires to call the Accused.

SEVIER: First I respectfully invite the Law Officer's attention to Page 516, Appendix 8a, *Manual for Courts-Martial.*

Judge Klein took the bait. Defense Counsel might have avoided Klein's reading from the book by stating: "The rights of the Accused have been explained to him and he wishes to take the stand as a witness." Lacking that, Klein might simply have asked the Accused if he understood his rights. Instead, he read them aloud in detail.

The questioning opened with McKeon's family status, education, and military record. Matthew McKeon testified that in 1942 at the age of seventeen he joined the Navy. He said, "I went through Boot at Newport, Rhode Island. Shortly afterwards I went on the commissioned carrier *Essex* at Newport News, Virginia. I stayed aboard it all the time, sir, until it was decommissioned." Sergeant McKeon was given only brief opportunity to mention the service of *Essex* and his comment was so sketchy anyone unfamiliar with the record of that gallant ship could scarcely appreciate what he said. Though we can't spare time for detail about *Essex,* we should pause briefly to consider her career.

Essex cruised the Pacific over a quarter of a million miles between May 19, 1943, and September 13, 1945. Her "yearbook," *Saga of the Essex,* lists eighty-seven actions in which she engaged, beginning with a raid on Marcus Islands August 31, 1943, and ending with one on Tokyo August 15, 1945. She supported invasions of the Gilberts, Marshalls, Marianas, Palau, Philippines, Iwo Jima, and Okinawa. A few places *Essex* attacked were: Rabaul, Tarawa, Truk, Pescadores, Formosa, Saigon, Hong Kong, Kure, Hokkaido. She was in both Battles of the Philippine Sea and later assisted in destruction of *Yamoto,* which ended effective power of the Japanese surface navy. *Essex* destroyed 1,531 enemy aircraft and probably destroyed another 800; she sank or damaged 419 ships. She took a *kamikaze* hit off the Philippines which killed fifteen and left *Essex* in flames, but nine days at an advanced base returned her to action. She rode out the typhoon which sank three destroyers. *Essex* was prototype of a class of World War II carriers; actually she was a class by herself. Matthew McKeon was just one of a 2,500-man, close-knit team which won *Essex* the Presidential Unit Citation. Seaman and admiral in carrier actions take equal risks: There are no foxholes.

When the witness had completed his all-too-brief description of forty months' service in the Navy he was still deficient in Showman Berman's requirements for public speaking.

BERMAN: Now then, following that—try and speak a little more distinctly. You don't help yourself by leaning right in the microphone. Keep your head up and speak into it.

MCKEON: I never spoke in one before.

McKeon went on to relate that two brothers, James and Edward, were marines in World War II. (He didn't mention that a sister was an Army nurse.) In 1948 he joined the Marine Corps to make it a career, he said, though he and his wife must later have been doubtful when in 1952 he stayed out of the service four months. Then he talked about his own Boot training at Parris Island with Platoon 82, which was taken into swamps and marshes on several occasions. Prosecutor Sevier wanted to strike that testimony unless it pinpointed Ribbon Creek, but after some vacillation, Judge Klein limited it to showing "a practice under similar circumstances." In any event Berman had on record his first sworn testimony concerning marches in the swamps.

McKeon continued with his experience as a seagoing marine, twice an instructor in Quantico, and in Korean combat. Then he described coming to Parris Island for DI School and his early experience with Platoon 71, particularly its falling off in discipline. It was the hour for noon recess; Berman's timing was precise.

Matthew McKeon remained on the witness stand two hours Tuesday afternoon and another two hours Wednesday morning. We have already pieced together his version of the Ribbon Creek tragedy. So in following the trial we limit our view to highlights in the proceedings which either reveal the spirit of the Court-Martial or do not appropriately fit into the story elsewhere.

Sergeant McKeon had difficulty translating his thoughts from informality of the parade ground to formality of the courtroom. Attorney Berman was guiding his client through the events of Sunday morning, April 8, when Technical Sergeant Scarborough showed up in recruit barracks:

Q. What was the general conversation?

A. Well, the general conversation was regarding the platoon on the Range—regarding their marksmanship—and the big topic was the discipline of the platoon. Sergeant Scarborough was kind of pee'd off at them.

Q. We say "tee'd off" around here.

A. Yes, sir. I'm sorry.

And like many of us Matthew McKeon had trouble pronouncing certain names. At this stage of his story it was Sunday evening and he had just sent Maloof and *Wood* from the DI room:

Q. All right then, with that did you—did they leave and did you ask for someone else?

A. Yes, sir. It was not immediately after—Private McPerson came in.

Q. Who?

A. Private McPerson.
Q. He pronounces his name "McPherson."
A. Yes, sir. I told you I would foul up.
Q. You are speaking of the same man, are you?
A. Yes, sir.

Then there was the matter of McKeon's controlling his emotions. Normally a hypersensitive person, the strain of four months reached a climax with the revelation in the courtroom of his private life. He was telling about slapping Private Langone Sunday evening:

Q. Was it a hard slap or was it with a closed fist? Were you out to hurt him? What was the circumstance?
A. Sir, I wasn't out to hurt him, sir. I slapped my kid—to be honest with you—harder than I slapped him.
Q. Which kid?
A. My five-year-old daughter.
Q. Well, what was the idea? All right. Take it easy now. Square yourself away.
A. Yes, sir.

But that was only a minor break. Matthew McKeon had been talking continuously an hour and a quarter Tuesday afternoon when he reached the point in his narrative where panic erupted in Ribbon Creek:

> I started swimming out toward this area here where they were and there was a kid looked like he was going the wrong way—he had his back toward me. I latched onto his dungaree jacket and pulled him approximately—oh, maybe ten feet in toward the ditch—and I stood up and asked him if he could stand up and he said he was all right. He said he was all right and I left him there and I started back out toward this group which at that time was almost parallel with me. Instead of back there [indicating on the mock-up], it was back here now. I started out and I seen this boy coming in. I thought he was going out all right and I was ignoring him for the simple reason that out there, maybe five yards further, there was a kid I could see the top of his head and I thought he was floating. That's the kid I was going for—but around this kid was possibly three or

four splashing—wasn't screaming or yelling or nothing—but they was splashing. I headed out toward that kid and, as I went by this other boy—this other man—he latched onto me—well, I can't just say—it surprised me—and when I did realize what happened the man had hold of my neck. I tried to break his hold, and every time I started treading water the both of us went down. We went down. And as we come up I told the guy to keep his head and I'd get him in. He was a colored boy. I don't know who it was, but I think it was Private *Wood* because I'd get hold of him and try to bring him around in front of me and he wouldn't leave go and I was looking at him more or less like this and he wasn't saying anything—wasn't saying a thing. He went down a second time, and the second time he went down it seemed to me like he went down further than the first time. While down there, all I was thinking of was getting to the top. I was pulling toward the top and this kid let go—this kid let go and that's the last I seen of him.

At this point McKeon broke down completely.

KLEIN: Perhaps this would be a good time for a recess.
HUTCHINSON: Yes, sir. The Court will recess for ten minutes.

It was twenty minutes before Sergeant McKeon resumed his story.

Playwright Berman didn't have McKeon's emotional outburst in the script. For ten days his client sat in the courtroom rigid and outwardly impassive. Spare uniforms, cleaned and pressed daily, were available in Father Maurus Cook's quarters so the Sergeant might change during the luncheon recess. Director Berman was portraying a stolid marine veteran, a fighting man. It is interesting to speculate whether Psychologist Berman could have avoided McKeon's breakdown had a recess been granted thirty minutes earlier. This is what happened when his witness reached the point where Platoon 71 was in formation in front of Barracks 761 ready to begin the march:

BERMAN: What is your pleasure, Mr. President? Shall we start this? This will be almost the last, but it may be a lengthy one. Do you think this is a good time for a brief break? I don't want to interrupt this phase of the testimony once I start.

HUTCHINSON: Suppose you continue and finish that up.

BERMAN: Fine.

At that time Witness McKeon left his chair and stood at a microphone near the Weapons Battalion mock-up.

During McKeon's direct examination it was important for Counselor Berman to reinforce the testimony of recruit witnesses about the depth of water in Ribbon Creek. This is how he did it:

BERMAN: What is the highest the water ever got on you at any time until something happened?

MCKEON: The water never got any higher than just about there. [McKeon indicated on his body.]

BERMAN: Hold that! Don't move your hand for a minute; will you, please? You are pointing to a spot directly over the second button; is that correct?

MCKEON: Yes, sir. Approximately there, sir.

BERMAN: What happened to the tape measure may I ask, Major Sevier?

SEVIER: We don't have one here, sir.

BERMAN: I thought we had one one day when we were measuring some distances. I think it might be important for the record and for the Court to see what that height is in measurement. I wouldn't vouch for my accuracy in using a straightedge—would rather have a tape measure—if we can get it.

SEVIER: We will have to go outside of the building to get it.

KLEIN: Hereafter see that there is a tape measure in the courtroom—or some kind of measuring wire of some sort.

McKeon went on with his testimony while a runner was sent out to find a tape measure. Ten minutes later he returned, but Lawyer Berman didn't want to interrupt his witness' story. Measurement was made dramatically just before evening adjournment, more than an hour afterward. That was a good figure for the Court to sleep on: The tape showed four feet eight inches.

Another point Berman wanted to underscore through McKeon was his favorite red herring: map scales. He accomplished this easily:

Q. I want to show you Prosecution Exhibit 27 and call your

attention particularly to an ink line which is drawn here. First I shall ask you in that regard did you sit down and study the scale of this map or have any idea of the scale of this map or know anything about the scale of this map?

A. No, sir; I didn't. The only thing regarding the map—I take it that's Sergeant Cummins'?

Q. I'm going to show you so you don't have to take anything. Just look at it. Now tell us whether or not did you draw that line, or how—just tell us what happened in connection with the map and Sergeant Cummins.

A. Well, he came in with this map and he says—words to the effect, "Now, they won't be exact." He said, "Can you find Building 761 on it?" It all looked like Greek to me, I couldn't find it. He pointed, drew a circle around Building 761 and explained to me where the ranges were. As a matter of fact I wasn't even thinking. I drew a line down the march we took—of the route we took to the creek and I told him when I got to the first target shed behind Charlie Butts we took a left and went out in the stream and I asked him at that time if they found any of them yet and he says, "They're looking out in this area here." And I said, "Well, about that vicinity there I think they went down." And he drew this circle here.

The fact that the Public Works map was drawn to scale is the only matter of importance. No one deals mentally with representative fractions when locating himself on a map. All the features are laid out in proportion and the map reader interpolates in proportion. Still, Berman's *non sequitur* registered in less analytic minds.

In his confession given to Sergeant Cummings early April 9 Sergeant McKeon made a few misstatements. Attorney Berman obtained from Major Sevier the original, Prosecution Exhibit 26, and questioned McKeon about discrepancies, particularly when McKeon said that he interrupted the morning field day, marched the platoon to noon meal, and then brought it back to barracks to resume the field day. These misrepresentations were quite easy to explain:

Q. Have you got any explanation of how that got into the statement?

A. Well, I didn't want to involve anyone else's name regarding the activities during that day.

Q. You mean the drinking?

A. The drinking.

Q. You didn't want to bring anyone else's name in so you assumed the whole day's activities yourself, is that it?

A. Yes, sir.

Q. But it isn't a fact that you secured the field day or took them to chow at all?

A. No, sir. I didn't secure it and I didn't take them to chow.

Matthew McKeon's description of Samuel Cummings' obtaining that statement reinforces Cummings' admission of coercion:

> They brought chow to me and then around a quarter past seven they came after me again. That is the time they brought me over to the Provost Marshal to Sergeant Cummins. That is when I met him, the first time I ever met him. He introduced himself and he also read Article 31 to me, explaining my rights to me—that stuff. He says, "We are in a rush. The General is waiting for a statement." And I told him I was ready to give anyone any statement, I don't care. "All right," he says, "Now I want to ask you some questions and you talk into this." And he gave me a microphone and a tape recording machine there and I spoke into that and I told him about what happened during the period of the day.

Major Sevier was cross-examining Sergeant McKeon on the same subject the following morning:

Q. Do you recall in your statement when you made it to Sergeant Cummings, and I quote, "The platoon still in column of twos marched at my command at route step into the stream and then beared right in water about waist deep along the bank"? Now that was made the next day?

A. Yes, sir. I don't recall it, sir.

Q. You don't recall that now?

A. No, sir. As I said before, Major, I don't recall what I said in that statement. Sergeant Cummins come in there stating that the General wanted a statement right away. I spoke into that tape recording machine first and then he shoved off with the tape recorder, I suppose. Major Holben come in and said, "Do you realize what you've done?" He sit down and started reading me out of a book. I didn't know what was going on.

Q. But you signed all that?

A. I would have signed anything, sir. I would have walked to the gallows—

It was McKeon's direct examination which concluded Tuesday's meeting. Though it was before quitting time Major Sevier wished to cross-examine in one session. Mr. Berman signed off with a request to begin earlier Wednesday morning: He had an important witness who must meet a time schedule. Everyone seemed to know that it was Commandant Randolph Pate, but that isn't apparent from the record. Tuesday's effective meeting time was three hours forty-five minutes, one hour less than Monday.

Wednesday, August 1, was twelfth day of the trial. To insure time for that important witness in the afternoon Court opened at 8:40 A.M. Matthew McKeon resumed his seat in the witness chair for cross-examination, which Prosecutor Sevier, by suggesting a recess, divided neatly into two 50-minute periods. Occasionally Sevier harassed McKeon, who was fair game in this situation; Berman's objections were generally overruled. Sevier followed events chronologically, which forced him at time to backtrack on topics pertinent to the offenses charged. These excerpts, rearranged by topics, reveal McKeon's attitudes and also show that Sevier was unable to shake him:

Q. I understand you testified yesterday that on many occasions you would give a man a slap—slap him into a position of attention.

A. Not many occasions, sir. Did I say many occasions?

Q. How many times did you slap those men?

A. To be frank with you sir, I didn't count them.

Q. It must have been more times than you could count then.

A. I can count quite a few times.

Q. It was quite a few times you slapped them?

A. I say I can count quite a few times—quite a few numbers—but it's not more than I could count.

Q. It must be a greater number than you can recall, because if it was one or two you would probably remember it.

A. If I slapped once or twice; yes, sir. I could recall that, sir.

Q. And what was the purpose of slapping Maloof then?

A. Maloof come in in kind of a relaxed position and he knows better than to enter the Drill Instructors' room in that kind of a position.

Q. So you slapped him into a stiff position?

A. Slapped him just to show that I disapproved of his position.

Q. You couldn't tell a man that you disapproved of what he was doing? You had to lay a hand on them?

A. I told them many times, sir—many times, sir.

Q. This night you laid a hand on him to show him?

A. I think I hit Maloof before, too, sir.

Q. Is this your normal way of speaking to the men; if you disapproved of what they were doing, to slap them?

A. No, sir.

Q. It wasn't normal for you then that day?

A. I don't understand.

Q. It wasn't your normal way? Had your drinks affected you?

A. No, sir.

Q. Now were you setting an example of discipline that day when you carried in there a vodka bottle and drank in front of a recruit, or—

A. I grant you, sir, that was a bad gesture.

Q. That was the example you were setting for this platoon you described?

A. I didn't show it in front of the whole platoon.

Q. Well, you know recruits talk?

A. I guess they certainly do, sir.

Q. Now while McPherson was in there you picked up this bottle?

A. Yes, sir; I did.

Q. And you gave him the impression you were drinking?

A. That is the impression I gave him.

Q. And that was the impression you intended to give him?

A. I told him I was a man and if I wanted a drink I could have a drink. I said, "You can't have any. When you become a man you can have some."

Q. And that was the mark of a man in the barracks?

A. I told you as I look back over it now it was a very poor gesture.

Q. Did you discuss this night activity you engaged in with Sergeant Huff?

A. Regarding the march? No, sir.

Q. You didn't ask his permission?

A. No, sir; I didn't.

Q. It was his platoon, wasn't it?

A. Yes, sir.

Q. Is that the example you were setting—of obedience to orders—to your troops?

A. Sir, I had a job to do—I was a junior sergeant—to help. If I thought in my duty as Drill Instructor—if something came to my attention, sir, I could handle without calling on Sergeant Huff, I would take care of it.

Q. Now had you ever informed that platoon—I say you, yourself—ever informed that platoon that they shouldn't lie on the grass in the rear of the barracks on a Sunday when it was their day off—or their day of decreased activity?

A. Sir, back at Mainsides here—at Battalion—we used to tell the boys to study their notes—notes they took in their classes—or to read their manual. If it was too warm in their huts they could go outside and study them outside. Many times they would have a tendency to sit down—human nature—and every time one of us would see them sitting down studying, he would tell them to stand up and study; if they wanted to sit down, to go back to their huts and sit on their locker-box.

Q. Why did you order that field day?

A. To teach them discipline.

Q. What method were you using there to teach discipline?

A. For the simple reason, sir—

Q. What method?

A. What do you mean, "what method"?

Q. You were using punishment to teach them a lesson?

A. I don't think it was punishment, sir. I don't consider any work done in the Marine Corps as punishment.

Q. Did you have any extra duty?

A. Extra duty, sir? Not that I recall.

Q. What do you call extra duty in the Marine Corps? It can't be anything else but for punishment.

A. I don't say it was punishment—it was inconvenience.

Q. You say you were just inconveniencing them then?

A. No, sir. I wouldn't say that.

Q. You deny then that was for punishment?

A. Yes, sir.

Q. Didn't you tell McPherson that the platoon would not fall out until after the movies started?

A. No, sir. I don't believe I said that, sir. I don't believe I said it, sir. I may have said it. I am not denying it, sir.

Q. And the reason you would not fall out until after the movie started was because no one would see you when you started out on this march—didn't you tell McPherson that?

A. No, sir; never, sir.

Q. Didn't you tell that to any of the other boys that night?

A. No, sir; not as regarding to fall out so no one would see us.

Q. Why did you take that route?

A. Well I was familiar with that area there, sir.

Q. Isn't it true that that was the best route you could take down that way and not cross a sentry post?

A. I will be frank: I don't know where the sentry posts are, sir. I never stood guard duty there.

Q. You went down through the middle between the widest distances?

A. I was familiar with that area. As a matter of fact I was familiar with the whole Range, you know. I coached down there at the Pistol Range and the .22 Range, sir. We walked back and forth across that, you know, taking the platoon back and forth to the barracks, and to chow, and from there. But regarding the sentry posts, sir, I don't know where they were, sir, to be frank with you.

Q. And didn't you say yesterday that you didn't know if the swimmers were around the nonswimmers or the nonswimmers mixed up with the swimmers?

A. Yes, sir; I said that. I didn't know.

Q. And there could have been nonqualified as well as qualified swimmers that weren't covering down, or out of the column?

A. Sir, I never got in the water over my chest and I figured if anything did happen—didn't figure on anything happening but, if it did happen, there would be enough men around there, sir, to prevent it.

Q. You were relying then on those recruits to prevent anything happening?

A. Not to prevent anything happening. I didn't think anything would happen, to be frank with you, sir. If I'd thought for one minute one of those kids would drown, sir, I'd never took them in.

Q. Did you check on what kind of discipline you were maintaining in that water?

A. Yes, sir. I told them a couple of times to knock off their fooling, and they did.

Q. But you never tried to maintain a column—never gave them the order to close up—never gave them the order to cover down?

A. No, sir; I didn't.

Q. Now was there a moon that night, did you say?

A. Yes, sir. There was a moon that night, sir.

Q. All the time you were in that water?

A. No, sir. When I noticed the moon gone, sir, is when I started coming back in after this accident happened, sir. That's when I noticed there was no moon, because I looked up.

Q. Do you remember whether there was a full moon?

A. Sir, I didn't actually take a reading on the moon, sir. There was a light on the water and there was a moon up there.

Q. You don't remember what kind—whether it was a full moon, quarter moon, or what?

A. I don't know much about moons, sir.

Q. Did you make a statement to Sergeant Cummings?

A. The next day, sir?

Q. Yes. Right.

A. Yes, sir; I did.

Q. Did you sign that statement?

A. Yes, sir; I did.

Q. And in that statement did you say—and I quote, "About three fourths of the platoon were squared away but the remainder were foul balls"?

A. I don't remember what I said in that statement.

Q. You signed it, didn't you?

A. Yes, sir.

Q. And you signed that you read it?

A. Sir?

Q. Are you denying that you made that statement?

A. No, sir. I'm not denying it, sir, but I don't recall what I said in that statement the next morning, sir. I'll be frank with you: I don't recall what went on.

When Sevier finally released Matthew McKeon, Colonel Hutchinson posed questions for the Court:

Q. Can you tell us what you understand to be the meaning of the term *disciplinary action* as it is used in the Marine Corps?
A. Disciplinary action, sir?
Q. Right.
A. All I recall, sir, as regarding disciplinary action is I read an order where it says disciplinary action will be taken—you know, sir—I believe that's Office Hours, going up to the CO.
Q. And when the CO takes action for an offense, do you understand that to be punishment?
A. Yes, Colonel.
Q. Do you think there's a difference between teaching discipline and taking disciplinary action?
A. Yes, sir; there is. I believe so, sir.
Q. Did you believe that your Battalion Commander held you responsible for teaching discipline?
A. For teaching discipline? Yes, sir; I believe he did.
Q. Did you believe that he held you responsible for taking disciplinary action?
A. No, sir.

Sergeant McKeon didn't flinch during cross-examination. He made only two errors, one in fact, one in perception. Sevier suggested that *Thomas* was a large man; McKeon agreed. *Jerry Thomas* was five feet six and a half inches; *Leroy Thompson,* whom McKeon obviously had in mind, was six feet one. The other discrepancy, which Major Sevier labored, probably recalling the classic defense made by Abraham Lincoln, concerned the moon. There was no moon. Counsel Berman knew that and ignored it. But there must have been a streak of light on Ribbon Creek, which could have come from Malecon Drive or some "standing light" at the Rifle Range.

Next on the witness stand for about ten minutes was Warrant Officer Volle, the surveyor. He had made a special reconnaissance, at Mr. Berman's request, of the Dredge Cut and the marshland behind Third Battalion area. Berman used Volle to show that conditions in both places were substantially the same as Ribbon Creek. Mr. Volle was questioned only for that limited purpose. Berman was through with him at 10:45 and calculated that there was adequate time to cross-examine before eleven, when the Court wanted to recess. But Sevier's habitual stubbornness prevailed; he asked for postponement, which Klein granted. When Volle returned four hours later he was on the stand nine minutes.

After a midday recess which lasted two and a half hours, the Commandant of the Marine Corps, Randolph McCall Pate, was called as a witness, duly sworn, and testified fifty minutes, enough to give the legion of newsmen their leads for the day. But to comprehend the significance of Commandant Pate's testimony we need first recall exactly where he stood in May; then we can examine some extracts from the record.

Careful study of Inquiry and Court-Martial shows that Pate had available all essential facts when he took action on the former. Actually the trial shed light on but one aspect of the whole case. While the Inquiry rendered the opinion "That Staff Sergeant McKeon at the time he marched his platoon into Ribbon Creek was under the influence of alcohol to an unknown degree," it stated at the same time he was "sane, mentally competent, responsible for his actions and aware of the difference betwen right and wrong." The Inquiry members had no doubt McKeon was sober. Had they disregarded the Bogens test and been more specific in their findings, the press would have been unable to suggest that liquor was a factor contributing to the incident. That point Mr. Berman disproved.

Isolating the Commandant's consideration of McKeon from his indictment of the whole Marine Corps when he commented on facts developed at the Inquiry, we find him rather brief:

> The Convening Authority has approved a recommendation of the Inquiry for trial by general court-martial of the acting Drill Instructor, Staff Sergeant McKeon, and I agree that this is necessary. Sergeant McKeon, an experienced marine, but an

inexperienced Drill Instructor, committed his egregious lapse. The Inquiry found that he violated the code of the noncommissioned officer by drinking in the barracks, by drinking while on duty, and by drinking in the presence of a recruit. The record also indicated that while under the influence of alcohol to an undetermined degree he unfortunately chose to order his platoon out on a night march because of a minor deviation from the very strict standard of conduct to which recruits must adhere. Subject to the foregoing remarks, I concur in the findings, opinions, and recommendations of the Court and the action of the Convening Authority thereon.

Thus with these Inquiry findings Pate agreed: That Matthew McKeon was guilty of illegal possession and misuse of alcohol, oppression of marines under his command, manslaughter through culpable negligence which cost the lives of six men. Administering mass punishment and conducting an unauthorized night march which led to the tragedy were included offenses. Conviction of these crimes might be punished with a dishonorable discharge, loss of all pay and allowances, reduction to private, and confinement at hard labor for twenty-three years. In Pate's estimate, this was no trivial misdemeanor. A special court-martial convened in a Recruit Training Battalion might adjudge a bad conduct discharge, loss of two-thirds pay, and confinement at hard labor for six months. McKeon's Commanding Officer, Lieutenant Colonel Robert A. Thompson, might summarily have deprived him of one stripe and taken administrative action to insure that McKeon was no longer associated with recruits.

Three months after the Commandant first studied this case he entered the courtroom. Most important was Pate's reversal of position, after a good deal of legal skirmishing which Berman finally won. In so-called hypothetical questions, Counsel summarized the whole case—from the Defense viewpoint—and asked for Pate's opinion. To an extremely long question there was an extended reply:

> There's no final say as to what an individual would do under all circumstances and, of course, I have not had the evidence that has been considered in this Court. I think you have

to take that into consideration. It's evident this drill sergeant did drink some vodka and I assume that it was against the regulations—the conditions under which he did it. I don't know. I think maybe I would take a stripe away from him for a thing like that. It's a fairly serious thing, of course, particularly when you are dealing with recruits.

As to the remaining part of it—it's a little fuzzy and hazy to me just what transpired—but I suspect I would probably have transferred him away for stupidity or, if you want to be a little more polite, for lack of judgment. I would probably have written in his Service Record Book that under no conditions would this Sergeant ever drill recruits again. I think I would let it go at that. That's not a final answer, I know. That's about what my judgment would be.

In April, Pate searched desperately for an order or local regulation which could be used to put McKeon on the hook. August 1, he felt differently. There was this exchange:

"Is it your view, General, from your large and long experience in the Marine Corps, that all training can be accomplished by lesson plans, syllabi, and regulations alone?"

"Oh, no. Of course not. I think syllabi and plans have to be used to guide the instructors. But at no time did I ever consider them as final and ultimate." [Yet these are promulgated as orders.]

The Commandant mentioned his own legal qualifications several times during his testimony. These remarks were most pertinent: "I have no objection to answering. I don't know the law business. You people know that. I think that's true, although I have not been a shipmate with the new Code as much as I could."

It was common knowledge that Pate acted upon the Inquiry—the full text of his comment, including his signature, appeared in New York *Times*. These extracts from the Court-Martial record stand by themselves:

BERMAN: Then I ask you, General—as we say in the law—as an expert, arising out of your official position as Commandant of the Marine Corps, based upon your broad views of this case, can you state an opinion, with a reasonable degree of certainty, as to what would have been your action in the event this matter had been allotted to you for action?

SEVIER: I—

KLEIN: I assume you object.

SEVIER: Yes, sir.

KLEIN: Do you mean the trial or after the—

BERMAN: Before the trial. Before there was ever a trial or a board of inquiry.

SEVIER: Sir, I think this is the ultimate issue that—

KLEIN: Objection sustained. If you want to ask him what he recommended, I will allow that.

BERMAN: I should like to state that this offer of proof is on the basis of opinion evidence from an expert.

KLEIN: But he has acted officially in the matter on a Court of Inquiry by making a recommendation—I assume.

BERMAN: I do not know anything about whether he has or not. [A copy of the Inquiry record was on Berman's counsel table and he referred to it during the trial.] I understand the Convening Authority is the Secretary of the Navy and I do not believe that any recommendations were made by the General.

KLEIN: I assume the General reviewed—and this is an assumption—reviewed the Court of Inquiry in this case. On the facts known to him at that time, he acted and either approved certain disciplinary action being taken, or did not do so. If you develop that and show he has not acted on Court of Inquiry information, that is another matter; but where we have on the record an official opinion of the General, I think that opinion should stand unless you seek to have that one modified.

Skirmishing continued. Attorney Berman eventually posed his hypothetical question and received the expected answer. Cross-examination, redirect examination, re-cross-examination followed. Finally it was Klein's turn at questioning. The matter about the Inquiry had been bothering him.

KLEIN: I have a question. General, did you take any action on a Court of Inquiry which inquired into the circumstances of the drowning of six men at Parris Island on April 8, 1956?

PATE: I did. I reviewed the Court of Inquiry.

KLEIN: And did you take any action concerning a recommendation for disciplinary action regarding the Accused in this case?

PATE: I made a recommendation to the Secretary of the Navy that the recommended action of the Court of Inquiry be implemented by him.

KLEIN: And do you recall what the recommended action—the recommendation for discipline—of the Court of Inquiry was concerning the Accused?

BERMAN: I object to that. That's no longer opinion evidence. That's like the matter of putting before the Court the action of a grand jury on the limited basis in which they knew the facts.

KLEIN: I appreciate that. But I do want to know whether at a prior time the same expert made another recommendation—other than the opinion of the expert you have submitted.

BERMAN: As I understand your question to the General, does he know what the recommended action of the Board of Inquiry was?

KLEIN: He said it should be implemented. The testimony is that he stated it should be implemented.

BERMAN: I am suggesting to you respectfully that your question to the General is, "What was the recommended action?"

KLEIN: I will withdraw the question on the basis of your—and I instruct—basis of your recommendation. I instruct the members of the Court to disregard my question. I now ask you: Did you recommend to the Secretary of the Navy that a recommendation for trial by general court-martial of the Accused be implemented?

PATE: I did, yes.

Earlier in the proceedings Mr. Berman produced the Commandant's unsigned policy statement.

BERMAN: I show you this paper, General, and ask you whether or not this brochure was put out, as an official document of the policy of your command, by you as Commandant.

PATE: I published and signed that, yes.

BERMAN: Will you sign that for me and I will take it home as my autograph?

PATE: I will be glad to. Do you have a pen?

BERMAN: I would take it in pencil—as this may have to be preserved for posterity, we'd better have it in ink, General.

The witness signed the document and handed it to Defense Counsel. Berman returned to the counsel table.

BERMAN: Excuse my back, General.

PATE: The best looking part? *Touché!*

BERMAN: *Touché.*

PATE: He will probably get back at me before he gets through with me.

Warrant Officer Volle followed General Pate after the 25-minute recess needed to get His Nibs clear of the area. Then Father Maurus F. Cook, OSB, appeared as a character witness.

Father Maurus is a man so absorbed in his vocation that he wins the respect of any right-thinking acquaintance, Catholic, Protestant, Jew, agnostic. He is a credit to the Order of St. Benedict. During their first few days aboard all recruits hear the "No. 1 Lecture" from a chaplain. Each platoon is divided for that purpose according to religion. Catholic boys have an opportunity to go to confession, which in many cases is the first time in years they have done so. After hearing a hundred-odd confessions through a sultry afternoon Father Maurus is completely whipped, nearly despondent.

Father Maurus spent years away from his Abbey at St. Leo, Florida, serving as a Navy Chaplain, particularly with Marine Corps units. He gave all he had rendering faithful service. But during eleven months following the Ribbon Creek tragedy Father Maurus was pushed around so inconsiderately that his life at Parris Island became intolerable. He asked and obtained his release. But if this were only one priest who figured in the Ribbon Creek incident we might suspect a personality weakness in him. Father Anthony Bielski, whom we met on Ribbon Creek during the recovery, suffered identical treatment until he felt obliged to resign from the Chaplain Corps.

Father Maurus felt an obligation to attend the Court-Martial. He was excluded by Judge Klein as a prospective witness, no matter it was only to McKeon's character. As McKeon would say, Father "latched on" to him April 9 and shepherded him until he left Parris Island. Without Father Maurus' religious solace, counsel, guidance, and firm belief in his innate goodness, Matthew McKeon might well have ended in the psychopathic ward. Father Maurus spoke briefly at the trial; his words were sincere:

Q. Now first will you tell us, in your opinion, what is the character of Sergeant McKeon for morality, veracity, integrity, and honesty generally?

A. All of those characteristics, sir, are of the highest, in my opinion. I have found him always to be truthful, to be dependable. He has been kind and gentle and deeply religious. He is a family man, very much devoted to his family—his wife and children—and, secondarily, devoted to the Marine Corps.

Q. Now then, in addition to your views that you have just testified to, are you able to express an opinion as to what Sergeant McKeon's reputation is with others, generally, aboard this base?

A. Since April 9 I have had occasion to hear—not that I have sought or solicited comments—but I have heard from time to time nothing but the highest comments in behalf of Sergeant McKeon.

When Father Maurus left the courtroom Wednesday it wasn't yet three o'clock, nor was Attorney Berman prepared to call additional witnesses. So he requested an early adjournment accompanied by one of his typical startling anouncements: He expected to conclude the defense next day. Wednesday's active trial lasted only three hours.

24

Judge Klein

THE ACT OF MAY 5, 1950 (Public Law 506, 81st Congress), entitled "Uniform Code of Military Justice," superseded the Articles of War, the Articles for the Government of the Navy, and the disciplinary laws of the Coast Guard, all rooted in the eighteenth century. Besides contributing to "unification," this new Code was expected to eradicate alleged harsh features of military law by grafting onto it "with true democratic spirit" our time-honored civilian practices. Among its real novelties were the Court of Military Appeals and the professional legal beagle.

Despite contrary insinuation the naval service had skillful lawyers before the new Code; some were admitted to practice before the Supreme Court. But all of these were primarily officers of the line—potential combat leaders—and secondarily law specialists. Each year a few career officers entered law school on a part-time basis while gaining practical experience in the Office of the Judge Advocate General. This program furnished an adequate number of attorneys to fill key billets ashore and afloat.

In addition, all line officers were trained in the elements of naval law and this was rightfully considered essential to command and administration. Throughout their careers they gained experience as judge advocate, defense counsel, and court-martial member. Inept performance led to knuckle-rapping in letters from reviewing authorities or in formal court-martial orders; inadequate knowledge led to failure on promotion examinations. But more pertinent to our view of Ribbon Creek was the tradition of foisting an undue share of law practice on marines, who received special training at Basic School in anticipation of that custom. Aboard ship the senior marine would expect to be the Captain's legal aide while the junior was summary court-martial recorder. Marines on naval staffs wrote court-martial reviews; at naval district headquarters they were habitually trial lawyers. And so any marine officer with a fair amount of service could in 1956 be presumed to have working knowledge of naval law.

Yet the new Code inaugurated a corps within a corps: All staff lawyers, court-martial law officers, and counsel at general courts-martial must now be certified by the Judge Advocate General. Winning certification requires law school attendance and admission to the bar. Peculiarly, while this new requirement for professional lawyers was being effected the Congress eliminated the old program for training career officers in law. This forced the Navy and Marine Corps to recruit civilians without being able to offer them monetary rewards that might compete with any well-established law practice.

Captain Irving Nicholas Klein, U. S. Navy, was on May 4 appointed Law Officer in the forthcoming case of the United States vs. McKeon. Fifty-three years old, as was Emile Berman, Irving Klein had entered the Navy as a Law Specialist during mobilization for World War II. He "integrated" from the Naval Reserve when the new Code made its demands on the regular establishment. Captain Klein was much junior to Colonel Edward Leigh Hutchinson, President of the Court-Martial, who made colonel four years before Klein's appointment to commander, one rank lower. Hutchinson also had ten years on Klein in length of service, but in the courtroom this had no significance barring riot or fire, when the senior would take over.

Under the old Code presidents of courts-martial functioned like judges in civilian courts. They were limited only by the provision that any member might respectfully object, then the court would be cleared while members voted on that question. Under the new Code presidents of courts-martial are an ambiguity: The statute itself is vague and leaves procedure to be approved by the President of the United States, as it was in the *Manual for Courts-Martial*. Basic law merely excludes the law officer from attendance while members deliberate or vote—and neither law nor regulation clearly defines *court*, which may variously be interpreted as "law officer," "members," or both. Thus the new Code passed Congress.

But then came the problem of drafting a new Manual. Realizing this would be "processed" in many bureaus and offices before approval, the writers tossed a few modest sops to the court-martial president. He keeps the title, though he is little more than jury foreman. He sets the time for trial. As presiding officer—whatever that means—he preserves order. He administers oaths to counsel, presides in closed session, and speaks for members of the court. Yet when you read the fine print you discover the law officer has the last word in everything except administering oaths. Even in determining upon recess or adjournment the law officer may call it an "interlocutory question" and make final ruling. Thus we see Judge Klein in command as the Ribbon Creek Court-Martial unfolds.

The nicest way to insult a baseball umpire is to show him the rule book, but courts-martial aren't like that. The law officer may demand formal arguments, require filing of briefs, or recess court to study the book. Judge Klein did just that after Counselor Berman entered McKeon's pleas on the second trial day.

Traditionally our courts recognize different forms of pleading: guilty, not guilty, guilty in a lesser degree than charged, guilty without criminality, *nolo contendere,* the accused stands mute. Military courts accept a plea of guilty when certain that it is voluntary, understood by the accused, not improvident, does not involve a capital offense, or the accused does not later set up matters inconsisent with his plea. All other pleas or a refusal to plead are entered in the record as "not guilty." The rule is that simple. This is what happened after Berman announced that on Charges I and IV "the Accused stands mute":

SEVIER: It is the understanding of Trial Counsel that the pleas to Charge I and Charge IV are to be accepted as pleas of not guilty and the Prosecution will proceed on all charges as if a not guilty plea was entered.

KLEIN: Trial Counsel will so proceed.

SEVIER: There are several preliminary matters I would like to take care of here now, sir.

KLEIN: Would you like to call a brief recess?

SEVIER: No, sir.

BERMAN: Pardon me, but I thought he said he would like to call a slight recess now.

KLEIN: I wish to call a recess for the purpose of checking the procedure we have followed. We have been confronted with something that is at the moment—that is, it is considered by me to be a very uncommon practice. Of course, it is a proper one under certain circumstances—it is one that can be made. I just want to verify it for the purpose of being technically correct and for this reason I recess the Court. *(After the recess Klein announced):* I'm satisfied that the procedure which we have followed in entering the not guilty plea is correct.

The following morning Judge Klein didn't look at his book:

SEVIER: I offer Prosecution Exhibit 2 for identification into evidence as Prosecution Exhibit 2. I request at the close of this trial that a true copy may be substituted. [This was an original Depot Special Order which for two years must remain in Parris Island files and then be retired to the National Archives.]

KLEIN: That pertains to all exhibits admitted.

But trial procedure requires the ruling Sevier requested, for example, Prosecution Exhibits 25 and 26, written statements of Matthew McKeon dated April 9, were appended in the original.

That same morning Prosecutor Sevier announced his desire to have the Court view Ribbon Creek that afternoon. Defender Berman agreed provided no testimony was taken at the scene, which Berman well knew is standard procedure. Members of the

Court were appointed by the Secretary of the Navy as "best qualified for the duty by reason of age, training, experience, length of service, and judicial temperament." They were all familiar with the rules and Judge Klein could presume that, but he read to the Court and into the record instructions contained in the Manual; cautious, late that afternoon he claimed his previous reading "paraphrased" and read those instructions the second time. Not thirty minutes after Klein's first reading this happened:

HUTCHINSON: Are questions by the Court appropriate at this time?

KLEIN: Yes, sir. Questions by the Court are proper if they have any that they desire to make, but I must tell the Court that they are not to initiate evidence. If a question is not clear, if a matter is not clear, by development of such a matter by the Trial Counsel or Defense Counsel, then the Court can interrogate for the purposes of clarifying and for further developing. The Court is not to inject any new matter, or initiate any new evidence in the trial. [Klein apparently forgot that his own questions were technically "by the Court."]

VALENTIN: *(appointed Defense Counsel):* Excuse me, sir—the admonition of the Court—they can only ask questions which have been brought before the Court by Counsel and that alone?

KLEIN: And that alone. Is that not your understanding?

VALENTIN: No, sir. I wanted to make it clear.

KLEIN: That is exactly what I told them.

HUTCHINSON: The Court understands that. No questions by any member of the Court.

Klein should have called a recess to read his book, which says:

> The Court is not obliged to content itself with the evidence adduced by the parties. When such evidence appears to be insufficient for a proper determination of the matter before it, or when not satisfied that it has received all available admissible evidence on an issue before it, the Court may take appropriate action with a view to obtaining available additional evidence. The Court may, for instance, require Trial Counsel to recall a witness, to summon new witnesses, or to make an investigation

or inquiry along certain lines with a view to discovering and producing additional evidence.

Court recessed for lunch fifteen minutes early and then convened thirty-two minutes late, probably waiting for Judge Klein to write the apology which he delivered when Court opened:

> In connection with a question that perhaps one or more of the members of the Court desire to ask of the last witness, I had instructed the Court concerning the extent to which their interrogation might go. I should like to change and amend and eat humble pie in connection with such instructions. Colonel Valentin rose to ask me whether that was my instruction. I mentioned that it was and asked him if he disagreed. At the moment he couldn't reach a reference. No other Counsel in the Court invited my attention to any other instruction on the subject, so perhaps I might feel free at this time not to feel too guilty in the present circumstances if my rule was the old Articles for the Government of the Navy rules and not in the new Manual, and to that end I will read and instruct the Court concerning the examination by the Court, or a member.
>
> The Court, including the Law Officer and its members, may ask a witness any question that either side might properly ask a witness. If new matter, not properly the subject of cross-examination of the witness on his previous testimony, is elicited by questions by the Court or its members, both parties will be permitted to cross-examine the witness upon the new matter. In questioning an Accused, should that be the case—should that come up in this case—the Court and its members must confine themselves to questions which would be permissible on cross-examination of the Accused by the Prosecution. Questions by the Court and its members, and evidence elicited thereby, are subject to the objection on proper grounds by either side and by the Law Officer and members of the Court. With that understanding—and corrected understanding—it is my intention to have Sergeant Manthey, who was last on the stand, recalled so that the members of the Court, if they so desire, have the opportunity to question Sergeant Manthey.

While he was at it Klein might have noted that exclusion of improper evidence elicited by the Court is particularly important because there is a natural hesitancy of the parties to object, and undue weight is liable to be given to such testimony. Further, in the interest of justice, a Court may always of its own motion exclude inadmissible evidence—this Judge Klein never did.

Klein's excuse about old rules was weak: As a Law Specialist he had presumably been working five years with the new ones; then he quoted a generality while in law there are always exceptions. True, the old rule said, "The Court should scrupulously avoid originating evidence, for to do so lays it open to animadversion. Evidence brought out by the Court should, in general, be limited to making clear the meaning of testimony already given." But Klein seemed to forget that the general rule was never invoked unless it seriously jeopardized rights of the accused. For 154 years under "Rocks and Shoals" every naval command from the China Station to Washington continually roasted courts-martial for basing their findings upon incomplete evidence. They were enjoined to summon witnesses themselves when the judge advocate failed to give them a full picture. In short, the exception was the general rule—and that is probably why this one was changed.

This excerpt from the record might indicate Judge Klein's sensitivity to differences between old Code and new:

BERMAN: I have just one question that I neglected to put. I will confine it to just this one; Mr. President, with your permission?
HUTCHINSON: Yes, sir.
BERMAN: I neglected to ask you—
KLEIN: I believe I rule on those questions as to whether you may ask a further question.
BERMAN: I'm very sorry.
KLEIN: You may proceed.
BERMAN: I certainly did not mean to have anyone usurp your prerogative.
KLEIN: You may proceed.
BERMAN: Thank you, sir.

Irving Klein was sometimes talking when he should have been listening; this was true the morning of July 24. Recruit

David McPherson, in whose sole presence Matthew McKeon was alleged to have taken a drink, was on the stand. McPherson had reached the point in his story where McKeon had a vodka bottle in his hand:

SEVIER: In your opinion, from what you observed at that time and that place, what did he do?

BERMAN: I object to that. What a person does is in a fact, and not the subject of opinion evidence.

SEVIER: I believe he can testify he saw the act and what he thought at that time he was perceiving.

KLEIN: What he was perceiving, yes. I think you have got enough in your record without insisting on that. I sustain the objection.

Judge Klein's remark was ill-advised. As it turned out, Counsel Sevier didn't have enough in the record: McKeon was acquitted of this charge. But more serious was the implication that Klein's observation might tend to influence the Court. Had there been a conviction on this charge, Attorney Berman would have had excellent grounds for appeal. It was such clear judicial misbehavior that it weighed on Klein's conscience. This is what happened after he had time to mull it over during the luncheon recess:

SEVIER: Let the record show that all parties to the trial who were present when the Court recessed are again present in the court.

KLEIN: In that connection—may I proceed?

SEVIER: Yes, sir.

Judge Klein spoke:

> In connection with testimony by a witness McPherson this morning he had said something to the effect that "I presume he did drink" in response to a question by Major Sevier, Trial Counsel. An objection was made by Mr. Berman, Defense Counsel, to the word *presume* and he moved that the answer be stricken and I granted the motion and directed that the answer be stricken. In connection with my ruling at that point I made the observation to Trial Counsel that "you have enough in the record." I was there referring simply to the questioning at that point concerning the taking of the bottle into his hand and the

raising of the bottle to his lips. My observation at that point was not intended—and is not intended—to be any opinion on my part regarding proof of any charge or specification in this case or any issue involved in this case. You gentlemen are the sole triers of the facts. I make this observation and you are to disregard anything that may appear to you as an expression of an opinion by me. You are the sole triers of the facts and of the question of ultimate guilt or innocence with regard to that specification and any other specification. You will again be charged on this matter and more fully in my instructions to you before you retire. I now have mentioned this to you so that you may completely disabuse your mind of any impression that I may personally have concluded that that charge or that specification has been here established fully. You are to completely disregard what may appear to you to be any opinion of mine on that subject.

HUTCHINSON: Thank you for the explanation, Captain. The Court did not get the wrong impression from your remark.

KLEIN: Is there anything that Counsel wants to air on that question? My purpose is only to insure that there was not any misunderstanding on the part of members of the Court concerning that matter.

BERMAN: I believe that the record has now been very appropriately corrected, sir. I think the record ought to show that this statement was made on your own initiative.

KLEIN: Has been so made only on my own initiative, and was not invited to my attention.

The day before he wrapped up his side of the case Prosecutor Sevier wanted to introduce a sequence of Depot Training Orders which placed out of bounds the swamps near Elliott's Beach. To appreciate the following conversation we must recall that up to the moment Defense Counsel had introduced four exhibits, none of which had been seen by Trial Counsel before it was shown in the courtroom. Sevier's exhibits are contained in the Inquiry record. A copy was on Mr. Berman's table.

SEVIER: I now show Prosecution Exhibits 17 through 23 respectively for the Defense's possible objection before I ask that they be admitted in evidence.

BERMAN: I ask the indulgence of the Court to look at these papers.

KLEIN: I would suggest that in the future when you have documents to offer, Mr. Trial Counsel, that you arrange during the recess the preliminary showing of the documents to Defense Counsel and try to obtain a reading of them so we don't have to sit here in Court while the time is being consumed for this purpose—if it can be so arranged.

SEVIER: Aye, aye, sir.

As a result of Emile Berman's maneuver four of these seven documents were never admitted. This had no effect on the trial one way or another because none was relevant, though each was otherwise technically admissible. An out-of-Court hearing was held during the recess which followed excusing the custodian of the seven orders. The next witness brought in another document which Judge Klein erroneously admitted: It was not "best evidence." There was a recess after the testimony of this next witness—and another out-of-Court hearing during which Klein would not back down. But right now it is entertaining to listen to clashing views in open Court when Hospitalman Billy Redmond brought in the Bogens Log:

SEVIER: Redmond, did you make the entries in this book?

REDMOND: I made the first entry in that Log, sir.

SEVIER: Did you have the duty to do so?

REDMOND: Yes, sir.

SEVIER: This Log is introduced and offered in evidence under the business entry exception to the hearsay rule.

KLEIN: Official record?

SEVIER: Official record—and this is a business entry—Log, too.

KLEIN: Admitted.

SEVIER: Sir, I would like—

KLEIN: It is admitted.

SEVIER: Is it admitted in evidence? I'm sorry. I'm not very fast today.

BERMAN: May I be heard on that for a moment?

KLEIN: Certainly.

BERMAN: I think that without being immodest I'm familiar with the rule which has ameliorated the old shop-book rule of common law days and I understand—I believe—the introduction of evidence on so-called official records or records of events—transactions and occurrences made in the regular course of business—but there are exceptions to that. One of the exceptions is that you can't get in by the official records rule something which is essentially hearsay and could not be established through the witness himself. And I propose to show that with regard to these entries this witness has no knowledge and could not testify to the ultimate facts.

KLEIN: Admitted.

BERMAN: I presume, in any event, that just as a matter of fairness, the doctor that did this examination will be put up by the Prosecution? I am asking that—having permitted this—the man who is responsible for the performance of the test will be brought here in connection with the offer of this exhibit.

Actually, Mr. Berman didn't get to prove that Hospitalman Redmond knew nothing about the Bogens. It was Dr. Atcheson's job to evaluate the test—and he was the one who knew very little about it. Redmond knew more about the Bogens than anyone else who appeared in that courtroom—except Emile Berman. The argument continued:

KLEIN: If you question the weight—

BERMAN: I am speaking about the performance of the test. Standing by itself, this has no validity at all.

KLEIN: This is a record which has gone in as a business entry record and as an official record, and has been so admitted.

BERMAN: That may be so, but that still does not lend it any scientific accuracy.

KLEIN: That will be for you to show.

BERMAN: Sir?

KLEIN: I think that if it does not contain what it purports to contain it will be for you to show.

BERMAN: It would seem to me that scientific evidence upon which this is based must come and should come from the man who made it. The obligation of the one who introduces a record under the rule of—business entry rule, would be to bring the man who it is said had the scientific knowledge to make the evaluation. This is not a burden I must assume.

KLEIN: The man has testified he had a duty to make this entry. The record is admitted with that duty.

BERMAN: Let me ask one question: You had a duty to make

an entry about what someone else who ran a test told you to put down?

REDMOND: Someone else didn't, sir. I stated that Fox and myself ran the test, that the doctor drew the blood.

BERMAN: Is that part of the test?

REDMOND: Yes, sir. That's the beginning of any test, the original source of your specimen.

BERMAN: Excuse me. Are you provoked with me?

REDMOND: No, sir. I'm not, sir.

BERMAN: And the matter of evaluating the test—the most critical of all—that's for the doctor to do?

REDMOND: Yes, sir. It is, sir.

BERMAN: And all that you have entered in this Log—in the regular course of business—is what you were told was the critical evaluation. Isn't that so?

REDMOND: Yes, sir.

BERMAN: And that, of course, was something that you were not required to do—to evaluate it for yourself?

REDMOND: No, sir. I can't do such.

BERMAN: I renew my objection to the proffer in evidence.

KLEIN: With regard to the entry concerning which you testified on April 8, 1956, at 2400, which bears the initials and name "B. G. Redmond," the entry is admitted.

Later that same afternoon Mr. Berman produced an unauthenticated paper stating the Commandant's policy on recruit training:

BERMAN: I think, Mr. Law Officer, that you are required to take judicial notice both of this paper and its authority.

KLEIN: I do take judicial notice of it.

SEVIER: I object to the introduction unless we can see what it is. I have never heard of taking judicial notice of an unknown document.

KLEIN: I am prepared to say on Mr. Berman's say-so that is a statement made by General Pate, the present Commandant of the Marine Corps.

SEVIER: When?

KLEIN: I don't care when. It contains a statement that he made —I take it—with regard to training recruits.

SEVIER: Then I request that I may be permitted to see it.

BERMAN: I thought this received unlimited distribution. I am referring to a paper dated May 1, 1956.

SEVIER: Then it is irrelevant. It is after the date of the incident of which the whole subject matter is about.

BERMAN: You mean the Major General Commandant changes his views between April 1 and May 1?

KLEIN: Will the Reporter read back the question?

REPORTER: Will you agree that the conduct of training must inculcate in each marine that sense of his own responsibility to do his part in battle so that his comrades do not bear his burden or suffer from his failure? Do you agree with that?

BERMAN: I will withdraw that.

KLEIN: Does that call for an answer? I think it is elemental. Certainly that is the function of every recruit. Do you expect the witness to disagree with that observation—that general observation—that very general one—that a man, any soldier, any sailor, any marine must not expect someone else to bear his responsibility? Is that what you are examining about?

BERMAN: Mr. Law Officer, that is not the question. The question is the conduct of training must inculcate that. I know what the duty of a soldier is. I am talking about this Commandant's statement.

SEVIER: *The conduct of training* is a very loose, elusive, and veiled term.

KLEIN: The objection has been sustained. I think we are getting a little remote.

BERMAN: I am compelled to disagree with you, sir. I believe these are the issues in this case. *(Then to the witness):* Do you agree there is an area of teaching in which each teacher or instructor—or a Drill Instructor—must impress upon his recruits his own responsibilities toward all?

SEVIER: I object. I don't even understand that question myself, sir.

KLEIN: I will allow the question.

SEVIER: Well, in an area in teaching—in teaching what?

BERMAN: The area of teaching which is a man's responsibility and his responsibility for all. *(Then to the witness):* Do you agree that that must be impressed on each recruit in the training program at the Recruit Depot?

KLEIN: I will allow that question.

SEVIER: I would like to know who is teaching. Who is the instructor?

KLEIN: Those responsible for training.

BERMAN: As long as that is the objection to it—the Drill Instructors. I thought we all understood who we were speaking about. The Drill Instructors are under obligation to impress upon each recruit his responsibility to himself and for all.

SILVEY: *(the witness):* Are you quoting from that paper?

BERMAN: I am asking you without regard to the paper. Do you agree that is appropriate and necessary for him for the training of recruits?

SILVEY: You say, "impress." What was the rest? Impress what?

BERMAN: To impress upon each recruit his own responsibility and his responsibility to all?

SILVEY: Yes, sir. I will agree with that.

BERMAN: That is all, sir.

SEVIER: Since I was not on the distribution list for this and—evidently—it has had wide distribution, may I ask Defense Counsel if I might see it.

BERMAN: Certainly. I am sure it must be in many headquarters of this command.

There was a 15-minute recess.

SEVIER: For the purpose of the record I would like to point out that an alleged policy—a statement which was the subject of some controversy prior to the recess—appears to be an unsigned document neither alleging distribution, promulgation, authenticity, and is in no way to be taken as any official document issued by any officer.

BERMAN: I don't know why he says that. What does it say on the title page?

SEVIER: I believe the Law Officer is familiar with the Navy system of publication and promulgation of orders.

BERMAN: I assume the title page speaks for itself. If you refer to the fact it is unauthenticated I will see that it is authenticated by bringing in some one from Headquarters of the United States Marine Corps, Washington, D. C.

KLEIN: Admitted, it is unsigned. Admittedly, it does not bear any authentication, but you might read for the record from that paper.

SEVIER: In line with my previous statement that it is unauthenticated, it is fourteen pages of printing not containing a distribution list or promulgation order.

KLEIN: On that score, I am rather certain that if Mr. Berman read it and questioned the witness from it, it is a document that he obtained either from the Marine Corps or which originated from the Marine Corps and is precisely what Mr. Berman purported it was.

SEVIER: I made no allegations. I merely wanted to call the Court's attention that it was not a duly promulgated order in any fashion.

KLEIN: Correct. And only in that sense do you mention it. I am sure you mean no aspersions.

SEVIER: Yes, sir.

Judge Klein might have called a recess, examined the document, and studied his book, beginning on page 257. A writing that is not authenticated may not properly be received in evidence—but proof of authenticity can be waived. This statement was genuine beyond doubt. The reason it wasn't blessed with an official "chop": Pate didn't send it through the mill; it came out his back door.

It is important to observe Judge Klein's behavior July 30 after Counselor Berman's motion to dismiss:

KLEIN: All the motions presented by Defense Counsel this morning have been denied.

BERMAN: Will the Law Officer inquire as to whether or not there is an objection from any members of the Court?

KLEIN: The Court has been informed that all of these motions have been made subject to their objection—each of them has been—all of the rulings upon the said motions, made by the Law Officer, are made subject to objection by each member of the Court.

HUTCHINSON: Before the Court makes a final ruling on the rulings by the Law Officer, I propose a recess until ten-thirty.

Colonel Hutchinson was within his rights to call a recess and to poll the Court privately. There was no reason why the members could not discuss this complex question among themselves. This, however, removed Teacher Klein from his pupils' classroom. He had twenty minutes to light off all boilers and cut in full power on his main steam line. His safety valve popped when the recess ended:

> In ruling, I prefaced my announcement of my rulings by the remarks, "subject to objection by any member of the Court." That does not call for or require that the Court recess to determine whether any member objects. The request, I assume, by the President of the Court, was for the purpose and only for the purpose of ascertaining whether any member objects and not to take any sort of a vote on the question of what shall be done with such objection. That is not the procedure. I now again ask whether any member objects and if any member does object to the ruling that was made—or of more than one—that any such member or members will announce in open Court, and I will let you know what the procedure is in that regard.

Judge Klein proceeded to read from the *Manual for Courts-Martial,* interpolating his own explanatory remarks between phrases. He covered the whole subject of Law Officer's rulings. Then Klein continued:

> But all of that is predicated—and I want to make this clear —and that procedure is predicated only upon the announcement of or the existence of an objection by any member of the Court. And now I call upon you, and each of you, to announce whether you have any objection to any of the rulings of the Law Officer.

BERMAN: Mr. Law Officer: I don't want to interrupt, but in order that the procedure you've just stated be plainer, would you instruct the Court—members of the Court—that in the event there is an objection, in addition to the Court being closed for their deliberations on the objection, what kind of a vote is involved in a seven-member Court?

KLEIN: Yes. I will be glad to.

HUTCHINSON: I don't believe that's necessary. We understand the procedure in the event of a vote and in this case no vote was taken. It was merely to determine whether any member had any objections to the rulings of the Law Officer—and I have to announce that no member of the Court objects to the rulings of the Law Officer.

KLEIN: And no member has objected to the ruling of the Law Officer?

HUTCHINSON: That's correct.

KLEIN: Since the request was made by Defense Counsel and

in order to comply with his request, despite the President's indication of a familiarity with the voting procedure in the event there is an objection to a ruling on a motion for a finding of not guilty, I will read from Paragraph 57. [Judge Klein read all of that, interspersing remarks, then continued]: I believe that is all. In order that the record might clearly reflect whether or not there was uttered any time from the moment the rulings were made an objection by any member of the Court, I desire each of you individually, starting with the most junior, to announce whether you have any objection to any of the announced rulings made by the Law Officer. Who is the most junior?

Those familiar with rank insignia could see that Lieutenant Bentley A. Nelson, Medical Corps, U. S. Navy, was most junior. Next in line was Major John G. Demas, whose gold leaves would represent a Navy lieutenant commander. Those familiar with rules for seating members at a court-martial—rules that have existed through the ages—know that in an odd-numbered court-martial, the most junior will be found on the President's extreme left.

Each member of the Court in response to an individual question answered, "No objection."

KLEIN: And do you each announce that at no time since such ruling did you have any objection? Do you each so announce?

Each member of the Court in response to an individual question answered, "Yes."

KLEIN: *(to Defense Counsel):* I think that satisfies you?
BERMAN: I think so, sir.

Polling the jury publicly is strictly civilian practice.

Judge Klein also had difficulties in his relationship with witnesses. Traditional court-martial procedure excludes prospective witnesses from the courtroom in order to prevent their subsequent testimony being influenced by any previously given. This rule should have been invoked when the Court met Monday, July 16. It was not. During out-of-Court hearings that afternoon, Judge Klein made the announcement the first time. July 18, before the first witness was called, he made it again. July 19, fourth day of the trial, this is what happened:

KLEIN: I just want to warn the witnesses that unless there is—I'm trying to find that warning about the persons in the courtroom. Will you be good enough to give that warning?

SEVIER: Unless they are required to be present for other reasons, all persons expecting to be called as witnesses in the case of the United States versus Staff Sergeant McKeon will withdraw from the courtroom.

After that Judge Klein made this announcement sporadically. He should have done it conscientiously each time Court opened after recess or adjournment. Nor is there any indication that prospective witnesses were excluded during the arraignment and opening arguments, times when the more suggestible might easily be influenced. The courtroom was continually filled with spectators both in uniform and mufti. Few oncoming witnesses were familiar with court-martial rules.

Another military convention designed to reduce opportunities for bias is the warning given to a witness who has testified. Let us first note the prescribed warning:

> You are instructed not to discuss your testimony in this case with anyone except Counsel or the Accused. You will not allow any witness in this case to talk to you about the testimony he has given or which he intends to give. If anyone, other than Counsel or the Accused, attempts to talk to you about your testimony in this case, you should make the circumstances known to Counsel for the side originally calling you as a witness.

Corporal Richard J. King, most junior ex-Drill Instructor of Platoon 71, was on the stand July 19 as a Prosecution witness. Sevier had conducted King's direct examination and Berman seemed finished with cross-examination. This is what happened:

BERMAN: I have nothing further. Is it customary to take a break?

HUTCHINSON: Yes, sir.

BERMAN: I suggest a recess.

SEVIER: I have no objection.

KLEIN: I'm agreeable to a recess.

BERMAN: I believe the witness is warned before the recess.

SEVIER: Yes; the witness should be warned.

BERMAN: I would like to make a request since the witness is actually in the process of interrogation that he speak to no one, both lawyers for the Defense or the Prosecution, any more than he would not have the opportunity to speak to anyone before we—

KLEIN: During the period of recess, which will be for about ten minutes—that period of time makes it satisfactory—you will not discuss your testimony with anyone. You will not discuss with anyone any matter concerning this trial whatsoever and you will have no discussion with Counsel on either side or with the Accused nor with any prospective witness. You are not to discuss the matter concerning which you have testified here, the matter to which you may testify to, or any matter concerning this trial during this period of time.

HUTCHINSON: The Court will recess until three-fifteen.

Defender Berman stole a base prodding Judge Klein into giving Witness King these instructions. Prosecutor Sevier was still making an effort to limit cross-examination to the scope of direct examination. Berman was conducting a vigorous, winning campaign to present simultaneously the cases of both Prosecution and Defense. Since Berman had succeeded in getting King to bring out matter not developed by Sevier, the Prosecution was adequately justified in conferring with its own witness.

Under the old Code, warning the witness before excusing him was mandatory; under the new Code it is optional. Except for such Top Brass as Generals Puller and Pate, Judge Klein normally issued the warning.

August 2, the last day witnesses were heard, Mr. Berman dredged up Sergeant Leland L. Blanding in a psychological offensive leading to the trial's climax. Blanding waived protection from self-incrimination and swore that he had taken five or six recruit platoons on unscheduled marches into the swamps, through water varying in depth from knee to neck, in daylight and in darkness. Berman wanted Blanding's hearing extended into the court of public opinion; the witness could speak more freely off the stand. Yet Berman feared a squared-away marine would obey orders: that Blanding would heed Klein's warning.

The record shows how little Judge Klein valued those instructions he had been giving for three weeks:

"Mr. Berman, would you state your question again, please?"

"I respectfully invited your attention to the fact that—in connection with the admonition you have given to this and other witnesses—many of these men, after they have testified, have been or attempted to be interviewed by the press. I don't know whether your admonition is intended to include that or not. But I think it would be clearer if these men could know, one way or the other, whether the admonition does or does not include interviews with the press. I am only making this reference for their benefit in their method of conducting themselves. It is not quite clear. In any event, I leave that with you, sir."

"The admonition of witnesses is a matter solely in the discretion of the Law Officer. He may admonish a witness and warn him concerning his testimony in any discussion of it. Where I have warned the witnesses, I have exercised that discretion. What the witness does after that is his own problem in every instance."

"Perhaps you misunderstand. I am not suggesting for a moment that admonitions should or should not be given. I am not clear—and I don't think that the witnesses are clear—whether your admonition includes interviews by the press."

"The admonition, when I give it, reads so, and I invite your attention to it." Klein read Blanding the standard warning. "I will not undertake to pass upon, in a general way, what occurs outside of this courtroom after I warn a witness. You are excused. Thank you, sir."

Captain Klein's rationalization in this instance defies logical explanation. Since he could omit this warning at will, why did he persist in giving it? Effective leaders issue an order only when they are confident that order is possible of accomplishment and that it will be accomplished.

25

Naval Justice

THURSDAY, AUGUST 2, was thirteenth day of McKeon's trial and the last when witnesses appeared. Court was in session only one hour forty-two minutes.

First witness was Sergeant Leland L. Blanding, product of Parris Island and veteran of Korea, who had just completed a 28-month tour as Drill Instructor. Attorney Berman called Blanding to verify the custom of night marches into swamps. Prosecutor Sevier unsuccessfully attempted to exclude this evidence as irrelevant and immaterial; but he was successful in striking from the record as hearsay Sergeant Blanding's statements insisting the custom was prevalent. This insistence, however, must have impressed the Court. Let's hear some of Blanding's story:

BERMAN: In connection with training and teaching platoons both discipline and morale, can you tell us whether or not you engaged in any exercises which were unscheduled?

BLANDING: Yes, sir; I have.

BERMAN: Direct yourself—if it is a fact—to the marching of men into swamps and boondocks and creeks.

BLANDING: I have had approximately five or six platoons in the swamp area and the water around Parris Island. Actually two of them in the area that I like to refer to as—in the fall of 1954 when I was a Drill Instructor—behind the Third Battalion area and one platoon

I had in the area behind the barracks at the Rifle Range—not behind the butts, but what is known as the Dredge Cut.

BERMAN: Tell me this: In taking your men into these areas were they in water?

BLANDING: They were.

BERMAN: What was the height of the water on you and on them?

BLANDING: Approximately anywheres from knee to neck-deep, sir.

BERMAN: And were these marches or exercises performed during the day or at night?

BLANDING: Both, sir.

BERMAN: And in connection with these exercises was it teaching discipline and instilling morale?

BLANDING: Absolutely.

SEVIER: Sergeant, what platoon numbers did you take on these marches?

BLANDING: Two of them I can give you an accurate account of, 272 and 403, sir.

SEVIER: What month?

BLANDING: If I remember correctly, sir, Platoon 272 I picked up in June or July of '54 and therefore that would put them in the area approximately in the month of August, sir, with our training schedule being at the Rifle Range at the time. Platoon 403, I believe, I picked up immediately after I dropped Platoon 272—and I'd say picked them up in the early part of September, I believe, sir—so that would make it in October and November for them being in the swamps. They were in the swamp area not only behind the Rifle Range but behind the Third Battalion itself, sir.

SEVIER: I ask the Law Officer to warn this witness under Article 31 of the Uniform Code.

BLANDING: I understand the Article fully, sir.

SEVIER: You don't require a warning?

BLANDING: No, sir; I don't. I know it fully.

SEVIER: Did you call anybody and ask for permission to do that?

BLANDING: No, sir. I took it upon my own initiative, sir.

SEVIER: Did you report back to the Officer of the Day after you had done it?

BLANDING: Sir, when a man reports something it's because he

feels like he had done something wrong. I didn't feel like I had done anything wrong.

BERMAN: By the way, on either one of these occasions were any commissioned officers in the vicinity of where these exercises were taking place at the time?

BLANDING: Yes, sir; one instance I remember very well. Coming back from Elliott's Beach I had my observers out in the marshy area —they were pretty well loaded down with mud and sand—they looked like they were in sad shape—more or less looked like combat marines. I had them on the road just prior to reaching the Rifle Range Road and had them flanked on both sides—was performing a few maneuvers coming back. An officer came down the road with a car—I was marching between my flanks at the front. As I went to move off to the side he stopped and asked me what my name was, what platoon, what company, and what Battalion it was. I told him, and I didn't see any reason for him asking me like that. When I came back I did tell my Company Commander that an officer did stop me and ask me those questions. He asked me if I knew who the officer's name was, and I said, "yes." He said, "I wouldn't worry about anything. Just let it go." I wanted to know why—and I talked to my Company Commander—I wanted to know why he wanted to know who I was.

SEVIER: Are you familiar with the Standing Operating Procedure for recruit training at or en route to and from Elliott's Beach?

BLANDING: I couldn't recite it from memory. If I look at it I might be able to remember it.

SEVIER: Did you ever see anything like that before?

BLANDING: Sir, are these exact copies of the orders given us as our recruit lesson plans? Seems like this contains more than I am used to reading. Yes, sir; this is vaguely familiar.

SEVIER: I read, "Picnic grounds, Whale Creek, beaches and all marshes are out of bounds." Are you vaguely familiar with that?

BLANDING: Not with the term involving Whale Branch.

SEVIER: Whale Creek.

BLANDING: Is that what is known as the Dredge Cut, sir?

SEVIER: No.

BLANDING: It is not. Well, in taking the platoon to Elliott's Beach, another one of the statements in there, the use of points, the main body, and the rear guards, and your flanks, I don't see how you could put out flanks and comply with the training order. Using flankers, a point, and a rear guard, I don't see how anybody could take them down the main road with traffic going up and down the road. I believe you would have to go off the roads.

Leland Blanding didn't realize what an important point he scored for the Defense: The Dredge Cut was never out of bounds, neither was 4,000 lineal feet of swampland generally parallel to Golf Course Road between Wake Boulevard and Elliott's Beach Road, part of the route of march required for this scheduled hike. Despite protests of Colonel David Silvey, Training Expert, to the contrary, his orders, when carefully read, demanded recruits march through the swamps, formed for usual march security, until November 1, 1954. After that it was tradition.

Next Defense witness was James C. Flaherty, Turtle Creek, Pennsylvania, ex-marine, fifteen months a corporal Drill Instructor. Flaherty claimed he worked with ten platoons. That is exactly twice the number he could have followed completely through the schedule in fifteen months, but perhaps he was pushed around. He did serve with four different Recruit Battalions. We hear Flaherty:

BERMAN: Now in connection with your duties as a Drill Instructor with ten platoons during the period of time you have told us about, did you ever have an occasion, for the purpose of teaching discipline and instilling morale and *esprit de corps,* to march your platoons on an unscheduled exercise into the swamps and waters surrounding Parris Island?

FLAHERTY: Yes, sir; I did.

BERMAN: How many of your platoons did you march in there?

FLAHERTY: At one time or another, sir, I took all of the platoons to the swamps.

BERMAN: Will you please tell us into what areas you marched those platoons?

FLAHERTY: I took them into what is called the Dredge Cut, behind the Weapons Training Battalion recruit barracks; I took them through the swamps and marshes on either side of the road leading to Elliott's Beach; and one time I had a detail of men down behind the butts behind Able Range, down around there.

BERMAN: Into the water?

FLAHERTY: Yes, sir.

BERMAN: Can you tell us whether or not you took the platoons in at night?

FLAHERTY: In the early evening, sir.

BERMAN: Can you tell us to what heights on you, for instance, into the water your platoons went?

FLAHERTY: The depths varied from my knees up to my chest, sir.

SEVIER: By the way, Mr. Flaherty, I believe you refused to talk to members of the Prosecution the other day?

FLAHERTY: Yes, sir.

SEVIER: Why did you do that? Did you have something to hide?

FLAHERTY: I have nothing to hide, sir.

SEVIER: Were you aware that under orders in effect at that time swimming in these waters surrounding Parris Island was prohibited because the waters were contaminated?

FLAHERTY: Yes, sir. I knew you couldn't allow them to go in the water for swimming purposes out on the beaches.

SEVIER: Then I assume you are testifying that you violated an order?

FLAHERTY: I never went swimming in the water, sir.

SEVIER: Because you didn't go through the motions of swimming? You were still in the water.

FLAHERTY: Yes, sir. Still in the water, but we weren't swimming.

Since April 9, Major Holben, Colonel Silvey, Major Faw—all Staff—were endeavoring to interpret Parris Island regulations strictly. Now we see that marines who carried out these orders did the same. There was just one difference in viewpoint: Staff maintained that any act not specifically authorized was prohibited; those who complied with orders held the contrary position.

BERMAN: The Defense desires to call to the stand Lieutenant General Puller.

HUTCHINSON: The Court will please rise.

To wind up the defense Mr. Berman pulled from his hat the biggest living rabbit he could find: Lieutenant General Lewis B. (Chesty) Puller, retired, is unquestionably the most colorful marine we've had since Smedley Butler—and just as controversial a figure when marines discuss values. Puller was hardly seated when he said in a parade-ground voice, "Now, if I don't talk loud, somebody back there sound off and I'll talk louder." Fifty minutes of testimony followed, but to appreciate it we should first meet the witness.

Chesty Puller enlisted in August 1918, took his Boot training at Parris Island, completed NCO school, received a commission, and was ready to go to France with a replacement draft at the Armistice. He spent more than twenty-two years overseas. He was in the *Gendarmerie d'Haiti* five, at Pearl Harbor four, in Nicaragua nearly five, in China or at sea on the Asiatic Station over five, with the First Marine Division—including Guadalcanal, Cape Gloucester, Peleliu—about three years, and then seven months in Korea with the original expedition: bad days around Pusan, triumph at In'chon, withdrawal from Choisin Reservoir.

Chesty wears five Navy Crosses, second only to the Congressional Medal of Honor. He is perhaps the finest patrol leader the Marine Corps ever produced. Paired with Warrant Officer Bill Lee in the *Guardia de Nicaragua* he habitually received the most difficult assignments. Puller and Lee patrols were denoted "Company M" in stateside literature; in Nicaragua they were more familiarly termed "the murder squad." When lawful government deemed it necessary to eliminate a more enterprising bandit, authorities called in Puller and Lee. In fact a few days before marines were evacuated from Nicaragua this team dressed in its discarded *Guardia* uniforms and successfully performed one last special mission.

Some American citizens have been squeamish about Marine Corps aggressiveness in banana countries. Yet at home, in a more civilized environment, they applauded J. Edgar Hoover's war against gangsters. As a matter of fact, taking a bandit down to a stream for a drink of water, releasing him, telling him to run, and shooting him when "he tried to escape," was no less fair play, no less practical, than the FBI's rubbing out John Dillinger —that is, when the marine thought to remove the rope from the bandit's neck.

But Chesty threw the book away long ago. During the three years he taught at Basic School he insisted that there is only one principle of tactics: A straight line is the shortest distance between two points. Under the check rein of Vandegrift, Thomas, and Twining at Guadalcanal, Puller's concept was quite useful. When sheer force seemed the only answer, when drive was more important than maneuver, Puller's battalion drew the assignment.

Though under different leadership in the next campaign, New Britain, the operation resembled bush warfare and Puller was quite at home. But when the Palau assault came Chesty had been fleeted up to regimental command. His First Marines in that fracas took 1,749 casualties, fifty-six per cent. Major Frank Hough stated in the official Peleliu monograph: "Although the 3d Battalion continued in its zone under regimental control for two days longer, the 1st Marines, as an assault unit on the regimental level, had ceased temporarily to exist." And a footnote adds: "Of the nine rifle platoons in the three companies of the 1st Battalion, 74 men—and no original platoon leaders—remained." [1st Battalion lost seventy-one per cent.]

Shortly after the First Marine Division was evacuated to Pavuvu, Chesty Puller was ordered back to First Training Regiment at Camp LeJeune. It was whispered in the corridors of Headquarters Marine Corps that Puller had been posted to his last combat command. He was passed over for promotion to brigadier at least once. But when the police action broke in Korea, Chesty was in exactly the right outfit—and we had a new Commandant.

Despite his eighteen years' acquaintance with hardship and suffering, Puller carries only two emotional burdens: the death of his brother Sam, whom Chesty so long overshadowed as a marine officer, in the Guam campaign; the inconsiderateness of Headquarters in forcing him to retire after thirty-seven years, four months and two days of service—just when he was seriously considering making the Marine Corps a career!

During his testimony at McKeon's trial Puller stated: "I have had experience training recruits not only here at Parris Island but at the Recruit Depot in San Diego. When I was on Parris Island as a recruit and later on a Drill Instructor in San

Diego—when I had charge of all drills and instruction in a recruit depot—Drill Instructors had practically unlimited authority."

Chesty's memory is faulty with respect to his service record. Elsewhere in his testimony Puller stated that at the end of World War I he lost his commission, re-enlisted, and went to Haiti. He later spent twenty-nine days in San Diego as a first lieutenant. It is most probable that those recruits he did train were Haitians and Nicaraguans.

Attorney Berman, master showman, used Puller to bring this spectacular drama to a climax. He requested a recess to escort his last witness into the courtroom. He made a point of introducing Chesty to Captain Klein, Law Officer, and to members of the Court. Then by questioning he drew out a summary of Puller's record, the modest admission that one unit on his beribboned chest represented five Navy Crosses. Now he was ready to capitalize on that one talent: A straight line is the shortest distance!

First came the mission of the Marine Corps:

> Well, I would like to say that the definition, my definition —a definition in the drill books from the time that General von Steuben wrote the regulations for General George Washington —the definition of the object of military training is success in battle. It wouldn't be any sense to have a military organization on the backs of the American taxpayers with any other definition. I've believed that ever since I have been a marine.

Parris Island's mission is carefully spelled out by the Commandant:

> To indoctrinate the recruit in the fundamentals of service life and develop pride, loyalty, self-confidence, discipline, physical fitness, initiative, adaptability, teamwork, and proficiency in small arms marksmanship. Recruit training is the initial step in implementing the basic aim of all training, which is to qualify all Marines to perform duty in the Fleet Marine Force in the field.

That mention of "initial step" is most important. Parris Island makes the *basic* marine. For eighteen months, one year before Puller retired at Camp LeJeune, all recruits had been sent there for advanced, or combat training. Parris Island molded the individual, LeJeune trained the team. Such fundamentals as scouting and patrolling, squad tactics, were specifically excluded from Parris Island's program. But that fact influenced neither Berman nor Puller:

"What in your view, based again on your long experience in so many places, is the mission of recruit training commands?"

"To prepare marines so that they will be successful in the next war."

"And in that preparation, what, in your view, is the most important training they must receive?"

"Well, I'll quote Napoleon: Napoleon stated that the most important thing in military training was discipline. Without discipline an army becomes a mob."

"Now then, in that context, can you tell us whether you have an opinion, based again on your experience, as to whether or not the training in discipline is for all situations confined to lesson plans, or syllabi, or training regulations?"

"No. The training of a basic marine is conducted almost entirely outside—in the field, on the drill ground, on the rifle range—that kind of work. The marine gets an idea of how the Marine Corps is run during this training, but his training is outside work."

There was need to wave the flag, to hammer on Berman's thesis contending that his only reason for coming to Parris Island was to help the gallant Marine Corps. This he accomplished with a single question:

"Can you tell us, General, of the things you learned here as a recruit?"

"Well, the main thing that I learned here as a recruit—that I have remembered all my life—is the definition of *esprit de corps*. Now my definition—the definition I was taught, that I've always believed in—is that *esprit de corps* means love for one's own military legion, in my case the United States Marine Corps. I also learned that this loyalty to one's Corps travels both ways, up and down."

Chesty Puller's last observation was personal philosophy,

not criticism of Randy Pate, the Commandant. This will be apparent later. It is doubtful that Puller ever achieved that rudimentary capacity for political analysis sufficient to discern Pate's utter failure to exercise loyalty down.

Emile Zola Berman, the craftsman, was ready to spring the trap. But Major Sevier was for once alert. He had been alert since the Government's case had virtually been demolished by Pate's testimony. Berman framed a long, hypothetical question regarding Puller's opinion concerning "oppression of troops."

SEVIER: I object. It is an invasion of the province of the Court. Also, Counsel is assuming facts not in evidence.

KLEIN: What facts?

SEVIER: Well, it assumes contrary to the testimony of the Accused. He was not in front of his troops the whole time, for one thing.

BERMAN: It is a hypothetical question.

SEVIER: Asking whether a certain set of facts is a crime is for these gentlemen to decide, not the witness on the stand.

KLEIN: It is only his opinion, which is submitted to the members of the Court for their determination. It is not in itself the ultimate issue. It is an opinion with regard to the ultimate issue.

SEVIER: It is an invasion of their province.

KLEIN: It is opinion evidence from an expert. It is permissible.

SEVIER: The witness has not been qualified as a legal expert. The Defense is asking him whether or not certain acts become a crime.

KLEIN: In that respect, you are correct. You mean from a military point of view, "Is that oppression?" Don't you, Mr. Berman?

BERMAN: The point is, oppression of troops is a military concept.

KLEIN: It is. It is also a legal concept.

BERMAN: I am asking him as a military authority.

KLEIN: Objection overruled, if you will qualify it with that understanding.

Klein had again been most helpful to Berman. The latter was ready to pull out the stops.

"I want you to assume what is evidence in this case. A Drill Instructor, on a Sunday evening, in an effort, an attempt to teach discipline and instill morale in a platoon—which he considered had poor discipline and no spirit—turned them out and marched them across a rifle range. Leading them at the head of the column into marshes and water, he stayed at their head without regard to the results. Do you have an opinion, which you can state with a reasonable degree of certainty, as to whether or not, from the point of view of a military man such as yourself, this is oppression of troops?"

"In my opinion it is not."

Berman continued to do most of the talking.

"Well, based again on your long and extensive experience in positions of command that you held throughout your life, can you state an opinion, with a reasonable degree of certainty, as to whether the leading of troops by one who commands them is or is not good practice?"

"Any kind of a commander or leader who does not lead his troops under all conditions is not worth his salt."

"I take it then that your answer is that it is good practice?"

"Yes. It is excellent practice."

Berman was getting ready to shoot the works.

"Now, by the way, would you like a drink of water?"

"No, thank you." Old tropical soldier Puller made a practice of keeping the lid on his canteen while on the trail in the daytime.

Berman started his next hypothetical question based on an assumption of evidence in the case. There was a brief legal skirmish. Sevier's objections were halfhearted. Klein cleared the atmosphere. Berman exerted all his energy in the stretch.

"I am going to ask you to assume that which is in evidence in this case: On April 8, 1956, a Junior Drill Instructor had his first platoon, the recruits of which had been aboard in training for about half of their scheduled course. The platoon was lacking in discipline, in spirit, in morale, in *esprit de corps*. He had tried other methods, such as speaking to his men of their mission in the training program. He gave them examples of the necessity for integrity of an organization, especially in combat, and of the need for interdependence of men in a military organization—so that each could rely upon the other. He had ordered field days and tried other similar methods. He had not found them successful. So, with the intention of teaching discipline, instilling morale, and developing *esprit de corps,* this man—this Drill Instructor—marched at the head of his men, unscheduled, on a Sunday night, across a rifle range, behind the butts, into the marshes and creek. In that creek he marched them upstream for a distance of approximately thirty feet, approximately five or six feet from the bank, parallel to it. When he came to that position, he made a left swing, that is, a half-circular turn, and, again at the head of his platoon, retraced his steps downstream. At this time, at the head of his platoon, the highest water was chest-high—or, as we measured it here—approximately four feet eight inches. While in that situation, in the dark, cries were heard and panic broke out. Now up to this point, quite apart from anything that happened later, do you have an opinion which you can render, with a reasonable degree of professional certainty, as a military man, whether his act in leading these men, for the purposes I have described, was good or bad military practice?"

Sevier objected. Klein overruled. Puller was set to answer.

"You won't have to repeat the question. I know it. In my opinion the reason that American troops made out so poorly in the Korean War was mostly due to lack of night training. If we are going to win the next war, I would say that from now on fifty per cent of the training time should be allotted to night training."

When Puller flew into Detroit after his service in Korea he said that American youth was getting soft. His prescription given to newspaper reporters: eliminate candy and soft drinks, provide a manly supply of beer and whiskey.

"So, in your opinion, was this act of this Drill Instructor in leading his troops, under those conditions and for that purpose, good or bad military practice?"

"Good."

"We have met before and discussed some of the problems of military training and practice—on other occasions—have we not?"

"Yes."

"I have also had the privilege of meeting your charming wife. Is that correct, sir?"

"That is right."

"Well, may I make this suggestion? If at any time you may want a break or may care to refresh yourself, just indicate it, and I am sure the President of the Court will entertain such a suggestion from you."

Klein intervened. "Do you desire a recess?"

"No; not a bit." Chesty Puller considered such treatment disparaging. To a veteran of days in battle without sleep, known in Nicaragua as *muy hombre,* what were a few minutes sitting on a chair in a hot courtroom?

Berman was confident in releasing his witness to Sevier. "You may inquire, sir."

"If we have a leader who blunders into a dangerous situation without prior reconnaissance, without any precautions, and leads his troops into a dangerous situation without good cause; it that good leadership?"

"No, not without cause. You are supposed to make a reconnaissance when you are in battle." But Chesty considered reconnoitering a minor factor. When you know where the two points are, you merely go from one to the other.

"And it takes some training for the leader in night work, too?"

"Well, we take it for granted that when a leader has been made a leader by higher headquarters the man is qualified." That is just Puller's philosophy. It is a leader's obligation to *know* that his subordinates are qualified, to train them when not up to standard.

"And if you were taking untrained troops into a hazardous situation, would you make some rcconnaissance or take some precautions for their safety?"

"Oh, yes. I would take safety precautions."

"Now, sir. You mentioned night training. No one will dispute the necessity for night training. However, do you believe that night training should be the initial training that any raw recruit should receive?"

"Well, the trouble is that not enough night training is prescribed."

"Yes, but—"

"And I know that in anything I have ever commanded I got most of the glory and I got all of the blame. I have willingly taken the blame. I would train my troops as I thought—as I knew they should be trained—regardless of a directive."

Sevier tried Berman tactics with the hypothetical. Berman used Sevier's gambit, denying linkage with the evidence. Klein, the Navy man, put in his oar. Berman withdrew.

"Assume that I have no control over this platoon not halfway through recruit training and, for the purpose of punishment, I decide to take them on a night march. I lead them into an area with which I am totally unfamiliar. I lead them into waters in which I have never been, of which I have no knowledge whatsoever. I make no effort to see that my troops are in formation. I have no reconnaissance, taken no precautions. I know that I have recruits who are nonswimmers. I lead these recruits into waters over their heads and I lose six of those men by drowning. Would you say that some action should be taken against me?"

"I would say that this night march was and is a deplorable accident."

"Would you take any action against me if I were the one who did that, if you were my Commanding Officer, sir?" Sevier was leading with his chin!

"Since I have been retired there was an accident similar to this down off the Florida Keys. It concerned the American Army. A soldier, acting as coxswain of a landing craft, took his landing craft around and outside the breakwater. The landing craft filled and sank. Seventeen soldiers were drowned. It hardly made the newspapers. As far as I know, there was no court of inquiry. As far as I know, there was no general court-martial—or any kind of disciplinary action. I think, from what I read in the papers yesterday of the testimony of General Randolph MacPate [sic] before this Court, that he agrees and regrets that this man was ever ordered tried by general court-martial."

Chesty Puller was respectfully excused and left the courtroom. There was a half-hour recess to get him over the side.

When Court re-opened Emile Berman rested his case to the consternation of Charles Sevier who had thirty-three Defense witnesses standing by. Arguments were deferred until Friday. Sevier announced his rebuttal would last no more than two hours that afternoon. Following the luncheon recess Berman re-opened his case to introduce McKeon's health record and service record. Sevier asked the Court to take judicial notice of moonset April 8, moonrise the next morning. Then Mr. Berman squeezed out the last drop of Marine Corps good will at the afternoon adjournment:

"Mr. President and Mr. Law Officer: I have never seen a Marine Corps review. I understand that General Puller will conduct a review tomorrow at eight-thirty. I should hate to leave here and not have seen a review."

Colonel Edward L. Hutchinson, President of the Court, showed the anticipated hospitality. "Very well. We will adjourn until nine-thirty tomorrow morning."

Friday morning, August 3, after giving Attorney Berman time to attend the review for General Puller, arguments were in order. These lasted one and a half hours with Berman and Sevier dividing the time nearly equally. We limit ourselves to the persuasive aspects of this oratory. Prosecutor Sevier gave his opening:

> We have the testimony of Private Grabowski who smelled liquor on the Accused's breath. We have the testimony of Private McPherson that he saw him with the bottle, saw him raise it to his lips. The Accused's explanation that he was just giving the impression he was drinking, gentlemen—that is impossible, that is unbelievable. We have further the evidence that at approximately midnight—or four hours later—the Accused had a Bogens test, a blood alcohol reading of 1.5 which corroborates the story that the Accused was drinking at that late hour in the evening—along about eight o'clock.
>
> There is no question that the Accused did order this night exercise, that it was unscheduled, did not obtain permission to deviate from the schedule. He did not obtain permission or seek permission from anyone in authority to conduct this night exercise. We further have the information that the Accused waited

until after the movie at the Rifle Range Lyceum started before he even fell his troops out to move out across that dark Range down behind the butts where there were no lights and no one in authority could find him or could see him. We have the testimony of the recruits, we have the testimony of the Accused that he did lead them into the water. There can be no other implication, there can be no other assumption or inference that non-swimmers led into the dark tidal waters of Ribbon Creek through deep mud and unknown waters without any supervision on the part of the Drill Instructor who was leading them produced fears: fear of injury, fear of drowning, fear of the unknown. Remember, gentlemen, you have seen these recruits: young lads, some of them seventeen, some of them eighteen, raw recruits with no combat swimming training who had never been in that area before.

You have also seen Ribbon Creek. You will have to imagine you were seventeen years old, you had never been in there, you were new in Boot Camp. What effect would that have on you if you were led into Ribbon Creek and then turned loose more or less on your own? The very results produced the oppression. Six potential marines were drowned that night. No one could say that those men were not oppressed. Private Leake was taken to the hospital—or Sick Bay. Four other men were taken to Sick Bay with him, all with subnormal temperatures. You have heard the description of the platoon when it left that water: naked, cold, wet, shook, scared, almost speechless with shock.

We pass to the charge involving manslaughter. There can be no dispute that the Accused did, while carrying out an act of oppression against these members, kill unlawfully *Thomas C. Hardeman, Donald F. O'Shea, Charles F. Reilly, Jerry L. Thomas, Leroy Thompson,* and *Norman A. Wood.* There is no doubt that these men are dead. Not one of those men went in there voluntarily. Not one of those men would have been in that stream that night except for the orders of the Accused. By his action he placed those men in a dangerous situation. That day six marines—six United States Marines lost their lives. Gentlemen, those are six marines who will not take their places in the Fleet Marine Force.

Let's assume that maybe the Accused was right, maybe he did have a bad platoon, maybe he was having a little trouble disciplining them; so he takes this platoon—a platoon which he admits he has no control over—on an unscheduled night march. He leads them out through the dark with more or less just a "follow me"—no orders to close up, no order to keep in column—and leads this mass out across the Rifle Range through the dark and into the stream—makes no effort whatsoever to maintain control—just plows on ahead through the dark. Is there a single instance shown even by the Accused's own testimony where he attempted to maintain any semblance of discipline on that march? Here is only one answer: He just took this platoon out there because he was mad and he wanted to punish them. He wanted to get them wet and cold. Absolutely no other reason.

We have the testimony of Privates Grabowski, Maloof, Nehrenz, Leonard, Moran, Daszo, Truitt and Brennan that they were in water over their heads prior to the time any panic broke out or prior to the time of any screams. We have testimony that some of the recruits saw the Accused himself swimming prior to the time this panic broke out.

Now I would like to take up a little bit the depth of that water. The Defense's witness, Warrant Officer Volle, stated that at the shallowest part of the creek there would be at least two and a half feet of water at low tide, and there was approximately five feet of tide water at the time the platoon went into the creek. Gentlemen, that is over seven and a half feet of water at the shallowest part of that creek, and that is not counting the depth of the mud or how far in that mud a man would sink. At places up on the edge of the creek, we find by the testimony of some of the recruits, they sunk in to their hips—one man to his waist—and the Defense's own witnesses said there were places there where a man could sink into the mud for a depth of four feet. Gentlemen, the story of the Accused as to the depth of the water that he was in at that time is impossible.

We see that down there at the stream the Accused stated that there was a moon. It's been shown conclusively by the tide table that there was no moon that night.

Now at the beginning of this trial the Defense attempted to make much out of some alleged practice for unscheduled night marches. So far they have produced two witnesses out of 300—or out of 208, which in open court they first called for. These two witnesses mentioned that they had been in the marshes on the march to Elliott's Beach. There is no unscheduled march to Elliott's Beach.

Each of the witnesses he produced here yesterday stated that he had been in one other area on one other occasion and it was shown that both witnesses acted in violation of Depot Regulations. They reported this to no one in authority; they asked permission from no one in authority. It was another attempt at a sneak march—to evade regulations and custom and orders of this base. If there had been such custom condoned, some of the witnesses who were subpoenaed could have no doubt gotten on the stand and supported the contention of the Defense. But only two witnesses were brought in front of you, gentlemen.

Gentlemen, on the basis of the uncontroverted testimony—the evidence, both direct and circumstantial—which has been presented here in the last eighteen days, I believe that each element of each specification under each charge has been proven. There has been substantial evidence—preponderance of evidence—to each one of these elements of proof. Gentlemen, based on the evidence—and I say all the evidence that has been presented by both the Prosecution and the Defense—I ask you to return a verdict of guilty to each charge and each specification thereunder.

Major Sevier's opening was exhortation. It contained exaggeration, like sinking into waist-deep mud, clearly an impossibility. He used the wrong psychological approach. Marine officers with long service, with extensive court-martial experience, prefer a statement of the evidence both concise and logical; they prefer to draw their own conclusions. In contrast to Major Sevier, we listen to Attorney Berman, who had no fear of pointing out minor flaws in his case and who realized the effect of persuasion:

May it please you, Mr. Law Officer, Mr. President, and officers of the Court: I suppose all of you at some time or another, gentlemen, have served as triers of the fact. And so you know that this is the opportunity given to lawyers to discuss with you, from the evidence, or from their concepts, what they believe correct judgment requires. I am going to make no attempt to repeat for you the day-by-day testimony of the many witnesses who were called. If that were so, it would be preferable that a reporter address you, rather than one who stands here for the protection of the rights of a human being.

I would be untrue to my own self-respect, gentlemen, if, at the very outset, I did not make it plain to you that no one is more aware that you—and you alone—have the sole responsibility, under your oaths and upon your conscience, to decide this case—yes, to bring to it your combined intelligence, wisdom and passion for justice. I surely need not remind you of what was said long ago by a great sage: If judges—and that is what you are of these facts, judges—if judges would make their decisions just, they should behold neither the plaintiff nor the defendant nor the pleader, but only the cause itself. I am satisfied that your combined wisdom and experience will bring that view to bear upon the facts of this case.

If I were to discuss this case with you, I would prefer to discuss it in an atmosphere of the living room of your home or mine, where I might sit down with you—both of us comfortable, and neither of us formal—to tell you what the evidence is in this case: That a fellow by the name of McKeon, from very ordinary circumstances, left high school after his second year at the age of seventeen to enlist in the Navy in the defense of his country and that he served some forty months. Speaking of kids—and kids have been referred to with great amplitude by Trial Counsel—he served in combat, he performed his duties, he received an honorable discharge. Wouldn't you have said, if we were talking in your living room or mine, "This is a good kid and he must have learned a lot from his experiences?" And if I went on to tell you—there in that more pleasant atmosphere—what is the evidence in this case, that this boy had a desire—maybe because his brothers had been marines, maybe because he had been exposed to marines in the Navy—a desire to become a marine and to devote his career to it, so that he enlisted and re-enlisted and presently is on his third enlistment, and that those various periods of practically his whole adult life—his entire grown-up estate—had him performing duties both in combat, in training and in teaching; and wherever he went—at whatever station, or whatever theater, anywhere—this man was well-regarded, highly looked upon and, on each occasion of the expiration of his enlistment, honorably discharged; is there one of you, in such an atmosphere, who would not have said, "A good boy, a good, dedicated marine," and that your service needs men of that type, dedication and devotion?

And then if I were to go on and say to you—what is the evidence in this case—that such a man, with such a reputation and with such grades and observations is assigned to a platoon, first, that he may not be the most articulate fellow in the world or even by any manner of means its greatest genius, but that he had a devotion to produce marines, basic marines. In fact, he even had a desire—if it could have been accomplished—to produce an honor platoon with men who were smart, well disciplined, well trained, independent marines with that *esprit de corps* that makes this service different from any other service in our country. What would you then have said, as you sat there listening to what is the undisputed evidence in this case, that this is the true spirit of a good marine, and that he's been acting in the highest traditions of a devoted Drill Instructor?

Now then, with this in mind, if I went on to tell you that Sergeant McKeon—incidentally, a man of family, a man of decency, a man of devout religion, yes, even of warm humanity—found this platoon of his, more than halfway through their training, not bad kids, no, but lacking in discipline; that is to say, actually not in discipline, but lacking in that sharp discipline which is so necessary for the equipment of men who are being prepared for war, and lacking in that spirit which is the heart of the *esprit de corps* so basic in every good marine, and if I told you, confronted with that, despite his own affliction, that this man did not give up, he didn't become lackadaisical, he didn't adopt an indifferent attitude—"Oh, what the hell do I care" attitude. Bound by his devotion to the Corps and by a New England conscience, he continued to attempt to perform his task, he kept trying with his own methods of trying to make basic marines. I say it's a fair intendment from the evidence before you that if McKeon had turned this platoon out in their present state—as described here—to take their places on ships and stations in this Corps throughout the world and go into combat, his conscience would have hurt him to his dying day.

What was this more rigorous exercise that this man was

going to undertake with those troops for such a purpose? Trial Counsel still talks in terms of punishment, punishment. He wanted to get them cold and wet. What about himself? Isn't that the key to his entire motivation? Do you punish someone by subjecting yourself to whatever rigors are to be accomplished even when you are less physically fit than those who are supposed to be punished and oppressed? This is lawyer talk; this isn't talk that's handled in life where people make decisions.

What about this practice that obviously other Drill Instructors—probably from the time this base was established—were confronted with, the necessity of doing other things not contained in the syllabi or lesson plans, that almost every Drill Instructor on this base knew that there was a practice for certain kinds of circumstances, in teaching men discipline, to take them into the boondocks or marshes or these creek waters? What for? For swimming lessons, for relaxation, in an attempt to ford a creek? No! But to get through under different circumstances the hard "slodging"—marching—to bring order, discipline and necessity on the part of boys and make them men.

Now who tells it to you from the stand? You have it from Sergeant Huff—he was a Prosecution witness. You have it from McKeon, you have it from Sergeant Blanding, and you have it from former Drill Instructor Flaherty. You would have had it from more than fifty had I not, in my judgment for which I take the sole responsibility, elected not to protract this trial. Well then, here was motivation, here was a mission, here was a dedicated and devoted marine with a record that was honorable. Here was a man who, by his own goofed-off platoon to the last man—you heard it here—was considered a decent guy, a straight shooter, a good leader. This, mind you, comes from what Trial Counsel would have you believe as "the oppressed."

Now in connection with that march Trial Counsel said McKeon never had control of the platoon. I submit to you that the evidence here has not been closely followed because he marched at the head of his column. They came to a ditch. He called attention to it, he had squads go over and hold up and he asked that the word be passed back to others that there was a ditch there, lest someone, perhaps inadvertently, might step in and break a leg or come to some other harm, and continued on at the head of his column to continue and conclude the exercise, which was a common practice. Does it require of Berman—I've never been a marine, gentlemen, never—does it require me to tell you that this is good practice in the highest military tradition? You have your own experiences, and you have the opinions of two great experts.

Everybody since this tragic event now talks about these dangerous waters—about what lurking pitfalls there were—but what did people think about this before April 8? Has there been one witness called to this stand, has there been a single regulation put in evidence, has there been a single statement made by anyone that Ribbon Creek was other than a meandering little creek in which people fished?

But nevertheless, both to show his leadership of his men and that he asked them to do nothing that he himself was not prepared to do, and also indeed to be the first to take that march in that mud and in those waters, he put his feet down so he would know whether there was any likelihood of danger to these troops that were following him. If you don't look upon things in the light of after-events, you'll find that this is a standard of care not only in the highest tradition of your service but in the exercise of judgment.

What happened? It's an unhappy thing. It's really a melancholy fact, gentlemen, that even with this trial, no one, no one will ever know precisely what happened. We do know that there was an accident and that there was panic, but I tell you this tragedy was not a result of danger. It was not caused by any carelessness. It was not because of any wrongdoing. It was not because of any heedlessness. The loss of these lives was due to panic.

Panic can never be predicted, panic can never be foreseen—not even by the most careful of reasoning men—because panic cannot be explained by reason. It has no foundation in reason or in logic, nor can its results ever be explained—as in this case—because we who undertake to analyze and explain can do it only by the process of our intellect, our reasoning and our logic, perhaps our experience combined. But this gives you no way of determining the myriad, the myriad of facts that occur, unreasoning, in a panic. That's why I say we will never know who started it. We'll never know what sheer, stark, unreasoning frenzy took place. We'll never know the acts by which these lives were lost, or even the over-all act by which this tragedy occurred. I submit to you with all of the sincerity that I am capable of, gentlemen, that this accident, this tragedy, was the result of panic, not lawlessness, not heedlessness, not carelessness, and not indifference.

Were I, then, maybe sitting with you in your homes, to go on and tell you that because of this tragedy, gentlemen, because of this tragedy—in the light of the after-result—because of public clamor, because of politics in high places—yes, even in the halls of Congress—and because of mistakes that were made in handling this matter, that this man whose life and career, whose devotion and dedication I have already told you about, was then charged with being a criminal, would there be one amongst you who would not have exclaimed, "What a shame! What an outrage! What are they trying to say? That this man who in his whole lifetime of exemplary conduct, of devotion to duty, of religion, of protection of family, all of a sudden and unaccountably turns out to be a criminal and behave like one?" Because make no mistake about it, oppression and manslaughter are crimes, high crimes.

I come to Charge I. I think it a fair interpretation of the regulation that what was being prohibited was carousing in quarters. It wasn't the drinking that was being prohibited. Nevertheless, my self-respect and my duty to deal fairly with the Court requires me to tell you that in my view there was a technical violation of that regulation. So I leave that matter for your own good judgment.

With respect to Charge IV, Sergeant McKeon is not being tried here for the appropriateness of a gesture or the weak kind of an illustration to prove a point. He is being charged with drinking. You have seen him on examination and cross-examination. You have watched his manner. You have observed the way in which he has testified. You have listened to him and you have studied him. Is there one among you who doubts his sincerity, his decency, and that the truth was told by him? I would be greatly saddened if after seeing him and hearing him there could be even one who would entertain the thought that this man was lying or trying to put on an act.

> The whole concept of justice, officers of this Court, demands that each man receive his just due. We have a right—I say we have a right to expect a verdict of acquittal on Charges II, III, and IV, not because I stand here before you to ask for it, but because the evidence, the opinions of outstanding experts, the facts, and the cause itself require it. Indeed because justice cries out for it. I have spent many, many weeks with my obligation and responsibility to Sergeant McKeon, and to the United States Marine Corps. I have tried to serve them both well—at least, to the best of my ability. At long last it comes to me to take this mantle of responsibility that I have carried heavily now for a long time and turn it over to you. You must assume that burden both for McKeon and the Court. I am confident that you will deal well with each. You have my thanks for your patience in listening to me.

Prosecutor Charles Sevier in accordance with regulations had the last word. He might have accomplished more remaining silent. But we must listen to him and sense his attitude:

> Much of the Defense Counsel argument appears to be immaterial and irrelevant to questions asked in the charges. I merely want to make a few comments in answer to Mr. Berman. Mr. Berman mentioned the highest traditions of the devoted Drill Instructor. I say the traditions require some precautions for the safety and welfare of his troops and clearly on the night of April 8 there were no precautions taken for the members of Platoon 71. In fact there was a definite lack.
>
> Again we have attempted to show a practice of marches—unscheduled marches—and again I ask, and I point out to you there was no evidence. There was an attempt to introduce some hearsay, an attempt to introduce some barroom talk, but only two witnesses—and very weak ones—were produced out of all those who were subpoenaed. The only permissible inference there in my mind is that the others would not support the contention.
>
> Again I point out there was no activity scheduled in the waters. No one expected a Drill Instructor so lacking in judgment as to take untrained troops—nonswimmers—into Ribbon Creek, and to continue in. So lacking in judgment is this man that after he got them into the creek he continued on leading

them into deep water, and into water over their head. The Defense contends that there was panic and perhaps there was. I am certain there was a panic but, gentlemen, how did that panic start? Why did that panic start? Who put those troops in a position to panic? Who took no precautions? Who disregarded his obligation for the safety of those troops?

I wasn't going to make any mention of this until Defense Counsel brought it out. Defense Counsel commented on the manner the Accused testified in Court—he was on the stand quite a while, gentlemen, and we all had an opportunity to observe him. I wondered how the Accused had certain things down exactly, measured and precise, but on other things—those things which could have been damaging or incriminating—he was vague, evasive, and did not remember. Now, there was some suspicion that there was a rehearsal. Do you recall the gestures? The answers? The manner? The voice inflections? Each time there was a "no, sir" the same inflection. Each time a "yes, sir" the same inflection. Reflect on that, gentlemen.

Sevier ended by reading an extract from one of John Thomason's early works describing the essence of Marine Corps tradition. It was hardly appropriate.

Following a 25-minute recess Judge Klein was prepared to read his instructions to the Court. His performance in this duty was far superior to anything else he had done in the whole trial and reasons were apparent: Each party had previously furnished him a thoroughly documented brief outlining the instructions they wished him to give, and he had plenty of time Thursday evening to do his homework. But Klein's instructions were still too repetitive and verbose; he spent too much time talking down the Court. We listen to only a small portion of his hour-long reading:

Oppression means the unjust or cruel exercise of authority or power, the subjection of unjust hardships through tyranny. To find the Accused guilty of oppression you must find more than the mere doing of a wrongful act. You must find that such act or acts upon which you base a finding of oppression, if you should so do, amounted to cruelty, undue severity, unlawful exaction and excessive use of authority. To make an act oppressive it must be done willfully, "under the color of law" and without legal authority.

Culpable negligence is a degree of carelessness greater than *simple negligence. Simple negligence* is the failure of a person, under a duty to exercise care, to exercise that degree of care for the safety of others which a reasonably prudent man would have exercised under the circumstances. *Culpable negligence* is a negligent act or omission, accompanied by a culpable disregard for the foreseeable probable consequences to others of such act or omission. It is a gross, reckless, deliberate or wanton disregard for the safety of others.

With reference to the evidence tending to show that the deceased, or any of them, failed to exercise reasonable care and caution for his own safety, you are advised that such is no defense if you are satisfied beyond a reasonable doubt that the Accused was culpably negligent and that his culpable negligence was the proximate cause of the death. The Accused is not relieved of responsibility therefor because the negligence of the deceased may have contributed in producing the result. However, the conduct of the deceased is material to the question of whether the Accused was culpably negligent and to the question of whether the Accused's culpable negligence, if any, was the proximate cause of the death of the deceased.

With regard to the offenses of involuntary manslaughter or the lesser included offense of negligent homicide, evidence of a common practice among the other Drill Instructors to do what the Accused is charged with having done, under substantially similar circumstances, is relevant to the issue of negligence and oppression and is admissible not to establish a legal standard, and not only is it admissible but it may be considered by you in your deliberations as evidence of the reasonableness of the Accused's acts from which, together with all the other facts and circumstances, the Court may determine whether the conduct in question was proper and justifiable.

Judge Klein asked for objections. Attorney Berman supported the brief he previously filed. There were two discussions between opposing Counsel and Law Officer off the record and out of hearing of the Court. Prosecutor Sevier wasn't sure about the ritual for members of the Court getting their meals during deliberations. Judge Klein set him straight. The Court closed at 12:45 P.M. Friday.

It was a long wait for Matthew McKeon. The brigade of newsmen was impatient. But Court members were thorough in their deliberation. Only they know the extent of their discussion —and they won't talk about it. Only they know the number of ballots and the tabulation, which they are sworn not to reveal. Finally, at 6:05 P.M. Judge Klein was called in to assist President Hutchinson in writing out the Court's findings in legal phraseology. At 7:25 the Court opened and all parties were reported present. Counsel Berman and Matthew McKeon rose, advanced, and stood before President Hutchinson, who read the findings. These were rather complicated and required that Berman explain them to McKeon later. We tabulate:

I.	Possession and use of alcoholic beverage:	Guilty
II.	Oppression:	Not Guilty
III.	(1) Manslaughter by culpable negligence:	Not Guilty
	(2) Manslaughter while oppressing:	Not Guilty
	But under (1) guilty of negligent homicide	
IV.	Drinking before a recruit:	Not Guilty

Judge Klein recessed the Court fifteen minutes to hold a conference with both Counsel. Court was then open just two minutes, long enough to convene and adjourn. Sentencing was deferred until Saturday.

Saturday, August 4, was fifteenth and last day of the trial. It took only twenty minutes to follow procedure required before the Court closed to determine upon a sentence. First, Major Sevier read McKeon's "personal data," which consisted of facts about his birth, pay, length of service, obligated service, and nature of any restraint imposed. McKeon had been confined in the Depot Brig forty-five days, from April 8 to May 23. Thereafter he was restricted to Parris Island with permission to spend nights at his home in Port Royal.

Next McKeon was given the opportunity to offer evidence in extenuation or mitigation. This frequently presents Defense Counsel with a dilemma: When Accused remains silent, Prosecution may only introduce evidence of previous convictions during the current enlistment; but when Accused once broaches the subject, Prosecution is free to offer evidence in rebuttal. In this case Defender Berman limited his remarks to conduct and proficiency markings, which were already contained in Defense Exhibit N but hadn't been mentioned by Prosecutor Sevier. He then made a brief plea with the announcement of an expected addition to McKeon's family, which may not have been known by the Court but was certainly known by thousands of newspaper readers:

> Mr. President and officers: I value and regard your own position too much to attempt to speak to you in any other way than on the solid facts. You will hear no emotional plea from me.
>
> I may be, however, of some assistance to you in the performance of your duties if I suggested to you that the maximum punishments to be found in the Code are, generally speaking, reserved for habitual wrongdoers.
>
> Sergeant McKeon's file shows something that must be of some importance to you and that is, in addition to his wife, he has two children, aged five and one, and his third child, gentlemen, is expected this week.
>
> You know that he is suffering from an ailment, what we call a "slipped disc," which is a painful matter and requires treatment.
>
> Now with respect to the violation or the offense of simple negligence, it may not be of concern to you but possibly of some interest. The military service of the United States is the only forum in which simple negligence is an offense, that is, a criminal offense—the only forum in the world. In all other forums simple negligence gives rise only to an action for civil damages and for myself as a lawyer, contemplating this for the first time, I have great doubt indeed whether or not the due process clause of the Constitution is not violated by making simple negligence a penal offense.
>
> I have two suggestions to make. This man has already served forty-five days in the brig. I cannot conceive how jail punishment will satisfy the needs of this case or will accomplish anything. Since April 8 until the present time this man has been reminded not only through the press, not only through this

trial, but by his own conscience, of the great tragedy which he participated in. No punishment that you could award will ever equal in severity and in its lifetime effect this pull upon his conscience. So I ask you to consider that and not confine him. Not alone because justice would not be served—perhaps this isn't a legal argument—but if there's one time he ought to be with his wife, this is the time.

Now one other thing I have to ask of you. This man has eleven years and two months in the service of his country. Aside from errors of judgment and the violation of this regulation, he has an impeccable record. The Government has spent a lot of money in training him and he has a dedication to the career of a marine. There are places in the Marine Corps where his experience and his talents and his devotion can well be used. There are ample methods available to you in regard to punishment, which I leave to your own discretion. I ask you not to send him to the brig, and I ask you not to take him out of this service.

When Attorney Berman returned to Defense Counsel table Judge Klein could exercise his option in instructing about maximum punishment. This he did at length, talking down to the Court as usual. His last words were: "In making these remarks to the Court, the Law Officer desires to make it abundantly clear that the Law Officer is not suggesting or inferring that any particular sentence he adjudged in this case." From first to last Judge Klein kept his finger on his number.

For illegal possession of an alcoholic beverage Matthew McKeon might have been sentenced to: dishonorable discharge, two years' confinement at hard labor, loss of all pay and allowances, and reduction to private. For negligent homicide the maximum penalty was: bad conduct discharge, one year's confinement at hard labor, loss of all pay and allowances, and reduction to private. These sentences could be cumulative. Those interested in evaluating human behavior may be concerned to note that our Table of Punishments gives double weight, in terms of imprisonment, for taking two or three illegal drinks of vodka when compared with negligently taking six lives.

Again the Court closed for deliberations and again there was prolonged debate and balloting. This time interested parties waited from 9:45 A.M. until 1:55 P.M. Court finally opened that hot Saturday afternoon. President Hutchinson handed a piece of paper to Major Sevier to hand to Judge Klein so that he might peruse the sentence.

KLEIN: Proceed, Mr. President.

The Accused and his Counsel arose, advanced, and stood before the Court.

HUTCHINSON: Staff Sergeant McKeon, it is my duty as President of this Court to inform you that the Court, in closed session, and upon secret written ballot, two thirds of the members present at the time the vote was taken concurring, sentences you to be discharged from the service with a Bad Conduct Discharge; to forfeit thirty dollars per month for nine months; to be confined at hard labor for nine months; and to be reduced to the rank of private.

Matthew McKeon had been getting $150.60 monthly from the paymaster, his wife received a "family allowance" check for $156.90 monthly, of which McKeon contributed $60. Now he would receive $92.60 monthly, turning back $30 of that for nine months, and his wife would get $136.90 with which to keep herself and three children.

All courts-martial are reviewed automatically. Besides, any accused, on request, may be represented by counsel before a Board of Review in the Office of the Judge Advocate General, and after that he may petition for a hearing before the Court of Military Appeals. When Emile Berman left Parris Island he was determined that Matthew McKeon would not receive a punitive discharge. If Berman didn't win out visiting the Navy Department, he would qualify to practice before the Court of Military Appeals. With his experience that would involve mere formalities.

26

Ink

OMITTING THE ROLE newsmen played in the Ribbon Creek affair would leave our account sterile indeed. Lacking interaction of news media, public opinion, and politics, the story would have less national interest than regimental amphibious maneuvers at Vieques. But unfortunately this is a strand in the hawser that won't pass rigid inspection. I must confess lack of completed staff work and recommend the Ribbon Creek incident as a graduate thesis for some marine studying either journalism or public relations. Radio and television were both hyperactive in April and July; I missed the major part of their coverage and have done no research to fill that gap. In those same months reporters and photographers swarmed over Parris Island and haunted promising sources in Washington. My day-to-day account comes from the New York *Times,* which I checked against *Life, Newsweek, Time,* and *U. S. News and World Report*. Other than that I'm limited to articles catalogued in *Readers' Guide to Periodical Literature*. So there is a serious omission of the viewpoints of many capable working newspapermen who wrote stories of tragedy and trial guided by individual wealth of experience and variant policies of their several publishers.

The news angle of our account begins when Brigadier General Robert Houston Pepper commanded Parris Island following his tour in Headquarters as Director of Personnel, where he became thoroughly acquainted with current Marine Corps problems as well as the wishes and philosophy of General Clifton Bledsoe Cates, then in office as our unsurpassed post war Commandant. *Life,* October 8, 1951, visited Parris Island and published in its unique style an essay on recruit training with photographs by Mark Kauffman. Obviously there was no censorship of pictures or cut-lines, no artificial slanting through the intervention of a skillful Public Information Officer—if Parris Island had one in those days.

The DI-hero of this story is Staff Sergeant William S. Trope, handling Platoon 268. Trope is described as deliberately rough and abusive, heaping maddening indignities on Boots, giving them every chance to crack up. Editorial rationalization claims this treatment pays dividends on the battlefield where toughness and discipline not only win, but save lives. (Our First Marine Division was then occupied in the mountains of Korea. Remember?) Pictures show a recruit with his cap over his eyes, standing with head in a corner for a half hour, shaving with head in a bucket, carrying in his mouth the belt he forgot, holding his left foot in the air for a grueling length of time, holding his rifle at arm's length for ten minutes. We see the naked hair-cut line at Hygienic; Sergeant Trope knocking a recruit's head forward and pushing his stomach in; Junior DI Corporal Wischmeyer yanking a recruit's shoulders into place; Trope tugging a recruit's cap visor over an ear to make him look like an idiot. In this story DI Trope seizes a Boot by the collar and twists, stamps on his right foot, then says, "Now pivot on the one that hurts." Unmasked recruits sing the Marine Corps Hymn in the gas chamber. Platoon 268 marches twice past one of their buddies collapsed at the side of the road. The entire platoon empties canteens on the march because one recruit drank without permission. Platoon 268, according to the text, began with strength of seventy-four and graduated fifty-nine. William Trope's chin is marred with scars from bar fights defending the honor of the Corps.

Life published seventeen letters in the issue of October 29 and five in that of November 19 to show public reaction. Some people contended this display of moronic brutality proved our

DIs were sadists and hoodlums; others offered testimonials to the effectiveness of Boot training. The Army's Commanding Officer, 13th Infantry Regiment, Fort Jackson, near Columbia, South Carolina, and rival for the state's share of Congressional pork-barrel legislation, said that he turns out first-class fighting men without being inhuman, undignified, and stupid. Marie Barbuscak, Fairmount, West Virginia, Sergeant Trope's sister, was sorry for the bewildered new recruits but impressed with the results her brother obtained. PFC Diego V. Del Valle, Platoon 268 alumnus then on the West Coast, claimed that he and his mates were proud they passed the test and proud of their Senior DI Trope.

Brigadier General Pepper was detached in January 1952 after a new Commandant, Lemuel Cornick Shepherd, Jr., took office the first of the year. Brigadier General Matthew C. (Jack) Horner held the post for a month until Major General Merwin H. Silverthorn, who had been lieutenant general while Assistant Commandant, took over. Silverthorn stayed until his retirement twenty-eight months later, played lots of golf, visited messhalls continuously, and periodically reminded Battalion Commanders and Staff that his major effort at Parris Island was devoted to eradicating maltreatment. Then Major Edwin Allen Pollock assumed command, forced dog-robbers to look and act like soldiers, judged maltreatment temperately during his eighteen-month sojourn, and was promoted out of the job when Randolph McCall Pate, Shepherd's cousin, became Commandant. Next in succession was Major General Joseph Charles Burger, University of Maryland lacrosse star, class of 1925, who initially came in the Marine Corps so he could play football. Joe Burger was aboard twelve weeks, still trying to dig in his spurs, when the Ribbon Creek story broke. We're going to follow this chronologically mostly in bulletin style giving credit to the New York *Times* unless otherwise noted. Date lines generally will be those indicating when the story was filed, not the publication date.

April 7—Estes Kefauver was in New Jersey yesterday compaigning for primary votes. Adlai Stevenson is a write-in candidate in Oregon. Dr. Simon Ramo, missile expert, predicts technicians will be our leaders in the future. Rain again spoiled two-day track meet at Quantico, where Villanova won the relay over NYU. Thursday Victor

Riesel, labor columnist, was attacked with acid. Wednesday an East Bronx factory fire killed six firemen, who left nineteen children fatherless; at nine o'clock Monday there will be Requiem Mass at St. Patrick's for five of the victims (the sixth was Lutheran).

April 8—Sixty-eight hundred Moroccan workers strike at U. S. bases. Harriman lists GOP failures. Spring snowfall hits northeast. Three marine flyers, Captain Ted Uhlemeyer, Jr., pilot, First Lieutenant Edward Myers Stimets, Jr., co-pilot; Second Lieutenant Robert Thomas Dietz, missing in SNB which took off from El Toro, fueled at Glenview, and cleared for Floyd Bennett so that one of the occupants could visit a sick relative. This is the anniversary of the surrender of Bataan. The American Management Association has its campus on Times Square.

[Anthony Leviero covers the story at Parris Island in April].

April 9—Israelis wipe out suicide band of five. Five thousand at services for the six firemen while fifty thousand line Fifth Avenue. Five marines die in swamp during Parris Island march; one still missing; initially eleven were missing but one stayed in camp, three soon turned up, and the fifth made his way back at midnight. Parris Island is a dense wilderness of cypress trees, man-high grass, and hummocks awash with tidal waters. At first report this was a night training exercise, later Captain Ralph Wood, Public Information Officer, said the men were dressed only in utilities and carried no weapons. General Randolph McC. Pate, Corps Commandant, is at the scene for a personal inquiry and to insure that appropriate steps will be taken to fix responsibility for the death of these young marines and to make sure nothing of this sort can ever happen again on a marine base. It is alleged Matthew McKeon, Drill Instructor now confined in the brig and unavailable to reporters, conducted the march as punishment for an infraction of discipline. Privates Clarence Cox, Dewin Leonard, Earl Grabowski, Donald Porter, David McPherson, and Eugene Ervin are interviewed and quoted. The sergeant didn't order anyone into deep water; he was first in and last out; he did all he could. The platoon was walking along the edge of the water and got lost in the dark, suddenly a lot of men were hollering for help, some survivors went under and lost their direction. Grabowski praises Porter for making the men grab hands to make a chain to pull themselves out. McPherson says it was just an unfortunate accident, some of the men drifted toward the center. The troops praise Sergeant McKeon. Colonel John Heles heads the Court of Inquiry.

April 10—President urging program to halt military turnover; forwards Defense Secretary Wilson's letter to Congress stressing fringe benefits. Hanson W. Baldwin, graduate of USNA in 1924 but *Times* military writer the past twenty-five years, tells that high pay and challenge lead construction men into Arctic to build DEW line. Court hears testimony from survivors of forced night march into treacherous tidal stream to teach the platoon discipline. McKeon issues statement through Counsel: He led men on ill-fated march to teach them discipline; he can't find words to express his grief; he says it is no excuse that he hadn't been in the area before and didn't realize it was a tidal stream nor that it was unusually deep for the area. Commandant Pate says McKeon had no authority for taking disciplinary action or for scheduling such a march; Pate orders Court to take testimony from all survivors; Pate believes Corps can handle this without a Congressional inquiry; Pate says "we have absolutely nothing to hide"; Pate asks that no premature opinions be formed on modifications to training until full evaluation of the facts has been made. Marine skindivers recover *Hardeman's* body. Mrs. Pearl *Thompson,* Brooklyn, is in deep mourning; her son left high school a year before graduation to join Marines since he thought Army and Navy would be too easy. Mrs. Aaron D. *Wood,* Bay Shore, says *Norman* one of six children, didn't complain, liked Marines. Mr. and Mrs. Peter *O'Shea,* Brooklyn, have two daughters; son *Donald* was in Marine Corps Reserve six months, scored 221 on Camp Lejeune Rifle Range last year. Mrs. Frank Bond, one of *Charles Reilly's* six sisters and three brothers who survive, collapses; both parents are dead but his stepfather, Samuel Savarese, lives at Port Byron; Mrs. Bond hopes McKeon gets all that is coming to him. Alson P. Coughlin, Alexandria, Virginia, is stepfather of *Jerry Thomas.* At Worcester, Massachusetts, a spokesman for Matthew McKeon's family says: "We all feel sorry for the families which lost their boys. How can we make judgment without knowing all the circumstances?" [Matthew McKeon's mother had a heart attack after she got word of the tragedy. She wrote letters of sympathy to the five surviving mothers and one sister.] Representative Kenneth B. Keating, Republican of New York, demands a report.

April 11—IBM increases earnings by 34.4%. Truman speaks at Des Moines. Armed Services Committee will investigate if Marines' own inquiry does not reassure the nation. Mrs. Coughlin, mother of *Jerry Thomas,* gets letter postmarked Monday morning: "It is like living in hell down here—some of the words I have for the island I can't write." General Burger talks to both AP and UP reporters: "I am completely puzzled by the whole thing. I have never known of a comparable situation." Had McKeon been drinking or did he become emotionally unbalanced? "I just can't answer—I just don't know." Editorial: The nation is shocked, grieved, angry; the public feels for the families bereaved; McKeon committed basic military error not familiarizing himself with the terrain; his zeal exceeded his judgment; but we should not soften training nor discredit a general policy of dispersal down through the ranks of authority to take command and initiative.

April 12—Israeli fliers bag an Egyptian jet. Marine Corps Recruit Depot sends away its dead with appropriate ceremonies; bodies of four arrive International Airport, Idlewild, where three are removed while that of *Reilly* goes on to Syracuse. Burger discloses a swamp march in 1954 followed by court-martial. In Washington, Pate is interviewed after visit with Richard Russell, Chairman House Armed Services Committee, where he went to report on the matter; Pate talked with Dr. Herlihy, psychiatrist, who said McKeon made an error of judgment, but Pate adds, "This is just one man's opinion."

April 13—Churchill asks British aid to Israel if Egypt attacks. Gruenther leaving NATO; Norstad named successor. Requiem for *O'Shea* at St. Brigid's, Brooklyn, which several thousand attend. Funeral for *Thompson* in Victory Temple of the Church of God in Christ, Brooklyn; body will go to Summerton, South Carolina, for burial. *Wood's* burial will be Monday from St. Mark's Protestant Episcopal Church in Islip, New York. *Reilly* will be buried tomorrow at Clyde, New York. All had or will get full military honors. Word from Fulton, New York, that *Reilly* wrote Sunday, April 8, to Allen M. Rice, Jr., a lifelong friend, telling him a DI made him drink nineteen bottles of pop as a punishment. Report from Parris Island that a brigadier general has been added to Inquiry so the Court will not be outranked by any witness called up for testimony. [It is apparent to any reader that Major General Joseph Burger, vested with full responsibility for both failure and achievement at Parris Island, will not testify. Had Pate wanted to investigate Parris Island, not just the Ribbon Creek incident, he would have been forced to convene the Inquiry himself.]

April 14—[Inquiry re-opened today after being inactive two days; since its doors are closed to the press, news is hard to come by. Leviero has already filed one story for tomorrow's Section IV: "Marine Training—Theory and Practice." He tells of DI barking one inch away from lobe of scared recruit's ear. DIs cite types of recruits: card sharp, sea-story artist, sea lawyer, crud, wise guy or snipe, mamma's boy. Quotes letters home saying one lad had to raise rifle two hundred times over his head for smoking; another had to drink nineteen bottles of pop. Pate shook NCO morale declaring McKeon was without authority to order disciplinary march; at platoon graduation the DI is a hero.] The drowning of six young recruits last Sunday night has raised serious morale, training, and legal problems. Basic policy toward NCOs—backbone of the Corps—is cloudy and ambiguous. Now that the Marine Corps is in trouble everyone in authority from Pate on down is throwing the book at Sergeant McKeon. Marine NCOs have a great deal of autonomy and discretion in administering and disciplining their platoons: There is tacit understanding that the DI must run his platoon with a firm hand but not get caught in the business of administering punishment. This is pushing NCOs into a legal No Man's Land. Most DIs worth their salt refrain from reporting minor infractions which might get the boy a bad record. Leviero recites the story he obtained from an unidentified surviver. "About ten P.M., when taps were sounding about a mile away, six of the recruits sank into a deep hole of the tidal stream. The officials of the base knew that night they had lost the youths, but did not make any public report until one P.M. the next day. . . . The undercurrent of feeling is against the poker-faced denial of the practice of marine discipline. Marine noncoms are notably uncommunicative to outsiders about any gripes they may have about the Corps. But in this case they have made their feelings known. . . . The rank and file of the Corps, however, are looking to their top leaders for a clearer definition of the responsibilities and the legal status of the Drill Instructor."

April 15—Drill masters curbed: nine on trial in sixteen months at Marine Recruit Base, which the Public Information Officer says is normal for the period. [Obviously Duane Faw, Legal Officer, counted only general courts-martial for maltreatment; he omitted special courts-martial and all trials for other offenses, such as extortion.]

April 16—President vetoes farm bill. Inquiry continues seventh consecutive day behind closed doors; will finish Wednesday at the earliest [Ralph Wood, Public Information Officer, was carrying out orders but fibbing: The Inquiry worked one hour nineteen minutes on the 12th, did nothing the 13th, was in session only during the afternoon of the 15th. It did finish Wednesday, the 18th.]

April 17—Bronx youth age eighteen slain in knifing at school.

April 18—Sightseers converge on Monaco for wedding today.

April 19—Court ends; PubInfo Officer says it completed work just after midnight; Court interviewed every survivor. [Twenty-three recruits appeared at the Inquiry; there were seventy-two survivors.]

April 21—Margaret Truman weds Clifton Daniel.

April 30—Alben Barkley dies of heart attack while delivering speech at Washington and Lee University. Eisenhower joins Dulles in pushing foreign aid plan. House will hold public hearing tomorrow; Carl Vinson says full report will be made to Armed Services Committee; Pate has already given findings and recommendations to Vinson and to Dewey Short, ranking Republican. [Three endorsements on the 425-page record of Inquiry, those of Commandant Pate, Judge Advocate General Nunn, and Secretary Thomas are dated April 30. Were these given Committee approval before signature?]

May 1—Dulles flies to Paris for NATO conference. The Marine Corps meets Congressional and public concern over its training program today by shifting key officers and ordering a manslaughter trial for Staff Sergeant Matthew C. McKeon, who is accused of being under the influence of vodka when he led Platoon 71 into Ribbon Creek; McKeon faces a maximum penalty of ten years in prison and dishonorable discharge under conviction for manslaughter; Major General Burger will be transferred for viewing the case too narrowly as a manslaughter action against one man and failing to recognize also a moral issue involving the whole Corps; Colonel William B. McKean, Commanding Officer of Weapons Training Battalion at the Boot Camp, will be reassigned; there will be closer supervision of training by officers, but Pate wants the NCOs to remain in full control; Pate will establish a Recruit Training Command at Parris Island with a brigadier general in direct control; Major General Edward W. Snedeker will be Inspector General for Recruit Training; the Inquiry recommended lesser disciplinary action against Staff Sergeant Elwyn B. Scarborough and Sergeant Richard J. King for joining in the vodka drinking; Representative Carl Vinson, Democrat of Georgia, complimented Pate for his courage and forthrightness in meeting the situation and recognizing current deficiencies in the recruit training system; the Committee requested Pate to report again in sixty or ninety days, but seemed satisfied with Pate's plan for closer supervision; Representative L. Mendel Rivers, Democrat of South Carolina, remarked: "I've heard it said that there is only one man between the recruit and God, and that is the DI." [Pate's picture is on the front page, those of Burger and McKeon on page nineteen. Full text of the Inquiry findings and Pate's comment is on page eighteen along with another picture of Pate and a special "man in the news" character sketch noting: He understands discipline better than any man I've known, says a close military associate; he is sensitive, he feels deeply, he felt a tremendous compassion for the families; he did not demonstrate anger, or that sort of thing; words most often used to describe him are quiet, studious, gentle, reserved, considerate; he has no nickname; he was president of his class four years at Virginia Military Institute and first in scholastic rank at graduation; in thirty-five years in the Corps he never commanded an outfit in combat smaller than a division; he used to be avid golfer but gave up the game after becoming Commandant. Note that Burger's comment on the Inquiry was not published; it probably was not released, since his remarks were not directed at the press.]

May 2—Marine Corps changes its mind; Major General David M. Shoup, winner of the Medal of Honor and British DSO, will get recruit inspection post instead of going to the Third Marine Division, now in Japan. Pate receives a letter from Patrick Murphy Malin, Executive Director, American Civil Liberties Union, asking public hearings to give recruits themselves a chance to have their complaints aired; ACLU has received complaints charging abusive treatment of recruits. Editorial: Drinking vodka helps to explain what the public found incomprehensible in the strange behavior of the leader of this death march; the Parris Island report required unsparing investigation and complete candor as to any top-level official laxity; Pate has dealt with this tragic incident in a spirit of compassion, firmness, but common sense that does not lose sight of the fundamentals; grueling training guaranteed victory over a cruel enemy, shortened wars, and saved American lives.

May 3—Hanson Baldwin analyzes Army's *esprit de corps*.

Bill Bockman, news commentator of radio station WBEU, Beaufort, maintains a reputation for calling his shots accurately. His criticism of Parris Island is often severe, always just. He made the following broadcast at one o'clock the afternoon of May 3:

> The Marine Corp is in disgrace. There are few marines scattered throughout the world today who are holding their heads very high. They can't, because their Commandant has cut the ground out from under a commanding officer—and he might just as well have cut out the ground of every marine in the business.
>
> The Commandant of the Marine Corps is telling you that everything about marine training needs to be changed. He's telling you that he has little confidence that the marine training under generals, colonels, majors, captains, lieutenants, and sergeants is being conducted in the proper manner. Yet this same training has molded the greatest striking force ever known.
>
> What a pity it is for any man not to have confidence in the men that have devoted their lives to the molding of the Corps. What a shame for a man in high authority not to back up his officers and men. What a blow to the morale of the Corps this must have been—and to know the top man most likely in the future will be swayed by forces so that he can run with the tide.
>
> It takes a great man to buck up: something that we apparently do not now have at the helm of the Corps.
>
> How can General Burger or any other commander look after every man on any base? He can't do it—not even General Pate. We wonder how General Pate would feel if this accident had happened while he was a commander of a base. Could he have prevented it? You answer this. For we are sure that your answer is the same as ours.
>
> Perhaps we should have been tipped off to this on the day after the tragic affair. That was the day the Commandant made his appearance at Parris Island and placed a lot of people squarely on the spot by changing texts of statements that had been made. We have carefully kept a special file on this Parris Island story and watched unsaid items creep into the stories bit by bit by sensational news gatherers. And Pate has been influenced by sensationalism and bowed to pressure.
>
> Well, Russia must be very happy with the new way of things that is going to be in the Marine Corps. Now they'll be prepared for cream-puffs and not the Marines of the past.
>
> Thank you, good afternoon and thirty.

May 5—Sniper at New York church kills one, wounds five. Marine swamp march leader faces Court May 14; names of Court members are not released; Law Officer will be Captain Irving N. Klein, now Legal Officer, Third Naval District, with headquarters in New York.

May 6—Destroyer *Eaton* rammed by battleship *Wisconsin*, commanded by Captain Frederick S. Keeler, USNA 1929. Weekly review of the news: Last month sergeants came into national controversy, which reminds one of *From Here to Eternity* where Sergeant Warden said he runs the company even though Captain Holmes is Commanding Officer.

May 7—*Andersonville* wins Pulitzer Prize. Marine Base at Parris Island hit by shake-up; Commanding General now only has jurisdiction over service troops; there is deep resentment among Drill Instructors and junior officers over Burger's transfer; Staff NCOs give Burger a farewell cocktail party; thirty-four officers and 116 NCOs are under orders to report to Parris Island; General Greene, now in direct command of recruits, says: "The present training plan is absolutely sound. No matter how much supervision you have, such an incident could happen."

May 8—Justice James B. McNally of the New York Supreme Court says a committee of judges and lawyers has been formed to aid Staff Sergeant McKeon; Emile Zola Berman, 52 Broadway, former lieutenant colonel during World War II has volunteered his services as chief counsel while Thomas P. Costello will assist, both without compensation.

May 10—Officers cleared in marines' deaths: Pate says the tragedy stemmed from acts of an individual that could not be prevented by the officer supervision in effect at that time; in letter to Representative Walter Norblad, Republican of Oregon, Pate says the reassignment of officers was not of a punitive nature. [No professional soldier, sailor, airman, or marine of any nation would be misled by Pate's denial of *punitive*.]

May 11—Navy postpones until July 14 the general court-martial of McKeon; delay was asked by Burman [sic], whose prior commitments would not permit him sufficient time to prepare his case if trial opened May 14.

May 12—Homer Litzenberg takes command at Parris Island.

May 13—Marines extend Boot Camp two weeks.

May 16—Joseph Burger takes command at Camp LeJeune.

June 1—Marine sergeant released from brig by order of the Secretary of the Navy; Ralph Wood, Public Information Officer, announces McKeon assigned temporary duties in Chaplain's Office. [Matthew McKeon was released from confinement May 23; apparently some newshawk discovered it nine days later.]

June 9—General Shoup, inspector of recruit training, speaks to Marine Combat Correspondents Association at their Third Annual Reunion dinner in the Gramercy Park Hotel; Shoup says that ruggedness is held basic to marines but that acts of personal humiliation and indignity will not be tolerated.

July 2—Marine Sergeant Arthur E. Ashcraft, Covington, Kentucky, is court-martialed for maltreating eleven recruits at Parris Island.

July 3—Ashcraft is convicted on three counts and gets one year hard labor and bad conduct discharge for striking recruits.

July 13—Navy names Court; Klein comes from Judge Advocate General's Office.

July 14—Marines will open trial of McKeon, which is no ordinary one because the Commandant said that the Marine Corps in a moral sense is also on trial; McKeon could get twenty-three years hard labor and dishonorable discharge. Thumping has been abandoned. Locked poll boxes have been set up where recruits can give their opinions of the DI.

[Wayne Phillips covers the trial at Parris Island for the New York *Times*.]

July 15—Emile Berman holds press conference in a schoolroom; he charges today that fear of reprisal is hampering the Defense; among Parris Island NCOs Berman has found a barrier of silence motivated entirely by fear of reprisal and punitive action; Berman releases text of his letter to the Secretary of the Navy requesting an order that no man who told the truth would be subject to reprisal; Thomas says such an order is not necessary; tomorrow Berman will move to dismiss trivial charges which may gravely prejudice the Defense on major charges. McKeon was not at the conference; today he attended Mass and then went to Yemassee to meet his brother and two sisters. [This was beyond the limit of McKeon's restriction.]

July 16—The Ribbon Creek tragedy has shaken morale of the Corps and raised questions about its training methods. Defense starts laying groundwork for a thorough review of recruit training in order to show the march was part of the training program approved by custom. Berman asks special training data obtained by Marine Corps Headquarters questionnaire and a list of names of marines separated from Parris Island to show evidence of custom; Sevier will refuse request on grounds of irrelevance, Klein will rule. Berman wants to sever liquor charges from those of oppression and manslaughter; wants separate trials usual in civilian procedure. McKeon sits at rigid attention during trial. Mrs. Maggie Meeks, mother of *Thomas Hardeman,* present in Court; she says, "He doesn't seem like a mean man. I've not got too much bitter against him; the Lord says don't hate nobody. But it seems that a grown man of that age—the Marines put such trust in him." *Hardeman* told his mother he saw a recruit who had his jaw broken for stepping out of line. [Picture of Berman and McKeon, page 11.]

July 17—Berman makes plea by press, radio, and TV asking all recently discharged marines who know of similar marches to communicate with him; phone calls and telegrams deluge Parris Island with offers to help McKeon; thirty lines between Beaufort and Parris Island are tied up, Western Union is running far behind, between 8:20 and 10:55 P.M. there were 119 telephone calls; off-duty women marines, joined by Mrs. Betty McKeon and two other marine-wife neighbors, are helping with traffic; Berman makes public the letter he will send to prospective Defense witnesses. Berman will present list tomorrow of marines he feels will have something constructive to offer in testimony. Public Information Officer says 1,450 veterans' names in file will be made available to Berman. [Reporter Phillips recalls Pate's remark of May 1: "I consider that my first moral and military obligation in this case is to take every lawful step available to me to insure that (those involved) are tried and punished to the fullest extent allowed by our Uniform Code of Military Justice."]

July 18—Court visits scene five minutes; press kept fifty yards away by MPs; Major Stanley M. McKeod [sic] tells reporter the stake with white rag in Ribbon Creek marks the deep hole gouged by the rushing current where the bodies were found. "Emile Zola Berman seized on every crevice to start wedging his defense into the record through cross-examination." Calls and telegrams continued to pour in; estimated 300 of each by evening; most contained expressions of sympathy and support rather than useful testimony. Berman will present a list of witnesses tomorrow. McKeon's disciplined lack of emotion cracks when he tries to express his sorrow to Mrs. Maggie Meeks;

McKeon says, "Hello, Ma'am. Your son was one of the finest boys in my platoon, and I am terribly sorry this all happened." Mrs. Meeks says, "The Lord says don't hate nobody. If you're guilty you will be punished." McKeon says, "If I'm guilty, I would rather be punished here than in the hereafter." McKeon chokes back a sob and his brother leads him away. [Front page picture of Mrs. Meeks and Sergeant McKeon.] Six survivors of the death march listed in misconduct status: two absent without leave since Friday; another declared deserter July 2 after thirty days' absence; a fourth AWOL since June 25; another awaiting office hours; another in the Camp LeJeune brig.

July 19—Lieutenant Colonel Robert A. Thompson [sic], Provost Marshal, recalled to identify pictures. Summary of testimony of Clement, Nolan, King, and Huff. Unsigned feature article on Berman: Arrived Parris Island a week ago Wednesday; lives at Roslyn Heights, Long Island, with wife, former Alice Rose Gaines of Clinton, South Carolina, and their two adopted children; graduated from New York University in 1925; most of his practice in negligence cases for either plaintiff or defendant insurance companies; has lectured on trial techniques at Columbia and NYU law schools; has been practicing continually in New York except for three years with Air Force in China-Burma-India theater where he won the Distinguished Flying Cross and Bronze Star; President, Metropolitan Trial Lawyers Association; Fellow, American College of Trial Lawyers; Trustee, International Academy of Trial Lawyers; a prominent New York jurist describes Berman's courtroom artistry second to none.

July 20—Senior DI Huff testifies he would have led platoon into marshes had he had time. Klein rules testimony concerning marches into swamps and waters will be heard in order to judge reasonableness of McKeon's action. Patrick, Taylor, Grabowsky, and Barber testify. Inquiry brought out that McKeon had morning drinks, part of a beer at lunch, and a single drink of vodka before the march. [There is no mention of that noonday beer by any witness or in any record until Matthew McKeon takes the stand and testifies July 31.]

July 21—Saturday, Court is adjourned. Eight members of Berman's staff have been working around the clock at Headquarters Marine Corps analyzing the four-page, unsigned questionnaires; Berman tells reporters the official survey, made in early May, indicates training should be tougher.

July 22—Sunday news summary by Phillips: Matthew McKeon

with sixteen battle stars, tall, ramrod-straight, hair cropped close, is the epitome of emotionless, disciplined fighting men turned out by the Marine Corps. [Reconstructs details of April 8, including McKeon's beer at the Staff NCO Club but the story reads like Berman.] Wire from San Diego: "You taught them what they taught you." Quote from unidentified DI: "I haven't got time to be a good guy." At first the Marine Corps was condemned by the public for what the Sergeant did, now it is being condemned for bringing him to trial.

Berman holds press conference: McKeon's Counsel will call 200 witnesses; Berman will battle to prevent reducing that number, which is necessary to establish proof that night marches were common practice; validity of that practice is denied from Headquarters Marine Corps down to Battalion officers at Parris Island. Sevier plans to call twenty-seven witnesses and will not approve bringing in substantially more Defense witnesses. Berman says night marches were not mentioned in the questionnaire; "apparently the people who prepared the questionnaire didn't put it in because they didn't think it was oppressive or in any way irregular"; but there was a question asking how often, when, and where officers were seen supervising. This close supervision under the new deal at Parris Island is undermining DIs' authority and has rallied these instructors to the defense of McKeon in opposition to commissioned officers of the Corps; many officers condemned McKeon, strongly and publicly, before the trial. Henry T. Stevens IV, Grosse Point, Michigan, former marine and member of lumber industry family, wires offer of $5,000, but Berman says no contributions are being asked or accepted; Stevens says, "No maltreatment was involved. It was the same treatment that has been going on at Parris Island since 1917." Telegram from Daniel K. Marlow, Miami: "Was in Platoon No. 273, First Recruit Battalion, 1951, under Drill Instructor Staff Sergeant Robert A. Olson. Forced marches in Ribbon Creek area at night routine for all platoons. Will testify at own expense if necessary." [First Lieutenant Robert A. Olson is again at Parris Island as Legal Officer, Headquarters and Service Battalion.]

July 23—Seven recruits testify; survivors depict McKeon as frustrated and depressed by his failure to instill discipline among them; testimony today indicates that even those classified as nonswimmers had been trained in dog-paddling, floating, and treading water. [This impression was derived more from Berman's questions than recruits' answers. "Qualification" requires swimming one hundred yards—in any fashion—and treading water thirty seconds, clothed in trunks.]

July 24—Six recruits testify; two survivors say McKeon was swimming and treading water shortly before, and four say they were in water over their heads before panic erupted. Last night Sevier had all sixty-eight survivors called in to check recollections of the march. In Washington, Brigadier General James Phillips Berkeley, G-1, son of retired Major General Randolph Carter Berkeley of Beaufort, says the trial will hurt enlistments: "We would be naïve and foolish to think otherwise."

July 25—*Andrea Doria* and *Stockholm* collide; 1,134 passengers abandon Italian ship in fog at sea; all saved, many injured; second vessel safe. According to evidence today, in contradiction to Corporal King's testimony, McKeon spent the afternoon of April 8 drinking vodka and mulling over the idea of taking his platoon into the swamps. [Phillips quotes from McKeon's confession of April 8 introduced by Sergeant Cummings.] Talking with reporters out of Court, Berman says the 1.5 Bogens measure is at the level between possible intoxication and intoxication. Eleven witnesses testified.

July 26—Italian liner sinks, *Stockholm* due tomorrow; seven dead, fifty-two missing, 1,652 saved in collision; *Times*man killed. The Government rested today after calling thirty-six witnesses. Berman subjected Silvey to blistering and at times shouting cross-examination. Quote from Commandant's statement: "The conduct of the training must inculcate in each marine that sense of his own responsibility to do his part in battle so that his comrades do not bear his burden, or suffer from his failure." This, Defense contends, is all that Sergeant McKeon was trying to do.

July 27—Berman sends request to Sevier this morning to order one of the Marine Corps' toughest generals, Lieutenant General Lewis B. (Chesty) Puller, Saluda, Virginia, out of retirement to defend McKeon.

July 28—Sevier assents, will ask Pate to order Puller to active duty for that purpose.

July 29—Review and summary: New York judges and attorneys with military backgrounds think Marines' traditionally tough discipline should be defended; they say outline of Defense case is already clear. [Phillips bases most of his story on Pate's policy statement of May 7.] When six men died in that nighttime panic in a tidal stream, there was panic also at Marine Corps Headquarters. Pate did not mention how the Marine Corps, by lowering its recruiting standards, was sending these DIs motley herds of indifferent teen-agers, some with IQs under eighty, that drove instructors to distraction. Marine training is now changed.

Berman holds press conference: Berman will move for dismissal of three charges; these motions will be the first decisions in the case made by the seven members of the Court. McKeon will take the stand this week to tell of events and his experiences as a recruit in 1948, when he was bitten by a marsh snake. Berman will call thirty-three witnesses, fourteen active-duty, eighteen civilians, and Puller. Scarborough will be first, otherwise the evidence might indicate McKeon was storing liquor in his room. Next witness will be a Navy hydrographer with scientific evidence concerning the characteristics of the bed of Ribbon Creek, because the testimony of various recruits is of such a confusing nature. Berman had estimated ten days to present his case but now says he will finish sooner "because of the weakness and the confusion in the Prosecution's case."

July 30—Klein denies Berman's motions to dismiss; Defense begins; Scarborough, Volle, and Kraynick testify. Defense opened today with an attempt to show no dangerous declivities in Ribbon Creek. The hydrographic survey will be elaborated tomorrow with a giant relief map.

July 31—With tears in his eyes Matthew McKeon told of the disciplinary march into Ribbon Creek; he was on the witness stand three hours and thirty-five minutes, not including recesses; when he came to that point where a Negro recruit disappeared under water, McKeon pressed his hands to his forehead and his eyes filled with tears; Berman suggested a recess. Pate will be next Defense witness; Puller will appear Thursday. [Excerpts from McKeon's testimony.]

August 1—Pate says McKeon should lose a stripe and be transferred for stupidity; previously Pate told Congress it was his first military and moral obligation to see that Sergeant McKeon was punished to the full extent allowed by the Code. Berman conferred with Pate in Washington over weekend and Pate flew down at Berman's verbal request. Entering the Defense Counsel room before the trial opened, Pate walks directly over to McKeon: "Hello, Sergeant." They shook hands. "I'm sorry to meet you under these circumstances. I'm here to help you all I can. How are you getting along?" No reply. "We are after justice, you know, and we know you are, too. My regards to your wife. Is she here now?" Speechless and rigid, McKeon shook his head. "I'd like to meet her before I go if I get a chance. Good luck to you, boy." Father Marcus [sic] F. Cook testifies. [Excerpts from McKeon's cross-examination and Pate's testimony.] Ninety-five-page Bill of Rights for recruits under Greene.

Christian Century—Liquor plus brutality are on trial with marine: Defense admitted that Sergeant McKeon had been drinking, but argues this fact is of no consequence and attempts to prove it standard procedure for the Sergeant to be drunk. The logic of this seems that drinking is universal in the Marine Corps and that the risk of tragedy in consequence of an officer's drunkenness is a hazard that has to be borne.

August 2—A living legend general comes back to help a sergeant; ramrod-straight, his uniform blouse ablaze with fifty ribbons, Puller sits in witness chair and testifies in drill-field voice. After the recess Sevier says he should have known better than try to cross-examine a legend. Pate was genial, bantering, fidgety, and flip; Puller was stern, emphatic, brusque, and rigidly dignified. Returning from Korea Puller said the Air Force was not much good at close support; and there was no reason why fighting men should not get a little beer —or even whiskey—if it made them fight better. Tonight the Staff NCOs had a beer party for Puller, who prefers the company of enlisted men to that of officers; Puller spoke to them: "Do your duty. If you do that, no one in a thousand years will ever destroy the Marine Corps." NCO sentiment here is compounded of what they would like to believe and of the skill with which the Defense sold the case outside the courtroom. Officers of the Court are an austere group that would not flinch from their convictions. [Excerpts from Puller's testimony in the *Times:* Q. Were you in combat? A. Yeah. Q. Were you decorated? A. Yeah. Excerpts from the record of trial: Q. How long were you in Korea with your organization, General? A. About seven months. Q. In combat? A. Yes. Q. Have you been decorated by your Government? A. Yes.]

August 3—McKeon acquitted of manslaughter, oppression, and conduct detrimental to the service; convicted of negligent homicide and drinking; verdict hailed as victory for Defense. The Court apparently agreed with Pate's opinion on oppression. Sevier crosses room, shakes hands with McKeon: "Keep on going like you are and you'll do all right. It was a fair verdict." McKeon answers: "Thank you for a fair trial." Sevier estimates case cost Government $100,000. Berman estimates it would have cost $25,000 for a similar defense in civilian courts. Staff NCO Club toasts Berman and staff. [Front page picture: McKeon, wife, Berman.]

August 4—McKeon dazed and speechless for minutes after sentence; Berman tight-lipped and angry-looking; Berman will appeal any sentence that would oust McKeon; Berman arrives New York by plane but will not comment on sentence. At the Ninth Annual Reunion of the First Marine Division Association at the Sheraton-Astor, four out of five in a random sample say either McKeon got a raw deal or shouldn't have been tried at all.

August 5—McKeon settles down for a long wait; he doesn't want that bad conduct discharge. At the Staff NCO Club there is a big glass jar to receive contributions for McKeon.

August 7—Editorial: If the Sergeant had been a better leader, his men wouldn't have gotten out of hand. While no military unit can be democratic in operations, it can in spirit. Let us be sure in developing competent soldiers we do not make a virtue out of cruelty.

August 8—At South Bend, William D. Webster, National Commandant of the Marine Corps League, says his group will appeal to Secretary Thomas for removal of the bad conduct discharge; Webster says for the Corps to run effectively we cannot allow a radical change to the system which has been successful for 180 years.

August 9—Letter of Ralph W. Howard, Philadelphia: "The fundamental tragedy of the issue is the correct conclusion by all concerned that our nation requires a fanatic corps of fighting men to defend our liberties; men who must be trained to love fighting for its own sake."

August 10—At Dallas, Timothy J. Murphy, Boston lawyer and National Commander of the Veterans of Foreign Wars, fears the court-martial of McKeon will tend to break down training in military survival; VFW favors programs that develop the ability of men to resist panic. At Lowell, Massachusetts, Representative Edith Nourse Rogers urges Secretary Thomas to void McKeon's conviction; she says the Sergeant's trial was staged to provide a scapegoat for higher-ups.

August 11—*Nation:* The Marine Corps quandary is that training methods which made the Corps one of the world's finest fighting forces today fail to yield similar results. Former marines who have seen action are grateful for tough training, but this makes little sense to new volunteers. Six of Platoon 71 were in the brig during the court-martial for trying to go AWOL.

August 12—At Dallas the National Council of VFW asks review boards to show leniency because McKeon's sentence is too severe for what appears to be minor infraction of base rules.

August 13—At Columbus, Ohio, AmVets ask Secretary Wilson to reduce McKeon's sentence. His valiant service in Korea was not adequately considered. Edgar L. Williams, State Commander, writes that Armed Forces recruitment will suffer because young men do not want to "suffer injustice of being the goat for a common practice of a branch of the service."

Life—Closeup by Joe McCarthy on Emile Berman entitled "The Man Who Helped the Sergeant": In three weeks Berman persuaded the public to do an about-face and then bewildered the Prosecution by calling Puller and Pate. Pate's testimony caused anguish in Navy Department. Berman, not the Prosecutors, defended Marine Corps traditions. Berman manipulates public relations angles of Court-Martial like a legal Barnum. His strength in courtroom comes from ability to argue against expert witnesses on medicine and engineering. Berman tells about his being named after Emile Zola, who defended Alfred Dreyfus against high brass of French Army, and Berman is quoted saying, "I thought the Marine Corps was using this boy to cover its own responsibility." In India he defended an aircraft crew caught flying medical supplies across the Hump and selling them to the Chinese; they were charged with smuggling; Berman obtained dismissal of that case by contending that smuggling is sneaking material into a country against that country's wishes—the Chinese were delighted to get the supplies.

August 16—At Dallas the 57th National Encampment of the VFW calls for an objective review and says the Ribbon Creek tragedy was an unfortunate accident. In Washington, Representative Edward H. Rees, Republican of Kansas, says Congress should probe more deeply into the drowning and tighten laws against liquor in military areas.

August 18—S. L. A. Marshall, National Guard general, newsman, established military author, writes from Detroit to comment on the *Times* editorial of August 7: McKeon is not a brute or sadist as Marshall originally thought. The court-martial atmosphere was unsatisfactory because the Government insisted that if slips within a training system and the breakdown of responsible inspection were factors contributing to a catastrophic failure by one individual, any such showing was still not pertinent to the fight by one man to save his honor.

America—Editorial on McKeon's trial recalls the Dreyfus *Affaire* and raises the question of ethics. Fr. Jerome A. Petz, SJ, in a two-page analysis of the ethical question notes that there is cause for alarm in the public thinking involved with this trial.

August 22—Copy of the record of McKeon's trial was received in the Office of the Judge Advocate General of the Navy early this week and it will take at least ten days for an opinion. Sergeant McKeon was ordered discharged in disgrace.

August 27—*New Republic:* In a letter to the Editor, John P. Roche, faculty member at Brandeis University and Army veteran of World War II, contends that it is increasingly difficult to justify the Marine Corps from a military viewpoint since it has outlived its original purpose: Marines were created by the British, Roche says, to protect officers from mutinous crews. The real issue in McKeon's trial was status of the Corps in American mythology. Marine training performs an egoectomy. Marines take an enemy strongpoint by storming while the Army waits judiciously for mortar fire. By Marine standards McKeon wasn't tough enough: With tight discipline, his men would have marched Indian file with each recruit keeping track of his neighbors. McKeon's sin was not losing six men—men are expendable—but doing it in such unshipshape fashion. The Marine Corps survives because of a myth in the collective subconscious of American people: Violence is forbidden fruit to a nation with civilian ideals; this brings ambivalence; the Marine Corps is a projection of the civilian hero wish.

August 31—The 33d Annual Convention of the Marine Corps League at Miami endorses tough training for recruits and has confidence the Navy will reach an appropriate decision as to McKeon's final punishment. At Beaufort Naval Hospital, Mrs. Betty McKeon gives birth to a seven-pound six-ounce baby girl, Alice Bridget.

September 4—Marine recruit dies of heat stroke at Parris Island.

September 17—Secretary of the Navy Thomas has received the court-martial record in McKeon's case and will spend considerable time studying it before taking final action.

September 19—Berman holds press conference to disclaim New York *World Telegram and Sun* story based on his off-the-record talk before a group of lawyers in Brooklyn Tuesday night. The WT&S said Berman said high officers of the Marine Corps had sacrificed Sergeant McKeon to save themselves from an investigation by Congress and attacks from public and press. Berman says the appearance of Pate and Puller should negate any suggestion that the Marine Corps abandoned McKeon upon trial. WT&S Editor responds that it was an open meeting and his newspaper was not committed to keeping Berman's talk off the record.

September 22—In Atlanta the WCTU says the bar and package store at the Staff NCO Club was the real culprit in the tragedy at Parris Island. WCTU wants Eisenhower to recognize that the Ribbon Creek tragedy was not in harmony with Defense Department's claim that drinking in military services is under control and to order Secretary Wilson to rewrite his drink regulations in harmony with existing law.

September 25—General Randolph McC. Pate, Commander of the Marine Corps, will begin a round-the-world inspection tour tomorrow flying to Europe on the first leg. He returns October 29 after visiting Marine units in Okinawa, Japan, and Hawaii.

October 5—McKeon's sentence is eased; he can stay in the Marines. Berman says the Secretary's action meets the needs of the case. McKeon says: "I believe it is a very just sentence and a very fair sentence. I believed from the beginning I'd be down to private and I will try to be the very best private in the Marine Corps." [Excerpts from Thomas' court-martial order. Picture of McKeon smiling.]

October 7—Editorial on justice and mercy: Something was wrong with the system of training as well as the Sergeant or it wouldn't have happened. It would have been tragic if one man were made scapegoat for errors in practice and judgment that were beyond his knowledge and control. The record of our courts-martial is good and there has been earnest and steady effort to make their procedure even more fully representative of what we believe are fundamental human rights within our society.

October 8—McKeon back in brig stripped of his sergeant's stripes; with good behavior he will serve only thirteen days more.

October 15—William S. O'Connor writes a letter to the Editor opposing the decision in McKeon's case; the punishment amounts to a slap on the wrist with the admonition to be a good boy.

October 19—McKeon will be released at seven-thirty tomorrow morning.

October 21—*Exclusive*—Unnoticed by the press a victory banquet is being held this evening at the restaurant of Mr. Bernard (Toots) Shor. Celebrating are the Accused, Counsel for the Defense —all of them—and such stalwart assistants as Rev. Fr. Maurus F. Cook, OSB, who stood by Matthew McKeon in his hours of trial. Emile Zola Berman picks up the check, including travel expenses.

October 22—*New Republic:* Eduard Bjorkman, Newark, writes a letter to the Editor; he is disturbed about Secretary Thomas' action. DIs can now go as far as they like. Parents now are more anxiously concerned. Had one deceased had connections, McKeon's fate would have been different.

Eleven months after the Ribbon Creek incident Parris Island was still making headlines. Periodically some Drill Instructor would be court-martialed for maltreatment and national wire services would carry the story. Monday, March 11, 1957, the Savannah *Morning News* published this editorial, unsigned but written by Joseph E. Lambright, Editor:

LET'S LAY OFF THE MARINES A WHILE

To date four drill instructors at the U. S. Marine Corps Recruiting Training Depot at Parris Island have been court-martialed for alleged mistreatment of recruits. And since the trial of Sgt. Matthew McKeon, who was in charge of the recruit platoon of which six men drowned on a creek during a night disciplinary march, each has been accompanied by considerable publicity at the hands of newspapers, radio and television. It cannot be argued that in the case of Sgt. McKeon a court-martial was justified. However, since the incident that led to that trial and its accompanying publicity, there hasn't been a single case in which a recruit suffered death or severe injury in which a drill instructor could have been held accountable.

Therefore, isn't it about time for the Marine Corps to get back to the business of making Marines out of recruits, and to stop permitting its principal recruiting base to be utilized as a locale for an endless series of courts and inquiries into every incident in which some recruit feels that he has been mistreated at the hands of his drill instructors? Unfortunately, the answer isn't up to the officers and men of the Marine Corps entirely. It's up to the public, especially the interested citizen who writes his congressman occasionally.

Americans must make up their minds whether or not they want a Marine Corps of the type we have had in the past. If not, then we may continue to supervise the training by public investigations and trials to insure that no recruit is mistreated in the process of becoming a Marine, and that drill instructors conduct themselves at all times according to Marquis de Queensberry rules. Some of the recruits will like it better that way, and maudlin meddlers with no concept of the mission of a Marine in battle will be pleased to know that the young men entering the corps are wet-nursed properly and tucked in every night. But heaven help the United States if the product of soft training techniques is ever thrown into battle against the Russian or Chinese Communists!

It might be well for all of us to become better acquainted with the U. S. Marine, his mission, and his traditions. You don't think of the Marines when you associate the military with learning a trade or seeing the world. You may do either in the Marines, but it's strictly secondary. Marines are and have been tough, highly disciplined fighting men, ready at all times to meet any enemy. They are usually the first to be thrown into action against an enemy. Their casualties are expected to be among the highest. They live with their rifle, and they know how to use it. Their shoes are shined and their dress uniforms immaculate. Their military bearing reflects pride in the tradition that marks him as an expert in the messy business of modern warfare.

Such were the men who fought the Japs for months on end in the rain-soaked jungles of Guadalcanal where neither side bothered much about taking prisoners. Such were the men who took Iwo Jima, inch by inch, so that American fliers would have protection on the long haul to Tokyo. Such were the men who led the attack in Korea. You may not always approve of their rigid discipline or their methods, but all Americans can be glad they're on our side when it comes to fighting.

Recently unification and recruiting regulations have required that the Marine Corps lower its sights on recruits. Formerly only men temperamentally and physically suited for the corps were accepted. Now regulations require that recruiting for Marines be less selective. As a result, training procedures must be more effective if the corps is to continue to live up to its reputation and accomplish its mission. The task is difficult. It cannot be done if drill instructors, who have the responsibility of transforming undisciplined scrawny boys into Marines, are afraid to get rough occasionally for fear of being court-martialed.

We for one believe that the continuation of a well-trained, well-disciplined, and proud Marine Corps is of greater importance to the future of this nation than the personal feelings of some recruit who may think that his drill instructor had no right to boot him out of his bunk or forcefully impress upon him the importance of obedience to orders. It may, at times, become necessary for a drill instructor to lay his hands on a recruit, the alternative being to produce an inferior Marine. It's time for the public, and Congress, to insist first on satisfactory results from the Marine Corps as reflected in the discipline and training of its men—not to hold a court-martial every time a drill instructor does something to a raw recruit that his parents should have done long before, but probably neglected.

April, 1957—*American Mercury:* G. Lincoln Rockwell writes "Who Wants Panty-Waist Marines?" Thesis: Communists and subversives through softhearted, mistaken Americans are systematically and coldly dismantling the machinery which makes superbly disciplined, fighting men—Marines—the nation's last bulwark.

News stories growing out of the Ribbon Creek incident were in sixty-three issues of New York *Times* between April 10 and October 21, 1956. Nineteen of these were on the front page. Only the collision of *Stockholm* and *Andrea Doria* during the Court-Martial moved them inside after they had been out front nine consecutive days. But this didn't end the Ribbon Creek story. It can't be buried with full military honors like those who drowned. Every time some marine recruit shows his bruises and claims the DI clobbered him, every time some knuckleheaded marine casts an unsavory shadow on Parris Island, journalistic practice requires the old story to be dug up from the newspaper morgue. It follows Matthew McKeon wherever he goes, whatever he does. It will follow him to the grave.

27

Afterthoughts

THE HONORABLE CHARLES S. THOMAS, Secretary of the Navy, signed General Court-Martial Order No. 1-56 on October 5. This was the first in his annual series because it is quite unusual for the Secretary to convene a court: Secretaries come and go without once publishing such an order. But McKeon's was an unusual case and Thomas' advisers didn't want current newsmen or future critics to draw comparisons with the Dreyfus *Affaire*. The three-page body of his order is routine: recitation of charges, specifications, pleas, findings, previous convictions, sentence, and then a paragraph denoting the Convening Authority's action.

Matthew McKeon was sentenced by the Court to a bad conduct discharge (BCD), forfeiture of $30 per month for nine months while confined at hard labor, and reduction to private. Charles Thomas approved only three months' confinement at hard labor and reduction. [Since confinement began officially when Colonel Edward Hutchinson pronounced sentence August 4 even though Matthew McKeon continued to spend his off-duty hours at home, since the Secretary's action was mailed Friday and not read on Parris Island until Monday, and since prisoners —actual or constructive—get time off for good behavior, in this instance three weeks, McKeon spent just twelve more nights in the Parris Island brig.]

But Secretary Thomas was not content to wind up such a

notorious case without editorializing. He attached a fifteen-page "opinion" well knowing it would be extensively quoted in New York *Times* and used as a handout for Washington correspondents. The style of his opinion, therefore, bears no resemblance to a typical legal digest. Let's see if we can follow his argument from some widely-scattered extracts:

> I am exercising the power of review conferred by Congress upon Convening Authorities. It is a one-way power: It can be exercised only in favor of an Accused—never against him. . . . The manner of exercise is one of the gravest responsibilities commanders meet. The wisdom with which it is exercised will influence not only the discipline, but also the morale and *esprit* of the entire command. This power presents an opportunity to temper justice with the human understanding and sympathy all worthy leaders feel toward the men entrusted to their command. . . . My review convinced me that the Accused received a fair trial in every respect.
>
> The Marine Corps is a very unusual organization. It earned its fame as a dedicated, disciplined, tough, hard, and finely trained corps. . . . It appeals to that type of young American who realizes the effectiveness of disciplined organization. All who serve in it know this high state of discipline, this rigorous training, saves vast numbers of lives in combat. . . . Discipline and toughness can never be abandoned if the Corps is to maintain its high standards of leadership and fighting. . . . On the other hand, the Marine Corps must ensure that in the course of this rigorous discipline and carefully conceived training no lives of American youths are risked or lost unnecessarily. It is Marine tradition to face danger forthrightly; it is no part of that tradition to face danger foolishly. . . . In battle the noncommissioned officer must demand instant response from his men. This system has stood the test of time, and of battle.

Noting he could reduce the sentence so as to condone misconduct or weaken its deterrent effect on future misconduct, Thomas considered first the BCD alongside the homicide conviction and quoted from the Manual it is "Designed as a punishment for bad conduct rather than as punishment for serious offenses of either civil or military nature. It is appropriate as punishment for an Accused who has been convicted repeatedly of minor offenses for which punitive separation from the Service appears necessary." Thomas noted that "simple negligence" is not as blameworthy as "culpable negligence"; that McKeon was acquitted of "oppression"; that a BCD would wipe out veteran's benefits for him and his dependents; that it would affect his entire future life and rehabilitation; and therefore it was inappropriate.

But Thomas' quotation was not in full context. Let's read the words which appear just prior to it:

> Dishonorable discharge should be reserved for those who should be separated under conditions of dishonor, after having been convicted of offenses usually recognized by the civil law as felonies, or of offenses of a military nature requiring severe punishment. A bad conduct discharge may be imposed in any case in which a dishonorable discharge may be imposed as well as in certain other cases. It is a less severe punishment than dishonorable discharge.

The Table of Maximum Punishments shows Mathew McKeon might have received a dishonorable discharge for the military offense of drinking on duty and a bad conduct discharge for negligent homicide, for which there is apparently no comparable civilian offense when the degree is "simple negligence." The major difference between the two types of discharge is in semantics: *Dishonorable* is worse than *bad conduct* because the Manual says it is. In practice the Veterans Administration treats the two discharges nearly the same; it merely reviews the case when a BCD is adjudged by inferior courts-martial.

Thomas noted McKean's excellent combat record, good reputation, and fine character. He said, "I believe that the real punishment will be always the memory of Ribbon Creek on Sunday night, April 8, 1956. Remorse will never leave him." The Secretary then decided that forfeiture of pay—in addition to what he would lose by reduction in rank—would serve no essential purpose and have its immediate impact against McKeon's family. This he remitted.

Next Thomas weighed drinking on duty and confinement at hard labor in the same balance saying, "It may be that he is not habitually a drinker of strong liquor, but not even one violation of such a serious character can be condoned or tolerated." He then reduced the brig sentence in consideration for the time McKeon had already spent in confinement or under restriction. That left the question of reduction in rank, for which we resort to more scattered extracts:

> In connection with the remissions in sentence determined above, all points in Sergeant McKeon's favor were considered and the finding of the Court was given decisive weight. With respect to the one determination remaining, however, the gravity of the consequences of his actions and the interests of the Service must be decisive. . . . The fighting men of our nation are entitled to the best leadership. The Accused—like any other officer, commissioned or noncommissioned—must be held accountable for his unjustified failure to meet the most fundamental responsibility of leadership. . . . He took his action on impulse with no previous planning, reconnaissance, evaluation or normal precautionary measures. Without regard to the very real danger which was clearly to be foreseen, McKeon subjected the men under his charge to risks which he had not calculated.
>
> To fail to hold a senior noncommissioned officer accountable for his proven failure to exercise reasonable care for the welfare and safety of his men would tend to destroy the very basis of the fighting-team concept which makes the Marine Corps great. Such teamwork requires instant and unquestioning obedience. The confidence in their leaders necessary to such instant obedience by the men was created by the officers, both noncommissioned and commissioned, being worthy of such confidence and loyalty. . . . The sentence in this case should recognize and preserve the principle of responsible leadership and never-failing loyalty of leaders to the men they lead. Men of the Corps might well soon lose their confidence if, after one had so signally and fatally failed in his trust, were to be retained in a position of that same trust. . . . Just one lapse resulting in such serious consequences is just one lapse too many.

Enforcing such strict accountability—particularly against

> a man who has otherwise proved his devotion to Corps and Country—is not an easy decision. It is, however, an inevitable decision, if standards are to be upheld. The Court reached the decision that Staff Sergeant McKeon should be reduced to private, a grade which does not carry with it command authority over men. I concur, and I will approve the Court's sentence of reduction from staff sergeant to private.
>
> By remitting the bad conduct discharge, I have restored to Sergeant McKeon the opportunity to build for himself a useful and honorable career. I hope and believe that he will avail himself of this opportunity. I am convinced of his fundamental dedication to the Marine Corps and to his Country. I recognize that the road back will be a hard one for Sergeant McKeon. I am giving him his chance.

Some material grafted onto the Secretary's Opinion was neither in the record of Court-Martial nor Inquiry. An example of this reveals how his essay tries to restore the Corps to public esteem:

> Since this tragic incident, however, the Corps has extended the supervision of its training in an attempt to guard against even such an unpredictable situation as we are concerned with in this case. This extension of supervision in no way weakens or basically changes the traditional Marine Corps system of recruit training.

That concept derives from Pate's "Policy Governing Recruit Training" dated May 1. It is a goal rather than an achievement and is being evaluated prematurely.

But one fallacy appears in Thomas' concluding paragraph: "I have restored to Sergeant McKeon the opportunity to build for himself a useful and honorable career." That statement is autism far removed from realism. Mathew McKeon is damned. Ribbon Creek will hound him wherever he goes in the Marine Corps. No selection board would make him technical sergeant as long as he lives.

Matthew McKeon was tried for *oppression,* which Emile Berman used as a rallying point in his strategy. Berman couldn't avoid the mention of *maltreatment,* but he succeeded in de-emphasizing its use and severing all connection *maltreatment* might have to *oppression.* Actually the two words are closely related, but there is a difference. *Maltreatment* implies cruelty; *oppression* implies cruelty through abuse of power or authority, *tyranny*—if you will. From the outset of the trial Berman weighted *oppression* with a host of unsavory, emotionally loaded connotations. Even during the first week he had an agent working on a list of all references to *oppression* in the Bible.

As a matter of fact the Court might legally have substituted *maltreatment* for *oppression* in the specification under Charge II, found McKeon guilty of the substituted word, and given him the identical maximum sentence under the charge: one year's confinement at hard labor with accessories. Since *maltreatment* was in the current vocabulary of everyone at Parris Island from Commanding General to newest Boot, it would have been completely familiar to every witness. But Brigadier Wallace Greene didn't seem to realize that fact at the Inquiry. The lackeys in the Judge Advocate General's Office who redrafted the specification knew nothing about Parris Island. What might have happened had the Inquiry been more perspicacious and less vindictive?

Matthew McKeon could have been peremptorily separated from the Marine Corps in April through either of two administrative devices. He might have been confronted with charges and specifications for trial by general court-martial and permitted to accept undesirable discharge in lieu of such trial; this would have left the option to him. Conversely, the Commanding General either by endorsement on the Inquiry or separate correspondence might have recommended an undesirable discharge because McKeon's behavior placed the Marine Corps in disrepute; the Commandant's approval would have made the discharge effective.

Separation of McKeon forthwith would have indicated that the Marine Corps is compassionate, not vindictive. It would have served the good of the Corps by killing further news stories after early May rather than furnishing material for a whole series from July into October. It would have served McKeon's personal welfare because his record gives him no practical chance "to build for himself a useful and honorable career" in the future. His discharge would void retirement equity but otherwise most probably leave his veteran's rights undisturbed. Whether this action would have been true justice I leave to the judgment of moral philosophers. I did recommend it to the Chief of Staff in mid-April, only to receive a courteous brush-off.

Had he been given the choice at that early date, I am sure Matthew McKeon would have accepted the first alternative. We remember this from the Court-Martial:

Q. Do you recall in your statement when you made it to Sergeant Cummings, and I quote, "The platoon still in column of twos marched at route step into the stream"? Now that was made the next day.

A. Yes, sir. I don't recall it, sir.

Q. But you signed all that?

A. I would have signed anything, sir, I would have walked to the gallows—

Civilians don't understand that short of trial by general court-martial and subsequent imprisonment or dismissal the worst punishment that can befall an officer is peremptory relief from his command. It is more damning than court-martial because the latter judicial proceeding gives the commander all legal privileges of a defendant. Relief from command is a punitive administrative measure from which there is no appeal. Through the ages an officer so relieved has borne that stigma to the grave. In the case of an important figure it carries on into history. Relief from command as a disciplinary measure implies negligence, incompetence, or malfeasance. Should the commander remain on the active list, it is inevitable that the respect and confidence of his subordinates is seriously impaired. This is bound to deprive him of that prestige and military character necessary to be effective in office.

As an outgrowth of the Ribbon Creek incident Randolph

Pate relieved Joseph Burger from command. This was announced on the front page of New York *Times*. The report stated Burger was relieved for "failing to recognize a moral issue involving the whole Corps." This clearly leads to the conclusion that such an officer is severely lacking in moral intelligence and judgment. Could there be greater calumny to military character?

But this is jumping the gun because I'm probably a moral idiot myself. Since that night at Ribbon Creek I've probed the aspects of marine behavior in the Parris Island environment; I've consulted editors, clergymen, journalists, philosophers, and professional soldiers, outlining the problem for them; I've read two standard textbooks on ethics, one Scholastic and one not. Still I'm powerless to define *moral issue* in this context. To "fight our country's battles" we train marines to kill and survive—we hope. To achieve perfect teamwork, dignity of the individual is sacrificed for good of the outfit. If shaved heads and duck-walking contribute to our achievement—and I'm prepared to defend either view of that premise—then shaved heads and duck-walking serve our mission even though they're "treatment incompatible with accepted American standards of human dignity." And as for human dignity, I can't erase from my mind the horrible vision of a damaged American destroyer pulling back from Corregidor with an unknown sailorman on her searchlight platform jackknifed backward over the rail with his guts hanging from belly to shoulders. Is that human dignity?

In a later news story Pate said no commissioned officer was blamable for the tragic march. He alleged that officers were relieved from command not to punish them, but to speed the fresh approach to the problem of supervision. Every professional soldier recognizes this statement for what it is: smoke screen.

Commenting on the Inquiry, without substantiating argument, Pate deduced that the supervision of Boot Training must be reorganized. He "recognized the need for closer supervision." When something goes wrong that cry is standard. The ultimate in supervision is achieved in the maximum-security prison; somewhat short of that is the psychopathic ward. Yet we seek leaders with initiative and energy, leaders willing to assume responsibility not only for carrying out instructions but for deciding what must be done to accomplish our mission. We can't develop such leaders using an omnipresent *Gestapo*. We can develop them by maintaining an atmosphere of mutual trust and confidence. This requires loyalty up and loyalty *down*.

The system involves calculated risk. So long as we deal with human beings some knucklehead is going to let us down. The solution is to clobber that character and be proud of the hundred other guys who carry on. Task Force Greene came to Parris Island, doubled the so-called Executive Staff, and installed "new supervision." Wallace Greene's first action, after receiving formal honors, was to schedule a conference of Battalion Commanders. There he admitted that any misguided DI could on any night lead his platoon into the waters of Ribbon Creek while any "system" would stand powerless to prevent it. But there's no need for worry about that: Tradition will keep Ribbon Creek safe as long as there is Parris Island.